Facing the Nazi Past

D1051159

'An excellent book, authoritative ... well researched, nuanced and percep-
tive ... remarkably and probably correctly upbeat about the effects of
reunification on German public memory.'

Richard Evans, *University of Cambridge*

Facing the Nazi Past provides a compelling insight into a nation coming to terms with
the horrors of its history. Since the unification of East and West Germany in
1990, contrasting perspectives on the past have fuelled the seemingly incessant
debate on the Third Reich in Germany.

Looking at the different ways that East and West Germans have remembered the
1930s and 40s, Niven argues that the unification of Germany has helped its people
confront the past more openly. Changes at concentration camp memorial sites, the
commemoration of 8 May 1945, and the image of resistance to Hitler in united
Germany are just some of the factors that have helped to shape a new perspective
on the past.

Facing the Nazi Past reflects on the most important developments and debates
affecting the way united Germany remembers its past today. This timely account
is set to provoke fresh discussion of this dramatic historical period.

Bill Niven is Reader in German at the Nottingham Trent University. He has published widely on the ways in which West and East Germany viewed the history of
the Third Reich. His recent publications include (with J. K. A. Thomaneck) *Dividing
and Uniting Germany* (Routledge, 2000).

Facing the Nazi Past

United Germany and the Legacy of
the Third Reich

Bill Niven

London and New York

First published 2002
by Routledge
11 New Fetter Lane, London EC4P 4EE

Simultaneously published in the USA and Canada
by Routledge
29 West 35th Street, New York, NY 10001

Routledge is an imprint of the Taylor & Francis Group

Typeset in Baskerville by
M Rules
Printed and bound in Great Britain by
TJ International Ltd, Padstow, Cornwall

British Library Cataloguing in Publication Data
A catalogue record for this book is available from the British Library

Library of Congress Cataloging in Publication Data
Niven, William John, 1956–
    Facing the Nazi past: united Germany and the legacy of the Third
Reich/Bill Niven.
      p.   cm.
    Includes bibliographical references and index.
    1. Germany – History – 1933–1945 – Historiography. 2. National
socialism – Psychological aspects. 3. Historiography – Germany –
History – 20th century. 4. Holocaust, Jewish (1939–1945) –
Psychological aspects. 5. Memory – Political aspects – Germany.
I. Title

    DD256.48.N58 2001
    943.086′07′2–dc21
                                    2001019953

ISBN 0 415 26281 X (pbk)
ISBN 0 415 18011 2 (hbk)

For Helene

Contents

Plates

Acknowledgements

In the course of carrying out the research for this book, I corresponded with and visited many institutions and individuals in Germany, west and east. To all of these institutions and people I owe a debt of gratitude. Time and again requests for information were answered with enthusiastic interest in my project, and with a will to help which went far beyond my expectations. I would particularly like to thank the Institut für Sozialforschung in Hamburg, whose support and library proved invaluable. Without Dieter Schröder, member of that Institute, I would have taken much longer to trace material than I did take. The staff at the Gedenkstätte deutscher Widerstand in Berlin, at the concentration camp memorial sites at Buchenwald and Ravensbrück, and at the Federal Archives in Berlin all helped me in my seemingly endless search for material. Thanks to the many interviews I conducted and the letters I received in response to queries, I was able to acquire insights, and to identify new questions. For these interviews and letters, I would like to express my appreciation to Ignatz Bubis (a.d.), Gisela Gneist, Hannes Heer, Ekkehard Klausa, Wolfgang Oleschinski, Hubert Polus, Thomas Rahe, Maternus Schmitt, Horst Seferens, Dagmar and Ulrich Seidel, and Christian Ude. For advice on specific passages of the manuscript, I should like to thank Ruth Bettina Birn and Stuart Parkes. For reading through the manuscript and offering invaluable advice on how it might be improved or added to, I am grateful to Richard Evans, Barbara Fennell, Marianne Howarth, Jim Jordan, Hamish Ritchie and Stuart Taberner. Stuart's enquiries as to the progress of the manuscript were always a source of encouragement, and I very much appreciate Barbara's clear and helpful advice at both the beginning and the end of the project. My thanks go too to the British Academy for financing one of my research trips, and Marianne Howarth, Head of the German Section at my home institution, for her help in securing a teaching-free semester just when it mattered most. Last but not least, I would like to thank Heather McCallum and Victoria Peters, my editors at Routledge, for their support, assistance and patience.

Bill Niven
The Nottingham Trent University, 15 March 2001

Chronology 1933–2000

(A) The Third Reich

1933   **30 January**: Hitler becomes Chancellor of the Reich.

27 February: The *Reichstag* is set on fire by Dutchman Marinus van der Lubbe. Nazis use this as pretext to begin persecution of communists and social democrats, many of whom are interned in the first concentration camps set up in March.

5 March: Nazis win 43.9% in *Reichstag* elections.

21 March: New *Reichstag* opened in Potsdam ('Day of Potsdam').

24 March: 'Enabling Law' passed in the *Reichstag*, enabling Nazis to introduce legislation without the permission of Parliament.

1 April: Boycott of Jewish shops.

7 April: Ruling that 'non-Aryans' (Jews) and 'opponents of the regime' be excluded from the civil service.

10 May: Organized 'book-burnings' of works by Jewish and left-wing writers.

June–July: Forced self-dissolution of political parties, Social Democratic Party banned. Germany now one-party state (NSDAP).

1934   **1 January**: 'Law for the Prevention of Hereditarily Diseased Progeny' comes into effect, marking the beginning of the sterilization programme.

30 June: Hitler, Goebbels, Himmler and Heydrich enlist the help of the army in dealing a crushing blow to the SA ('Röhm Affair'). The downgrading of the SA is followed by the rise of the SS.

2 August: Reich President von Hindenburg dies. Hardly an hour later the German army swears unconditional obedience to Hitler, who becomes Supreme Commander of the Armed Forces.

1 November: A special department responsible for collecting data on homosexuals established in Gestapo headquarters.

1935   **16 March**: Military service introduced, in violation of the Versailles Treaty.

15 September: Nuremberg Laws proclaimed (marriages and sexual relations between Jews and Germans forbidden; Jews lose German citizenship).

26 November: Ruling by Prussian Minister of Interior extends Nuremberg Laws to cover Sinti and Roma.

1936   **7 March**: German forces march into demilitarized zone of the Rhineland, in violation of the Versailles and Locarno Treaties.

1 August: Olympic Games opened in Berlin. The staging of the Games provides the pretext for the quasi-internment of 600 Sinti and Roma in Marzahn on the outskirts of Berlin.

18 October: Nazis proclaim a Four Year Plan designed to force the pace of rearmament.

1937 *30 January*: 'Enabling Law' extended for another four years.

5 November: Hitler presents his plans for territorial expansion to military and civilian leaders.

1938 *4 February*: Hitler takes personal control of the *Wehrmacht*.

12 March: German troops march into Austria. Austria is 'annexed' to Germany (*Anschluss*).

27 August: Ludwig Beck, Chief of the Army General Staff, resigns over disagreement with Hitler's war policies.

29 September: Britain, France, Italy and Germany reach an agreement in Munich conceding the Sudetenland to Germany.

1 October: German troops march into the Sudetenland (Czechoslovakia).

9–10 November: Nazis organize country-wide attacks on synagogues, Jewish property and, in some cases, Jews themselves (*Reichskristallnacht* pogrom).

1939 *15 March*: German troops enter the remaining part of Czechoslovakia.

23 August: Hitler–Stalin Pact of Non-Aggression.

1 September: Germany invades Poland.

3 September: England and France declare war on Germany.

October: Hitler personally authorizes a 'euthanasia programme' in the course of which 70,000 people are killed (by August 1941).

9 November: Georg Elser tries to blow up Hitler in the Munich *Bürgerbräukeller*.

1940 *9 April*: Germany occupies Denmark and parts of Norway.

May–June: Holland, Belgium and France surrender to Germany.

1941 *April*: Capitulation of Yugoslavia and Greece.

22 June: Germany invades Russia ('Operation Barbarossa'). Behind the front, the slaughter of Russian Jews by the SS and other elite units begins – with the support of the *Wehrmacht*.

11 December: Germany and Italy declare war on the USA after Japan attacks Pearl Harbor.

1942 *20 January*: Wannsee Conference in Berlin ushers in the 'Final Solution' against European Jewry. The mass slaughter of Jews claims the lives of 6 million people.

22 November: Soviet army completes encirclement of Germans at Stalingrad.

1943 *2 February*: The remains of the German 6th Army surrenders in Stalingrad.

18 February: Goebbels makes his notorious 'Do you want total war?' speech in Berlin's *Sportpalast*.

13 May: German–Italian Africa corps surrenders in Tunisia.

13 July: National Committee for a Free Germany set up by German POWs with Soviet support in Krasnogorsk.

24 July: Bombing raid on Hamburg signals the beginning of heavy Allied bombing of German cities.

25 July: Fall of Mussolini.

28 November–1 December: Teheran Conference: America, Britain and the Soviet Union agree on the partition of Germany.

1944   **6 June**: Normandy landing of Western Allies.

20 July: Claus von Stauffenberg attempts to kill Hitler with a bomb in Rastenburg (East Prussia). Hitler is only slightly injured. Stauffenberg and some 200 people linked with his conspiracy are subsequently executed.

11 September: Allied armies reach the the boundaries of the German Reich.

11 October: Soviets reach East Prussia.

1945   **January–May**: Five million civilian Germans flee from the eastern territories of the Reich as the Soviets advance.

27 January: Liberation of Auschwitz.

4–12 February: Yalta Conference (Roosevelt, Stalin, Churchill) seals division of Germany into Allied zones of occupation.

13 February: Bombing of Dresden by the Allies.

April: Liberation of Buchenwald (11 April), Bergen-Belsen (15 April), Sachsenhausen (22 April), Dachau and Ravensbrück (29 April).

25 April: Soviet and American troops meet at Torgau (Elbe).

30 April: Hitler commits suicide.

5 May: British troops reach Neuengamme camp, but find it deserted.

7–9 May: German capitulation in Reims and Berlin.

(B) The Two Germanys

1945   **5 June**: Allied representatives proclaim division of Germany into four zones of occupation. The eastern zone (later GDR) is controlled by the Soviets, the three western zones (later FRG) by the USA, Britain and France. As of July, Berlin occupied by forces of all four Allied powers.

2 August: Allied Conference at Potsdam ends with agreement on demilitarization, economic dismantling, denazification and democratization of Germany. Pending a peace settlement, Allies approve loss of German territories east of the Oder and Neiße rivers to Poland and the Soviets. Allies effectively sanction the expulsion of Germans from these territories. Germany to pay reparations. It is agreed that Germany should be treated as an economic unit.

20 November: International Military Tribunal begins with trials of Nazi leaders in Nuremberg.

1946   **21–22 April**: Under Soviet pressure, German Communist Party and Social Democratic Party merge in Soviet-occupied zone to form the SED (Socialist Unity Party). Otto Grotewohl and Wilhelm Pieck are elected as chairmen, Walter Ulbricht as deputy chairman.

16 October: Ten leading Nazis sentenced to death by International Military Tribunal in Nuremberg.

1947 *1 January*: American and British zones economically unified as 'Bizonia'. In the course of the year, the 'Economic Council' gains in political profile.

10 March–24 April: Allied Foreign Ministers fail to reach agreement on a Peace Treaty for Germany.

5 June: US Foreign Minister Marshall proclaims European Recovery Programme (Marshall Aid), but Soviet Union refuses participation.

28 October: Americans step up anti-communist campaign in their zone.

1948 *1 June*: Six-Power London Conference agrees to set up west German state.

18 June: Currency reform carried out in western zones. Soviet Union subsequently protests at reform by blockading Berlin, and the airlift to Berlin organized by Western Allies begins on 26 June.

1 September: Parliamentary Council for the western zones meets in Bonn.

1949 *12 May*: End of Berlin Blockade.

23 May: Proclamation of Basic Law.

21 September: Federal Republic of Germany (FRG) comes into existence, after the Christian Democratic Union (CDU) and Christian Social Union (CSU) win first elections to West German Parliament. Coalition government formed with the Free Democrats (FDP). Konrad Adenauer (CDU) becomes FRG's first Chancellor.

7 October: German Democratic Republic (GDR) proclaimed in East Berlin. Five days later first GDR government is announced (under Otto Grotewohl of the SED).

11 October: Wilhelm Pieck becomes President of the GDR.

1950 *January*: Dissolution of the Soviet Special Camps at Bautzen, Buchenwald and Sachsenhausen.

6 July: Poland and GDR recognize Oder and Neiße rivers as the official border between them.

25 July: Walter Ulbricht becomes General Secretary of the SED in the GDR.

19 December: NATO Council assents in principle to West German rearmament as Cold War intensifies.

1951 *10 April*: West German Parliament votes for bill which paves the way for the rehabilitation and re-employment of civil servants removed from employ in the course of Allied denazification.

18 April: FRG and five other Western states establish the European Coal and Steel Community.

27 September: Adenauer announces intention to pay compensation to Jewish victims of Nazism.

1952 *10 March*: First of a series of notes from Stalin on a possible Peace Treaty for a united Germany, but Western Allies sceptical.

21 May: First significant steps in the GDR towards setting up military forces.

23 July: Regional *Länder* dissolved in the GDR. 1952 generally sees greater imposition of centralized socialism.

10 September: Reparations agreement between the FRG and Israel.

1953 *5 March*: Death of Stalin.

16–17 June: Mass strikes throughout the GDR in protest at increase in work norms lead to a rebellion against the SED.

20 October: Christian Democrats again strongest party in elections; new West German coalition government formed under Adenauer.

1954   **25 March**: Soviet Union recognizes GDR as sovereign state.

28 September–3 October: Western states at London Conference agree to rearmament of FRG within NATO.

1955   **9 May**: FRG becomes a member of NATO; a few days before this, the occupation statute had been lifted and FRG had become a member of the Western European Union.

14 May: GDR and Soviet bloc countries sign the Warsaw Pact.

8–14 September: Diplomatic relations established between the Soviet Union and the FRG. Soviets agree to release remaining German POWs.

9 December: West German Foreign Office stresses intention to implement Hallstein Doctrine (FRG will not recognize countries which recognize the GDR, although an exception is made in the case of the Soviet Union).

1956   **18 January**: GDR Parliament (*Volkskammer*) approves setting up of National People's Army (NVA).

7 July: West German Parliament approves a bill introducing military service.

17 August: West German Constitutional Court declares the 'Communist Party of Germany' (KPD) to be illegal.

1957   **25 March**: FRG signs Treaty of Rome, thereby becoming a member of the European Economic Community (EEC).

1958   **10 November**: Soviet leader Khrushchev demands that West Berlin be declared a Free City and threatens to transfer all responsibility for East Berlin to the East Germans. Second Berlin crisis results. Exodus of GDR citizens intensifies.

1959   **24 December**: Cologne synagogue (FRG) daubed with swastikas and anti-semitic slogans. Wave of far right extremism in FRG.

1960   **14 March**: Adenauer agrees to pay secret military aid to Israel (amounting to 320 million marks).

4 May: West German Refugees Minister Theodor Oberländer (CDU) resigns following allegations of involvement in Nazi crimes.

23 May: Adolf Eichmann, one of those responsible for implementing the Final Solution, seized in Argentina and brought to trial in Israel.

1961   **10 March**: Adenauer expresses concern that Eichmann trial will create the 'wrong' impression that more Germans were convinced Nazis than actually were.

12–13 August: GDR forces begin to seal off the border to FRG; the Berlin Wall is built within a matter of days.

1962   **24 January**: GDR introduces compulsory military service of 18 months for men between the ages of 18 and 26. In February, FRG also increases length of service to 18 months.

31 May: Adolf Eichmann executed in Jerusalem.

2–8 July: Adenauer and French President de Gaulle take salute at first joint parade ever held by French and German armies (Mourmelon, France).

1963 *12 January*: GDR and Cuba establish full diplomatic relations; two days later FRG breaks off relations with Cuba in line with Hallstein Doctrine.

22 January: Adenauer and de Gaulle sign Franco-German Treaty of Cooperation in Paris.

11 October: Adenauer resigns; Ludwig Erhard (CDU) becomes West German Chancellor 5 days later.

17 December: First of a series of agreements enabling West Berliners to visit East Berlin.

20 December: Auschwitz Trial begins in Frankfurt (ends 20 August 1965).

1964 *12 June*: GDR and Soviet Union sign 20-year Treaty of Friendship, Cooperation and Mutual Assistance.

1965 *21 April*: In the face of much conservative protest, FRG's 20-year Statute of Limitation on prosecution of murder (and therefore murderous Nazi war crimes) is extended by making it run from 1949.

2 May: FRG takes up diplomatic relations with Israel, whereupon several Arab states break off relations with Bonn.

1966 *30 November–1 December*: Federal Chancellor Erhard resigns and is replaced by Kurt Kiesinger (CDU). 'Grand Coalition' formed between the CDU/CSU and the Social Democrats (SPD).

1967 *31 January*: In a significant departure from the Hallstein Doctrine, FRG takes up diplomatic relations with Romania.

10 May: GDR Minister President Willi Stoph writes to Kiesinger about possibility of establishing normal relations between the two German states. Exchange of notes follows.

2 June: Shooting of student Benno Ohnesorg by police in West Berlin triggers months of student protest and unrest.

1968 *9 April*: FRG submits proposals for better relations with Warsaw Pact countries to Soviet ambassador.

11 April: Left-wing student leader Rudi Dutschke shot and severely wounded in West Berlin, triggering new wave of unrest.

20 August: GDR plays a part in Soviet invasion of Czechoslovakia.

30 October: FRG agrees to pay 7.5 million marks in compensation to Czech victims of Nazi camp medical experiments.

1969 *11 June*: West German Parliament decides to extend Statute of Limitation on prosecution of murder by 10 years.

21 October: Willy Brandt becomes West German Chancellor. SPD/FDP coalition now in power. Brandt immediately sets about establishing better relations with Poland and paying compensation to victims of Nazism there.

8 December: Talks between FRG and Soviet Union on non-aggression treaty.

1970 *19 March*: Willi Stoph and Willy Brandt meet in Erfurt (GDR). On 21 May, the two then meet in Kassel (FRG). *Ostpolitik* begins in earnest.

12 August: FRG and Soviet Union sign Treaty of Moscow, which includes a non-aggression agreement. Both countries agree to respect the current boundaries of all European states, including the GDR's border to Poland and the border between GDR and FRG.

7 December: FRG and Poland sign Treaty of Warsaw respecting Oder–Neiße line as GDR frontier to Poland. Brandt falls to his knees at the Warsaw Ghetto Memorial.

1971   *3 May*: Erich Honecker replaces Walter Ulbricht as First Secretary of the SED in the GDR (till 1989).

3 September: Western Allies and Soviet Union sign Four-Power Berlin Agreement.

1972   *19 November*: SPD wins elections in West Germany. Brandt continues as Chancellor.

21 December: 'Basic Treaty' signed by FRG and GDR. FRG *de facto* recognizes GDR. Subsequently, a number of NATO countries recognize GDR.

1973   *18–22 May*: Leonid Brezhnev becomes the first General Secretary of the Soviet Communist Party to visit the FRG.

September: GDR and FRG become members of the United Nations.

1974   *16 May*: Helmut Schmidt (SPD) elected Chancellor after Brandt resigns following the discovery that one of his aides, Günter Guillaume, was an East German spy.

1975   *1 August*: Final Act of Helsinki Conference on European Security and Cooperation signed by all European powers (except Albania), including GDR and FRG.

1976   *3 October*: SPD win 8th Federal elections. Helmut Schmidt remains West German Chancellor, SPD remains in coalition with FDP.

1978   *4–7 May*: Leonid Brezhnev, Soviet President, pays state visit to FRG. 25-year economic agreement signed by Soviet Union and West Germany.

1979   *3 July*: Federal Parliament votes to lift the Statute of Limitations on the prosecution of murder.

12 December: NATO 'Twin-Track' Decision to station 572 US medium-range nuclear rockets in Western Europe as of 1983, while simultaneously offering negotiations to the Soviets aimed at reducing the number of nuclear weapons in Europe.

27 December: Soviets invade Afghanistan. USA subsequently threatens economic and political sanctions against Soviet Union.

1980   *8 May*: Schmidt and Honecker talk at Tito's funeral and agree that both the GDR and FRG should try to avoid international political repercussions of Afghanistan invasion.

5 November: Schmidt reelected West German Chancellor.

1981   *25 February*: FRG rejects Brezhnev's suggestion of a moritorium on deployment of new nuclear missiles.

10 October: Mass demonstrations in Bonn against escalating nuclear arms race in West and East.

1982   *18 June*: American President Ronald Reagan steps up economic sanctions against the Soviet Union.

20 September/28 September: FRG and GDR reach agreement on youth exchange programme and environmental protection.

1 October: Schmidt is toppled by a constructive vote of no-confidence. Helmut Kohl (CDU) becomes Chancellor of a CDU/CSU and FDP coalition, which is confirmed in power in March 1983 elections.

1983 **29 June**: First billion mark credit for the GDR organized through Bavarian Minister President Franz-Josef Strauß.

15 September: Richard von Weizsäcker becomes the first mayor of West Berlin to meet Honecker.

22 November: West German Parliament agrees to stationing of nuclear weapons in FRG (SPD and Greens vote against).

1984 **25–30 January**: Kohl visits Israel.

6 June: Neither FRG nor GDR is invited to take part in commemoration of D-Day landings.

4 September: Honecker postpones planned visit to the FRG for the second time under Soviet pressure.

1985 **10 March**: Death of Chernenko. Mikhail Gorbachev takes over as General Secretary of the Soviet Communist Party.

5 May: Kohl and Reagan visit Bitburg military cemetery and Bergen-Belsen memorial site to mark the coming 40-year anniversary of the end of the war.

8 May: Historic speech by Federal President von Weizsäcker stressing German responsibility for remembering the crimes of Nazism.

14–16 June: Kohl provokes indignation by speaking at the annual meeting of Silesian expellees. He maintains that Polish border issue is still legally open.

1986 **4 April**: Soviet Union protests at West German support for Reagan's Strategic Defense Initiative (SDI).

6 May: Cultural Agreement signed by GDR and FRG.

1987 **25 January**: CDU/CSU win elections, coalition formed with FDP.

7–11 September: Honecker pays a working visit to FRG. First time a GDR head of state has visited FRG in official capacity.

8 December: Reagan and Gorbachev reach agreement on destroying all medium-range nuclear missiles.

1988 **17 January**: Arrest in GDR of dissidents at the Rosa Luxemburg remembrance parade. Beginning of sporadic protests and small demonstrations in the GDR.

17 October: Honecker meets Edgar Bronfman, President of the World Jewish Congress, in East Berlin and agrees in principle to pay compensation to Jewish victims of Nazism (hitherto GDR had accepted no responsibility).

24–27 October: Kohl makes large-scale official visit to Soviet Union, during which many inter-government and trade agreements are signed.

10 November: President of Federal Parliament Philipp Jenninger has to step down after making a speech interpreted by some as a defence of German conduct during the Third Reich.

1989 **20 January**: George Bush becomes President of the USA.

30 January: Citizens' action group 'Perspective Berlin' calls for the construction of a Holocaust Memorial in Berlin.

25 February: Soviet troops complete withdrawal from Afghanistan.

19 March: NATO and Warsaw Pact meet to discuss reduction in conventional weapons.

7 May: Opposition movement in GDR finds evidence of manipulation in East German local elections.

10 September: Hungary opens its western border for GDR citizens, about 50,000 of them leave for the West.

6–7 October: GDR's 40th anniversary celebrations attended by Gorbachev, who criticizes Honecker's unwillingness to reform.

9 October: First large-scale demonstration in Leipzig, in which 50,000 people take part.

18 October: Honecker resigns and is replaced by Egon Krenz.

23 October: At least 300,000 East Germans demonstrate in Leipzig against the East German government. Danger of violence averted.

9 November: Opening of Berlin Wall. Thousands of East Germans pour into West Berlin.

13 November: Hans Modrow becomes East German Minister President.

28 November: Kohl presents a ten-point plan for a German confederation.

16 December: SED changes its name to SED-PDS as part of a process of reform.

1990   **8 February**: Modrow declares that the whole German people is responsible for the Nazi past.

11 February: Gorbachev states that Soviet Union has nothing in principle against German unification.

18 March: CDU-dominated 'Alliance for Germany' wins first free GDR elections.

5 May: First 'Two Plus Four' negotiations between Foreign Ministers of Allies, the GDR and the FRG.

1 July: Treaty on currency union between FRG and GDR comes into effect.

23 August: GDR Parliament decides on the accession of the GDR to the Federal Republic.

29 August: Greens propose a motion in Federal Parliament for the rehabilitation of *Wehrmacht* deserters – without success.

31 August: GDR and FRG sign Unification Treaty.

12 September: 'Treaty on the Final Settlement with Respect to Germany' is signed in Moscow by the former occupying powers. Precondition for complete sovereignty of united Germany.

3 October: Unification of the GDR and the FRG.

4 October: Federal Parliament declares Berlin to be the new capital.

(C) Post-unification Germany

1990   **9 November:** Gorbachev and Kohl sign good neighbourhood and cooperation treaties.

14 November: Germany and Poland sign a treaty confirming the

Oder–Neiße line as their joint border.

2 December: First all-German elections, which are won by the CDU/CSU/FDP coalition.

1991   **17 June**: Germany and Poland sign a Friendship Treaty guaranteeing minorities' rights in both countries.

20 June: Federal Parliament decides to move from Bonn to Berlin.

18 August: Remains of Frederick the Great and his father reburied in Potsdam at Sanssouci.

1992   **27 February**: Kohl and President Havel sign good neighbours' treaty in Prague.

23–26 August: A hostel for asylum seekers in Rostock (Mecklenburg-West Pomerania) is attacked over several nights.

26 September: Neo-Nazis set fire to Hut 38 at the concentration camp memorial site in Sachsenhausen. Several thousand people demonstrate against xenophobia at Sachsenhausen on 3 October.

6 November: Agreement reached that about 50,000 eastern European Jews who had not been able to claim compensation as victims of Nazism will receive payments of 630 billion US dollars from Germany between 1992 and 2000.

8 November: 300,000 people take part in a mass show of solidarity towards foreigners in Berlin.

23 November: Racist attack in Mölln (Schleswig-Holstein) claims lives of three Turks.

1993   **30 May**: Five Turks die in arson attack in Solingen. Germans and Turks organize protest demonstrations around the country.

2 July: Federal Parliament votes for deployment of Federal Army (*Bundeswehr*) in Somalia – within the framework of a UN peace-keeping mission, but outside of NATO area.

14 November: Kohl's national memorial, the *Neue Wache*, dedicated to 'the victims of war and the rule of violence', is opened in Berlin.

23 November: Regional Court in Schleswig-Holstein condemns the two men responsible for the attack in Mölln to life-long imprisonment and a 10-year youth sentence respectively. With some exceptions, courts begin to impose harsher sentences for right-wing radicalism.

24 November: SPD and Greens propose a motion to Federal Parliament for rehabilitation of *Wehrmacht* deserters. CDU/CSU reject the motion.

1994   **1 March**: German première of Steven Spielberg's film *Schindler's List* in Frankfurt. Millions of Germans flock to see it. Over a million copies of the book by Thomas Keneally on which the film is based sell in March and April alone.

26 April: Federal Constitutional Court (BVG) confirms that it is a punishable offence to deny the facts of the holocaust ('Auschwitz Lie').

April: The Circle for Promoting the Construction of a Memorial to Europe's Murdered Jews, the Berlin Senate and the Federal government launch competition for a Holocaust Memorial.

12 July: BVG rules that out-of-area deployment of the *Bundeswehr* under certain conditions is consistent with the Basic Law.

20 July: Official commemoration of the 50th anniversary of Stauffenberg's attempt to kill Hitler.

20 September: BVG confirms that the Kurt Tucholsky quotation 'Soldiers are Murderers' (used on a car-sticker) is a defensible expression of opinion which does not represent an insult to the *Bundeswehr*.

16 October: CDU/CSU/FDP narrowly win Federal elections and continue their coalition.

1995   **March**: 'Crimes of the *Wehrmacht*' exhibition first shown in Hamburg.

28 April: Federal Parliament, together with the Federal Council, commemorates the end of the war and the National Socialist rule of violence.

8–9 April: 50th anniversary of liberation of Buchenwald commemorated.

13 April: Regional Court in Schleswig imposes prison sentences of between 30 and 50 months on four people found guilty of an arson attack on a Lübeck synagogue in March 1994.

8 May: Official state commemoration of the end of the war in Berlin, attended by representatives of four Allied powers.

30 June: Chancellor Kohl expresses his disapproval of the Jackob-Marks design for the Holocaust Memorial.

1996   **26 January**: German *Länder* agree to delay the return of fugitives from Bosnia-Herzegovina, 340,000 of whom have taken refuge in Germany.

27 January: First official commemoration in Germany of the 'Memorial Day for the Victims of National Socialism' (anniversary of the liberation of Auschwitz).

16 April: In Geneva, Foreign Minister Klaus Kinkel criticizes China's lack of respect for human rights, leading to tension between the FRG and China.

April: First reviews of Goldhagen's book *Hitler's Willing Executioners* appear in German newspapers. German translation published in August. Goldhagen visits Germany in September.

8 May: Federal Parliament debates pros and cons of a Holocaust Memorial in Berlin.

1997   **10 January**: First of three colloquia in Berlin on the theme of the planned Holocaust Memorial.

21 January: German and Czech Heads of State and Foreign Ministers sign German–Czech Reconciliation Declaration. Germany acknowledges responsibility for injustices done to Czechs during the Third Reich. Czech Republic acknowledges and regrets fact of expulsion of Germans from Czechoslovakia at the end of the war.

24 February: 'Crimes of the *Wehrmacht*' exhibition opens in Munich, triggering mass interest and, soon, national debate.

3 March: Parliamentary Commissioner for the *Bundeswehr*, Claire Marienfeld, points in her yearly report to an increase in right-wing extremism in the German army.

5 March: 30,000-strong police presence required to enable the transport of nuclear waste (burned-out fuel rods) to Gorleben. Tens of thousands of people demonstrate against the dangers of such transports.

6 June: Unemployment figures reach highest level since 1949 (11.4% of the potential work-force).

29 December: German and Czech governments agree to set up a 'Fund for the Future', into which Germany will pay 140 million marks, the Czech Republic 25 million; to be used *inter alia* to compensate surviving Czech victims of Nazism.

1998   *6 March*: Turkish President Mesut Yilmaz, angry at EU's refusal to consider Turkish membership, compares Germany's EU policies with the expansionist politics of Hitler.

19 April: Left-wing terrorist organization Red Army Faction (RAF) announces its dissolution.

23 April: Federal Parliament votes for EU currency union as of 1 January 1999 (introduction of euro).

26 April: Far-right German People's Union (DVU) wins 12.9% of the vote in Saxony-Anhalt.

22 May: Kohl, who has expressed his sympathy for the Eisenman/Serra Holocaust Memorial design, agrees modifications with the designers.

28 May: Federal Parliament approves bill annulling sentences based on 'specifically National Socialist injustice'. The bill covers some sentences passed against deserters and homosexuals, and sentences imposed by the notorious People's Court. However, it does not allow for a general rehabilitation of all deserters and homosexuals sentenced by Nazi courts.

18 June: Parliamentary Committee (CDU, FDP and SPD) publishes a report disclaiming the existence of extreme right-wing structures within the *Bundeswehr*.

7 July: Volkswagen announces intention to set up private fund of 20 million marks as compensation for those who worked as forced labourers for VW between 1944 and 1945. Siemens follows suit on 29 September.

27 September: SPD wins Federal elections and forms a coalition with *Bündnis 90*/The Greens. Gerhard Schröder (SPD) becomes chancellor.

11 October: Martin Walser makes a controversial speech in the Frankfurt *Paulskirche* in which he inveighs against over-exposure to the Nazi past in the media.

20 October: In their coalition agreement, SPD and Greens agree to pass decision on Holocaust Memorial to Federal Parliament. They also stress historical responsibility to Poland and Israel.

12 November: Following the threat of court cases in the USA, six insurance companies under leadership of *Allianz AG* decide to set up fund to pay claims of Jewish victims. After meetings between Bodo Hombach (SPD) and victims' organizations in the USA, several German firms agree to join together to finance compensation for forced labourers and other Nazi victims.

18 November: Federal Parliament votes for *Bundeswehr* participation in NATO special force in Kosovo.

1999   ***24 January***: Opening of Daniel Libeskind's Jewish Museum in Berlin.

8 March: Schröder and Czech Prime Minister Zeman declare that they hope to draw a line under the past. Schröder rejects demands by Sudeten German Expellees, who want to make German support for Czech entry to the EU dependent on a Czech commitment to return German property confiscated after 1945.

1 April: Amsterdam EU Treaty comes into force.

19 April: Federal parliamentarians conduct plenary business for the first time in the reconstructed *Reichstag*.

1 July: Johannes Rau (SPD) takes over from Roman Herzog (CSU) as Federal President.

1 December: American Defense Minister Cohen complains that Germany's military budget is too modest.

2 December: Federal Parliament sets up first committee to investigate so-called 'Party Funds Affair' (undeclared donations to CDU, notably to Kohl).

10–11 December: European Council confirms that progress has been made in negotiations for EU entry of Cyprus, Hungary, Poland and the Czech Republic.

2000   ***3 February***: European Parliament declares that it may have to suspend relations with the Austrian government if the far-right 'Free Party of Austria' (FPÖ) under Jörg Haider, which has recently formed a coalition with the Austrian People's Party (ÖVP), threatens to break the principles on which the EU is based.

23 May: Commission set up to look into structural reform of *Bundeswehr* proposes a reduction in the size of the army from 320,000 to 240,000.

13 June: Government negotiators Graf Lambsdorff (for Germany) and Stuart Eizenstat (USA) finalize agreement on issue of compensation for victims of forced labour during the Third Reich. The fund from which the payments are to be made will be 10 billion marks in total: 5 billion will be contributed by German industry, 5 by the German government. In a 'Statement of Interest', American government will recommend that court cases in the USA against German firms relating to compensation issues be dropped.

23 June: Foundation stone laid for Dresden's new synagogue.

17 July: German–American government agreement on legal protection for German firms concludes negotiations on issue of forced labour.

9 August: State secretaries of Federal and Regional Ministeries of the Interior agree to set up a commission to look into possibility of banning the extreme right-wing NPD (National-Democratic Party of Germany).

9–10 December: Federal Parliament apologizes for the persecution of homosexuals during the Third Reich, and asks government to come up with proposals for compensation. Parliament also decides to join the German government and the Federal Council in appealing to the Federal Constitutional Court for a ban on the NPD.

Introduction

The inclusive picture

'I would like to understand why, in this decade, the past is being presented as never before.'

(Martin Walser 1999: 12)

Why now?

The above quotation is taken from the text of a controversial speech given by the author Martin Walser, in which he expressed consternation at the degree to which a preoccupation with the National Socialist past had taken hold of the public realm. Walser's speech addressed an apparent discrepancy. In consequence of the 'Two Plus Four' Treaty of 12 September 1990, the Allies had passed complete sovereignty to the Germans, relinquishing rights deriving from occupation. On the one hand, then, Germany, as a united country, had put behind it that period of its history directly or indirectly linked to National Socialism, without which there would have been no Third Reich, no post-war state of defeat and ruin, no Allied occupation, no division of Germany and no integration into the competing power blocs. Yet while the political impact of National Socialism and its aftermath had come to an end, there was a veritable explosion of discussion about the National Socialist past in the public realm. The media, intellectuals, politicians of all parties and the general public were involved in this discussion. Indeed the Germans set about debating the Nazi past as never before. To a certain extent, this discussion was a response to special anniversaries. 1994 was the year of the 50th anniversary of Stauffenberg's attempt on Hitler's life. In 1995, Germany and other countries took part in ceremonies to mark the 50th anniversary of the end of the war. To a certain extent, too, discussion was triggered by spectacular media events, such as the showing of the Hollywood film *Schindler's List*. It can also be explained by the fact that views of Nazism were presented in the public realm – in exhibitions, speeches, books or films – which broke with images of the Third Reich typical of East or West Germany, or of both Germanys. Yet these views would never have attracted as much public and media interest had there not been a readiness to consider them. Indeed it seemed as if they only had the effect they did because the time was right. Interest in the National Socialist past was driven by its own momentum, absorbing influences, feeding on them, but not always impelled by them. It was this dynamic which puzzled Walser. Was this, as Walser suspected, some kind of German sado-masochism? Was Walter Benjamin's angel of history stuck permanently in retrospective horror, unable to look forward?

It is my contention that many of the views of Nazism presented in the public realm after 1990, and certainly the interest in them, must be understood not as a contradiction of unification, but as a result of it. Unification brought to an end both the post-Hitler period and a certain way of looking at the Third Reich, one which was itself a product of German division, the Cold War and conflicting political ideologies. As long as Germany was divided, guilt for National Socialism could be passed back and forth over the German–German border. The existence of two Germanys as of 1949 – here the GDR (East Germany), there the FRG (West Germany) – meant that one Germany could always blame the other, for past as well as present ills. This was made easier by the fact that these two German states were markedly different in economic and political character. The GDR was a communist state. In identifying capitalism as the source of fascism, the GDR was able to draw comparisons between West Germany and the Third Reich. In identifying totalitarianism as the prime element of fascism and socialism, West Germany was able to vilify East Germany as but the socialist equivalent to National Socialism. Both states were encouraged in such mutual recriminations by their respective allies, the Soviets in the case of the East Germans, the British, French and above all the Americans in the case of the West Germans. East and West Germany, after all, were situated at the geopolitical divide of the two power blocs. The result of such recrimination was that neither state adequately came to terms with the National Socialist past. It was felt, in each case, that it was the other German state that had to do this, given that the continuities were 'there', rather than 'here'. Inculpation went hand in hand with self-exculpation. East Germans were invited by their government to identify with the anti-fascist resistance against Hitler, while in the West, West Germans were invited by the political establishment to identify with the military resistance to Hitler. It was even possible, in the climate of the Cold War, to imagine that there was less to come to terms with than was actually the case. West German anti-communism for a long time blocked proper empathy both with the communist victims of National Socialism and with the Soviet Union, devastated in Hitler's war. The anti-Zionist stance of the GDR, moulded in the anti-capitalist and anti-American spirit of communism, blocked empathy with the victims of the holocaust. When Germany was united in 1990, this ritual of buck-passing and systematic self-exoneration became obsolete. Of course, some west Germans continued to berate the GDR even after it had gone. Equally, some east Germans continued to portray the FRG as a neo-fascist state. But, essentially, unification meant that the games-playing would have to stop, sooner or later. Responsibility for the National Socialist past had to be centred within one nation.

The key term here is ownership. What had all too often been foisted on to the other set of Germans on the other side of the Berlin Wall was now the inheritance of all Germans. If the country were to be psychologically united, then this would have to be on the basis of accepting a common past, a common past not least of crime and atrocity. Awareness of this partly explains the pace and intensity with which the Germans, since 1990, have gone about facing the issue of perpetration during the Third Reich. New exhibitions in Berlin focusing on the bureaucratic planning of the holocaust and other massacres have opened, attracting much public attention. Concentration camp memorial sites have set about integrating SS and other 'perpetrator areas' into the landscapes of memory, particularly in the east, but also in the west. Numbers of visitors to these sites are steadily on the rise. Germans streamed into podium discussions with Daniel Jonah Goldhagen in 1996, proving to be deeply interested in the question as to *why* the Germans killed Jews. They visited the 'Crimes of the *Wehrmacht*' exhibition between 1995 and 1999 in hundreds of thousands, horrified by the realization that regular soldiers, not just elite killing troops, had been involved in massacres behind the eastern front. All levels at which there was involvement in perpetration, from the highest, namely Hitler himself, down to that of the 'ordinary German' – a catch-phrase of the 1990s – have moved into sharper focus. It seems as if no stone is be left unturned, as German thoroughness is at last applied to an area it frequently tended to shun.

Increased interest since 1990 in the true extent both of crime, and of involvement in it, has been matched by increased interest in learning about the range of victims. The two German states had acknowledged victims. However, their understanding of who the victims were was in some respects limited. The GDR focused on communist victims of National Socialism, more or less excluding Jews from the picture. In West Germany, there was greater acknowledgement of Jewish suffering. But for a long time, the main victims in the eyes of many West Germans were the Germans themselves, who had been 'forced' to serve in Hitler's army, bombed by the Allies, treated unjustly in Soviet camps during and after the war, or expelled from their homes by the Czechs and Poles in 1945. Even when the Jews moved more into the picture, it was as partners-in-victimhood, whose suffering in the concentration camps had been comparable to that of the Germans at the front – war was understood as fate, not as something the Germans had started and waged. Neither in East nor in West Germany were Sinti or homosexual victims of National Socialism of much commemorative interest. Things did change slightly in West Germany in the 1980s, as 'forgotten' victims were discovered. But it was only with the discussions in the 1990s surrounding the proposed Holocaust Memorial in Berlin that the fate of Sinti and homosexual victims of National Socialism moved into the centre of media, political and public attention. In eastern Germany, it was not until the post-1990 period that the fate of Jews and Sinti was appropriately recorded at concentration camp memorial sites. Helmut Kohl's much-criticized *Neue Wache*, opened in 1993 and dedicated to all the 'victims of war', erased differences between Germans under Hitler and those upon whom they inflicted war and inhumanity. But the massive Holocaust Memorial will, once it has been built, shift the central commemorative focus onto Jewish victims of Nazism. Here again, the end of division has played a crucial role. As long as Germany was divided, many Germans could nurture a feeling of being victims. After unification, this is not possible to the same degree.

As the above paragraph demonstrates, it is not my intention to deny that East or West Germany endeavoured to face up to the National Socialist past before 1990. Both countries, with different emphases and outcomes, had conducted trials in connection with National Socialist crimes, and compensated different sets of victims to different degrees. West Germany paid some 3.45 billion marks in compensation to Israel and the Jewish Claims Conference; East Germany, abnegating responsibility for the holocaust, paid no such compensation, though special pensions were paid to 'victims of fascism'. In time, the system of mutual inculpation was significantly undermined by *Ostpolitik*, the politics of *rapprochement* between the two German states which began under West German Chancellor Willy Brandt in the 1970s. Particularly in the 1980s, West Germany began to confront the National Socialist past more self-critically. Federal President Richard von Weizsäcker's groundbreaking speech on 8 May 1985 placed Jews, Poles and Russians higher up the list of victims than the Germans themselves. East Germany 'discovered' the Jewish victims of Nazism in the late 1980s, commemorating them vigorously at state level in 1988. In the course of this book, I will have cause to point to these and other pre-1990 developments in the process of coming to terms with the past (*Vergangenheitsbewältigung*). Moreover, the impact of generational shifts, in the 1960s and again in the 1980s, cannot be underestimated. To an extent, the developments of the 1990s were a continuation and radicalization of a process of coming to terms with the past, rather than its first phase.

But as long as Germany was divided, this process was always going to be promoted to a greater degree in West Germany, which proved to be the less blinkered of the two states. It was always going to be slowed down and held back by existing tensions between the two Germanys, and there was always the risk that an intensification in the Cold War might reverse trends. Attempts by conservative historians in the mid-1980s in West Germany to declare bolshevism the primary and greater evil, and to play down the holocaust, were an indirect result of the nuclear arms-race. Even apparently positive moves had their negative sides. Thus the GDR's developing sensitivity towards the terrible fate of the Jews and its interest in the July 1944 attempt on Hitler's life were in part attempts to extend its self-congratulatory concept of anti-fascism. Only the end of the geopolitical divide created the ideal preconditions for a more open and persistent confrontation with the National Socialist past. In contrast to the pre-1990 period, moreover, this confrontation took the form not just of political and legal measures (such as the recently agreed payments for forced labourers), but also, and in far greater measure, of public discourse. The task of coming to terms with the past, long the preserve of historians and politicians, was taken up by the population at large. Freed from Cold War politicization, the period 1933–1945 was 'released' into the public realm for re-evaluation. Only once in the pre-1990 period, in West Germany with the showing of the American TV series *Holocaust* in 1979, had the wider German public been so shaken by the theme of German atrocities. In the course of the 1990s, a sense of shock was the hallmark of an intense public interest and discussion.

National identity

The thesis of this book, then, is that the presentation and understanding of the National Socialist past in united Germany has become more inclusive than it was in the pre-1990 period. There is now a broader awareness of the true extent of National Socialist criminality and of the range of victims. It is a positive thesis. I would, nevertheless, not wish to argue that inclusive implies conclusive, or even comprehensive. There will always be areas of the National Socialist past, as there will be of any past, that still need to be addressed. Inclusiveness might be understood as an ongoing process of broadening understanding, or as a mental attitude, a willingness. Inclusiveness towards the past is, perhaps, a parallel process to that of inclusiveness towards foreigners, towards the 'other', in the present. In accepting the mistakes of the past, Germans will be more able to welcome the multi-cultural society that is becoming the norm today. A critical picture of National Socialism founded on a broad-based awareness of past national guilt, collaboration and complicity, of perpetrators and victims, but also of the scope for resistance, can help to keep Germans alert to weaknesses in their society and political order and strengthen 'civil courage' (*Zivilcourage*). The National Socialist past – with its combination of political dictatorship, total media control, racism, chauvinism and militant aggression – is everything today's Germany does not want to be. It is, from today's perspective, the 'opposite', the 'anti-normal'. It thus forms the essential negative foil to Germany's democratic national identity.

Against this positive thesis it can be argued that there has been in united Germany, and still is, considerable resistance to making critical memory of German crimes a cornerstone of German national identity. Unification animated many conservatives into calling for a more robust Germany. At last, so these conservatives hoped, Germany could be a dominant force again, as a political and economic leader of Europe. They have argued that historical shame cannot function as the psychological motor of self-assertion. If it were to, the argument continues, it would be the wrong kind of self-assertion, defensive, neurotic and resentful. Hence Germans, it is claimed, need to put the holocaust behind them, take pride in aspects of their pre-1933 history, in the achievements of post-war democracy, or in unification. One group of conservatives, the New Right, is sceptical of Germany's supposed subservience to the west and to the Americans. This loosely connected group of intellectuals and politicians would set Germany free of its western moorings and allocate it a pivotal role at the heart of central Europe (*Mitteleuropa*); it would also resuscitate spurned values such as German inwardness (*Innerlichkeit*), often blamed for the slide into the Third Reich (for the views of the New Right, see Schwilk and Schacht 1994). More traditional conservatives stress Germany's commitment to the west and argue that, while Germany after 1945 had 'received' the gift of western democracy, its role is now to confer this gift upon others, such as Poland and the Czech Republic. For both these groups, any norm of national identity which turns on memory of German crimes under National Socialism is bound to result in a crippled national psyche and an immobile

Germany. It is this fear which has led these conservatives to resist bitterly the process of inclusiveness, for the more the Germans become aware of past crimes, the more they may be inclined to base their self-understanding as Germans on a sense of historical shame.

Many west German conservatives have sought to keep the totalitarianist theory alive in post-unification Germany. Equating the GDR with the Third Reich was always problematical. Now that there is no longer any Cold War or any GDR, such equation also appears politically pointless. But it can still serve a purpose. Before 1990, the function of equation was to discredit the GDR morally and politically. Now, its function is both to prevent any renascence of socialist thinking and to provide a basis for what Stefan Berger has called the 'renationalization' of German identity (Berger 1997). Highlighting the crimes of GDR socialism enables conservatives to play these crimes off against those of National Socialism, one set of crimes as it were 'cancelling' out the other. In stressing that Germany had seen two dictatorships come and go, one imposed by Hitler, the other by the Soviets, these conservatives can argue that totalitarian rule was a world-wide or at least European problem, and abnegate any specific German responsibility. This paves the way for a more self-assertive German identity. If totalitarianist theorists do admit German responsibility, then only east German responsibility. They often imply that the east Germans, who, it is claimed, lived far longer under totalitarian rule than the long democratized west Germans, should take the lion's share of responsibility for any process of coming to terms with the German past. Post-1990 championship of the totalitarianist theory thus also represents an anachronistic attempt to continue the tradition of inculpation and self-exculpation. Quite a number of memorial sites and exhibitions which address the issue of Germany's 'double past' have been opened since 1990, most of them in eastern Germany; some of these appear to interpret history along the lines of the totalitarianist paradigm.

The term 'double past' is not a misnomer. There was political repression in the GDR, as well as under National Socialism. It is to the credit of the Germans that, as of 1990, they sought to come to terms with the injustices committed in the name of socialism during the period of the Soviet occupation of eastern Germany (1945–1949), and in the GDR (1949–1989). It is also to their credit that they reacted with a swiftness that was in marked contrast to the dilatoriness with which the two Germanys had faced the National Socialist past: legal, political and social measures were quickly put in place to redress the wrongs of socialism. Both the last government of the GDR and the first one of united Germany were keen to avoid a repetition of what writer Ralph Giordano has called the 'second guilt', a term he applied to the failure of both the FRG and GDR to come to terms with National Socialism (Giordano 1987). Without doubt, too, the intense concern in the period 1990–1992 with the crimes of socialism served to enhance interest in the National Socialist past. The two pasts were compared. Yet this very process revealed more differences than similarities. In the GDR, as in the Third Reich, political opponents were persecuted, freedom of opinion was suppressed, and rights of movement were denied – most brutally by shooting fugitives at the border. But there were qualitative differences in the degree and extent of this persecution; the methods of East Germany's Socialist Unity Party (SED) were not generally murderous and certainly not genocidal. Moreover, in contrast to National Socialism, the GDR was, on paper at least, committed to equality and social justice, not destructive nationalism. It also, arguably, realized this commitment in certain areas. Those who subscribe to the totalitarian paradigm would elide these differences.

The identity debate has not yet been resolved, but it is unlikely that it will be won by the right. Over the last ten years, I would argue, the historical focus in the public realm has gradually shifted away from socialism towards National Socialism. A case in point might be the 'Crimes of the *Wehrmacht*' exhibition, which has triggered more media, political and public discussion than any other historical exhibition in the history of either the FRG or the GDR. An exhibition on the *Stasi* in Munich in 1997, which ran more or less at the same time as the magnetic 'Crimes of the *Wehrmacht*' exhibition, attracted hardly any interest. It was as if the German public had understood where the greater criminality lay, namely in a past common to all Germans – in west and east. Looking back over the 1990s, one gains the impression that this exhibition, as well as Goldhagen's *Hitler's Willing Executioners* and the discussion surrounding the proposed Holocaust Memorial, acted as a counterblast to totalitarianist equationism. Certainly the hope of some conservatives that one set of crimes would be understood as cancelling out the other has been severely dented. German national identity, I argue in the final chapter of this book, will probably be based on an inclusive model of memory. By remembering National Socialist crimes and the victims of these crimes, Germans will maintain a sense of the need to uphold and defend democracy.

Structure and layout

I have structured the book in chronological accordance with the main discussions on the National Socialist past since 1990. Each of these discussions centred around views of National Socialism in the public realm which sought either to bring to public attention aspects of this period which had hitherto been inadequately faced, or to combine the best of West Germany's model of memory with the best of East Germany's. These views were therefore inclusive, while opposition to them was based on principles of exclusion. To enable the reader to understand these views and the accompanying debates in context, many of the chapters deal in some detail with various aspects of divided memory in the two German states between 1949 and 1989. To summarize briefly the contents of the chapters: Chapter Three looks at the image of German resistance which prevailed in 1994, an image reflecting the contribution of both communists and the military elite to German resistance, rather than focusing on just one of these. Chapter Four examines the controversial manner in which 8 May was commemorated in 1995. The East German tradition of remembering this day as one of liberation was combined with the West German tradition of remembering it as one of German pain and loss.

Chapter Five explores the impact of Goldhagen's *Hitler's Willing Executioners* in 1996, a book which led to greater awareness of the guilt of the 'ordinary German'; prior to this, Germans had tended to blame Hitler and the SS for Nazi crimes. Chapter Six examines the reception of the 'Crimes of the *Wehrmacht*' exhibition, which impacted on the general public in a manner comparable to Goldhagen's study. Martin Walser may have given a rather revisionist speech in 1998, but the complex reception of this speech, the subject of Chapter Seven, led among other things to an awareness that Germans in the present and future must take personal responsibility for remembering Nazism, instead of delegating responsibility to the state. Chapter Eight looks at the evolution of the plan (beginning in 1988 and ongoing) to build a Holocaust Memorial in Berlin, a plan that inspired a debate about principles of inclusion and exclusion. Should the memorial 'just' commemorate the Jews? Should it be 'just' a memorial?

I have prefixed these chapters with a chapter on changes in the commemorative and documentary landscapes at former concentration camp sites (Chapter One), and a chapter on memorials at sites with a 'double' past (Chapter Two). A consideration of developments at concentration camp memorial sites since 1990 reveals most clearly how previously neglected areas of Nazism have been included in the landscape of memory. The analysis of developments at sites with a 'double' past both demonstrates the dangers of totalitarianist equationism and points to examples of the way such dangers can be overcome. I have not included a chapter on legal responses to the legacy of National Socialism since 1990, as I wished to concentrate in the book on debates relating to 'representations' in the public realm, be these in the form of exhibitions, speeches, political acts or books. There are, however, references in passing to legal questions, and the still current issue of the compensation of forced labourers is examined in Chapter Nine. The chosen debates do not represent the only ones since 1990, but they were – or still are – the most important. Where possible and relevant, I have included references to other debates, such as that triggered by the showing of *Schindler's List* (in Chapter Three), or the publication of Victor Klemperer's diaries (Chapter Five). The final chapter (Chapter Nine) looks at the role played by the National Socialist past in the Berlin Republic – the term applied to Germany since the parliament moved to Berlin in 1999. It also examines the impact on coming to terms with the past of the 1998 change of government. In September 1998, the Social Democrats (SPD) and B'90/Greens formed a coalition, taking over the reins of government from the Christian Democrats (CDU/CSU) and Liberal Democrats (FDP). What will be Germany's attitude to the National Socialist past in the new millennium?

Throughout, I have sought to write a book that will be of interest to the general reader, specialist and student alike. I was very aware when I began this project that there is, to date, no book which provides an overview of the post-1990 debates in Germany on the Third Reich, despite the fact that several of these debates are now discussed in university courses at German and history departments in Britain and in the USA. The largely thematic approach I have adopted will make it possible for the chapters to be used as 'modules', as well as understood as parts of a larger whole. Each chapter is therefore largely self-supporting, providing the necessary historical background required for an understanding of the issues addressed. For overview purposes, a chronological table of the main events of the period 1933–2000 in Germany is provided at the start of the book.

The book draws *inter alia* on a wide range of newspaper reports. References to these have been kept as brief as possible, so as not to disturb the flow of the text (a key to the abbreviated names of newspapers is provided at the end of the book). I have also drawn on academic secondary literature. The bibliography features only a proportion of the books and articles relating to issues of coming to terms with the Nazi past which have appeared in the last ten years. However, the ones listed are, I believe, the most important. Together with the present book, they will provide a corpus of material for university courses.

1 Concentration camp memorial sites

'It is a fact that we either want to learn from the past, or we condemn ourselves to repeating old mistakes. The facts of concentration camp conditions, the causes of the atrocities there, the assessment of degrees of guilt and the naming of the victims are, taken together, important areas of information which must never be repressed nor forgotten.'

(Schafft and Zeidler 1996: 7)

Sites of crime, sites of memory

Concentration camps have long been a method of terrorizing and neutralizing groups identified as 'the enemy'. The very first of these were set up in Cuba in 1896 (*campos de concentración*), where the Spanish governor 'concentrated' Cuban rebels in camps in an attempt to break their resistance to Spanish colonial rule. In 1900, the British established 'concentration camps' in South Africa during the Boer War. Arguably, it was during the Weimar Republic (1918–1933) that the first concentration camps were created in Germany. Reich President Ebert used emergency decrees in 1923 to quash political unrest: communists were taken into 'protective custody' in former prisoner-of-war (POW) camps. These camps, and those set up in the early 1920s in Stargard and Cottbus-Sielow to 'concentrate' Eastern European Jews who had fled from the Poles and Russians, were in some very limited respects precursors to the Nazi camps (Drobisch and Wieland 1993: 16–21). Although conditions in the Weimar Republic camps could be poor, they were not murderous; and they were not a typical feature of the Weimar political system. It was the Nazis who institutionalized, perfected and made a murderous machine of the concentration camp system. After the arson attempt on the *Reichstag* on 27 February 1933 – which the Nazis blamed on the communists – the regime set about incarcerating communists in prisons and camps. The earliest camps were 'ad hoc affairs, set up by local Party bosses, the police and the SA' (Burleigh 2000: 198–9). The most notorious 'wild' SA camp was probably that at Oranienburg (Morsch 1994). But it was under the SS that the concentration camp system was to be developed into a monstrous instrument. The first SS-run camp to be established was Dachau, opened in March 1933. In the course of the 1930s, the whole concentration camp empire was coordinated and centralized by SS leader Heinrich Himmler, who placed it under the authority of Theodor Eicke. Eicke had become Commandant at Dachau in June 1933. He was responsible for building up the notorious Death's Head units, from which camp guards were recruited. Other camps followed Dachau: the main ones were Sachsenhausen (1936), Buchenwald (1937), Flossenbürg (1938), Neuengamme (1938) and Ravensbrück (1938–1939), the latter for women prisoners. The new camp at Sachsenhausen was valuable because of its proximity to Berlin – it could be used to incarcerate 'enemies of the Reich' quickly in case of war. But economic factors played an increasingly central role in the choice and development of sites, as the SS sought to turn the camp empire into a thriving economic concern. Thus prisoners at Sachsenhausen slaved away in nearby brickworks; bricks were needed to fuel Speer's rebuilding programme in Berlin. In Flossenbürg prisoners were put to work in quarries. Many satellite camps were set up at the site of armaments firms.

The number of inmates rose rapidly in the course of the first five years Hitler was in power. The composition of the inmate population changed over time and was different from camp to camp. A few generalizations, however, can be made. Prior to 1937, it was principally political opponents of Nazism who had been held – social democrats and communists, but also 'dissident' members of the clergy; among the communists and social democrats, however, were many Jews. Increasingly, racial politics played a part in reasons for internment. In 1938, the Nazis stepped up their campaign of terror against Jews. In the course of the 'Action Workshy Reich', and subsequent to the *Reichskristallnacht* pogrom of 9–10 November 1938, thousands of Jews were detained in the concentration camps, many of them, however, only for a short period. Thus between April and December 1938, 13,687 Jews were sent to Buchenwald by the Criminal Police and Gestapo (GB 1999: 76). The sharpening of the laws against homosexuality in 1935 led to the imprisonment of homosexuals in the concentration camps, although their number remained relatively low. Another group to suffer incarceration was the Sinti and Roma, many of whom were arrested in April and July 1938 along with the so-called 'asocials' in line with the 'Basic Ruling on the Preventative Combating of Crime' (Wippermann 1999: 50). Jehovah's Witnesses, who refused allegiance to Hitler and military service, were interned in concentration camps as of 1935, and particularly from 1937: by the end of 1938, the number of Jehovah's Witnesses in Buchenwald had reached 477 (GB 1999: 70).

Following the outbreak of war in 1939, more and more foreign nationals from the occupied countries – Czechs, Poles, Dutch, Russians, French – were deported to the concentration camps within Germany, either as hostages, because of their role or alleged role in resistance, as prisoners of war, because they were Jews or in other ways 'racially inferior', or for purposes of slave labour (often motives were mixed). In 1942, as the Nazis stepped up their programme to make Germany 'Jew-free' and, ultimately, exterminate them in the 'Final Solution', most Jews in concentration camps within Germany were deported to work or annihilation camps in Poland, such as Auschwitz. Those considered too weak for deportation were killed: thus many of Buchenwald's Jews were gassed at Bernburg, a euthanasia centre (GB 1999: 128). The 'detention camp' at Bergen-Belsen, set up in April 1943, was something of an exception: it was used to hold 'exchange Jews', Jews of foreign nationality whom the

Nazis planned to exchange for German POWs. In the course of 1944, it developed into a full concentration camp. As the Red Army pushed the *Wehrmacht* back in 1944 and 1945, the Nazis were forced to evacuate the work and annihilation camps in the occupied territories. Thousands of Jews died during the transport to Buchenwald, Dachau and other camps. In the overcrowded camps in Germany, the mortality rate in the final months of the war – as a result of hunger, disease and murder – was catastrophically high. As the Allies approached the concentration camps, further evacuations, or 'death marches', claimed the lives of thousands. In a terrible error of 3 May 1945, British bombers attacked two ships in Lübeck Bay that were full of evacuated prisoners. More than 7,000 of them died (see AIN 1995).

Generally speaking, the concentration camps within Germany were not centres of industrialized genocide, in contrast to the annihilation camps in Nazi-occupied Poland where the 'Final Solution' was for the most part carried out. But systematic slaughters and innumerable gratuitous killings were still the norm. One of the most notorious massacres was the methodical execution of Soviet POWs. With the cooperation and collaboration of the *Wehrmacht*, political commissars, state and Communist Party functionaries and other 'undesirable elements' among the Soviet POWs were rounded up, deported to Sachsenhausen and Buchenwald, and then killed in their thousands by means of a specially constructed apparatus which delivered a fatal shot to the neck. Eight thousand Soviet soldiers died in this way at Buchenwald alone between the summer of 1941 and the summer of 1942. Many concentration camp prisoners died when they were deported to Nazi extermination centres in Poland. Others perished as a result of labour, starvation and disease in the concentration camps. Thus, all in all, about 50,000 people lost their lives at Bergen-Belsen, 56,000 at Buchenwald. Those who survived till liberation died soon afterwards, or lived with lifelong traumas – victims of a concentration camp system notorious for its injustice, exploitation and murderous brutality.

After the end of the war, Auschwitz-Birkenau, site of the mass murder of over a million Jews, lay beyond the East German border in Poland, and far enough away from West Germany for its citizens to be tempted to forget it had once existed – at least until the 1963–1965 Auschwitz trials in Frankfurt. But the former camps at Bergen-Belsen, Dachau, Flossenbürg and Neuengamme became potential sites of memory for West Germans; Sachsenhausen, Buchenwald and Ravensbrück potential sites of memory for East Germans. More than anything else, the post-war treatment of these sites was going to be a measure of the preparedness of Germans to face up to the criminality of National Socialism. This chapter will demonstrate that, while memorial sites were set up at the former camps in both Germanys (more resolutely in East Germany, and also with more staff), these sites were subjected to the process of divided and one-sided memory outlined in the Introduction. Ideology, with its attendant overemphases, distortions and omissions, made its mark on forms of representation at the memorial sites (more so in East Germany). From the immediate post-1945 period onwards, moreover, most former camps were subjected to a process of refunctionalization, and thus of historical estrangement. Only as of the 1980s, but particularly after unification, did a concern to create a more rounded picture of camp life, of victims and perpetrators, and to recover the original topographies become noticeable. This concern has resulted in significant changes to the exhibitions at all concentration camp memorial sites, especially in eastern Germany, where the ideological imprint was more pronounced than in the FRG. It has also resulted in an 'expansion' of the memorial sites, as they reach out to encompass the original extent of the camps – the inclusive model of memory at work.

Putting to a new use

After liberating the camps, the Allies did, to a degree, confront Germans with the atrocities there, as, for example, when the Americans made the citizens of Weimar face piles of corpses at Buchenwald. In November 1945, moreover, the Americans were instrumental in arranging for a small exhibition on SS crimes to be shown at Dachau, concurrently with the staging of the first Dachau Trial. But the Allies also set a precedent of erasing traces and of new utilization. In the case of the burning down of prisoners' huts by the British in Bergen-Belsen, such erasure was a necessary response to the danger of typhus. Faced with the need to intern or relocate so many people, moreover, the Allies cannot readily be blamed for turning the former concentration camps into internment or relocation camps. Practical exigencies were paramount, and the concentration camps in any case were associated with such dire suffering that it might, at first, have seemed perverse to want to 'preserve' them. With hindsight, however, it is unfortunate that the Allies inscribed new historical narratives into the sites, because to a degree these overwrote the first narrative. There was an additional problem. While some of these narratives, as in the case of the imprisonment of SS men by the Western Allies, appeared at least to stand in punitive relation to National Socialist crimes, others created new legacies of injustice. Thus at 'Special Camps' set up by the Soviets in Sachsenhausen and Buchenwald *inter alia*, thousands of Germans died of malnutrition and disease after 1945. This was a narrative East Germans were not able to relate until 1990, but when it was related, there was a danger it would divert the focus away from the atrocities of the concentration camps (see Chapter Two). Even when the former concentration camps had become well established as memorial sites, the Allies continued to use parts of them for military purposes, particularly so in East Germany. Ravensbrück Memorial Site, for instance, opened in September 1959, was perched on the lakeside at the edge of the original camp topography, while the Soviets continued to use the area of the former camp huts, not least for tanks and as materials depots, right up to unification in 1990. Their officers lived in the yellow-painted settlement formerly used by the SS administration and camp guards, and a number of new buildings were constructed for canteen, commercial, industrial and living purposes. A whole new military culture encrusted itself around the fig-leaf memorial site. In Dachau in West Germany, too, the area of the SS camp remained under US military control until 1972, including the camp's entrance-building and the so-called *Bunker*, a set of cells in which prominent or significant prisoners had been interned. After this, the Bavarian riot police took over these areas, sealing off the original entrance to Dachau camp.

The use of parts of the camps by the Allies continued beyond their immediate post-war remit. The resulting constriction of the memorial sites served to trivialize the past; memorial site visitors left Ravensbrück and Dachau with the impression of an altogether smaller camp complex. The Germans were also quick to allocate other uses to the camps, and here the concern was both one of practicality, and one of hiding an uncomfortable past. When Flossenbürg and Dachau were passed over to Bavaria, the Bavarian Regional Parliament ruled on 29 April 1948 that they should be used to house Germans expelled *inter alia* from the Sudetenland (in Czechoslovakia). Within the space of a few years, Flossenbürg had seen a series of different occupants come and go. It thus continued to function as a 'transit' camp, a role which it had had in the Third Reich. After liberation in 1945, it was used to imprison SS men. From 1946 to 1947, it was used as a United Nations Relief and Rehabilitation Administration camp, housing displaced persons (DPs) such as former concentration camp inmates, forced labourers and prisoners of war. As of 1947–1948, it served as collection camp for Germans who had been forced to leave the Sudetenland and other areas east of the Oder and Neiße rivers. In the mid-1950s, the community of Flossenbürg tore down the former concentration camp huts and sold the ground to the expellees. Family homes replaced the traces of terror as the expellees became a permanent feature of the landscape. The presence of these expellees was a political and psychological statement to the effect that the Germans chose to empathize with *this* group of victims, rather than with the victims for whose sufferings the Germans themselves had been responsible. The sense of injustice at the expulsion from and loss of the eastern territories was inscribed stubbornly over the narrative of National Socialist perpetration. Street names, such as Sudeten Street and Silesian Way, functioned as signposts to this injustice. A similar practice of street-naming was established near Dachau's former concentration camp (see Chapter Three).

A different, yet comparable situation, obtained at Neuengamme. In 1948, the city of Hamburg took over the former camp site from the British and promptly turned a significant part of it into a massive prison [Plate 1.1]. The former SS main guard house together with a watchtower became the entrance to this new 'Institution for the Implementation of Justice' (*Justizvollzugsanstalt*), and the crematorium and a number of wooden huts were torn down to make way for it. A year before, in 1947, one legal councillor had opined that setting up a model prison would represent an 'act of making good', a means of 'restoring Hamburg's honour and reputation' (quoted in *FR*, 8 May 1997). Certainly the prison was well intended, but it also represented a rather hurried and defensive attempt at demonstrating self-improvement. Hamburg sought to avoid confronting its past by asserting that it was now operating a penal system in accordance with the highest standards of justice. Worse, there was an all too pervasive implication that the problem under the National Socialists had been the inhumane way the camp was run. Of course this had been one of the problems, indeed the main one. But the other problem had been that the people incarcerated under Hitler were innocent. It was not just the penal environment that was criminal in Neuengamme camp, but the fact that people had been imprisoned there in the first place.

Plate 1.1 Neuengamme Memorial Site. In the background, a prison built after the war by the City of Hamburg.

When, in 1991, the building of a supermarket at Ravensbrück hit the headlines, there was a national outcry – not least from west Germans keen to point the finger at east Germans. Yet in 1991 the prison still stood at Neuengamme despite years of protest from former camp prisoners, and it seemed set to stay; indeed a second prison, a youth detention centre, had been added in 1970. Moreover, in 1973, a wharf company was allowed to lease the east wing of the former concentration camp's clinker brick factory, and even to use a canal built by camp prisoners. Commercial use was no exception in the West. At Flossenbürg, the SS canteen, first used as a cinema after 1945, became a restaurant. The Upper Palatinate Stone Industry used the quarry area, with its huts and SS administrative buildings, as of 1950; the camp laundry-room and kitchen, together with the roll-call area, was used for years by the French firm Alcatel. In line with this commercial use, new factories were built on the site in the 1970s and 1980s. Nor did the GDR shy from industrial use. One firm (*VEB Spezialbau*) built technical equipment for the *Stasi* and SED near Ravensbrück. In Buchenwald, an agricultural collective kept grain in a former concentration camp building until 1985. Both the GDR and FRG used camp sites for military purposes. Traces of the presence of the GDR's National People's Army (*Nationale Volksarmee*) at Sachsenhausen are still visible today, and the West German army (*Bundeswehr*) used the concentration camp at Esterwegen, where the publicist Carl von Ossietzky had been held, as a depot. Other institutions also made use of former camp sites. In Oranienburg (East Germany), the concentration camp where the anarchist writer Erich Mühsam was murdered vanished altogether under a new building for the police; the camp at Moringen (West Germany) was smothered by a regional hospital and clinics as of 1955.

The uses described above reduced or even removed the space available for memorialization. In giving the camp sites new functions, the GDR and FRG created new associations for these sites, linking them to the present or future, thus stifling associations with the past. Indeed the former sites were used as a vehicle for demonstrating the self-transformational energies of the perpetrator nation, at the cost of empathy with the victims. West German camp memorial sites became the focus of a constant struggle, principally led by organizations representing camp victims, to 'win back' those areas of the camps now used by industry or state institutions. Victims insisted on the revisualization of the true parameters of their agonies. They thus soon found themselves engaged in a new struggle against discrimination, this time in the area of memory. While such protest often went unheard, it could not be articulated, or not to the same degree, in East Germany. The reason for this was the centralized running of Buchenwald, Ravensbrück and Sachsenhausen, and the state cooption and control of the streamlined victims' organization.

The memorial sites in the West

Against this background, it will come as no surprise that the areas reserved for remembering the National Socialist history of the camps were themselves shaped in accordance with certain 'diversionary' tactics. In the case of West Germany, forms of remembering were often heavily Christianized. This was particularly so at Dachau Memorial Site. In 1960, in front of 50,000 people, the 'Chapel of Christ's Fear of Death' was dedicated. In 1963, the foundation-stone was laid for a Carmelite Monastery. Construction of the Protestant Church of Conciliation began in 1965. Given that these confessional buildings were constructed on the site of the former camp vegetable garden and disinfection building, one might see here a certain covering up of traces. Christian opponents of Hitler were incarcerated in Dachau, and Christian forms of remembrance were needed by a considerable number of Dachau's former inmates. In providing spiritual support, the Protestant and Catholic Churches could make some amends for the degree to which, as institutions, they had tolerated and even collaborated with National Socialism. But there was, equally, a danger that their role in administering consolation in the present would obscure their failures in the past. Moreover, the focus on Christ's prefigurative agonies invited visitors to the memorial site to view the sufferings of Dachau's inmates as derived and secondary, or as part of mankind's condition. Unveiled in September 1968, the International Memorial by Nandor Glid portrays emaciated figures whose thin bodies are so contorted and drawn out that they have become indistinguishable from barbed wire [Plate 1.2]; there are echoes of Christ's suffering on the cross. Setting camp suffering within a Christian context lends it an air of inevitability and stresses that it can be overcome through divine love and grace. The focus on the consolations of the life after death also usefully deflects attention from issues of immediate human responsibility and redress on earth. As

Plate 1.2 The International Memorial at Dachau Memorial Site.

they walk from the top of the memorial site, which houses the exhibition, to the bottom, where the Christian buildings predominate, visitors take part in a ritual of salvation. The journey symbolizes the transition from earth to heaven, or even hell to heaven.

In the former Flossenbürg camp, the Chapel of Atonement 'Jesus in Prison' was opened on 25 May 1947. It was constructed from granite stones taken from torn-down camp watchtowers. The Chapel was built at the instigation of former prisoners, notably Poles, but can nevertheless be read as an image of Catholic Bavaria's ingestion and reprocessing of the past; the vigilant eye of National Socialist guards is replaced by the merciful eye of Christ. Three original watch-towers do remain, one of which is connected to the Chapel by a walkway; but this link implies that the Chapel can transform perpetration into grace and forgiveness. As in the case of Dachau, it seemed that the state of Bavaria preferred to delegate coming to terms with the past to the Christian Church. While it was necessary to lay out graveyards, this could, moreover, serve a dubious purpose, in that the National Socialist past could then be buried along with the bodies. In 1957, 4,387 people who died during death-marches from Flossenbürg were exhumed from provisional graves. They were then reburied in what became the 'Honorary Cemetery' with a 'Park of the Last Place of Rest' at Flossenbürg Memorial Site. To make way for this cemetery and park, another original concentration camp build-ing, the Disinfection Building, was torn down. Giving the dead a last place of rest was instrumentalized as a means, to put it provocatively, of 'disinfecting' the site of associations with the perpetrators. 'Greening over the past' was common practice at memorial sites in both West and East Germany. Significantly, the Bavarian Administration of State Castles, Gardens and Lakes was responsible for Dachau and Flossenbürg Memorial Sites right up to 1990. In the GDR, trees were planted at post-1950 Buchenwald, and a park-like setting was created at Sachsenhausen Memorial Site. In East and West, a certain touristy prettification prevailed.

To be fair, the suffering of non-Christians, notably of Jews, was commemorated in the West by means of various memorials. Jewish prisoners in Bergen-Belsen erected a wooden memorial in 1945; it was replaced by a memorial of stone in 1946, which still stands at the memorial site today. There are also Jewish memorials at Flossenbürg Memorial Site. But there was often a time-lag. It was not until 1967 that the Jewish Memorial Temple was dedicated at Dachau Memorial Site. A sign in Dachau pointed to 'Religious Memorial Centres – Protestant, Catholic, Jewish', setting the priorities clearly. Memorials at West German memorial sites dedicated to all victims of National Socialism, such as the memorial slabs naming the countries of the victims at Neuengamme (1965), or the wall of commemoration in different languages in Bergen-Belsen (dedicated in 1952), reflected the will to honour the dead in all their diversity. But there were omissions. The Sinti and Roma were not allocated a place on the Bergen-Belsen wall until 1982, and an application put in by Dutch Sinti and Roma for a memorial at Bergen-Belsen has, to date, not been approved. Moreover, there was a problematic tendency to lump German war-dead together with camp victims. In 1951, a number of former French camp prisoners wrote to Hamburg's Senate asking for a memorial to be erected at Neuengamme in honour of French victims. In response, Hamburg's Cemetery Office seriously suggested constructing one not at the former camp site, but in Neuengamme's village cemetery – in close proximity to a planned monument honouring local German soldiers who had died in the 1939–1945 War (Neuengamme 1951).

Only gradually did the realization set in that memorial sites should not function solely as places of commemoration, but also, especially given continued evidence of right-wing radicalism in West Germany, as places of historical enlightenment. Initial attempts at documentation, with its inevitable focus on the crimes, were resisted. A small exhibition opened in Dachau's crematorium was closed in 1953; instead, in 1955, Dachau's Regional Council sought to have the crematorium removed, and was stopped only by the Federal Republic's signature under the Paris Treaties. It took Dachau until 1965 to construct a serious permanent exhibition – which it did not least as a result of pressure exerted by Dachau's International Committee of former prisoners (set up in 1955). Bergen-Belsen followed suit in 1966. In Neuengamme, the first exhibition was opened in 1981: at Neuengamme Memorial Site, as at Dachau, it was an association of former prisoners, in this case the 'Amicale Internationale de Neuengamme' (founded in 1958), which was the motor behind developments. Flossenbürg is only now in the process of establishing a permanent exhibition. In line with the Cold War, West German exhibitions understressed communist resistance in the camps, while overstressing Christian resistance. Dachau's standing exhibition, in its presentation of the

Weimar Republic, implicitly equates communists with extreme right-wing groups. While it does contain a reference to the fact that between 2,000 and 3,000 of Dachau's inmates in 1933–1934 were communists, this reference is hidden away in a quotation from the *Manchester Guardian*. By contrast, an enlarged photograph of a statistical table listing the various kinds of religious prisoners hits the visitor full in the face. Communist resistance is subsumed under generalizing terms such as 'opposition', or ranked after that of clergymen and social democrats. To an extent, the victims' group responsible for the exhibition, the International Dachau Committee, was gradually purged of communists and fell under the sway of Christians such as the Munich Bishop Johannes Neuhäusler, a Dachau prisoner whose integrity was later compromised by his intervention on behalf of National Socialists standing trial. The Christianization of Dachau went hand in hand with an anti-communist exhibition agenda.

The same agenda was visible in the lack of sympathy for the fate of Russian soldiers. Until April 1990, Bergen-Belsen Memorial Site neglected the early history of Bergen-Belsen as a *Wehrmacht*-run POW camp. Between 1941 and 1943, tens of thousands of Russian soldiers were either murdered, or died of maltreatment, starvation and disease at Bergen-Belsen. At Dachau's Memorial Site, the murder of 6,000 Soviet POWs in nearby Hebertshausen by the SS was inadequately documented – not least because the Russians destined for execution had come from POW camps where the *Wehrmacht* cooperated with the Reich Security Main Office in sifting out execution candidates. The reason for this commemorative neglect was not just the Cold War, but also West Germany's blinkered idealization of the *Wehrmacht*, not revised until the post-unification 'Crimes of the *Wehrmacht*' exhibition (see Chapter Six). In a letter of 12 December 1998, Bergen-Belsen historian Thomas Rahe also pointed out to me that the 1966 Bergen-Belsen exhibition was pitifully small, as well as didactically and historiographically unsound: not until the end of the 1980s was there a 'collection of photographs, documents, personal recollections or artefacts'. He also writes that Bergen-Belsen was 'a memorial site without staff'; before 1987, the whole complex was 'run' by a janitor. A similar situation existed in Dachau. The recent commission responsible for suggesting changes to Dachau's Memorial Site was critical of lack of staffing: 'Dachau is the camp memorial site with the highest number of visitors in Germany (in 1995 about 700,000), but with the comparatively lowest staffing numbers' (Fachbeirat Dachau 1996: 2). Dachau in the early 1990s had four permanent members of staff, while pre-1990 Buchenwald had about a hundred.

The memorial sites in the East

Concentration camp memorial sites in West Germany were the responsibility of regional ministries and local government, with considerable involvement on the part of groups representing former prisoners. This tendency to 'leave things up to the regions' resulted in a degree of neglect. In the GDR, there was the opposite problem of overcentralization. Not that centralization was only negative. The SED's interest in promoting its moral credentials as the 'better' German state did at least have the benefit that 'National Sites of Warning and Memory' were opened at Buchenwald (1958), Ravensbrück (1959) and Sachsenhausen (1961) earlier than the fully-fledged memorial sites at Dachau and Neuengamme (1965). Public donations helped towards their construction. Ulbricht himself oversaw preparations for the opening of the memorial site at Sachsenhausen, to which some 200,000 people came: the streets of Oranienburg were lined with flags to mark the occasion. But, in the final analysis, centralization meant uniformity, monopolization and politicization of memory. The VVN, or 'Association of Those Persecuted by the Nazi Regime', had been set up in March 1947 to represent the interests of victims of Nazism. Its dissolution in the GDR (disguised as a 'self-dissolution') in February 1953 was followed by the setting up of a Committee of Anti-fascist Resistance Fighters, run largely by SED functionaries. From now on, management of the past was streamlined to reflect both the 'heroic' role of communist resistance in the concentration camps, and the GDR's self-understanding as heir to its spirit in the struggle against western capitalism.

This streamlining was ensured by a quasi-legal statute of 28 July 1961 which fused Buchenwald, Ravensbrück and Sachsenhausen into one national memorial site. The second article of this statute outlined the various functions this mega-site was to have (see MfWFK 1992b: 13). It was to depict the following: the struggle of all democratic forces and of the German working class against fascism; the role of the Communist Party as the central force behind resistance; the common struggle of all European nations – particularly the Soviets – against the 'SS terror'. The result of this mandate was a uniform picture at all three memorial sites, which told the same tale of communist-led resistance. This narrative was embedded, again in accordance with the mandate, within the wider one of the struggle of the international and revolutionary working class against the 'renascence of capitalism and fascism' in West Germany in the present. West German Christianity imposed sense on camp suffering by placing it within the narrative of man's difficult spiritual journey towards the promise of the after-life. East Germany's stress on communist resistance located this suffering within the narrative of man's social and political journey from fascist capitalism to socialism, and the promise of paradise on earth.

Strikingly, then, there were unexpected structural and semantic similarities between the West and East German models of remembering. Indeed, underlying the heroization of communist resistance was East Germany's secular version of the Passion. The glorification of German communist leader Ernst Thälmann (killed at Buchenwald) or Rosa Thälmann (interned at Ravensbrück) had Christian overtones. The figures in Fritz Cremer's monumental sculpture on the Ettersberg (1958), which celebrates camp resistance and solidarity in Buchenwald, bear the face of Ernst Thälmann. His suffering, like that of Christ, is everywhere. The message is: he died so that you might live. Clearly, this nimbus of martyrdom surrounding Thälmann idealized suffering as effectively as some forms of Christian cross. The imposition of sense on suffering removed the need to ask how the suffering came about. The significant difference between East and West Germany lay in the concept of victimhood. In the West, camp inmates were often seen as passive, helpless pawns in a devilish game. In the East, the communist inmates, at least, were seen as active. They suffered, but they transcended their suffering by directing energies towards resistance, even liberation. Thus the GDR made much of the fact that camp inmates had helped to liberate Buchenwald, transforming their assistance of the American liberators into an act of self-liberation.

The more active the prisoners appeared, the less they came across as victims. The active prisoner had another essential asset: he was forward-looking. The GDR's self-legitimation was in part based on the claim that it was continuing the struggle for which all anti-fascists in Buchenwald and Sachsenhausen, not just the communists, had given so much. Indeed it had already fulfilled some of the goals of these anti-fascists in setting up a socialist state which had overcome the evils of capitalism and was opposed to capitalist imperialism throughout the world. At frequent junctures the GDR stressed this role as worthy successor in an ongoing battle. An appendix to a Central Committee meeting of 28 April 1958 ruled that the opening ceremony at Buchenwald's new memorial site on 14 September of that year was not to be exclusively dedicated to commemoration and mourning, but 'must make reference to the current tasks facing democratic and socialist powers in the struggle to maintain and secure peace' (SAPMO 1958). The minutes of the same meeting point to the 'clerical fascist and military reaction in West Germany' (SAPMO 1958). The GDR avoided confronting German guilt for National Socialism by identifying with the 'good' Germans in the camps, playing down the element of victimhood, and foisting responsibility for continuing National Socialist traditions on to the FRG.

Not just official commemorative acts, but exhibitions and catalogues were often little more than illustrations of this model of memory. In 1986, the memorial centre at Buchenwald published a small brochure designed to act as a guided tour to the site. The account it provided was structured in accordance with a 'negative–positive' perspective, a consciously bipolar perception of individual buildings and events. Thus the description of Quarantine Block 17 pointed out not only that this block housed British and Canadian military destined for liquidation, but also that the solidarity of anti-fascists had saved the lives of four of these 'patriots' (Ritscher 1986: 10). The section on the *Effektenkammer* informed the reader that this was where the prisoners had to hand over their clothes and possessions, and where anti-fascists hid the three-year-old Jew Stefan Jerzy Zweig (Ritscher 1986: 11). Suffering and resistance at the GDR's Buchenwald Memorial Site were presented as preconditionally linked; it was the mystery of communism which functioned as the alchemistic transformer of one into the other. A teleological superstructure was imposed on camp life which, if unintentionally, legitimized its horrors. In the same way, memorial statues such as Cremer's figures on the Ettersberg, or Willi Lammert's *The Carrier* (1957) and Cremer's *Mothers of Ravensbrück* (1959–60) at Ravensbrück all transformed misery and death into a kind of muscular spiritual energy focused on defiant mutual support and solidarity.

Visitors to today's Sachsenhausen still have a chance to view part of the old GDR main camp exhibition dating back in part to 1961, and in part to 1974. They will be struck by the contextualization of the history of the camp within the broader history of the 'patriotic' anti-fascist struggle in past and present, and within the history of the war, represented in terms of the Soviet defeat of the Germans at Stalingrad, the Soviet liberation of eastern Germany, and Soviet victory in 1945. National Socialist Germans are presented in the exhibition as 'fascists', camp prisoners as 'anti-fascists', conveying the impression that camp life was about an interlocking of well-matched opponents, and the dynamic tension between these. By means of enlarged photographs of emaciated figures, as well as stylized drawings, suffering is resignified as spiritual strength. An artistic representation of camp inmates on glass – culminating in a figure with rifle in hand, and accompanied by a heroizing text by Brecht – imposes a positive narrative structure. The glass is illuminated from within, creating a transcendent glow. The negative–positive principle dominates throughout. Thus a photograph of neatly aligned skulls, displayed to demonstrate the destructiveness of slave labour capitalism, is contrasted with photographs of individual resistance figures, or with a close-up photograph of a few determined-looking faces at roll-call dubbed 'The Face of the Anti-Fascist' [Plate 1.3]. Blown-up photographs undermine, rather than enhance, the reality of what is portrayed. In the pathology building, enlargements of photographs of detached limbs rob these of their natural dimensions. The overall impression is one of an unreal chamber of horrors.

The GDR understood fascism to be a barbaric form of capitalist exploitation. Anti-semitism and racism were regarded at best as secondary manifestations, or mere by-products. Given this fact, there was little room for the history of racial

Plate 1.3 'The Face of the Anti-Fascist': exhibit in the GDR's main exhibition at Sachsenhausen Memorial Site.

persecution in GDR representations of camp life. Sinti and Roma were virtually excluded from representation. The fate of the Jews was underemphasized, in part also as a consequence of Stalinist anti-semitism and the GDR's anti-Israel stance. It is true that a Jewish memorial stone was laid at Buchenwald Memorial Site in 1964, and an exhibition on the Jewish prisoners opened at Sachsenhausen in 1961 – albeit only after Jewish and particularly Israeli protest at the planned exclusion of a specific section focusing on Jewish suffering from Sachsenhausen's museums (Titz 1995: 15–24). But the fate of the Jews was presented one-sidedly. At Sachsenhausen, the exhibition on the Jews presented the visitor with little concrete information on Jewish suffering, focusing instead on acts of resistance such as the revolt of Jewish prisoners in the face of imminent deportation to Auschwitz on 22 October 1942 (zur Nieden 1996: 275). The persecution of the Jews, moreover, was viewed from the perspective of communist sympathy and solidarity. Thus while the exhibition made mention of the Jewish victims of the November 1938 *Reichskristallnacht* pogrom (dubbed 'Fascist Pogrom Night' in GDR terminology), it highlighted the fact that the German Communist Party had protested against the November pogrom in a 1938 edition of its newspaper *The Red Flag*. In GDR remembrance ceremonies, the pogrom was principally associated with communist courage, only secondarily with Jewish suffering. Buchenwald's memorial stone to the victims of the pogrom was therefore a symbol of communist pride.

At Buchenwald Memorial Site, there was a particular focus on the fact that the camp resistance groups had saved the life of a young Jew, Stefan Jerzy Zweig. The hiding of Zweig was presented to the outside world by the GDR as proof of communist grit and pro-Jewish sentiment. Not that all former communist prisoners relished the focus on Zweig; they regarded him with suspicion, accusing him of being either a *Stasi* spy or the state's darling. Zweig left the GDR in 1972. The GDR was quick to politicize the theme of Jewish suffering. The final section of the Sachsenhausen exhibition on the Jews featured the not unfounded claim that West Germany had failed to overcome the legacy of anti-semitism, and the unfounded claim that the GDR had succeeded in doing so (zur Nieden 1996: 277). In reality, the GDR, certainly in the 1950s, was hardly friendly towards Jews, some of whom fell prey to an increasing anti-Zionism following the Slansky trial in Prague in 1952; many left for the West, reducing the Jewish community in the GDR to a few hundred. Jewish victims of Nazism were treated as second-class victims following a ruling of 1949. This ruling made distinctions between (mostly communist) 'resistance fighters' and (mostly Jewish) 'victims', the former receiving more compensation than the latter (Herf 1997: 95). The VVN was gradually purged of individuals of whom the SED had grown suspicious, and Jewish members were also excluded prior to its dissolution (Leo 1996). It was only in the 1980s that the GDR appeared to 'rediscover' the fate of the Jews between 1933 and 1945, and even then the motive may well have been economic as the SED, in 1988, sought to establish business links with the President of the Jewish World Congress Edgar Bronfman (Wolffsohn 1995: 344ff.).

The real attitude of the GDR towards the Jewish victims is perhaps best exemplified by the case of Jamlitz. Here, the *Waffen*-SS had run a labour-camp with predominantly Jewish inmates between November 1943 and February 1945. From 1956 onwards, a stone sculpture by a Hungarian Jew imprisoned at Jamlitz served as a memorial. In May 1971, a mass-grave with 577 bodies was uncovered. In a macabre imitation of Nazi practice, the Ministry for State Security (*Stasi*) in Cottbus removed the gold from the teeth of the victims before passing the bodies on for cremation – in contravention of GDR laws (Weigelt 1999: 54). The Jewish memorial was removed in September 1971. In the same month, a new one was erected in nearby Lieberose in honour of the generalizing 'victims of fascism'; it showed a large red triangle, symbol of communist resistance. By moving the memorial to Lieberose, the local SED sought to resignify it, loosening its associations with Jewish suffering at Jamlitz. The SED wished to detract attention from Jamlitz for another reason: it had served as a Soviet Special Camp after 1945 (see Chapter Two).

The new generation

Were it not for the engagement and persistence of surviving victims, the major concentration camp sites in the West might have fallen into complete neglect. As it was, the developing memorial sites were long perceived as centres of commemoration for certain groups of victims or their families, not as places for Germans to reflect on their nation's crimes. The work of processing the past was left to the Christian Church. In the East, camp memorial sites were so heavily politicized that only certain groups of victims were remembered, and then only in so far as they were useful. Their agony was not the central issue. It took a new generation of West Germans, not least schoolchildren and students, in the 1970s and particularly the 1980s to draw attention to the need for Germans to remember their victims. To a lesser degree, generation changes in the GDR had a similar impact.

It was West Germany's then Federal President Gustav Heinemann who, in the early 1970s, first promoted the idea of regular nationwide German history competitions among the younger generation. By the late 1990s, some 75,000 young people in the FRG had submitted all in all some 15,000 projects on various aspects of local German history. Many youngsters, such as the daring Anja Rosmus in Passau, chose to probe into the National Socialist past. Thanks to their energies, many previously forgotten sites of pain and perpetration came to light. In Regensburg, a group of students from the local Technical College drew attention in their project to the existence of a small concentration camp in Regensburg itself, known as 'The Colosseum'. As of 1982 a youth group under the auspices of the League of German Unions began to research more thoroughly into this camp (a satellite of Flossenbürg). In East Germany, too, schoolchildren researched into remote sites. Laura, a satellite camp of Buchenwald, was opened as a memorial site on 6 May 1979. But the 'rediscovery' of Laura dates back to the mid-1960s, when a group of schoolchildren in Wurzbach first uncovered the history of the site (Gropp 2000: 5). In the West, schoolchildren and students did much to bring into sharper relief the history and topography of camps which already had memorial sites. In the summer of 1982, Hamburg's Cultural Authorities helped to set up a first international work camp in Neuengamme; twenty young people from eight countries uncovered railway tracks, collected artefacts such as the remains of shoes, and constructed a signposted walkway around the camp indicating the where-abouts and function of its various buildings. Hamburg's Senate then put Neuengamme under a preservation order in 1984. It was also a group of students and academics who, in 1980, began to undertake serious research into the history of the Emslandlager camp.

Younger generations, of course, had nothing to hide, unlike the war generation. Indeed they often had an urgent desire to uncover. The work of these young people helped, in West Germany at least, to make possible a shift towards a more self-critical commemoration of victims, and towards the conceptualization of camp memorial sites as places of historical learning. For a long time, documentation had very much taken second place in relation to commemoration. Arguably, moreover, it was the youth-driven peace movement in both West and East Germany which best understood the legacy of the concentration camps as one of warning against war and destruction. In 1985, peace protesters made their way along a 'path of peace' from Munich's 'Square for the Victims of Fascism' to Dachau and to Hebertshausen. This walk became a regular yearly occurrence. On 1 October 1987, this time in East Germany, several thousand largely young people from peace and environment groups took part in the Olaf Palme March from Ravensbrück to Sachsenhausen. The march was partly coopted by official GDR groups, such as the Free German Youth (FDJ). But it nevertheless represented a determined attempt by the GDR peace movement to interpret the legacy of the camps in the interests of peace and freedom of movement, *against* the anti-fascist instrumentalization by the state.

The peace movement in the FRG and GDR demonstrated, at grass-roots level, a commonality of East–West interest. Towards the end of the 1980s, as Gorbachev began to pursue his policies of *glasnost* and *perestroika*, first tentative steps towards a depoliticization of memory became possible in the two Germanys. This also affected camp memorial sites. In response to a cross-party initiative, the Regional Parliament of Lower Saxony ruled on 18 April 1985 that changes needed to be made at Bergen-Belsen Memorial Site. An advisory commission was convoked. In January 1987, it recommended transforming the exhibition to take account, among other things, of the use of Bergen-Belsen as a POW camp prior to its use as a con-centration camp. A path was laid, linking the Soviet POW cemetery at Hörsten with Bergen-Belsen itself. The acknowledgement of German inhumanity to Soviet prisoners, and the broadening of focus to include the history of the Second World War, represented a significant development. Bergen-Belsen was no longer to be understood merely as a case of SS brutality, but also as an example of a system of warfare and violence in which the *Wehrmacht* was implicated. In East Germany, there was no development that can be compared with that at Bergen-Belsen, but there were noteworthy attempts to adopt a less aggressive policy towards the West. Thus the new-look 1985 Buchenwald exhibition scaled down the attacks on 'fascist continuities' in West Germany. A new 'resistance' museum at Ravensbrück gave different nations from Western and Eastern Europe the chance to create their own rooms of remembrance. The idea was not new; Sachsenhausen's international resistance museum dates from 1961. But at Ravensbrück's new museum, individual countries were given more conceptual and artistic freedom, leading to a fascinating diversity of styles and perspectives beyond all centrality of focus on resistance.

A greater focus on historical documentation, and to a degree therefore on the facts of perpetration, also found its way into the catalogue of changes formulated by the Bergen-Belsen advisory commission in 1987. The commission called for documentation at the memorial site of the history of the National Socialist rise to a mass movement, its ideology and practice of discrimination, Bergen-Belsen's position in the overall camp system, the history of the POW and concentration camp Belsen, the history of other camps situated in Lower Saxony (such as Moringen), and the history of post-war Belsen, as well as of the trials conducted against the perpetrators. The greater stress here on contextualization, the commitment to throwing connections, processes and systems into sharper relief, revealed a concern to move towards what I would call 'embedment'. Not only is a fuller picture a prerequisite for fuller understanding; it also enables the visitor to trace processes back to points of inception and acquire a sense of the need to resist such processes *as and when they begin*. The pedagogical aims of the new concept were reflected in the plan for a larger, better-documented, in part audio-visual exhibition with work-folders for groups of schoolchildren. They were underpinned by the decision to house the exhibition in a new building accommodating a seminar room and a library, and by the provision of an organized visitors' service with guided tours. The increased interest in pedagogy reflected the awareness that young people needed to be informed, especially in view of the danger of neo-Nazism. But it is noteworthy that it was often young people who first undertook the job of enlightenment frequently eschewed and indeed resisted by the older generation.

The *Wende*, unification and the chance of greater change

By 1989, while the situation at concentration camp memorial sites in the GDR was still largely one of monolithic idealization of anti-fascist resistance, the situation at the West German ones was slowly becoming less tendentiously commemorative, more self-critical and less half-hearted, but there was still much to be improved. In the ten years between 1989 and the time of writing in 2000, the topographies of memory at both east and west German camp memorial sites have either been radically transformed, or are in the course of such a transformation, whereby problems of inadequate financial support, degrees of ideological stonewalling and disputes with local communities or organizations representing groups of victims are slowing down the pace of change.

In the west, this change is a continuation of developments in the 1980s, but would not have proceeded as it has done without a number of additional factors.

Gestures of good will extended to eastern European camp inmates in the 1990s at Dachau Memorial Site, for instance, were made possible by the end of the Cold War, as was the erection there of a Russian-Orthodox Chapel in 1995. The tentative post-1990 development of Flossenbürg towards a fully-fledged memorial site and documentation centre has in part been the result of the fact that surviving Soviet and Polish prisoners (the majority of Flossenbürg's inmates) have recently been able to add their voices to calls for such a development. The reunification of Germany, the problem of neo-Nazism, fears abroad of renascent German nationalism, and Germany's awareness of its need to demonstrate its democratic intent provided the wider political backdrop to decisions in 1991 and 1994 respectively to set up advisory commissions for restructuring the memorial sites at Neuengamme and Dachau. The 50th anniversary of the end of the war in 1995 was bound to attract enormous international attention (see Chapter Four). The date of 8 May 1995 became a focal point either for the completion of changes or, at least, for the expression of a will to change. Thus in Neuengamme the new exhibition was opened on 4 May 1995, while at Flossenbürg a Jewish Memorial Centre was dedicated on 7 May 1995. Undoubtedly, too, the indignation expressed in the press and among west German historians at the distortive impact of anti-fascism on the GDR's representations of camp life boomeranged somewhat, so that a critical rethinking of representations of camp life in the west of Germany was reinforced.

Developments at east German camp sites were more significantly affected by the end of the Cold War. Soldiers from the USA – whose role in liberating Buchenwald had been played down in the GDR – were invited to take part in large-scale acts of commemoration at Buchenwald Memorial Site in 1995. It was also in 1995 that the new concentration camp exhibition was opened at Buchenwald. In parallel to the situation in Dachau and Neuengamme, advisory commissions were set up in 1991–1992 by the relevant regional authorities to recommend changes to the camp topographies in Ravensbrück, Sachsenhausen and Buchenwald. But changes in the east of Germany have been much more radical because of the collapse of socialism. Had West Germany collapsed, it is not unthinkable that the Christian encrustations at Dachau and Flossenbürg would have fallen prey to victorious socialist excision. History has decided otherwise. GDR anti-fascist renderings of camp history, not least monuments or exhibitions, were summarily removed or shut down in 1990 or subsequently. It may be the case that the west of Germany – it is largely west Germans who now run the camp memorial sites in the east – has an ideological interest in delegitimizing anti-fascism and imposing its own paradigms on the formation of memory at Buchenwald, Sachsenhausen and Ravensbrück. There are signs of creeping Christianization since 1990 at eastern memorial sites, as is demonstrated by the Christian crosses erected in memory of those Germans who died in Soviet camps at Sachsenhausen and Buchenwald after the end of the war (see Chapter Two). However, it can hardly be disputed that GDR representations of concentration camp life were highly ideological and in need of revision – something recognized in the course of the *Wende* by GDR citizens themselves.

Extending the topography

Overall, changes at both eastern and western camp memorial sites over the last ten years reflect an enormous improvement over the pre-1990 situation. The post-1990 period has seen a remarkable push towards the inclusion within memorial sites of previously excluded parts of the original camps. Also, surroundings of relevance to the camps, such as the sites of related work camps, quarries and factories, have been included or themselves designated as memorial sites, creating an integrated network which provides a more comprehensive picture of the realities of imprisonment. The culture of integration (or reintegration) is the culture of post-unification Germany, and it would have been a surprise had this cultural discourse stopped short of sites of memory. Because national and international media attention has tended to focus on Ravensbrück and Sachsenhausen, where this integrative process has been most dramatic, it has often gone unnoticed that the same process can be observed in Flossenbürg, Neuengamme and Dachau. Some facts will illustrate the parallel developments in east and west.

At Sachsenhausen, the post-unification memorial site has expanded to integrate 'Zone II', where Allied POWs were held. Plans are also afoot to integrate into the memorial site the so-called 'industrial complex' (*Industriehof*), where prisoners slaved away for SS firms. Not far from Sachsenhausen is the site of an almost forgotten clinker brick factory, where prisoners were also subjected to slave labour. After 1945, it was used by the Soviet army and then the East German army. In 1998, part of it was declared a 'historical park' and memorial site. Moreover, houses on the Diana Street, once used by SS officers and currently lived in by local residents, have been put under a preservation order to prevent their decay or transformation, a 'semi-memorialization'. At Ravensbrück, the departure of the Soviet military in the course of the early 1990s freed up for the memorial site whole areas of the former concentration camp, such as the grounds on which the inmates' huts had stood, the former Siemens slave-labour camp, many SS houses and even a whole satellite concentration camp, Uckermark, where the National Socialists imprisoned children, and which had an attached annihilation complex.

In the west, at Dachau, the *Bunker* building has recently been integrated into the memorial site and fitted out with a small exhibition. The 1996 plan of the Dachau advisory commission envisaged the provision of access to the site via the original prisoners' route and entrance-building (*Jourhaus*). Negotiations are under way to persuade the Bavarian Riot Police to cede this building to the memorial site. In 1989, after years of wrangling, the Hamburg Senate agreed to move the prison away from the former concentration camp site at Neuengamme. The need for this move was reinforced by the Neuengamme advisory commission in 1992, but it was not until July 1996 that Hamburg's Justice Senator Wolfgang Hoffmann-Riem was in a position to announce formally that the prison was to be closed and the institution moved to Billwerder. Organizations representing former prisoners hope to install exhibitions in the vacated buildings. In autumn 1997, the French firm Alcatel offered its whole industrial park at Flossenbürg to the State of Bavaria – for a symbolic price of one mark. Finally, it has become possible to include the camp kitchen, laundry-room and roll-call area in the memorial site.

The 'expanding' memorial site is a post-unification phenomenon which has not gone unresisted. Ravensbrück in the east and Neuengamme in the west became the sites of symbolic struggles over how to weight the past in relation to the present and the future. In 1991, following the departure of the Russian military, a supermarket was built on the grounds of the former concentration camp's potato-store and joinery at Ravensbrück, next to the road which leads to the memorial site – a road built by camp prisoners in part from human ashes. But the supermarket never opened. Following international protest and the intervention of Minister President of Brandenburg Manfred Stolpe, it was agreed that an alternative location should be found. The building which would have housed the supermarket still stands there at Ravensbrück today, unused. The supermarket scandal, as it became known, was a perfect example of unscrupulous east–west commercial cooperation. In 1990, the town of Fürstenberg sold off dirt-cheap 3,000 hectares of the former concentration camp grounds to a west German property speculator. A west German supermarket chain, Tengelmann, contracted the construction of a supermarket on the site, and subsequent attempts to stop the building were resisted by local mayor Wolfgang Engler, formerly SED, now SPD. But the scandal had another, equally significant dimension: the clash between the need for a community of east Germans to confront the National Socialist past and their perceived right in the present to consumer goods and chances of employment.

The people of Fürstenberg, who defended the need for a supermarket at the former concentration camp site and even blocked a motorway to express their anger, were not neo-Nazis. They were east Germans who felt that, for years, they had had to endure not just life in the GDR, but also, particularly, the obligation of ritualistic anti-fascist commemorations at Ravensbrück and the massive Soviet military presence there. After 1990, hopes of economic improvement had been dashed as Fürstenberg's few local industries collapsed under the strains of capitalism. Unemployment had grown. The supermarket was a lifeline. Now, the past was 're-emerging' and threatening to deprive locals of the chance of a present. Whether they would have been more open towards the idea of the 'expanding' memorial site had they not come to associate Ravensbrück with GDR propaganda is a moot point. Local feeling ran high and was encapsulated by a number of, one suspects, deliberately provocative remarks by the town's mayor. He opined that the 'pulse of normal life' was returning to Fürstenberg, and that it was unacceptable for the memorial site at Ravensbrück to 'crush' the town, given the prospects of employment for up to 80 women (*taz*, 6 July 1991). On another occasion, he remarked that the former concentration camp was 'ideal for commerce because it has a rail-connection' (*ND*, 8 July 1991). Engler was implying that a normalization of life was under way which was being blocked by an abnormal intrusion of the past. By means of a curious inversion, he created the impression that it was not commercialism which was intruding into the territory of memory, but the concentration camp memorial site which was intruding on areas of commerce; that it was not the camp inmates who were victims, but the local townspeople. In line with this inversion, Engler, the press and eventually the Brandenburg government found themselves caught up in a macabre discussion about the need to compensate the builders and the supermarket chain should the construction be halted. Thus it was the present-day 'victims' of the memorial site who needed to be compensated, not the slave labourers of Ravensbrück concentration camp, whose calls for compensation had gone unheeded for years.

One element of the Walser debate, namely the fear that the past had become an irresponsible moloch threatening the German chance of normality (see Chapter Seven), was anticipated here. It was also anticipated in the west. Disagreements within the Hamburg Regional Parliament, and resistance from the Bergedorf district authorities responsible for the site to which Neuengamme's prison is due to be moved, have delayed this move for almost a decade. Unusually, Bergedorf's CDU, FDP and Greens came together in 1993 to try to thwart the SPD's plan for the new prison at Billwerder. The Greens objected to the fact that the new prison was to be built in an idyllic country environment. CDU local politician Bernd Capeletti also warned of possible damage to the ecosystem (*BGZ*, 20 April 1993). At regional level, the SPD's attempts to force through the plans were resisted again by the CDU, but also by Hamburg's STATT Party, whose parliamentary leader Frank-Michael Bauer suggested it would be cheaper to modernize the existing prison at Neuengamme than to spend 100 million marks on a new one (*BGZ*, 4 November 1993). Regional CDU parliamentarian Gert Boysen argued that it would be 'manipulative to heal misguided decisions [i.e. to turn part of Neuengamme into a prison, BN] by simply covering up the traces' (*BGZ*, 28 May 1993). There are curious inconsistencies in the CDU's espousal of Green thinking, and in Boysen's concern at covering up the traces, an argument the CDU would be less keen to use in reference to the National Socialist past. Behind the objections to the move are normative systems which place economic considerations, notions of the irreversibility of past misjudgements and, above all, issues of environmental protection above considerations of greater acknowledgement of the past.

Nevertheless, the SPD-run Hamburg Senate has continued to press for the move, and it will occur in the next one or two years. Nor will the CSU's reluctance since 1996 to provide adequate funds for the proposed expansion and revision of Dachau Memorial Site prevent changes in the long run. The discrepancy between the memorial sites and the true extent of the camps they memorialized was the physical manifestation of the German reluctance on both sides of the Iron Curtain to remember the whole story. The 'expanding' memorial site represents the present wish to overcome this limitation. With almost criminological zeal, memorial sites since 1990 have embarked on a large-scale process of archaeological retrieval. A commitment to *Spurensicherung*, a term from police vocabulary meaning 'securing the traces' in an effort to track down criminals, represents a conscious contrast to the process of covering up the traces so typical of the post-war era in both Germanys. It demonstrates a wish to recover what can be recovered of the *univers concentrationnaire*. The more complete the topographical impression, the more 'authentic' the site seems, the more irrefutable. As more and more is recovered, more and more has to be faced. In a manner reminiscent of digging up unpleasant truths from the subconscious, projects are under way to uncover 'overgrown history' (*zugewachsene Geschichte*). Whether it be the satellite camp at Uckermark, SS officers' houses or the forced-labour Gustloff Works at Buchenwald, vegetation has to be stripped away, ruins or foundations revealed.

Even *within* the confines of the memorial sites as they used to be, a certain expansion is taking place. At Sachsenhausen, the former camp sick-bay areas (*Revierbaracken*), used by the GDR for archive and library purposes, were repaired in the 1990s and will be used for an exhibition as of 2001. In the course of repairs, the cellars were cleared of rubble with which they had been filled after 1945. This led to the discovery that the original pathology rooms were situated beneath one of the sick-bay huts. These underground rooms are to be made accessible to visitors. It is significant that it is not just the topography of the victims, their huts or places of labour, which is now emerging in more detail, but also that of the perpetrators. The current generation of Germans is taking upon itself the responsibility for pointing up effect and cause, the crime and its criminals. This will certainly help in proving, in an age where it is possible to deny Nazi atrocities, that they really happened. There could hardly be a stronger indication of a shift from a tendency to regard memorial sites as being for 'them' (the victims) to one of regarding them as being just as much for 'us' (the nation from which the perpetrators came). But there is a danger of an unintended countereffect. Some, notably neo-Nazis, might see in the process of revealing the remains of perpetrator buildings, and particularly in their restoration, an implicit celebration of these perpetrators. More generally, there may be a danger of former camp sites being understood as a set of archaeological remains, associated more with scientific and distanced recovery than with active memory. Placing ruins or restored buildings under 'monument protection' in line with this respect for the traces can appear, moreover, to transform them into sacrosanct relics, more of a 'hands-off' than a 'hands-on' experience. It is to the credit of the regional authorities responsible for Sachsenhausen and Ravensbrück that they have entrusted designers with the task of integrating recovered traces into an overall artistic plan which seeks to prevent such distancing. Of course any aesthetic accretion in the present may create a new form of alienation. But the chosen models are characterized by a self-consciousness which encourages critical reflection in the visitor.

The case of Polish architect Daniel Libeskind will demonstrate this. In 1990, the GDR's People's Police (*Volkspolizei*) vacated whole areas of the former SS troop complex in Oranienburg (the site of an SS training camp as well as a concentration camp). At first, the town of Oranienburg simply wanted to transform parts of this topography of terror into a 'lively city neighbourhood' with apartments (Wiedmer 1999: 193). Now, however, it appears that the area will be memorialized. Libeskind's original 1994 proposal for the former SS troop complex envisaged flooding it in water and constructing across it a 'Hope Incision', a building in which space would be made available for cultural, social and business purposes. The whole project Libeskind termed 'Dawn of a New Mo(u)rning'. While, at first glance, Libeskind seemed more committed to trace obliteration than preservation, this was not so. The use of water was intended as a reference to the Baltic

(*Ostsee*), in the direction of which thousands of Sachsenhausen's prisoners were marched on the notorious death-marches in 1945. Visitors, on bridges, would have been able to see the troop complex through the water. Libeskind hoped to encourage reflection on the erosive and submersive effects of time, the susceptibility of memory and the apparent inevitability of the past becoming the past. Nevertheless, his plan was felt to be a threat to the original buildings, and the design was only accepted by the town of Oranienburg (on 25 October 1999) after Libeskind agreed to limit the water element to one or two small 'water gardens'. The revised plan combines recovery of the troop complex with a degree of discreet commercialization in the 'Hope Incision'. But there will be no supermarket. In contrast to the situation at Ravensbrück, moreover, nothing of the past will be obscured. Indeed it will remain distinctly visible, intruding into the present, a constant reminder of what once was. Visitors will be encouraged to reflect on the fact that the human energy which was destructively channelled at the SS troop camp was positively rechannelled after 1945, a rechannelling which occurred at the expense of memory.

It was the Frankfurt architects Braun & Voigt who drew up the model for the reconstruction of Sachsenhausen's Jewish Huts (*Jüdische Baracken*), burnt down in a neo-Nazi arson attack in 1992. Here too, a dialogue between past and present has been set in motion. Thus a dividing wall in the reconstruction bears traces of the arson-attack, reminding the visitor how destructive the desire to forget or repress can be. The reconstruction is itself a reconstruction of a reconstruction. The GDR rebuilt the huts in the early 1960s, using material from a number of similar period models. The 'new' reconstruction also contains, in addition to a few innovations such as a covering of rusted steel, elements taken from another original hut of the same type. Thus the Jewish Huts represent a reconstituted and compromised, indeed staged originality. Yet they still convey an impression of the past reality, and represent an act of attempted resistance against the corrosive present.

At Ravensbrück, all traces of the Uckermark children's camp were well-nigh obliterated by post-war Soviet use. In accordance with a prize-winning model by Stefan Tischer and Susanne Burger, Uckermark is to be covered in blue flowers, except for the annihilation complex, which is to be the site of archaeological diggings. Former victims have objected to the blue flowers. It is true that growing flowers will result in a prettification, despite the prizewinners' assertions that they reflect in their 'fragility and temporary beauty the fates of the victims' (Stadt Fürstenberg/Havel 1998: 44). But the contrast to the archaeological site will create a dialogue between beauty and horror, surface and depth, present and past, covering and uncovering.

Tischer and Burger clearly want visitors to reflect on this dialectic. After 1945, the Soviets tore down concentration camp huts in Ravensbrück and erected new buildings at the site. The Tischer and Burger proposal envisages the removal of these post-1945 buildings and the gradual archaeological recovery of the remains of the foundations of the concentration camp huts. It also stipulates that the area around these remains, as they are revealed, be covered with slack taken from a heap visible to visitors. The slack will therefore highlight these remains and mark out the basic groundplan. But it will also constitute a 'layering' of the present over the past, encouraging us to reflect on the conundrum that this past cannot be brought to light without applying an arguably subjective language of representation. Given that the uncovering of these foundations is likely to take several years, the heap will dwindle very slowly, symbolizing both the ongoing process of recovery, and the arduous struggle against forgetting.

Where uncovering pre-1945 use means removal of post-1945 buildings, it has been objected that *Spurensicherung* can result in the undesirable erasure of subsequent layers of narrative. In line with Giordano's theory that the Germans must also confront their 'second guilt' of not coming to terms with the Nazi past (Giordano 1987), it was felt by some that while the penal institution at Neuengamme should be moved to Billwerder, not all the post-1945 parts of the prison should be removed, as this would be tantamount to a deconstruction of the traces of this second guilt. And is not German *Vergangenheitsbewältigung* as much about facing this guilt as the primary one? Accordingly, suggestions have been made that a part of the post-1945 cell tract at Neuengamme be retained for an exhibition on post-war use. The issue is at the time of writing still undecided. The question of whether or not to represent the post-1945 camp use by the Allies is a particularly sensitive one, as doing so may seem like wanting to shift the focus and play down German guilt. But that responsibility for 'burying the National Socialist past' must be shared to a limited degree is surely undeniable. At Ravensbrück, while the Tischer and Burger project envisages the more or less complete removal of Soviet barracks, the post-1945 entrance-building will remain, offering an exhibition on post-war use.

Representing the victims

The process of inclusion at post-unification memorial sites has extended beyond buildings and grounds. Again, it is particularly the east that has been affected. The GDR's focus on anti-fascist resistance had led to a marginalization of groups whose suffering could not be interpreted as an element in the narrative of political struggle. The general critique of Stalinism which set in in the GDR in late 1989 did not stop short of the GDR's official anti-fascism. In the early 1990s, as state controls relaxed, GDR camp memorial site staff began to adopt a critical stance towards the distortions of anti-fascism. On 2 March 1990, the Ravensbrück Memorial Site issued a statement stressing that it wished to focus on 'new insights', particularly in 'neglected areas such as Christians, the victims of "racial" persecution, children and *bürgerlich* resistance' (Lagergemeinschaft Ravensbrück 1991: 1–2). Also in March 1990, Hans Jacobus of the Committee of Anti-fascist Resistance Fighters criticized the fact that many victims of National Socialism, including Christians, Jehovah's Witnesses, homosexuals and victims of forced sterilization, had not been acknowledged in the GDR (*Der Morgen*, 3 March 1990). It would be easy to dismiss such statements as attempts to turn with the tide, and they will have been this to an extent. But GDR staff at both Buchenwald and Ravensbrück Memorial Sites claimed after the *Wende* that they had been doing research into Jews and Christian groups since the mid-1980s. They had had, however, little scope for implementing the results of such research.

The emerging understanding of the need to remember the full range of victims led the Ravensbrück Memorial Site in April 1990 to set up an international room of commemoration in the Cell Building. This provided rudimentary information on underrepresented victims such as Jews, Sinti and Jehovah's Witnesses. In the summer of 1990, a 'Room of Contemplation' was opened for Christian remembrance. In the course of the 1990s, the Memorial Site opened additional rooms dedicated respectively to July 1944 Plot victims (see Chapter Three), Jews, Sinti and Roma and Christian resistance. It saw no problem in adducing these rooms to the eighteen rooms from GDR times which housed exhibitions on national groupings (such as the Polish, Russians and French). Sachsenhausen did not follow this path, closing down its 'Museum of the European People's Anti-Fascist Struggle for Freedom' in 1990 because it was deemed too ideologically tainted and heroic. The national rooms at Ravensbrück are, in part, of high artistic quality, and the ideological and patriotic rhetoric is, in general, not overbearing. In maintaining the GDR's national rooms, the memorial site perhaps sought to imply that what mattered was not so much the ideological colouring of some (but by no means all) of the rooms, as the fact that they represent a plurality of approaches to memory and a variety of national narratives. In this sense they were ground-breaking, certainly as far as the GDR was concerned. If the rooms on national groups did rather understate racial, religious and non-communist political reasons for incarceration, the new rooms placed these more in the foreground, while not necessarily denying other motives.

Post-1990 Buchenwald gives the fate of Jews, and to a lesser extent of Sinti and Roma, homosexuals and Jehovah's Witnesses, a significant place in the new exhibition and in the various guided tours of the site as a whole. Lectures, temporary exhibitions on and research into these groups are a standard part of Buchenwald's current programme, as they are at Ravensbrück and Sachsenhausen. Thus, in August 1993, the exhibition 'Jews in Mühlhausen' was first shown in Buchenwald. The Buchenwald Memorial Site has also taken exhibitions elsewhere, notably 'The Survivors are the Exception', an exhibition on the Sinti and Roma shown in Heidelberg between October and December 1993. In October 1997, an exhibition on Jehovah's Witnesses first shown in Ravensbrück was opened in Buchenwald. Moreover, the commemorative landscape at Buchenwald has been redesigned to include new memorials. The Jewish Memorial by Tine Steen and Klaus Schlosser, located at the site of Block 22 which was occupied largely by Jewish prisoners from April 1939 onwards, was dedicated on 10 November 1993. The notorious 'Gypsy Block' at Buchenwald, Block 14, is the location for another new memorial, in this case to the Sinti and Roma. It was dedicated in April 1995. Both the Sinti and Roma Memorial, designed by Daniel Plaas, and the Jewish Memorial use stones as a commemorative motif, evoking memories of the nearby quarries where prisoners endured slave labour. The Sinti and Roma Memorial organizes them into a sequence of decreasing size, symbolizing death and erasure from memory, while the Jewish Memorial organizes them into a sloping structure of similar symbolic force. Again, the dialectic of past and present is addressed. Since 1990, plaques dedicated to the memory of Sinti and Roma as well as homosexual victims have been mounted at Sachsenhausen Memorial Site.

But it would be wrong to suggest that it was only in the east that such inclusions were necessary. An exhibition on homosexuals which opened at Oranienburg Castle on 21 April 1995 pointed out that paragraph 175, used to discriminate against homosexuals for generations, was not completely scrapped in the Federal Republic until 1994; the GDR abolished an equivalent paragraph in 1988. The first memorial to homosexual victims at a concentration camp memorial site took the form of a plaque unveiled in Austria's Mauthausen in 1984. Similar plaques were put up in Neuengamme (1985) and Sachsenhausen (1991), as well as on Berlin's Nollendorf Square (1989). At Dachau, where the exhibition made no mention of homosexual victims, the International Dachau Committee in 1986 refused to allow a commemorative plaque to be mounted. In 1988, it was given 'right of refuge' in the Protestant Church of Conciliation, and finally placed in Dachau's Room of Commemoration in 1995. The wall outside the Church of Conciliation also carries a plaque commemorating Sinti victims of Nazism and the 'occupation' of Dachau Memorial Site by a group of rejected Sinti and Roma asylum-seekers in 1993 [Plate 1.4]. It is to be hoped that the new permanent exhibition at Dachau will provide detailed information on the sufferings of Sinti and Roma, homosexual and communist prisoners, as is indeed planned. The small

Plate 1.4 The 'Protestant Church of Conciliation' at Dachau Memorial Site. The plaque in the foreground reads 'In Memory of the Roma murdered in Dachau concentration camp. Donated by their fellow Romanies, who sought refuge here. May 1993'.

exhibition in the *Bunker* building, opened in 1999, features a computer database which provides information on communist prisoners, and quotations from an account by Walther Buzengeiger, a KPD prisoner, are displayed in two of the cells. This is a positive development.

Also in the west, attempts by the Gay–Lesbian Archive in Hanover to secure for homosexual victims a place on the wall of commemoration at Bergen-Belsen have so far been rejected on the grounds that this wall only commemorates national and ethnic groups (Rahe 1997: 10). Strict adherence to national and ethnic groupings represents here an act of exclusion. It also denies the basic realities of National Socialist persecution as an often multilayered phenomenon. For a while, there was a danger that the planned house of commemoration in Neuengamme would be Christianized, or at least called a 'Chapel' whatever the function of its rooms. But the building, which was opened in 1995, has been designated a 'House of Memory' (*Haus der Erinnerung*), and contains all the known names (about 20,000) of Neuengamme's victims. It may be that this absolute personalization is the only way to overcome the possible exclusion of victims. Blank scrolls in the building await the addition of new names, or at least symbolize the need to remember those whose names have not been recorded.

Groups, boundaries, persons

The example of Ravensbrück demonstrates a possible way forward. In the early 1990s, the main GDR Ravensbrück exhibition with its heavy anti-fascist line was completely revised, being replaced with two new exhibitions which were opened in 1993 ('Topography and History of the Women's Camp') and 1994 ('Women of Ravensbrück: On the Lives and Fates of Former Female Prisoners') respectively. The second of these focuses largely on women incarcerated for their part in staging resistance, but in such a way that the visitor is made aware of the whole gamut of possible forms of, motives for and sources of resistance, and of the infinite possibilities of overlap between political, racial and ideological discrimination by the National Socialists. Thus we read of German-Jewish woman Irmgard Konrad and her contacts with socialist ideas; of German woman Hildegard Schaeder, a member of the Confessing Church imprisoned for protecting Jews; of French nun Elisabeth Rivet, who hid weapons for the *résistance*; and of British WAAF member Yvonne Baseden, who helped organize resistance in the French Alps. The exhibition consists of biographical overviews, which include photographs of the women. Personal items, even paintings, are also on display. Camp experience is contextualized within particular life-stories, stories which began years before Ravensbrück, only to end there, or continue in broken form afterwards. The advantage of this shift from the macronarrative towards the micronarrative is that individual contours and complex realities emerge. Empathy becomes possible because the visitor is not confronted with anonymous group suffering. In a sense the biography is a counter-narrative to all group narratives, which can force affiliation at the cost of difference. It is interesting that one or two of the biographies reappear in slightly altered form in the cell block rooms dedicated to Jews, or Sinti and Roma. Should we see Irmgard Konrad as a victim of racial or political discrimination, or both? Should we see her in terms of her German-Jewish background, or of her socialist affiliation? Boundaries become fluid.

The exhibition on Jewish prisoners which opened in Sachsenhausen in 1997 also highlights individual biographies, each with its own complex mix of the personal and the general. The visitor can even listen to taped interviews with survivors or members of their families (a similar facility is provided in a 'listening-shell' in Neuengamme Memorial Site's new 1995 exhibition). A series of contrasting slides projected onto opposite sides at the centre of the exhibition impresses on the visitor the need to understand suffering in both collective *and* personal terms. On the right, looking down from above, we see a series of slides of Jews and other victims being ridiculed, deported, made to assemble in groups, trodden on and shot. On the left, we see a series of facial shots of some of those individuals whose biographies are featured in the exhibition. This critical dialogue between the impersonality of photographic representations of the holocaust and the very personal nature of the victims is complemented by a display of tattered remains of leather shoes under a glass-case extending between the sets of slides. It is hard to believe that these remains were once part of individual items with individual owners; yet their very fragmentation triggers an inchoate impulse in the viewer to want to reconstitute the pieces into a whole or wholes. Of course one cannot reconstitute disparate pieces; and the victims whose faces we can put a name to in the one set of slides are not the same people we see being brutalized on the other set. Repersonalization remains a process fraught with obstacles. What matters, ultimately, is that the visitor be made aware of it as a *desirable* process.

And what of the perpetrators? Should they also be represented in the form of detailed biographies? The Dachau commission suggested providing an 'overview of SS careers which began in Dachau, short biographies and portraits' (Fachbeirat Dachau 1996: 8). Similar recommendations were made by the relevant commissions for Sachsenhausen, Buchenwald and Ravensbrück Memorial Sites. So far, new exhibits relating to the SS are still in the planning stages at most sites. At Buchenwald Memorial Site, however, the new 1995 exhibition features, in addition to a comprehensive overview of SS structures and activities, biographies of notorious figures such as Camp Commandants Karl Koch and Hermann Pister, or SS man Martin Sommer, known for his atrocities at Buchenwald and Sachsenhausen. Just as the victims were not anonymous, nor was the SS. Exemplary biographies can moreover demonstrate the diversity of possible paths to commitment to National Socialism and to involvement in atrocities. Indeed in the case of the perpetrators, repersonalization is *rehumanization*: they lose the 'beast' status they tended to have, particularly in the GDR. There is, however, a danger that biographies might render SS men too 'colourful'. A case in point might be Waldemar Hoven, a doctor in Buchenwald who, we learn in the new Buchenwald exhibition, not only committed atrocities, but also had a brief, if peripheral fling at a career in Hollywood (GB 1999: 308). Representing the SS remains generally a controversial issue. When advising against making camp watchtowers accessible to the public, Dachau's advisory commission warned against presenting the 'perspective of the perpetrators' (Fachbeirat Dachau 1996: 7). Neuengamme's commission in August 1992 advised marking the SS areas and rendering them accessible, but it was against making the buildings themselves accessible or staging an exhibition on the SS. Behind these reservations are fears of misinterpretation, leading to the buildings becoming places of pilgrimage for neo-Nazis.

Decentralization

At concentration camp memorial sites, then, the focus is now constantly widening to encompass not just the various groups of victims and perpetrators, but also the variety of individuals among these. The result is a degree of complexity and a multi-perspectival view of camp experience. Because memory is no longer organized around a structuring principle such as anti-fascism, a certain decentralization has set in. It was Sachsenhausen Memorial Site, under director Günter Morsch, which in a 14 April 1999 press statement defined the new concept for Sachsenhausen as one of 'decentralization'. Instead of one major exhibition and one or two minor ones, as in pre-1990 Sachsenhausen, Morsch plans ten smaller ones. The drive to decentralization reflects the inherent polylocality and multi-narrative of camp life. Morsch seeks to allocate to buildings and rooms exhibitions describing events or people associated with these locations. Each location 'tells its own story'. Thus his plan envisages *inter alia* an already completed exhibition on Jews in Hut 38, exhibitions on the SS in Tower A and the Camp Commandant's Office, an exhibition on medical experiments and National Socialist racial anthropology in the sick-bay huts, and a series of exhibitions in the cell block on individual prisoners such as Georg Elser (see Chapter Three). Tischer and Burger's plan for Ravensbrück also includes a 'decentral exhibition' landscape (see Stadt Fürstenberg/Havel 1998: 45), featuring for instance an exhibition on the SS in their living quarters, on camp admission procedures in the bath house, on medical experiments in the sick bay, and on forced labour at the Siemens Camp. In the west, the Dachau commission in 1996 advocated – in addition to the main exhibition – setting up separate exhibitions in the *Bunker* building (on the history of Dachau's punitive system), the crematorium building (on executions and death in the camp) and Hut A (on illnesses and medical experiments). Neuengamme plans – in addition to the new exhibition opened in 1995 – an exhibition on Neuengamme's satellite camps.

All the memorial site advisory commissions have stressed the need for carefully differentiated presentation of the victims in these new exhibitions. Neuengamme's new main exhibition charts the fates of women, hostages, Jews, homosexuals, Soviet POWs, 'criminal' prisoners, resistance fighters, forced labourers, Roma and Sinti and Jehovah's Witnesses. Buchenwald's new main exhibition carefully documents the experiences of different national groups, such as Poles and Russians, but also those of 'criminal' prisoners, homosexuals, Sinti, and Jews. If more examples of the multinarrative approach be needed, one could point to the process of *wider embedment*. This process can be *synchronic and physical*, whereby links between concentration camps, their satellite camps and industry are stressed, or between the camps and local towns or cities (Buchenwald and Weimar, Ravensbrück and Fürstenberg, Neuengamme and Hamburg). At Buchenwald, the memorial site topography has been extended since 1990 to reconnect the camp to the wider system of National Socialist repression of which it was both expression and endpoint. The restoration of Buchenwald Station, completed in 1995, has made it possible to imagine the camp's connection to the outside world of the Reich with its institutionalized persecution and deportation. In Buchenwald's permanent exhibition, an art-work by Jozef Szajna (*Appell*) made up of photographs of Auschwitz victims encourages reflection on the wider network of camps of which Buchenwald was but a part. Wider embedment can also be *diachronic and conceptual*, as in the representation of Buchenwald's and Sachsenhausen's two 'dictatorial' pasts (see Chapter Two). And it can embrace the whole issue of coming to terms with the past (or not) after 1945, as is planned for Dachau, Neuengamme and Sachsenhausen. In Buchenwald, an exhibition on the GDR's (mis)management of memory at the memorial site was opened in October 1999.

The post-modern

An 'ideal' concentration camp memorial site might be one in which the whole topography is visible, where there is detailed documentation of the history of the camp, where there is comprehensive scope for commemoration, and where bias and idealization are replaced by a respect for complexities and multiple narratives. This ideal is closer to realization in Germany now than at any other point in the post-1945 period. Visitors to the rapidly changing memorial sites will have to bring much more time with them than was the case before. Instead of being offered a neatly packaged version of camp history, they will be invited to construct their own interpretations. Buchenwald's new concentration camp exhibition is divided into numbered sections, rather like a library, offering a multiplicity of points of view in considerable detail from which the visitor can choose. Repeated visits, indeed, may be necessary – in accordance with the library principle, and in stark contrast to the idea that an exhibition can be readily absorbed as it was in the typical GDR one-day Buchenwald-Weimar school outing (first the horrors, then the more restful and uplifting legacy of Goethe). That the visitor must actively participate in generating his or her own impression is underpinned by multimedia installations, as at Neuengamme, where computers provide information on the many satellite camps. Drawers, folders and other means are employed at Neuengamme and Buchenwald to encourage such participation. The separation of enlightenment and commemoration reflected in developments at Neuengamme and Bergen-Belsen has unburdened the exhibitions somewhat; they are no longer expected, at least not only, to inspire pain and pity, but to inform – all the more important for today's generations who have no communicative memory of the Nazi past. Of course there is a danger of didactic overkill, and of schoolchildren sweeping through complex exhibitions on a wave of helpless confusion. But here it is the task of teachers to plan and prepare the visits properly. At Germany's concentration camp memorial sites, the post-modern and pluralist spirit of the present lends itself to uncovering and discovering the complexity of camp life. We might even go so far as to claim that, with the trend away from historical master-narratives, the time of imposing sense on the senselessness of the holocaust has itself come to an end. As we shall see in the next chapter, however, one historical master-narrative is proving difficult to overcome . . .

2   The 'double past'

'There were many different Buchenwalds.'

(Pierre Durand, quoted in Zimmer 1999: 63)

The legacy of socialism

The Russians liberated the east of Germany from Hitler in 1945, but it was a liberation which, for many Germans, was experienced as injustice. While the Soviets
used denazification statutes in the main to arrest National Socialist functionaries,
they also arrested quite a number of Germans, including women and even children, who were in no way guilty of any involvement, administrative or otherwise,
in National Socialism. Many Germans were held for years without trial, or tried
without even a semblance of fairness, and sentenced to extremely high sentences,
often involving labour. Some were deported to the Soviet Union to labour camps.
Increasingly, as the Soviet Union tightened its ideological grip on the Eastern
zone, political opponents of sovietization from the ranks of the Social and
Christian Democrats, but also 'renegade' communists, were sentenced and incarcerated. Some unfortunate individuals, such as the Social Democrat Robert Zeiler,
were imprisoned under the National Socialists *and* the Soviets. The Soviets held at
least 130,000 Germans on the basis of denazification directives in so-called Special
Camps, ten of them in all. Conditions there were appalling. At least 43,000 people
died, including 700 who were sentenced to death by Soviet military tribunals
(Niethammer 1999: 109ff.). Illnesses such as typhus, dysentery and tuberculosis,
resulting not least from undernourishment and from the unhygienic condition of
the camps, accounted for many deaths. When the last three camps were dissolved
in 1950, over 3,000 internees were transferred to the Saxon town of Waldheim,
where draconian sentences, including 24 death sentences, were imposed by East
German courts (Werkentin 1998: 12–16). Prison sentences were subsequently
served in GDR prisons. Life after internment in the Special Camps was not easy.
The subject of the Special Camps was taboo in the GDR. The truth hardly corresponded to the propagated image of the Soviet 'brothers-in-combat'.

   Injustice and repression were also characteristics of the GDR's political and legal
system. Between 200,000 and 250,000 political sentences were passed throughout

the 40 years of the GDR's existence (Werkentin 1998: 99). Prisoners included politicians, critical thinkers, journalists, editors, authors, film-makers and other intellectuals. Many others were imprisoned simply for attempting to leave East Germany illegally. Every year from the late 1950s until the peaceful revolution in 1989, some 2,000 to 3,000 of those held in GDR prisons were people convicted of having illegally planned or attempted to cross the German–German border. Indeed, many of those who filed applications for exit visas, even after the formal legalization of a 'right to apply' under Honecker in 1983, received prison sentences. Others were sentenced on the grounds of having helped those who wanted to leave to devise and carry out their plan. In GDR prisons, conditions were often appalling. Not only were cells notoriously overcrowded, damp and cold, but it was common practice to put 'criminal' prisoners in with political prisoners to make life for the latter difficult to bear. Food was bad, and hunger, with accompanying severe weight loss, weakness and illness was a problem, especially in the 1960s and even 1970s. Right up to the *Wende*, prisoners were often given days, even weeks of solitary confinement as punishment for misdemeanours. The confinement in so-called 'tiger-cages', where there was hardly enough room to stand, let alone sit or lie, was especially brutal.

It was the *Wende* in 1989–1990 that brought the injustices of the 1945–1989 period to the surface. The GDR's reform movement called not just for democracy in the present and future, but also for the redress of wrongs committed in the past. The first general amnesties for political prisoners serving sentences in GDR gaols were passed in late 1989. On 5 January 1990, the GDR's Supreme Court annulled the sentences of 26 July 1957 which had led to the imprisonment of publishers Walter Janka and Gustav Just. On 15 July 1990, it was the turn of dissident Rudolf Bahro to have his sentence repealed by the Supreme Court. On 29 June 1990, the GDR Parliament (*Volkskammer*) passed the 6th Criminal Code Revision Law. This law regulated the abolition of those penal rulings which had been abused for purposes of political jurisdiction, such as §213 (illegal crossing of the border), §214 (inhibiting state activity), §215 ('rowdiness') and §219 (illegal establishment of contact to the West). Annulment of sentences passed according to these laws led to the release of many more prisoners. Finally, and perhaps most significantly, the GDR passed a Rehabilitation Law on 6 September 1990 to regulate criminal, administrative and professional rehabilitation – the first steps towards coupling annulment of wrongful sentences with some form of restitution. This law also regulated the rehabilitation of those unjustly interned by the Soviets between 8 May 1945 and 7 October 1949. In the course of the 1990s, the Soviets themselves began to annul some of the sentences passed by their military tribunals against Germans.

In uncovering traces of injustice between 1945 and 1949 in the Soviet-occupied zone, the reform movement sought to reveal the origins of the system of injustice subsequently imposed in the GDR under Ulbricht and Honecker. The most important post-*Wende* group to lobby East Germany's government for rehabilitation, the Organization for the Victims of Stalinism, represents to this day the concerns of victims of both Soviet occupation and the SED. Horrifying discoveries during the *Wende* confirmed this tendency to see the 1945–1949 and 1949–1989 periods in parallel. Thus several sites of mass graves of Germans who had died in Soviet internment between 1945 and 1949 were uncovered at the same time as horrific stories about planned *Stasi* internment camps were circulating. In late March 1990, a mass grave of thousands was discovered in Fünfeichen near Neubrandenburg, one of the sites of the Soviet Special Camps. It was also in March 1990 that the Erfurt Investigative Committee reported on the *Stasi* internment camp in Tambach-Dietharz, in which members of the Christian opposition were to be incarcerated (see Thomaneck and Niven 2001: 60). Gradually, this sense of parallelism left its mark on the exhibition landscape. Between 22 June 1990 and 19 August 1990, the Berlin Museum for German History showed an exhibition entitled 'Against Forgetting', in which biographies of German victims of Soviet internment, or deportation to Siberia, were set side by side with biographies of victims of SED repression such as the members of the Weißensee Peace Circle, arrested for trying to gather evidence of the election trickery of May 1989.

The 'double past'

Clearly, the memorial site landscape of eastern Germany – dominated before 1989 by commemoration of the victims of National Socialism – was going to have to change to incorporate this narrative of injustice under Soviet occupation and GDR socialism. In the course of the 1990s, intense research into the Special Camps began, aided by the opening of Soviet archives; equally, research into the injustices of the GDR penal system proceeded rapidly. The results of this research are gradually becoming manifest in the form of publications and new exhibitions. Collections of interviews with former prisoners at last able to talk of their experiences after years of enforced silence, as well as autobiographical accounts, have appeared in book form (Bautzen-Komitee 1992; Knechtel and Fiedler 1991). It is right and proper that united Germany should commemorate and document the injustice and suffering of the 1945–1989 period. Moreover, because many of the political prisoners were opponents of state socialism, or people who insisted on basic freedoms, they embody a tradition of democratic awareness and courage in eastern Germany which contributed to the *Wende*. Commemorating their suffering means acknowledging their engagement for the process of change.

At some sites, however, the process of documenting and commemorating their suffering has been complicated by the fact that these sites already had a 'past' – as sites of National Socialist injustice. For practical purposes, the Soviets used former concentration camps such as Sachsenhausen and Buchenwald as Special Camps. These were closed in February 1950. The prison complex at Bautzen, by contrast, had an even longer history. The National Socialists imprisoned political opponents such as the communist leader Ernst Thälmann at Bautzen. After the war, it became a Soviet Special Camp (until February 1950). In the GDR, Bautzen was a notorious prison for political prisoners and would-be fugitives right up to 1989. It still functions as a prison today. Other sites, such as the 'Red Oxen' (*Roter Ochse*) in Halle or the 'Munich Square' (*Münchner Platz*) in Dresden, were also used for political prisoners from 1933 right through to 1989. While it would be more correct to talk of sites with 'two' (National Socialist and Soviet) or 'three' (National Socialist, Soviet and East German) pasts, in united Germany it has become the norm to refer to all sites characterized by National Socialist and socialist injustice – whether from 1945 to 1950 or from 1945 to 1989 – as sites with a 'double past' (*doppelte Vergangenheit*).

Sachsenhausen, Buchenwald and some other sites of National Socialist injustice, such as Dresden's 'Munich Square', had already been memorial sites in the GDR. Could commemoration of the victims of the Soviets and the GDR simply be grafted onto the commemoration of the victims of National Socialism? Should both histories of injustice be documented at the same place? There are good reasons why they should. In terms of arbitrary violence, disregard for principles of legality and repression of political opponents, there were striking similarities between the conduct of the National Socialists and that of the Soviets. Sites of 'double memory' could offer a legitimate opportunity to compare. To a degree, too, the post-war history of Buchenwald and Sachsenhausen might be read as a lesson in the iniquities of vengeance; that Germans after the war were incarcerated and, in their thousands, died in camps built and run by the National Socialists is a cruel, but telling irony. It is a history which demonstrates that it was particularly the East Germans who were made to suffer for the war unleashed against the Soviets. Sites with a 'double past', however, can also demonstrate that Germans in the GDR were only too willing to adopt practices introduced by the Soviets (or, seen from another perspective, inherited from the National Socialists). Over two regimes, Germans practised injustice, from 1933 through till 1989. It is important that Germans be confronted with this fact. Facing a 'double past' is rather like having a double dose of injections. It is good immunization therapy against injustice in the future. It is important too for future generations to understand that injustice was not only a characteristic of negative ideologies, such as National Socialist racism. Even commitment to a better society under utopian socialism could take on self-contradictory and destructive forms.

However, there is the danger of such 'double sites' being instrumentalized. Balanced comparison of periods and regimes between 1933 and 1989 is valuable because it can highlight both continuity and difference. Equation of these periods, however, is distortive. Some have argued that National Socialism and Soviet communism were mirror images of each other. While the National Socialists launched a 'racial war' (*Rassenkrieg*), it is argued, the Soviets waged 'class warfare' (*Klassenkrieg*). While Hitler implemented a 'brown holocaust', Stalin staged a 'red holocaust'. When such equations are applied to the histories of Buchenwald and Sachsenhausen, they become particularly problematical. Apart from the 'criminal' prisoners, the National Socialists incarcerated people on political, religious and racial grounds. After the war, *most* people interned by the Soviets at Special Camps were interned because they were (albeit small-scale) National Socialist functionaries. This in no way excuses the fact that they were subsequently not given a fair trial, or that innocent women, children and – increasingly – political opponents, were also incarcerated, but it does make it clear that the Soviets were in broad outline acting in accordance with Allied internment and denazification directives.

Moreover, while the Soviets did deport prisoners for purposes of what was effectively slave labour, there is very little evidence to support the contention that those who died in the Special Camps were victims of deliberate starvation and deliberate medical neglect. The immediate post-war period was generally one of high food shortages, especially in the east of Europe. Certainly the Soviets can be accused of indifference to the fate of the inmates. Indifference is appalling, but not surprising given the suffering that the Soviets had had to endure at the hands of the Germans during the war. Like it or not, while most of the Germans in Special Camps were victims of arbitrary justice and awful conditions, many were not innocent of administrative or moral responsibility for National Socialism. Their victimhood was a qualified one. Jews, Sinti and communists under National Socialism were absolute victims. Attempts to erase this difference, and with it the whole issue of cause and effect, are motivated by the unsound wish to 'cancel out' German crimes with reference to Soviet ones, and bracket everyone together in the category of 'victim', thus playing down the issue of German responsibility for National Socialism. Such attempts have been fuelled by the adherents of the totalitarian paradigm (see the Introduction), who are largely west German, and by former Special Camp internees keen to absolve themselves of all responsibility for having acted as cogs in the National Socialist machine.

If the equation of Soviet Special Camps with concentration camps is problematic, the equation of the GDR with National Socialism is largely untenable. Such equation ignores qualitative differences between political repression in the GDR and the Third Reich. As Jürgen Habermas has pointed out, the GDR did not start a war leading to 50 million deaths, or launch a genocide. Nor was the political criminality anywhere near as destructive (Habermas 1995: 28). The oft-quoted definition of the difference between the two regimes as one between 'piles of bodies' and 'piles of (*Stasi*) files' is not so well worn as to be no longer true. Moreover, while it would be difficult to find any aspects of National Socialism that were not tied in some way to imperialism and aggression, many social, economic and cultural aspects of the GDR had their roots in a genuine will to create a fair society. Put on trial, the GDR would have more to say in its defence than the Third Reich. There is therefore a danger that such 'double sites' be used not to point to similarities, but, in keeping with the totalitarianist paradigm, to obliterate all differences. The GDR political system might come across as one of socialist fascism. Was it perhaps the wish to present such a view of history that motivated the Federal Government in 1993 to offer ten years of central funding to a number of 'double past' sites including Buchenwald and Sachsenhausen, while Dachau and Neuengamme still had to rely entirely on regional funding?

We may have to wait another ten years before we can properly judge how, and indeed if, east Germany's 'double past' memorial sites have dealt with these potential dangers of equationism. While the history of the Special Camps is now documented in permanent exhibitions at Buchenwald and Torgau, Sachsenhausen's exhibition on this subject is temporary and out-of-date; a new one is planned. Current exhibitions on the topic of GDR injustice are temporary and often rather flimsy, especially in the case of Bautzen Memorial Site. But new exhibitions are planned for Bautzen, the 'Red Oxen' and Dresden's 'Munich Square'. In terms of commemoration (memorial plaques, monuments), the process is also by no means complete. What follows, then, is an overview of an interim *status quo*. More can be said at present about the treatment of the Special Camps because in this case there already are one or two permanent exhibitions. I will argue that Buchenwald Memorial Site has resisted the temptation to equate the 1933–1945 and 1945–1949 periods, that Sachsenhausen Memorial Site is likely to, and that the Documentation and Information Centre at Torgau, by contrast, has opted for equationism. The chapter concludes by analysing new historical exhibitions in Bonn, Leipzig and Dresden. These exhibitions are not physically situated at sites with a 'double past', but they will serve as an illustration of how the totalitarian paradigm has been applied to the GDR. It is to be hoped that memorial sites at Torgau, Bautzen and the Munich Square will not plough this furrow.

The principle of hierarchy: Buchenwald and Sachsenhausen

In 1991 and 1992, the advisory commission set up by the Thuringian Minister for Science and Art made a set of recommendations for the redesigning of Buchenwald's landscape of memory. Firstly, the focus should be on the history of both the concentration camp and the Soviet Special Camp. Secondly, the emphasis should be on the former. Thirdly, remembering the Special Camp should 'come after' remembering the concentration camp (*nachgeordnet*). Finally, the sites of remembering should, in physical terms, be clearly separated (GB 1992b: 10). By and large, these recommendations have been followed by the memorial site staff, who have thereby institutionalized a hierarchical system of memory. The advisory commission for redesigning the landscape of memory at Sachsenhausen also stressed the need to document and highlight both the National Socialist and the Soviet use of this camp site. But it also came up with the following formulation: 'NS crimes must not be relativized by means of the crimes of Stalinism, nor must the crimes of Stalinism be trivialized with reference to National Socialist crimes' (MfWFK 1992a: 231–2). This appeared to warn against the dangers of playing off one past against the other. On paper, the Sachsenhausen commission made no commitment to a hierarchical system of memory. There are indications, however, that Sachsenhausen's memorial site staff intend to practise the same prioritization of the National Socialist over the Special Camp past – perhaps even to a greater degree.

There are persuasive arguments for setting priorities in this way. The National Socialist camps came first, chronologically. Without these camps, there would have been no Special Camps. These constituted a *reaction*, albeit one characterized by injustice. Only in the National Socialist camps was the quality of victimhood in most cases absolute. Above all else, Buchenwald and Sachsenhausen were the locus during the war of international suffering, after the war – by and large – of German suffering. Germany has an international community of former concentration camp prisoners and their families to consider. Placing primary emphasis on German suffering after 1945 could appear to symbolize a 'turning away' from this community, a belittling of their pain. Even worse, it could be construed as a *post hoc* rehabilitation of National Socialism. While some of those former Special Camp internees to whom crosses have been erected at various grave sites since 1990 were genuine victims of arbitrary arrest, this does not hold true for all. In February 1990, Buchenwald Memorial Site allowed crosses to be placed just beyond the periphery of the camp site, where the bodies of Germans had been disposed of by the Russians. The children of Otto Koch placed a cross in memory of their 'dear father, Mayor of Weimar from 1937–1945', who died in Buchenwald Special Camp in 1948. Otto Koch was responsible among other things for organizing the ghet-toization of Weimar's Jews in 1941 (GB 1999: 232). At Torgau cemetery in September 1996, a memorial plaque in honour of Friedrich Timm was mounted at the instigation of the Organization for the Victims of Stalinism. Timm was a Special Camp internee; but he was also an active member of the National Socialist party, and had passed a doctoral thesis exploring the social behaviour of Buchenwald prisoners with tattoos. This doctoral thesis drew the attention of Ilse Koch – camp commandant's wife at Buchenwald – to this group, and led directly to the fabrication of 'souvenirs' made from tattooed human skin. Because Timm had already been rehabilitated by the Soviets, the Foundation of Saxon Memorial Sites had contributed to the cost of the plaque. Later, it realized it had made a mistake. Equally, the decision at Buchenwald to accept the erection of crosses in 1990 so close to the camp was slightly foolhardy. Staff at the time did not realize, perhaps, how easily the injustice of the 1945–1950 period could be instrumentalized. Such experiences only confirm how important it is to separate strictly private memory – where such abuse can hardly be prevented – and sites of official memory.

With almost exemplary precision, Buchenwald has observed the principle of hierarchy – concentration camp first, Special Camp second. This can be well illus-trated by a comparison of the two buildings housing, respectively, the exhibition on the concentration camp and the exhibition on the Special Camp. The exhibition on the National Socialist camp is housed in an original camp building, the *Effektenkammer*, used as a store-house for prisoners' clothes and personal possessions. The Special Camp exhibition is housed in a building constructed after 1990 specif-ically to hold this exhibition [Plate 2.1]. As at Sachsenhausen, a decision was taken not to mount the new Special Camp exhibition within any of the original build-ings, as these had been used by the National Socialists before they were reused by the Soviets. There was a reluctance to weaken their association with the concen-tration camp. The concentration camp exhibition at Buchenwald is in a two-storey building, the Special Camp exhibition in a one-storey building. The former is accordingly more extensive than the latter. The Special Camp exhibition building is within the original camp site, but at its very edge. It is not visible from the main gate, unlike the *Effektenkammer*, which dominates the background to the view to the right when passing through the entrance gate. Only as you approach the *Effektenkammer* does the Special Camp exhibition building become visible beneath. It therefore appears implicitly as the 'offspring' or by-product of the building above it. When entering the Special Camp exhibition, you look up over the flat roof to the *Effektenkammer* above. The National Socialist past dwarfs all.

Plate 2.1 The Special Camp exhibition building at Buchenwald Memorial Site, with the *Effektenkammer* housing the concentration camp exhibition in the background.

   The Special Camp exhibition building is devoid of expression or profile. The winning proposal for this building by architects Frese and Kleindienst was modified when Volkhard Knigge, director of Buchenwald Memorial Site, and Thuringia's Science, Research and Culture Ministry objected to the 'memorializing' aspects of the design. The proposed bridge which was to connect the building with the forest graves of post-war German victims was not built. Plans to erect a number of beechwood poles or 'steles' outside the building in memory of the dead were also dropped. The more research was done on the Special Camps, the more convinced Knigge became that at least 80% of Buchenwald's post-war inmates had had connections to National Socialist organizations, and the more wary of any too generalized a nod in the direction of pity. While there are memorials to the dead Jews and Sinti and Roma within the camp grounds, there is not to be one to the dead Special Camp inmates. Such memorials are also *Mahnmale* – warnings, not least to the Germans of subsequent generations. It would not be appropriate for the Germans to issue a warning to the Russians, especially not where former National Socialists are concerned, however badly the Russians treated them. The steel poles erected by the German War Graves Maintenance outside the camp perimeter to mark the graves arguably reflect precisely the kind of dubious memorialization that Knigge was keen to avoid. These poles bear the inscription 'unknown', as if the Special Camp inmates had died in battle. This can be construed as heroization and distortion.
   A single, thin, vertical window-slit is all that allows a visitor to the Special Camp

exhibition a view of the forest behind; only a very few of the steel poles can be seen through this slit. We are not immersed in images of mass-graves, but invited to reflect instead on individual guilt and responsibility, on cause and effect. At Sachsenhausen, too, the building that will house the new exhibition on the Special Camp is to be situated peripherally, outside the main camp triangle (Zone I). It will be located in the area where Allied soldiers were imprisoned during the war, and where those sentenced by Soviet military tribunals were held after the war (Zone II). The exhibition on the National Socialist camp is housed within the camp triangle. The winning design by Till Schneider and Michael Schumacher for the Special Camp exhibition building at Sachsenhausen, selected in April 1999, is every bit as sparse and bare as its Buchenwald counterpart. The building is to be sunken, so that its flat roof is flush with the top of the wall surrounding Zone I; it will therefore only become visible from Zone I when the visitor reaches the top corner of the camp triangle. There will be narrow slits with limited views to the nearby cemetery for those who died in the Special Camp, and to the huts where some internees were held. The surface of the building will be machined in such a way that the surrounding, rather barren landscape will be reflected. The building will thus be integrated more into the grave site than is the case in Buchenwald, but its simple profile and withdrawn character will prevent any maudlin expression of pity or pain.

The exhibition on the Special Camp in Buchenwald was opened in 1997 – two years after the opening of the new exhibition on the concentration camp, in line with the principle of hierarchy. Section Three of this exhibition, with its subsections 'Undernourishment and Isolation', 'Inactivity and Monotony', and 'Hunger and Death', in no way shirks from openly confronting the theme of injustice and inhumanity within the Special Camp. But this theme is deliberately placed within an interpretative framework which makes three things clear: firstly, that Germans in eastern Europe had at Hitler's instigation enslaved and decimated the populations of various peoples; secondly, that the Soviet Special Camps must be understood at least initially as a denazification measure, whatever the apparent similarities to the GULAG system and the subsequent use of the Camps for political prisoners ('sovietization'); and thirdly, that while the inmates were often treated appallingly, many were not free of moral responsibility for their internment. The exhibition offers a selection of over twenty inmate biographies. The majority of these are of people with National Socialist affiliations. Thus Anna Siegert was a Nazi Party member and a functionary in the Nazi Women's Organization (*NS-Frauenschaft*); Friedrich-Emil Krauss ran a firm which made weapons for the German army (*Wehrmacht*), and he was a troop leader in the SA; Otto Koch, as we have seen, was mayor of Weimar. The biographical section does provide examples of inmates who had no, or no significant, National Socialist affiliation, and the exhibition also features interviews with survivors who assert their innocence. But because the exemplary biographies are predominantly of people with a significant National Socialist background, and because they run the length of the exhibition hall, accompanying the narrative from 1945 to 1950, they impress on the visitor the importance of not forgetting German responsibility for National Socialism, and of understanding Soviet post-war maltreatment of Germans as a deplorable, but nevertheless in some respects comprehensible overreaction to the suffering inflicted on the Soviet Union by the Germans.

This principle of hierarchy has not been to the liking of surviving Special Camp prisoners, who believe they are being treated as second-class victims. In a sense, they are. It is, however, a genuine conundrum that most of those Special Camp survivors now able to tell of their experiences are either people interned for political reasons in the later 1940s, or people so young at the time of their imprisonment that they were either innocent of involvement in National Socialism, or at least too immature to be accorded much blame (though, as we shall see later, not blameless) – in contrast to the majority of Special Camp inmates. Inevitably, they, or their relatives, feel hurt by the implicit insistence in Buchenwald's Special Camp exhibition that most inmates were National Socialists.

A step too far?

Advisory commissions at Buchenwald and Sachsenhausen were composed mostly of west German historians. Most of these were left-liberal in orientation. Choosing historians with predominantly right-wing sympathies would have resulted, possibly, in anti-communist exhibitions on the Special Camps. But in the view of those representing former inmates, choosing left-liberal historians has led at Buchenwald to an exhibition too friendly towards the Soviets, and too critical of the camp inmates. This argument is largely self-interested; the Buchenwald exhibition is generally fair. The representatives are on firmer ground when they complain that both Buchenwald and Sachsenhausen currently employ staff who formerly had links to the SED or even the *Stasi*. Given that the staff has been in large measure responsible for implementing the recommendations of the historians' commissions (admittedly under the leadership of west Germans), this seems a questionable tolerance. Bodo Ritscher, as research leader, was on the GDR staff at Buchenwald. He produced a distortive brochure on Buchenwald camp life in 1986 (see Chapter One). As IM Jochen Philipp, he collaborated with the *Stasi* as unofficial informant. The head of the Youth Centre at Buchenwald, Helmut Rook, has a GDR past as border-guard, FDJ agitprop secretary and *Stasi* collaborator. At Sachsenhausen, one of the researchers is Lutz Prieß, formerly of the GDR Institute for Marxism-Leninism and one of the four heads of the PDS Historical Commission. Prieß has a record of heavily doctrinal publications in the GDR. Both Prieß and Ritscher have been involved in research into and publications on the Special Camp. One can well understand the anger at their employ.

There is also reason to believe that, at Sachsenhausen Memorial Site, surviving Special Camp inmates and their relatives have been subjected to a discriminatory campaign of obstruction. At present, a head-high revolving turnstile opens onto Zone II, where a graveyard for the dead of the Special Camp has been laid out. But because the turnstile rarely works, officially because its electrical system has been damaged by lightning, it prevents rather than allows access. Even when it does, it functions by voice-system: only after the visitor has announced his or her wish to pass through is it opened electronically (or not) by a member of the site staff. When I visited, it was padlocked, ostensibly to keep out right-wing radicals, a curious argument given that they can easily clamber over the walls. A somewhat unsympathetic sign saying 'Paths not cleared in winter!' is affixed to the turnstile [Plate 2.2]. People who enter here, in other words, do so at their own peril, at least when it snows. This turnstile has been the focus of a grotesque battle between relatives of victims unable to reach the graves, and the memorial site staff. With the completion of the new exhibition, the problem is to be rectified.

A new exhibition is certainly needed, because Sachsenhausen's temporary Special Camp exhibition – tacked on to the old GDR exhibition on the concentration camp – is deficient. It conveys the impression that the Special Camp was but a slightly unpleasant form of holiday camp. A section on life in the camp mechanically informs the visitor of the daily routine from getting up in the morning to going to bed; it reads like the instructions to a guest at a dingy hotel. Another section, 'Cultural Activities', tells us that the culture group in the camp organized

Plate 2.2 The faulty revolving turnstile at Sachsenhausen. The plaques read 'Access to the mass graves 1945–1950' and 'Paths not cleared in winter'.

'colourful programmes' and performed 'songs and ballet'. It mentions actor Heinrich George's theatrical activities in post-war Sachsenhausen, but not his terrible death there. The theme of death, hunger and inactivity – what most sticks in the minds of the surviving inmates – is addressed in very general fashion, but the trivialization of the generally poor camp conditions borders on the cynical. Nor do the signs at Sachsenhausen providing basic information on individual parts of the area do much justice to the theme of the Special Camp. Thus it is claimed that the dead were 'laid to rest' (*bestattet*) in Schmachtenhagen Forest. In fact they were tossed into shallow graves. An angry survivor or relative has rubbed the word *bestattet* out. It seems, then, that a residual spirit of prejudicial anti-fascism is still present within Sachsenhausen's memorial site staff.

Defining the difference between the concentration camp and Special Camp inmates in terms of 'primary' and 'secondary' victims is defensible, but it should not be overdone. Certainly representatives of the Special Camp prisoners feel that, at Sachsenhausen, it has been. But they are not alone in feeling unfairly treated. Representatives of the communists and other political opponents of National Socialism imprisoned at Sachsenhausen and Buchenwald, furious at the removal of anti-fascist memorials and signs from the landscape of memory since 1990 (see Chapter Three), have also taken offence at the redesigning of this landscape to include reference to the Special Camps. They claim that Buchenwald and Sachsenhausen are being turned into National Socialist shrines by the capitalist west, and that the Special Camp exhibition building at Buchenwald is little more than a 'National Socialist Valhalla' (for a good, if biased overview, see Zorn 1994). In April 1997, a group of anti-fascists pulled bin-bags over 300 of the steel poles marking the graves of the Special Camp dead at Buchenwald (300 represent 80%, a reference to the fact that 80% of the Special Camp inmates were National Socialists). Also, both the Central Council of the Jews in Germany (*Zentralrat der Juden in Deutschland*) and the Central Council of German Sinti and Roma (*Zentralrat Deutscher Sinti und Roma*) have persistently protested at what they perceive to be a massive presumption. The Jews and Sinti and Roma have, at last, been given a place in the memorial and documentary landscape at Buchenwald and Sachsenhausen. Yet now, they believe, they are being asked to share their status as victims with the dead of the nation and indeed of the political organization which persecuted them. This charge can take dramatic form. Thus Romani Rose, head of the Central Council of German Sinti and Roma, exclaimed that he did not want 'to bow down to the perpetrators' at Buchenwald and would resist any 'lumping together of the victims' (*taz*, 13 April 1992).

In the case of both Buchenwald and Sachsenhausen memorial sites, representatives of victims of National Socialism are overreacting, even if their sensitivity on the issue is understandable. Knigge has made his position on the Special Camp inmates at Buchenwald quite clear, arguing that they were largely civil functionaries who 'stood in a direct relationship of guilt, or at least responsibility to the concentration camp prisoners' (quoted in GB 1997: 12). The new-look memorial site in no way seeks to exculpate them. In the case of Torgau, however, the situation is rather different.

The principle of equation

In 1998, an exhibition on Torgau's *Wehrmacht* prison was opened in a tower (*Flaschenturm*) in the grounds of Hartenfels Castle in Saxony. The exhibition was the result of pioneering research work undertaken by the Documentation and Information Centre Torgau (DIZ). The DIZ was set up after 1990, not least thanks to the initiative of west German historian Wolfgang Oleschinksi. It is now supported by the Foundation of Saxon Memorial Sites. Prior to unification, Torgau was known in the GDR, and indeed in the FRG, as the town where the American and Soviet armies had met on 25 April 1945. The meeting was symbolized in the famous handshake between American Second Lieutenant Bill Robertson and Soviet Sergeant Nikolai Andrejev on the ruins of a bridge over the Elbe. This meeting was commemorated regularly in the GDR, in honour, of course, of the Russian contribution to liberation in 1945. Yet Torgau had also been the site, at Fort Zinna, of two dreadful prisons for *Wehrmacht* soldiers. Here, deserters and other soldiers considered in need of disciplining for 'undermining defensive morale' were imprisoned. In 1941, Fort Zinna became a centre for selecting which 'miscreant' *Wehrmacht* soldiers were to do service at the front in the murderous *Bewährungstruppe 500* (a 'probationary troop'), or to be allocated to Field Punishment Camps where they were either arbitrarily shot or exposed to an often fatal programme of military drill, maltreatment and starvation. In 1943, Torgau played host to the notorious Reich War Court, which passed some 1,200 death sentences, many against deserters. This brutality was a fact which the post-war political orders in both German states were at pains to forget. In the course of the Cold War and remilitarization, there was little room for self-critical reflection on the issue of military justice and the moral right of desertion. As Haase and Oleschinski put it, the GDR and FRG required 'deployable soldiers, not "underminers of morale", deserters and "traitors to the fatherland"' (Haase and Oleschinski 1993b: 17). However, it has to be said that the GDR did at least conduct trials against Fort Zinna staff in the 1950s. By contrast, the military judges who had imposed draconian sentences for desertion (some 50,000 in all) not only got away scot-free, but were able to continue their judicial careers unhindered in West Germany.

It is all the more laudable, then, that this dark chapter in the history of German military justice is now documented in the new exhibition and its accompanying book (Eberlein, Haase and Oleschinski 1999). The exhibition is detailed and frank in its depiction of the wanton cruelty of the *Wehrmacht* penal system, and invites the visitor to understand the act of desertion as a positive moral decision within the context of the war of annihilation unleashed by the *Wehrmacht* and SS in eastern Europe (see Chapter Six). Superimposed upon this exhibition, one floor up in the *Flaschenturm*, is a second exhibition, this time on the use of Fort Zinna in Torgau as a Soviet Special Camp between 1945 and 1947. The DIZ is also the architect of this exhibition on the second 'taboo' in Torgau's history. Fort Zinna was also used as of 1946 as a transit prison for Soviet citizens convicted by Soviet military tribunals on charges of collaborating with the Germans, desertion, plundering and rape. A third exhibition, on the use of Fort Zinna as a GDR prison after 1950, is planned for the third floor of the *Flaschenturm*. The DIZ aims to portray all three 'levels' of the history of injustice and silence.

Unfortunately, the exhibition on the Special Camp is not good. It attempts to exonerate the inmates of moral guilt by means of an unrepresentative selection of biographies. Most of the examples are of young people whose guilt would seem to be in doubt, or qualified by their youth. Where arrested individuals did have connections to National Socialism, the exhibition seeks to play this down, or stress the fact that the Soviets arrested them for political reasons such as supposedly disseminating anti-Soviet propaganda. The biography of Ulrich von Fresenius, the NSDAP mayor of Wernigerode who was later imprisoned by the Soviets in Torgau, is noticeably lacking in any account of his activities between 1933 and 1945. By contrast, the biography of Stella Kübler, a Jewish fashion designer who survived National Socialism by betraying Jews who had gone into hiding to the Gestapo, is not lacking in such an account. While Kübler's betrayal led to many deaths, the implication that a Jew imprisoned in post-war Torgau was guilty, while the imprisoned Germans were not, leaves an unsavoury aftertaste. The exhibition fails to mention that, according to Russian statistics, of the 7,672 people held in Torgau in January 1946, 5,406 were active members of the National Socialist Party, and 498 were members of the Gestapo, SD and other National Socialist punitive organizations (*Straforgane*). This information, at least, is provided in the accompanying book (Oleschinski and Pampel 1997: 73), which also points out that about half the prisoners were over fifty, and only 45 under twenty (Oleschinski and Pampel 1997: 27 and 73).

The exhibition seeks to portray the imprisonment of the Germans as exclusively the result of Soviet power politics. Thus we read on one text board that the Soviet Special Camps were set up 'under the cover of common Allied interests', and that they followed the 'inner logic of the Stalinist machinery of persecution' and 'countenanced the suffering and deaths of thousands at former sites of horror in order to support the new power relationships'. This implies that the Special Camps were on a par with concentration camps, and comes close to attributing genocidal intentions to the Russians. It also implies that the Special Camps were designed only as a mechanism of throttling potential opposition. Not only do former National Socialists emerge from this picture as total victims, they are also indirectly transformed into anti-Soviet resistance fighters. It is not legitimate to use the fact that the Soviets did, increasingly, intern political opponents of communism as a means of morally whitewashing all the prisoners. Nor does the fact that most Special Camp inmates were either not given a fair trial or not tried at all, mean that all were free of legally determinable guilt. It must be stressed again that, while the Germans were treated terribly by the Soviets, this cannot be attributed to Stalinism alone, at least not in the 1945–1946 period. Reactions which can be put down to arbitrary vengeance were a reaction to German atrocities. And it was a vengeance that, in the case of at least 70% of Torgau Special Camp inmates, was imposed on National Socialists.

The Torgau Special Camp exhibition appears to have been shaped by a spirit of anti-communism. An image of the Soviets as unfeeling, primitive beings is projected, an image which bears an uncanny resemblance to the anti-bolshevist views of the National Socialists. In contrast to the memorial sites at Buchenwald and Sachsenhausen, moreover, Torgau's various exhibitions on the 'double past' are not in different buildings, but superimposed within one dizzying tower, escalating from, as it were, the atrocities of National Socialism at the bottom to those of the Special Camp, and, above, those of the GDR penal system. This is also a principle of hierarchy, only now the GDR penal system – much less dreadful than either that of the Soviets or National Socialists – will be at the top, suggesting it was more dreadful.

When, in 1992, the Organization for the Victims of Stalinism initiated plans for erecting a cross in memory of the victims of the Soviets and the GDR at Fort Zinna in Torgau, there was considerable protest from former victims of National Socialism, such as Ludwig Baumann, a *Wehrmacht* deserter. As it now stands, the cross is dedicated to the 'victims of the rule of violence'. But this lumps together all Nazi and post-1945 victims. The fact that *Wehrmacht* deserters had, in their way, staged an act of resistance, while many of those interned by the Soviets after the war had been National Socialists, is obscured. In 1998, against the will of Baumann and other Nazi victims, the Saxon Foundation of Memorial Sites inaugurated a competition for a 'collective' commemorative memorial at Fort Zinna. It was won in June 1999 by Klaus Madlowski and Claudia Diehl. Their design is simple. An asphalted surface runs over four gradated levels. The first and lowest level represents the present. The second commemorates the victims of SED injustice, the third those who suffered in the Special Camps, the fourth the victims of National Socialism. While the memory of suffering under National Socialist atrocities is placed 'above' that of suffering under subsequent injustice, the shared memorial suggests an equal moral status as victim. Baumann and historian Manfred Messerschmidt reacted sharply: 'by means of an incredible distortion of history, everything here is being lumped together' (Baumann and Messerschmidt 1999: 32). They also objected both to the fact that the cross in memory of Soviet and GDR victims would now cast its shadow over the level designed for the Nazi victims, and that the surface-area to be allocated to the memory of the former is greater than that envisaged for the latter.

To be fair to the competition's organizers, they were aware that not all inmates of the Special Camps should be commemorated alongside *Wehrmacht* deserters or political prisoners of the GDR. The guidelines stated clearly that the post-1945 commemoration was for 'arbitrarily arrested people', notably 'youths accused of *Werwolf* activities'; not, in other words, for National Socialist civil functionaries (Haase 1999: 36). The texts planned for the 'Wall Plates' on each commemorative level will make this clear. Yet this only complicates matters. There is an erroneous assumption that arrests on the grounds of *Werwolf* activities were always arbitrary. Erroneous because these activities did take place, and young people were involved in them. According to historian Perry Biddiscombe, the *Werwolf* movement, which organized terrorist attacks against the Allies before and after the end of the war, was responsible for some 3,000 to 5,500 deaths

(Biddiscombe 1998: 276). Thuringia, where Buchenwald is situated, was a hotbed of *Werwolf* violence. Neither the GDR nor the FRG acknowledged the existence of the *Werwolf* movement adequately, and the subject has been one of historiographical neglect. The focus in both Germanys was on resistance to National Socialism, not on resistance to the Allies. Nor should it be forgotten that the *Werwolf* movement is known to have strung up deserters in 1945. To Baumann, it must seem as if perpetrators and their victims are being granted the same right to commemoration.

In Bautzen, there is now a cemetery for some of the dead of the Special Camp No. 4, including those prisoners who died after 1950 following their transferral to the GDR's penal authorities. The cemetery, laid out between 1994 and 1997 on a hill in Bautzen (*Karnickelberg*) with support from Bonn and from Saxony's government, is also, in more general terms, a site of commemoration for the 'victims of the communist rule of violence', as the entrance plaque puts it. A memorial inside the graveyard reinforces this, and there is a special chapel for prayer and commemoration. Those accustomed to commemorative sites in west Germany honouring the 'victims of the National Socialist rule of violence' will recognize a certain parallelism of formulation here. Bautzen is one of many new sites of memory in the new *Länder* equipped with an inscription referring to the 'communist rule of violence'. It is hard not to see in this a process of commemorative relativization, whereby references to socialist injustice are being used to reduce the stark impression left by National Socialist atrocities. One might well ask why there is no correspondingly vast memorial to the victims of National Socialist Bautzen between 1933 and 1945.

The planned exhibition on the history of Bautzen's prisons, to be housed in the former prison Bautzen II, may adopt a more differentiated approach. On the wall as one enters the building is a statement of intentions which points to the need to give 'each period of persecution its specific weight', to avoid relativization and to be wary of seeing recent history simply in terms of victims and perpetrators. 'Overhasty moral judgements do not do justice to the complex situation.' The documentation site is to be a 'place of open learning', without a prescribed route (*Rundgang*), thus avoiding an 'artificial logic'. It remains to be seen whether the stated need for an awareness of moral complexity will or will not degenerate into defending Special Camp inmates against any suggestion that they might, in any sense, bear responsibility for National Socialism. The fact that the Hannah Arendt Institute for Research into Totalitarianism in Dresden is involved in the planning of Bautzen's permanent exhibition does not augur well (see Chapter Three). Bautzen's current exhibition is very understated, but still displays apologist tendencies, declaring Soviet measures to be fundamentally political in motive. Bautzen could learn from the current documentation site at Halle dealing with the history of the 'Red Oxen' prison. Despite its simplicity, this temporary exhibition is exemplary because it presents the 1933–1989 history of the prison graphically, but with a welcome objectivity of tone and without sweeping judgements.

Prison cells and the Wall: what remains of the GDR?

As stated earlier in this chapter, it is not yet possible to make general predictions as to how the memorial sites with a 'double past' will present the theme of GDR injustice in their permanent exhibitions. There is certainly a danger that they may be influenced by the totalitarianist theory into presenting this theme too drastically. There is a disturbing trend in united Germany towards an exhibition and memorial site landscape which conveys an absolutely negative view of the GDR. The post-unification removal of anti-fascist relics was motivated in part by the desire to overcome the GDR's understanding of itself, its history and pre-history in terms of heroes and villains (see Chapter Three). Yet if we were to take new historical exhibitions and memorial sites in eastern Germany which relate to the post-1945 period and understand them as a gallery with several rooms, then we would have to say that most of these rooms are hung with pictures of heroes and villains. Only now the villains are the Soviets, GDR socialism, the SED and of course the *Stasi*, while the heroic victims are those who opposed the GDR, those who fled to West Germany and from there agitated against the GDR, those who demonstrated in 1989 and, last but not least, the anti-communist West Germany itself. That the GDR offered its citizens not just repression, but a range of exemplary social and economic benefits has been somewhat obscured, as have the weaknesses of West German democracy. Moreover, in this black-and-white scheme of remembering there is no place for the mass of 'normal' GDR citizens who were neither villains nor heroes. Unhealthily, they are constrained into identifying themselves with one or the other category.

A tourist in the east is invited to come to the conclusion that the GDR must have been about prison-cells – by implication, then, was itself a prison. At Bautzen, Halle and the 'Munich Square' in Dresden, or at Hohenschönhausen in Berlin, the visitor is guided round gloomy, dingy, decrepit gaols. If he or she should also visit Sachsenhausen or Ravensbrück, where cells can also be viewed, then it will be hard to resist a cumulative impression of the 1933–1989 period as one of persecution and incarceration. This impression will be reinforced by a visit to the numerous new sites documenting and memorializing the history of the Berlin Wall. The Museum at Checkpoint Charlie, a privately run, robustly anti-communist exhibition on the Berlin Wall and the inventiveness of those East Germans determined to reach West Berlin, long predated unification. It is now embedded in a network of sites in Berlin supported by regional and Federal funds which focus on the Berlin Wall, such as the Memorial Site and Documentation Centre Berlin Wall in the Bernauer Street, the Commemoration Site Emergency Camp Marienfelde (formerly used for GDR fugitives) and the Allied Museum in the Clay Avenue. There is now also a memorial site at the former border crossing-point in Marienborn.

In many senses, of course, living in the GDR was like living in a prison, especially for those who wished to leave. Remembering the concrete and barbed wire at the German–German border, moreover, will keep fresh the memory of the pain of division, in part a consequence of Hitler's imperialism, as a warning against unleashing any wars in the future. Moreover, the wish of East Germans to move to West Germany, and the risks they took in trying to do so – leading to 1,000 deaths, in many cases as a result of mines or shots from border guards – are a legitimate point of historical reference for a now united country. It is also here, however, that the problem lies. That some GDR citizens persecuted by the SED have felt drawn to the CDU is no surprise. Helmut Kohl, after unification, had a strong interest in presenting the history of the GDR teleologically, as one long and painful road to unification. The GDR was the wound that he, Kohl, had healed. Victims of the GDR felt represented by Kohl's insistence on the need to remember the crimes of socialism, but have perhaps not recognized that he instrumentalized their suffering as proof of the illegitimacy of the GDR and the legitimacy of the FRG, and as justification for the largely westernized process of unification. Undoubtedly, any development towards a culture of memory which reduces the history of the GDR to one of imprisonment and repression, and blames it for division, would play into the hands of conservative west German politicians. Furthermore, the more diabolic the GDR appears with hindsight, the easier it is to equate it with National Socialism. The two pasts can only be effectively dovetailed by excluding from representations of the GDR the positive elements of anti-fascism and socialism.

Attempts to establish a negative, indeed totalitarianist narrative are deeply political, blinkered, unhistorical, even propagandistic. As evidence, let me point to two exhibitions where this narrative has taken on disturbing proportions. Both are exhibitions developed under the auspices of the West German-dominated House of History. One, focusing on West German history, is in Bonn. It was opened in 1994. The other, focusing on the history of East Germany, is in Leipzig, and was opened in 1999. The House of History was one of Kohl's long-cherished dreams, and came about thanks to strong government interest. Its advisory board is composed largely of handpicked conservative historians, the odd east German historian highly critical of the GDR, and one or two fig-leaf left-liberal historians who were included after protest. Both of these exhibitions aim, essentially, to laud the Federal Republic and demonize the GDR. They achieve these aims very well. The measure of their success in doing so is also the measure of their dubious merits as pictures of history.

Both exhibitions construct a typically west German historical narrative of German suffering during and after the war, a narrative to which an additional chapter, relating to the victims of the Special Camps, has been added. The Leipzig exhibition particularly focuses on the vengefulness of the Soviets, their plunder, rape and persecution of Germans. A section on the Special Camps seeks to illustrate by means of four videotaped interviews the innocence of many of their inmates. There is only a cursory reference to the fact that National Socialists were also interned. Both exhibitions handle the history of German atrocities in a very gingerly fashion. Thus in Bonn's exhibition, the portrayal of the holocaust is encased in a black box (see Chapter Eight), while at Leipzig the history of the German invasion of the Soviet Union is banished to a three-sided 'cupboard' whose contents are easily overlooked. Both exhibitions use German suffering to relativize German guilt. In the Bonn exhibition, the suffering of the Germans expelled by the Poles and Czechs is set beside that of Jews, while in Leipzig the German war-dead are ranked numerically after those of the Soviet Union, but without any distinction being made between aggressors and defenders. This picture of German agony serves to set the tone for the portrayal of post-war divided Germany: here the West, liberated from dictatorship, there the East, where the Soviets and then the SED continue rule by dictatorship. 'Anti-fascism is used as a legitimation for a new totalitarianism', declares the Bonn exhibition. To help the visitor gain the desired impression, the Bonn House of History uses heavy symbolism. In one room, we are presented on the right with a wide area containing seats. On the back wall is a screen onto which films of politicians making speeches in the West German Parliament are projected. The visitor, at the touch of a button, can select from a range of speeches and politicians. On the left, the political world of East Germany is represented in the form of one large sepia-coloured photograph showing an SED session. In front of the photograph is a steel frame, like camp wire, bearing quotations such as one by Adenauer: 'in the Soviet Zone there is no free will of the German people'. With all due respect to the differences in political freedom between West and East Germany, the symbolism here plays with images of free choice and the lack of it, open and closed space, the moving and the static in a way which utterly discourages critical analysis of the West German system, and unambiguously invites condemnation of the East German system. The visitor, ultimately, is left with no choice at all.

But it is the exhibition in Leipzig which perfects the portrayal of the GDR as little more than a continuation of National Socialism. Outside the building is a sculpture by Wolfgang Mattheuer. According to the catalogue, it symbolizes the 'relationship of the Germans to both totalitarian systems in the 20th century' (Stiftung Haus der Geschichte 1999: 42). The sculpture is an elongated figure, the right arm stretched upwards and outwards in the National Socialist salute, while the left arm is raised – bent at the elbow, fist clenched – in socialist defiance. Mattheuer's creation is entitled *The Century Step*. The outstretched leg symbolizes the manner in which fascism and socialism stepped out across the century. Mattheuer, a GDR sculptor, intended his 1984 sculpture to signify the conflict between fascism and socialism. But it is now being used to signify the equivalence of these. Inside the building, this equational thinking is consistently maintained. It operates firstly by means of stressing continuities between National Socialism and GDR socialism. Certainly it is illuminating to learn that Kurt Säuberlich, an SS man, later became a member of the GDR People's Chamber, and that Kurt Schumann, President of the GDR's Supreme Court, worked for a National Socialist war-court. But such high-level continuities were largely untypical of the GDR, and much more common, indeed typical, in West Germany. A passing reference to Hans Globke, who wrote the official commentary for the 1935 Nuremberg Race Laws and later became Adenauer's chief aide in the Chancellery, hardly does justice to this fact. Secondly, the exhibition consistently seeks to convince the visitor that most events and developments in the GDR were shaped by a cynical and repressive politics. Anti-fascism is discredited as but a front behind which power politics concealed its ugly face. While this is undeniably one side of anti-fascism, it surely cannot be denied that some in the GDR sincerely believed in and sought to realize its purported ideals, and were genuinely concerned at restorative tendencies in West Germany. GDR cultural ideals, land and economic reform, centralization and coming to terms with the past are all presented only in terms of their negative aspects. There are some references to the GDR's social building programme and its industrial achievements, but these are 'squeezed' in between the negative focal points.

These negative focal points are: 1953, the year of the workers' uprising in East Berlin; 1961, the year when the Berlin Wall was built; and 1968, the year of the Prague Spring in Czechoslovakia. One positive focal point, the year of the *Wende* (1989), stands in contrastive (and victorious) relation to these negative foci. Each of the negative events is thrown into larger-than-life relief. The section on 1953 features three video installations showing the same scene from the uprising, and it also includes an enormous enlarged photograph of the Soviet intervention. The GDR is presented as the history of rebellion and counter-rebellion, protest and repression. Much space is devoted to the history of the reform movement and its suffering. That the exhibition was opened on 9 October 1999 – the tenth anniversary of the first large-scale Monday demonstration in Leipzig – was an acknowledgement of the achievements of the GDR reform movement and those people who took to the streets. Such acknowledgement is undermined, however, by the absence of any reference to the fact that many reformers and ordinary citizens initially wanted a reformed GDR, not unification, at least not on FRG terms. A tiny reference to the call 'We are the people' does little to offset the effect of the calls for unity on which the exhibition focuses. The GDR reform tradition is thus instrumentalized as a prefiguration of German unification under West German auspices. It has to be said, too, that the understanding of the GDR in terms of repression and resistance exactly mirrors the West German and East German understanding of National Socialism. But given that the West Germans 'won' the Cold War, Wolf Biermann and Rudolf Bahro can now be set alongside Stauffenberg in the gallery of those who paved the way to the partial, then total triumph of West German democracy on German soil. The ultimate impression of this exhibition is one of noise, as it seeks firstly to prevent critical thinking, and secondly to contrast the dissidence and violence of the GDR with the redemptive harmony of unification. Screams and the crunching sound of tanks give way to chants for unity.

The exhibition brochure claims that the exhibition is directed against tendencies to justify the SED dictatorship and create myths (Stiftung Haus der Geschichte 1999: 7). But creating new, demonic myths will only make east Germans sympathetic to those who want to whitewash the SED. It seems, too, that the Bonn and Leipzig Houses of History are intended as much as a glorification of West Germany as a deconstruction of the GDR. In the same measure as National Socialism and the GDR are equated, the FRG is distanced from National Socialism. This is also the agenda at the new Museum of Military History in Dresden, a creation of the Federal Army (*Bundeswehr*) and the Office for Research into Military History. On the one hand, the museum stresses the role of *Wehrmacht* officers in building up the *Kasernierte Volkspolizei*, forerunner to the GDR's National People's Army. On the other, no mention is made of the role of former *Wehrmacht* soldiers in building up the West German army. The National People's Army's espousal of dubious Prussian military tradition is highlighted, but where the *Bundeswehr*'s nostalgia for *Wehrmacht* traditions is conceded, then this is attributed to 'individual soldiers', not the *Bundeswehr* as an institution. Yet 'individual soldiers' were not responsible for naming barracks after German generals.

The injustices of the National Socialist and 1945–1989 periods should be represented at sites with a 'double past', or indeed in historical exhibitions. But problems begin when negative images are arranged into patterns and placed in perspectives that predispose towards certain types of reaction. Neither the House of History in Bonn, nor that in Leipzig invites us to reflect on the past, it tells us how it should be read. Inclusive memory, in this case, is only apparently inclusive, because reference to injustice is not balanced by reference to positive aspects. Effectively, Kohl's House of History in Bonn and Leipzig is a Cold War relic, rather than an exhibition. Of all the chapters in this book, this one is the most sceptical of post-unification *Vergangenheitsbewältigung*, pointing to the ways in which the totalitarianist reading of the 1933–1989 period has made inroads into exhibitions in eastern Germany. Yet Sachsenhausen and Buchenwald memorial sites, at least, are striving to present their 'double past' with more feeling for differentiation. As will become clear from the rest of the book, moreover, the far greater ugliness of National Socialism, if not the more positive sides of GDR socialism, have come so much to the fore in the public realm in recent years that the totalitarianist theorists have found themselves fighting an increasingly rearguard action. Even their attempts to discredit communist resistance during the Third Reich and thereby strike at the very roots of GDR anti-fascism have not been crowned with success, as the next chapter shows.

3   Resistance

'20 July is a day of commemoration for all those who rebelled against the regime of injustice [. . .] We in the Federal Republic should not make the mistake fifty years after the event of categorizing the resistance politically and morally.'
(from an FDP statement, published in *FDK*, 18 July 1994)

The instrumentalization of resistance traditions

All in all, there were about forty attempts on Hitler's life between 1933 and 1945. None of them was successful. Georg Elser, a carpenter from Wurttemberg, attached a bomb to a pillar in a Munich beer-cellar (*Bürgerbräukeller*). It blew up, as planned, on the evening that Hitler gave a speech there on 8 November 1939. But Hitler had already left the beer-cellar, earlier than anticipated. On 13 March 1943, Henning von Tresckow, an officer in the *Wehrmacht*, and his adjutant Fabian von Schlabrendorff succeeded in getting a bomb (disguised as an innocent bottle of cognac) placed in Hitler's plane. It failed to explode. Claus Schenk Graf von Stauffenberg came closest to success when, on 20 July 1944, he planted a bomb at the Führer's headquarters in East Prussia (the so-called 'Wolf's Lair'). It went off, and it killed four people, but none of them was Hitler. In fact Hitler was well-nigh unscathed, and able to address the German people by radio that same evening, when he claimed that 'a very small clique of ambitious, wicked, and stupidly criminal officers forged a plot to eliminate me' (Fest 1996: 278). At the time, and even with retrospect, it seemed as if Hitler had led a charmed life. To an extent, he had. One other factor played a significant role in his survival, however: those who had tried to kill him were to a degree the victims of their own poor planning, delays and nervous indecision. This was even true of the courageous Stauffenberg himself, who, briefly disturbed as he activated the timer for the first bomb, failed to place the second bomb in his briefcase. Had he done so, the first would surely have set it off, and Hitler would have died (Fest 1996: 257).

Resistance to Nazism, of course, cannot be defined merely in terms of spectacular (or spectacularly unsuccessful) attempts on the Führer's life. In his overview of German resistance, Ger van Roon divides up anti-Nazi resistance *inter alia* into communist resistance, social democratic resistance, resistance by the Confessional (Protestant) Church, Catholic resistance, the Goerdeler Group (civil resistance), military resistance, and resistance from exile (Roon 1994). These divisions suggest the existence of a set of group-oriented, principled, indeed organized resistance groups which sought to curb the impact of Nazi rule. In post-war Germany, where both states were desperate to find some positive legacy from the Third Reich, there was a tendency to focus principally on one of these. In East Germany, the emphasis was on communist resistance. In West Germany, it was largely on military resistance, particularly on the 20 July 1944 assassination attempt. However, because a number of civilians were also involved in this plot to a greater or lesser degree, the West German emphasis on the 20 July conspiracy was thus an emphasis on a supposedly widespread (and largely conservative) resistance.

Both German states tended to exaggerate the achievements of their chosen group. In the GDR, little attention was paid to the fact that the communist resistance within Germany was effectively smashed by Hitler within the first few years of his rule – not least because its organizational methods and naïve optimism made it easy prey for the Gestapo (Burleigh 2000: 668). Most German communists by 1937 were either dead, in concentration camps, or in exile. There was a brief flurry of relatively organized communist anti-Nazi activity in Berlin in the 1940s under Robert Uhrig and Anton Saefkow, but it could achieve little. The workers and their unions, the basis of communist support, had already been in part successfully wooed by Hitler in 1933, and by 1941–1942 a large proportion of these workers was fighting his war against, not least, the Soviet Union. As for the military resistance, this did indeed, as West Germany liked to point out, gradually escalate within the *Wehrmacht* and the Military Intelligence, which Hans Oster, in the words of Joachim Fest, had turned into a 'hotbed of resistance' (Fest 1996: 106) by 1938. Stauffenberg's bomb-attempt of 20 July 1944 was an act of individual courage, but it was also the result of long-standing plans hatched across a range of military men and civilians for a *coup d'état* (by means of 'Operation Valkyrie') and the establishment of a state based on the rule of law. However, Stauffenberg's attempt to kill Hitler came very late. Military resistance was, for long, something of a lame duck. It was not typical; officers and generals, after all, are paid to fight wars, and war was what Hitler offered. Many soldiers who disapproved of Hitler still felt they had to be loyal to their vow to serve him. Given that Hitler was so dependent on the military, given too that it had the best access to him and the power to overthrow the regime, disgruntled generals and officers had a greater responsibility to act on their dissatisfaction, one which, arguably, they should have discharged long before the start of the war.

But West and East Germany in the first post-war decades were not so much interested in identifying weaknesses or failures in their chosen resistance group, as in emphasizing strengths. This was because of the inevitable politicization of resistance discourse in the GDR and FRG as a result of the Cold War. In striving to appear as the 'better Germany', each state had an interest in claiming that it was heir to a grand resistance tradition: historical legitimation was, after all, an important factor in identity building. Thus the GDR tended to glorify and exaggerate communist resistance, while the FRG glorified and exaggerated military resistance. It was also inevitable that each Germany would seek to denigrate the resistance tradition espoused by the other state, because in so doing, it could undermine its legitimacy. Thus in West Germany, it was argued that the communist resistance celebrated in the GDR had been manipulated by the Soviets and directed towards the establishment of another dictatorial state. In East Germany, it was argued that the high-ranking military and civilian resistance celebrated in West Germany had aimed to establish a state based not on justice and freedom, but on traditional class interests and authoritarian values. The communist resistance was discredited in West Germany as inherently totalitarian, the military and civilian resistance dismissed in East Germany as inherently reactionary. Accordingly, communist resistance was for a long time barely acknowledged in the West, and the military and civilian resistance around Stauffenberg not acknowledged in the East.

This did change somewhat, not least as a result of *Ostpolitik*. West German and, a little later, East German historians began to acknowledge the 'other' resistance tradition, as did politicians. In West Berlin in the 1980s, the Memorial Site for German Resistance embarked on creating a new exhibition based on the 'integrative concept', whereby hitherto excluded resistance groups were to be featured alongside the lionized Stauffenberg. What started in earnest in the 1980s continued after unification. It was now complemented, however, by a process of demythologization. Changes to the permanent exhibition at Buchenwald Memorial Site since 1990 have led to a more, if at points too critical view of communist resistance at the camp. Equally, while the pre-1990 historiographical picture of high-ranking military and civilian resistance in West Germany was to a degree critical, critical appraisals never penetrated the public realm to the extent they did in 1994, the year of the 50th anniversary of Stauffenberg's attempt on Hitler's life. The success of the Memorial Site for German Resistance in defending and extending its integrative concept after unification despite objections was a measure of the extent to which communist anti-Hitler resistance is now – albeit somewhat grudgingly – accepted in the western canon. In the east of Germany, changes to street names have led not just to a necessary reduction in signs dedicated to communists, but also to a wider introduction of names associated with the 20 July conspiracy. There is a move, a tentative but noticeable one, towards a (critical) inclusiveness in west and east.

The picture of resistance in the GDR

As a self-proclaimed socialist state of workers and peasants, the GDR naturally sought its heritage in the resistance of communists and socialists between 1933 and 1945. Without doubt these groups had staged the earliest resistance, and had paid the highest price in terms of the number of those arrested and incarcerated after Hitler's accession to power. In 1961, within the GDR's Institute for Marxism-Leninism, a working group drew up principles for a 'history of the German anti-fascist resistance struggle between 1933 and 1945' to be taught at universities. The resulting proposal emphasized that resistance was to be understood in terms of the 'leading role of the working class and its Marxist-Leninist Party in the struggle against fascist German imperialism'. Students were to be taught that the working class, as well as ideas of peace and progress, gained in influence even during the Third Reich, and that the working-class-led fight against Hitler was the precondition for bringing about 'the political-moral unity of all honest and nationally conscious forces within the German people' (SAPMO 1961). The true nationalism of the working class was set against the false nationalism of German imperialism. This view, which remained typical throughout the history of the GDR, was more than distortive. To identify the working class with communism is to overlook the fact that there was also a Catholic and social democratic workers' movement when Hitler came to power. It is also to overlook the fact that the Nazis managed to a significant degree to sever the nexus between the workers and the left-wing political groupings by means of massive repression of the latter, the absorption of the workers into Nazi organizations and various re-employment programmes. The new nationalism which Hitler offered to workers was racially based and virulently anti-Marxist. In the course of the 1930s, communist resistance dwindled away to a few disparate underground cells; the workers could not be mobilized to rise up against Hitler.

The GDR's picture of a united anti-fascist resistance constituted a misrepresentation of the 1935–1936 *Volksfront* idea, according to which the social democrats and communists, among others, had agreed to work together against Hitler (prior to this, the enmity between communists and social democrats had played into Hitler's hands). The SED strove to accredit to the communists the outstanding role in such resistance, one which it did not in all cases have. As we saw in Chapter One, this led at Buchenwald Memorial Site to an underrepresentation of the variety of national and political groups involved in planning resistance within the camp. It also led to a misappropriation of the famous 'Buchenwald Oath'. After liberation on 19 April 1945, an international group of anti-fascist (but not exclusively communist) Buchenwald prisoners swore an oath in which they committed themselves to the 'annihilation of Nazism at its very roots' (GB 1999: 247). Subsequently, SED politicians consistently identified this as a specifically socialist pledge. They were also at pains to imply that the GDR was the German state which had heeded the 'Buchenwald Oath'. 'Hitler fascism was [. . .] pulled out at the roots only in one part of Germany, the German Democratic Republic', claimed Minister President Grotewohl in his 1958 speech opening the new Buchenwald Memorial Site (Buchenwald 1958: 7). Thirty years later, in a talk in commemoration of the victims of the November 1938 *Reichskristallnacht* pogrom, General Secretary of the SED Erich Honecker said: 'The German Democratic Republic has fulfilled its duty to destroy fascism and its ideas at the roots for ever honestly and genuinely' (SAPMO 1988). Given the relative indifference to Jewish suffering in the GDR, this was a strong claim.

The desire to inflate the importance of communist resistance also resulted in a misrepresentation of the various resistance groups loosely coordinated by Arvid Harnack and Harro Schulze-Boysen. The Gestapo labelled them 'Red Orchestra' (*Rote Kapelle*), as part of an attempt to portray them as Soviet agents. In the GDR, they were also understood to have been loyal servants of the Soviet Union. But while the Harnack/Schulze-Boysen organization in the summer of 1941 did indeed seek to inform the Soviets of Hitler's war-plans, this was in an attempt to end the war and preserve Germany's status as an independent state; it was not a gesture of communist solidarity. Both Harnack and Schulze-Boysen had been involved in opposition to Hitler since the mid-1930s or even earlier, and the people they gathered around them were of varied social, professional and political background. 'Red Orchestra' was a forum for critical discussion, not a communist platform. The image of resistance from within the National Committee for a Free Germany (NKFD), a group with which the GDR particularly liked to identify, was also in part distortive.

Set up at a German POW camp in Krasnogorsk in the Soviet Union on 13 July 1943, not long after the huge defeat of the Germans at Stalingrad, the NKFD aimed to bring together soldiers of different backgrounds and persuasions in the fight against Nazism. By means of leaflets and other forms of propaganda, members of the NKFD sought to encourage German soldiers at the front to desert. Some NKFD members fought in the Red Army. In September 1943, a number of the officers, notably generals, of the defeated armies at Stalingrad formed the League of German Officers (BDO), a parallel organization to the NKFD. Both the NKFD and BDO came about with the express interest and support of the Soviets, and of German exile communists such as Walter Ulbricht and Wilhelm Pieck, who were later to play a significant political role in the GDR. Increasingly, too, the Soviet manipulation of the NKFD turned it into an instrument of Soviet policy. But the motives of German soldiers and officers in forming or joining the NKFD and BDO were diverse. Not all members were communist. Moreover, while the NKFD did have a considerable influence on communists within the Reich, it was regarded by some with a degree of scepticism because of its emergence from the conservative *Wehrmacht*. When the Institute for Marxism-Leninism set out to establish exactly when the Berlin branch of the NKFD had been set up, it not only failed to establish a clear foundation date, but also came across a concerned statement by the communist Saefkow Group in Berlin stressing that it would be 'wrong, a hundred thousand times wrong for the proletariat to form fighting groups in "Free Germany" [. . .] The workers belong in their class organizations' (SAPMO 1955b).

The SED thus not only misrepresented the extent of communist resistance, but also tended to paper over the cracks that emerged in the relationship between communists in Moscow, in the Soviet POW camps, in German concentration camps and in German cities such as Berlin. Given the geographically far-flung and disparate nature of communist groupings, given too the Hitler–Stalin Pact of August 1939, which alienated many German communists within the Reich from Moscow's leadership, such cracks were not surprising. After the end of the war in 1945, mutual distrust and rivalry escalated, as former camp communists, exile communists and members of the BDO and NKFD became caught up in a messy wrangle for power in eastern Germany. In Dachau in April 1947, the Americans began with the trial of some of Buchenwald's SS guards and the prisoners who collaborated with them. Fearing that the Americans would use whatever they found out to fuel an anti-communist campaign, the SED hastily set about gathering positive information on the conduct of Buchenwald's communists which could be used as counter-propaganda (Niethammer 1994). In the event, it was the negative rather than the positive information which proved useful to men such as Ulbricht, an exile communist keen to diminish the political power of the former concentration camp communists. Some of Buchenwald's communists, such as Walther Barthel and Robert Siewert, were expelled from the SED. The Soviets, suspicious of a communism that had evolved in Buchenwald and not in Moscow, supported the German exile communists, deporting former camp inmate Ernst Busse to a Soviet work-camp in 1950, where he died. Yet the so-called *Inland-Kommunisten* such as Erich Honecker, who had spent the Nazi years in a prison in Brandenburg, could give as good as they got. Secretary of the Central Committee's Security Commission at the time, Honecker was instrumental in drawing up a proposal which led to a Politburo ruling of 15 February 1957 that phased in the removal of former BDO and NKFD officers from the East German army (Niemetz 1999).

The GDR's portrayal of communist resistance as the most dominant and coherent force within German resistance thus depended on a degree of overemphasis, readjustment and plain distortion. The picture of the supposedly 'illegitimate' resistance around Stauffenberg, while marked rather by underemphasis, was also distorted. In the proposal referred to above, the Institute for Marxism-Leninism dismissed the whole 20 July 1944 plot, prepared as it was by individuals from the 'wrong' classes, as 'antinational in character', and as 'the attempt by reactionary representatives of German finance capital to prevent the inevitable collapse of German imperialism' (SAPMO 1961). In similar vein, the SED newspaper *Neues Deutschland* on 19 July 1954 dismissed the plot as 'an attempt to save German imperialism'. This reduced the motives of the conspirators to one of self-interest, and stripped the projected plans for a post-Hitler Germany of their diversity and constructive elements. But in the black-and-white world of GDR Marxist-Leninism there was little scope, at first at least, for differentiation. The 'positive' motives of the legitimate communist resistance, namely to create a society based on freedom and equality, were contrasted with the 'negative' ones of the group around Stauffenberg. This dichotomy extended into the GDR's view of the post-war era. The GDR, 'born' of communist resistance, understood itself to be in opposition to the combined imperialism of West Germany and the United States, an alliance in turn traced back to the wish of some involved in the 20 July plot to arrange a separate peace with the western Allies and continue the war against the Soviets. Hence the view of the 20 July conspirators in the GDR of the 1950s as being anti-Soviet.

In the late 1950s, following the 50th Party Conference of the Soviet Communist Party, and more so in the 1960s, GDR historians turned to neglected areas of resistance, such as that of Christians, social democrats and the 20 July plot. But initial interest was marginal. Something of a breakthrough was achieved with Kurt Finker's biography of Stauffenberg, which appeared in the GDR in 1967 and was quickly sold out. In 1971, a second edition appeared, and by 1989 the book had run to seven editions. Gradually, in the late 1960s and 1970s, GDR historians and politicians developed a principle of selectivity whereby 'progressive' and 'reactionary' elements within the 20 July group were distinguished. Given that

Stauffenberg had sought contacts to communists and shown indignation at the atrocities in the east, he was ranked as a progressive. Carl Goerdeler, by contrast, former mayor of Leipzig and head of a civilian group linked to the 20 July assassination attempt, was rejected as reactionary because he entertained ideas of German hegemony in Europe. Increasingly, too, there was a tendency to evaluate Stauffenberg's deed *as a deed*, in terms of its immediate aim of destroying Hitler. From being viewed as a putsch, it came to be regarded as a courageous act.

A real change in attitude came in the late 1970s and early 1980s. In 1980, the East Berlin City Council sought to name a street after Stauffenberg. His widow Nina turned down the request, arguing that there was already a Stauffenberg Street in West Berlin. In December 1983, SED Politburo member Kurt Hager said at an SED Central Committee conference that 'history knows examples where representatives of the exploitative classes, without actually overcoming the limitations of their class-determined understanding, are able to maintain a sense of reality or to acquire this sense through bitter experience' (quoted in Finker 1984: 4). This quotation was circulated widely in the GDR press and journals. By 1984, Stauffenberg, as well as the Kreisau Circle around Count Hellmuth von Moltke which had had links to Stauffenberg, had been somewhat acrobatically embraced by the GDR's concept of anti-fascist resistance. Thus, during the course of the 40th anniversary commemoration of Stauffenberg's attempt on Hitler's life in 1984, GDR television showed several programmes on the topic. Two principal reasons can be adduced for this change of policy. One was the GDR's reaction to the stationing of nuclear arms on German soil. SED politicians called for a 'coalition of reason' across national and political boundaries to overcome the threat this posed. Stauffenberg, who had consulted with people of various political persuasions in developing his plan, was seen now as having been motivated by common sense or a feeling for *Realpolitik*. Needless to say, in claiming Stauffenberg for itself, the GDR also began to refute the right of the supposedly aggressive West Germans to 'keep' him for themselves (see *FAZ*, 21 July 1988). Secondly, in its attempt to anchor itself more within a variety of traditions in German history and thus take firmer root, the GDR in the 1980s developed an interest in Prussian history and historical figures. The inclusion of Stauffenberg and Moltke in the anti-fascist appropriation of Prussianism might seem less surprising when we consider a fact from the history of the post-war Moltke Circle. This is an international group of some 5,000 people committed to the memory of the Kreisau Circle's most significant figure. In 1979, the West German branch of the Moltke Circle approached the GDR to discuss the setting up of an East German branch. In the course of negotiations, Freya von Moltke, Moltke's widow, opined that she believed the GDR 'to have done much and realized more than her husband had envisioned. Here there is order, discipline and hard work' (SAPMO 1979). She certainly saw much that was Prussian about GDR socialism.

In 1986, the GDR put up a plaque in Potsdam cemetery in honour of one of the four men directly involved in the assassination attempt of 20 July 1944, Albrecht Mertz von Quirnheim. In 1988, in Bornstedt, a memorial stone was unveiled to another of the military leaders involved, General Major Henning von Tresckow, who had been a member of Potsdam's Infantry Regiment No. 9. Finally, shortly after the *Wende*, a memorial was erected in honour of Stauffenberg outside the former seat of the GDR's Defence Ministry in Strausberg. The GDR's concept of anti-fascism had proven more flexible than at first seemed possible, but the emphasis on communism was maintained to the bitter end, and the yardstick for evaluation remained the degree to which resistance could be interpreted as linked to socialist ideals. In the case of Stauffenberg, much tweaking and twisting had been required to make him 'fit', and even then he fitted awkwardly. The one group never to find favour was the group around Carl Goerdeler, whose ideas remained too elitist for the GDR.

The picture of resistance in West Germany

If Stauffenberg and the July 1944 conspirators were long neglected in the GDR, they were not always celebrated in West Germany either. The view that Stauffenberg had committed high treason was prevalent in West Germany in the 1950s and even the 1960s. At election rallies of the extreme right-wing Socialist Reich Party (*Sozialistische Reichspartei*) in the early 1950s, Otto Ernst Remer, who had been actively involved in quashing the attempted coup in Berlin which followed the assassination attempt, accused the 20 July plotters both of treason and of being paid Soviet agents. He was taken to court by CDU Minister of the Interior Robert Lehr on the charge of insulting the memory of the dead. At the end of a famous 1952 court case in Brunswick, Remer was given a three-month prison sentence, not least as a result of the impassioned plea by state prosecutor Fritz Bauer. The judges moreover acknowledged that the 20 July conspirators cannot be branded traitors because they wanted to help Germany, not damage it. This view gradually established itself as it became clear from other trials connected with Nazi atrocities just how criminal Hitler's regime had been. When the West German army (*Bundeswehr*) was founded in 1955, one of the criteria for recruitment to the officers' caste was whether or not the applicant had a positive or at least understanding view of the July 1944 conspiracy. That *Bundeswehr* soldiers swore an oath to the constitutional principles of justice and freedom, and not, as in the Third Reich, to the ruling powers, was a nod towards the primacy of conscience, precisely that quality which had motivated Stauffenberg and others to act. The principle of 'inner leadership' (*Innere Führung*) espoused by the *Bundeswehr* reflected this primacy, as did the 1965 Decree on Tradition (*Traditionserlaß*), which stressed the notion of 'faithfulness to conscience'. When, in 1968, an article (Article 20,4) was introduced into the West German constitution anchoring the right to resistance, it seemed that Stauffenberg's right to act had been legally enshrined.

Yet this is only half the story. One must remember that the *Bundeswehr* was built up by former *Wehrmacht* soldiers whose real views on Stauffenberg were often different to those they might appear to hold. The Defence Ministry was often equally ambivalent. Thus while there were barracks named after military men connected to the conspiracy such as Ludwig Beck (the former SS *Ordensburg* Sonthofen became the Ludwig Beck Barracks in 1956) and Stauffenberg (in Sigmaringen in

1963), other barracks were named after the more 'loyal' variety of *Wehrmacht* general, and even after some involved in criminal acts against the civilian population during the war. It was not until 1995 that the Ministry of Defence changed the name of the notorious Eduard Dietl Barracks in Füssen into the more harmless-sounding Allgäu Barracks (Dietl was a rabid anti-semite and allegedly involved in violations of human rights in Finland during the war). Far-right elements and a degree of cultivation of *Wehrmacht* traditions have dogged the *Bundeswehr* right up to the present. CDU politician Volker Rühe, Minister of Defence in the Kohl government as of April 1992, tended to dismiss right-wing extremism in the army as the result of the social milieu from which the soldiers hailed – despite clear evidence that the climate in some *Bundeswehr* garrisons was conducive to extreme right-wing thinking.

In legal terms, too, ambivalence long remained the order of the day. While Remer's trial ended in an affirmation of the legitimacy of Stauffenberg's attempt on Hitler's life, the acquittal of SS judge Otto Thorbeck by the Federal Court of Appeal (BGH) in 1956 implied by contrast that Nazi judges had been justified in passing death sentences against members of the resistance (in Thorbeck's case against theologian Dietrich Bonhoeffer) where they believed the latter to be guilty of high treason. Until 1998, when the Bonn coalition of CDU/CSU and FDP finally made a move to establish a Germany-wide law declaring all unjust sentences passed by Nazi courts to be null and void, the precise legal status of these sentences was unclear and contentious. Regional variations were one reason for this. Thus while Bavaria had a ruling from 1946 declaring those sentences imposed for acts of resistance to be null and void, Berlin's 1951 'Law for Making Good National Socialist Injustice' ruled that the annulment of a sentence had to be explicitly applied for. Each case had to be settled in court. After 1990, it became clear that there were no regional rulings in the new *Länder*. But the problem was not merely a legal one. That it took the West German government till the 1980s to address this problem properly, and the united German government to solve it, implies a long-standing lack of political will. Or rather a surfeit of the wrong kind of political will: one which aimed to protect the Nazi judiciary, many of whose representatives had found a place in the West German legal system.

Politically, Adenauer walked something of a tightrope between defending the conduct of the Germans under Hitler, and seeking to build a new state on the democratic principles which most had either actively helped to throw overboard, or whose destruction they had accepted. This same ambivalence characterized the political reception of German resistance in the 1950s, not just in the CDU. A good example is provided by Federal President Theodor Heuss's famous speech of 1954 to mark the ten-year anniversary of Stauffenberg's assassination attempt. Heuß (FDP) set out to justify the fact that the 20 July conspirators had chosen to break their military vows of allegiance, a fact which still caused indignation among those Germans who had served loyally to the bitter end. He highlighted the 'fundamental ethics' behind the conduct of the conspirators (GDW 1984: 53). His whole speech, an exercise in democratic re-education, sought to convince the West Germans that the tradition of loyalty to authority is not binding when the latter departs from the road of human rights. But he was equally careful to present the average German soldier as a victim of Hitler, referring as he did to the 'terrible [. . .] spiritual situation of hundreds of thousands, millions of soldiers' (GDW 1984: 57). He stressed the bravery of the *Wehrmacht* soldiers and their 'constant inner conflict', while arguing that the real moral blame lay with the military leaders. Well into the 1960s and even later, political pronouncements on the 20 July conspirators sought to square the circle by praising their disobedience while upholding the right of the mass of *Wehrmacht* soldiers to practise unconditional obedience. Only when the 'Crimes of the *Wehrmacht*' exhibition exploded onto the scene in 1995 did the direct and indirect moral responsibility of the ordinary soldier for the atrocities of Hitler's war come into sharper relief (see Chapter Six). This in turn led to the realization that the ordinary soldier could also, to a degree, have been expected to disobey. That deserters sentenced by Nazi courts were not offered the prospect of rehabilitation until the late 1990s was symptomatic. Desertion is the ultimate form of the ordinary soldier's disobedience. To recognize it as an act of conscience is to admit that the ordinary soldier could, and perhaps should, have made his stand.

But in the 1950s acceptance of West German democracy depended on not alienating the war generation, and any criticism of the ordinary soldier certainly would have resulted in alienation. It was rather a question of encouraging a not too self-critical identification with Stauffenberg, and of persuading the Germans that they were partaking of his moral legacy – in that they were living and working in a free democratic state. That West Germans often came to imagine in some vague and illogical way that they had fought the war for 'Stauffenberg's West Germany' cannot be denied. A similarly bogus identification resulted from East Germany's obsessive presentation of the GDR as the legacy of communist resistance. From the mid-1950s, West German politicians sought to anchor 20 July 1944 in West German consciousness. On 20 July 1953, Berlin's mayor Ernst Reuter (SPD) unveiled the 'Honorary Memorial' to the 20 July conspirators in the Bendler Block, where Stauffenberg had had his office and where he was executed together with Werner von Haeften, Friedrich Olbricht and Albrecht Mertz von Quirnheim on the evening of 20 July 1944. From now on, 20 July was accompanied each year by wreath-laying and speech-making, either in the Bendler Block or at Plötzensee, where other 20 July conspirators had been executed. The two major parties, SPD and CDU, alternated from year to year in making the keynote speech. The tenor of the speeches was to celebrate Stauffenberg and those associated with planning the assassination attempt as harbingers of freedom, democracy and even the European idea. Where it was admitted that the 20 July conspirators had varied and often anti-parliamentarian notions of government, this was explained away as an inevitable by-product of the time. It was, moreover, as much from the deed as a 'rebellion of conscience' that a commitment to democracy was inferred.

Why was there no comparable degree of commemorative interest in West Germany in Georg Elser, the simple carpenter who tried to blow up Hitler in 1939? The Gestapo view that Elser was a paid British agent was for a long time accepted in West Germany. Even when it became clear that Elser had acted on his own, this did not make him any more 'useful'. Indeed it made him even less so. Elser was an outsider, and an individual. Stauffenberg was an insider, and the executor of a plan which had long occupied and brought together members of the military and civilians. The support for his plans could be seen as evidence of strong humanist traditions within state institutions such as the army, diplomatic service and administration. That the plan was not just to assassinate Hitler, but to seize the centres of power within the Reich, could be taken as proof of a widely networked, worked-out political will for change. This was the key value of the 20 July 1944 conspirators. They could be functionalized in West Germany's attempt to create a dichotomous view of the Third Reich: there the National Socialists and their organizations, here the morally conscious high-ranking army and bureaucracy. By suggesting that there had been this 'other Germany' distinct from Hitler, West Germany could claim that the traditional elites upon which it had to build after 1949 were not essentially corrupted by Nazism, indeed these professions embodied an *unbroken organic* German tradition of loyalty to a sense of justice and freedom, principles enshrined in West Germany's Basic Law. This was a very useful tool of self-legitimation in the struggle to be accepted as an equal among the Western states, and in the Cold War, where issues of legitimacy vis-à-vis the GDR played a vital role. Elser was 'another German', but not 'another Germany'. He remained entirely self-referential, useless in the symbolic system of post-war Germany.

At CDU party-political level, of course, the value of the above argumentation was that it made a clear distinction between humane conservatism and National Socialist despotism. Given the involvement of social democrats in the wider spectrum of the 20 July conspiracy, the SPD also benefited from the focus on Stauffenberg. Over the years, speeches made on 20 July did concede that there had been other resistance groups and individuals beyond the Stauffenberg group. West Germany was after all a pluralist state, and the SPD, FDP, CDU, Catholic and Protestant Churches, to name the most important parties and institutions, sought to promote memory of the resistance offered by those they had a wish to remember (overlooking often the degree of collaboration with Nazism). But just as all roads lead to Rome, so all officially commemorated roads of resistance were understood well into the 1980s as having led to Stauffenberg. He remained its ultimate expression. That it took him until July 1944 to attempt to kill Hitler was not highlighted. Indeed the lateness of the attempt made it possible to regard it as a kind of apogee. 'The resistance against the injustice of National Socialism found its visible expression on 20 July 1944', said SPD politician Gerhard Jahn in 1973 (GDW 1984: 127). The fact that politicians increasingly referred to other resistance groups, yet did so on 20 July, enhanced the impression that these groups were being subsumed under the also-rans, at best bunched together as the forerunners to Stauffenberg.

Particularly affected by neglect and denigration was the communist resistance. West Germany's pluralism had its boundaries, exemplified by the banning of the German Communist Party (KPD) in 1956. As late as the mid-1980s, the Berlin Senate rejected an initiative by a number of students who wanted to rename the main building of Berlin's Technical University after a communist resistance group around Herbert Baum. On 18 May 1942, this group had tried to set fire to a Nazi anti-Soviet propaganda exhibition called 'The Soviet Paradise' in Berlin. In 1954, Theodor Heuss compared Stauffenberg's attempt on Hitler's life to the 17 June 1953 uprising in the GDR (GDW 1984: 42). In so doing, he opened the door – consciously or not – for the delegitimation of the communist resistance to Hitler. As the Cold War escalated in the 1950s, totalitarianist theories were applied to the history of communist resistance, which, it was argued, was organized by people only interested in replacing one dictatorship with another. This being the case, the argument continued, communist resistance was not a legitimate form of resistance, but merely the tool of Stalinism.

In a curious parallelism with the GDR, West German politicians and historians long regarded the 'Red Orchestra' and the NKFD as agencies of the Soviet Union. But in the case of the FRG, this was a reason to condemn rather than praise them. Even a well-meaning person such as the author Carl Zuckmayer, who expressly praised 'convinced communists' in his 20 July speech of 1969, fell prey to a certain bias when he chose Harro Schulze-Boysen and Arvid Harnack as examples (GDW 1984: 110). Whatever Harnack's interest in the Soviet economy, or Schulze-Boysen's links to national bolshevism, their politics were too fluid to be categorically defined as communist. The most extreme expression of anti-communism in connection with the 20 July 1944 commemorations came in 1978, when Stauffenberg's son protested so vigorously against the choice of Herbert Wehner as speaker that Wehner withdrew; Wehner, an SPD politician, had formerly been a communist. He was replaced by Dietrich Stobbe (SPD). 'Wehner was a communist and has never denied this or even so much as played it down', Stobbe said in his speech. But he went on to state that, once Wehner had dissociated himself from communist ideas, he committed himself to democracy in West Germany (GDW 1984: 153). This rather suggested that Wehner had first to recover from a bad illness. It appears not to have occurred to Stobbe that communists might also entertain democratic ideas. If it was one-sided to present the GDR purely in terms of repression, it was even more unjust to assume from the negative aspects of GDR socialism that this was what communists in the resistance had wanted. The more the German communist resistance could be associated with Stalinism, of course, the more it could be presented as the lackey of the Soviet Union, dismissed as un-German (in contrast to Stauffenberg) and even – always unspoken – stigmatized as treachery. While West German politicians gradually freed Stauffenberg of the stigma of betrayal, they did much to attach this stigma to the communists.

Historical research, however, was more varied in West Germany than in East Germany, and tended to be several steps ahead of the political image of resistance. As of the 1960s and 1970s, there was increasing historiographical criticism of Stauffenberg and Carl Goerdeler for their collaboration with Nazism and their conservative views. The flourishing of regional history in the 1970s led to an interest in grass-roots resistance in the trade unions and among the workers. This inevitably led to research into communist workers' organizations. The historians' view of communist resistance, a view which outlined the evolution of differences between German and Soviet communism (not least as a result of the Hitler–Stalin pact), was more multi-faceted than that offered by the politicians. Theoretical principles for defining resistance which sought to transcend politically motivated criteria were developed among others by Peter Hüttenberger (see Steinbach 1994: 59). In the 1970s, a research group under Martin Broszat in Munich developed the notion of *Resistenz*, a concept of resistance based not just on active resistance but on the idea of maintaining alternative, non-Nazi cultures in the face of state ideology. This enormous breadth did filter through to the politicians, but it took Richard von Weizsäcker to start a process which, up to unification and beyond, was to influence decisively the portrait of resistance in the public and political realm.

The Memorial Site for German Resistance before 1990

Before 1980, the memorial site at the Bendler Block was dedicated to the 20 July conspirators. In 1955, Bendler Street was renamed Stauffenberg Street. In 1960, a plaque with the names of those shot in the Bendler Block was unveiled, and in 1968 a 'Memorial and Educational Site Stauffenberg Street', as it was then called, was opened. An exhibition documenting the course of the assassination attempt and occupying a modest three rooms was also opened in 1968. In 1979, the Berlin Senate agreed to release funds for changes to the memorial site, and the Federal Government, owner of the Bendler Block, made more rooms available between 1980 and 1983 for additions and changes. In 1983, Berlin's then mayor Richard von Weizsäcker entrusted Passau historian Peter Steinbach with the task of representing German resistance to Hitler in its 'whole breadth and diversity' (Steinbach 1994: 11–12). That Steinbach was the right candidate for the job was clear from his contribution to the international five-day conference on resistance in Berlin in 1984, where he stressed the need to free the picture of resistance from political instrumentalization in the present.

Over the course of the next six years, and reaching completion in 1989, a new exhibition was put together in the Bendler Block extending over twenty-six rooms and – faithful to Weizsäcker's brief – including all areas of resistance. Each area was presented in considerable detail. By July 1986, nine rooms had been completed, outlining the history of the Weimar Republic, the impact of National Socialism, resistance within the workers' movement and Christian circles before 1939, the opposition within military, diplomatic, liberal and conservative circles, and the whole history of the 20 July 1944 assassination attempt. By July 1987, four further areas had more or less been integrated: resistance in the arts and sciences, the 'White Rose' (a Munich resistance group largely comprising students), the 'Red Orchestra', and Exile and Resistance. In July 1989, the (for the time being) final section was opened, covering *inter alia* the history of the NKFD and the BDO. The exhibition is, however, so designed as to be extendable, and a section on resistance by the Sinti and Roma was added in 1998 (there is also a section on Jewish resistance). Now the activities of the 20 July 1944 conspirators are one resistance narrative among many. Their activities still stand at the centre of this multinarrative, but without the same sense of teleology. Down below in the courtyard, the memorial is still a memorial to the heroes of 20 July. But the spirit of breadth in the exhibition has reached out and touched this memorial too, so that, very gradually and not without ferocious controversy, the 20 July 1944 conspirators have ceased to be the group under which all others are subsumed, but have become symbolic of resistance as a whole in a much less assimilatory manner. In keeping with the new spirit, the memorial site was renamed 'The Memorial Site for German Resistance' in 1985.

The integrative concept pursued by Steinbach has led to the reinstatement of communist resistance, be this in the sections on resistance in the workers' movement before and after 1939, or in the sections on resistance in the arts and sciences, exile and POW camps. It has also led to the inclusion of a section on desertion and other forms of non-cooperative or subversive behaviour in the German army. The term 'integrative' is double-edged. It refers not just to the inclusion of all individuals, groups, organizations and institutions from which resistance emerged, but also to the inclusion of information or photographs which cast, where necessary, a critical light on these. CDU and Christian circles in the late 1980s reacted with some indignation to photographs in the exhibition showing Catholic dignitaries in Berlin-Neukölln, or Protestants such as Dresden's Bishop Friedrich Coch, raising their arms in the Hitler salute in 1933. Steinbach, however, was committed to showing the *whole* truth, which was, after all, a mixture of collaboration and resistance across many institutions. Thus the military is shown to have collaborated with Hitler in a war of annihilation before seeking to remove him. In the case of the communists and social democrats, the exhibition points out that some wanted to cooperate with Hitler, and that they certainly did not want to cooperate with one another, the KPD dismissing the SPD as 'social fascists', the SPD dismissing the KPD as undemocratic.

Also pointed up in the exhibition are the highly conservative views of some of those involved in the high-ranking military, diplomatic or civilian resistance. Ulrich von Hassell, one-time German ambassador in Rome, passed a memorandum to the British in February 1940 outlining the plans of the opposition group around Carl Goerdeler and Ludwig Beck, Chief of Staff of the Armed Forces between 1935 and 1938. These plans called for the end of the war, we are informed, but also for the return to Germany of territories lost after World War One. We are also told that Carl Goerdeler thought in terms of a strong post-war German state, constructed around self-administrative political units built on principles of class. Nor is there any pretence in the exhibition that many of those involved in the 20 July Circle conspiracy had not, for long, been very misguided. Henning von Tresckow's initial welcome of the National Socialist takeover in 1933 is mentioned. The integrative concept also works against a false homogenization, resisting blanket definitions and identifications. This is especially so when it comes to the portrayal of the 'Red Orchestra' and the NKFD. These groups are separated out into their various elements, making it clear that the post-war West German and East German view of them was undifferentiated. Thus while the role played by the NKFD and BDO in Soviet power politics and in the Soviet war effort is highlighted, it is also made clear that some German soldiers joined these organizations for their own anti-Hitler motives, and that these motives were what governed their activities in the NKFD, not pro-Soviet sympathies. Among the NKFD groups working at the front were a number which operated independently of central Moscow guidance, as Steinbach pointed out in defence of the exhibition (*FR*, 4 July 1994). The exhibition, which also focuses on the membership in the NKFD of 100 members of the clergy, gives the lie to the theory that the NKFD was composed simply of communists or communist sympathizers.

The integrative concept did not please everyone. One important pre-unification objection was voiced by Maria Hermes, daughter of Joseph Wirmer, who in the Third Reich had tried to establish contacts between oppositional trade unionists and the civilian resistance around Goerdeler. In the summer of 1987, Maria Hermes complained in a letter to West Berlin's School Senator Hanna Renate Laurien (CDU) and Steinbach about the absence of an exhibition section on 'men and women from Christian Democratic resistance circles'. Dissatisfied with the lack of response, she wrote to Kohl, asking him to intervene 'to bring about an appropriate honouring' of this group (*DAS*, 3 January 1988). Kohl then wrote to Laurien on 28 September 1987 and asked her to ensure that 'flaws in the exhibition' were removed (*Spiegel*, 7 December 1987) – by which he presumably meant not just the supposed lack of focus on Christian Democratic resistance, but also the alleged overemphasis on workers' and communist resistance, to which Maria Hermes had also objected. Laurien, however, vigorously defended the exhibition against the charges, and Kohl's intervention had little impact. Politicians of the Catholic Centre Party had opposed Hitler, and their contribution to resistance is documented in the exhibition. But there had been no Christian Democratic resistance in any party-political sense between 1933 and 1945; the CDU was a post-war creation, albeit one which Centre Party politician Andreas Hermes, Maria Hermes's father-in-law, helped to found. Hermes and Kohl wanted lines to be drawn from present to past, creating a desirable pre-history for the CDU.

The exhibition's inclusion of the NKFD and of Ulbricht and Pieck also gave rise to vehement objections, particularly from Count Franz Ludwig von Stauffenberg, Stauffenberg's son, and from Hartmut von Hösslin, brother of one of those executed in connection with the 20 July plot. Hösslin staged a spectacular protest at the official opening ceremony of the extended exhibition on 19 July 1989. He read out a letter accusing the NKFD of practising 'psychoterror' (*Welt*, 20 July 1989). Hermes perceived in the exhibition an SPD-driven, anti-CDU agenda. Hösslin saw in it an unacceptable concession to *Ostpolitik*. But Steinbach's aim was to free the picture of resistance from politicization. The inclusion of the NKFD was an admission that West Germany had long overlooked this organization because of its communist links. As the two German states grew closer together, from the 1970s onwards, there was less need to reject historical traditions embraced by the other state. Steinbach was granting the NKFD the status of resistance, but he was not – as Hösslin and Franz von Stauffenberg implied – thereby sacrificing truth for the sake of appeasement. The view of the NKFD in the exhibition does not mirror the GDR view. On the contrary, it demonstrates that the NKFD was far less homogeneous than the GDR liked to think.

20 July 1994

The situation after German unification was potentially both productive and coun-
terproductive for the Memorial Site for German Resistance. As of 3 October
1990, it became the central resistance exhibition and commemorative location for
the German nation, not just for a part of it. East Germans, as well as west
Germans, could now acquire a more rounded picture of resistance. They would
not feel marginalized, for the history of communist or communist-linked resistance
was judiciously covered. It seemed possible, too, that the collapse of East Germany
would put an end to calls for the removal of the sections on the NKFD and BDO.
But it was also possible that the demise of the GDR would have the opposite
effect. Given that *Ostpolitik* was now obsolete, so the conservative critics of the integrative concept could argue, then surely there was no need any more for
'concessions' to the GDR in the Memorial Site for German Resistance. The post-
unification situation was therefore finely balanced. On the one hand the political
unity of west and east Germany strengthened the case for a united picture, with
both resistance traditions, east and west, integrated in a value-free environment. In
this way, the very different sense of historical identity in the two Germanys could
be respected. On the other hand, with the demise of the GDR and the SED, it
could be argued that most East German traditions and emphases, including communist resistance, were things of the past. The justification for this argument was
that western liberal democracy had triumphed over repressive eastern socialism:
not only was this socialism irrevocably discredited, but so was the whole anti-fascist
legacy on which it was based.

In the course of 1994, in the lead-up to the 50th anniversary of 20 July 1944,
critics and supporters of the integrative concept became locked in an at times
embittered and entrenched debate. Clearly, the symbolic significance of this
anniversary was enormous, especially with Federal elections due to be held in the
same year on 16 October. The struggle for 'control' of the date was therefore pre-
programmed. The tactics of the conservatives were, in essence, simple. They
sought to devalue communist resistance. In this way, they tried to undermine the
integrative concept. The tactics of those who opposed these conservatives were
equally simple. They defended the communist resistance and the integrative concept against attack. In this way, 1994 itself became a 'year of resistance'. The
integrative concept, as a basis for documentation and commemoration, and as
manifested in the combination of these at the memorial site, won this battle,
though not without wounds. To a degree, it was the supporters of the integrative
concept within the CDU who made this victory possible.

In 1994, the conservative critics based their critique of communist resistance on
what might be termed moral, semantic, political and utilitarian criteria. Morally,
they argued that what mattered, primarily, was what you were fighting for, not who
you were fighting against. Communist resistance was discredited by pointing out
that some of those involved in it had gone on to become repressors in the GDR.
Semantically, the contention was that you could not properly stage resistance from
within a POW camp (NKFD and BDO) or from the general security of exile, but

only from a position of threat and potential persecution within the boundaries of the order you wished to resist. The extreme form of this contention was the claim that only those who had risked life or limb could be understood as having resisted. Politically, it was maintained that those who cooperated with the enemy in any act of resistance were in essence fighting their war. Finally, as a general didactic principle, it was asserted that today's united Germany was based on an anti-totalitarian consensus, not an anti-fascist one. The true resisters were those who had been against both National Socialism and communism. Accordingly, only those communists who opposed National Socialism and, subsequently, state socialism, such as the intellectual Robert Havemann, were acceptable as role-models. By applying these criteria, conservatives argued that communist resistance was compromised, ambivalent, insincere or irrelevant; some even believed that it could not be defined as resistance. Certainly it was clear for the conservatives that the communist resistance was a rotten apple, and that any inclusion of it among the 'good apples' such as the 20 July conspirators might lead to contamination.

The first focus of conservative attack, predictably, was the exhibition again. On 27 June 1994, Franz von Stauffenberg issued a press statement dismissing it as a 'conglomerate of Western historical traditions and Eastern historical propaganda ideology'. He went on to protest at the inclusion of photographs of Ulbricht and Pieck, leaders of German communism first in the Third Reich and then from exile. Ulbricht and Pieck, Stauffenberg argued, had made no sacrifice to 'freedom, justice and honour' (the motto on the bronze plaque near the exhibition). They had betrayed party comrades. In the GDR, they had killed thousands (presumably a much-inflated reference to those killed trying to flee), driven out hundreds of thousands, and repressed millions. Stauffenberg found it scandalous that Berlin's politicians could honour the victims of 17 June 1953, and yet tolerate the 'honouring' of the 'gaolers and murderers' at the exhibition. 'Pieck and Ulbricht will always remain two of the most despicable villains of German history' (for excerpts from the statement, see *FAZ* and *STZ*, 28 June 1994). For some weeks, Stauffenberg applied pressure in the hope that Steinbach might remove the photographs and the references to the NKFD. He was supported by CDU and CSU politicians. Thus CSU politician Michael Glos inveighed against any equation of those men and women he considered to be 'true' resistance fighters with 'communist repressors and murderers' (*BK*, 2 July 1994). But neither Peter Steinbach nor Berlin's Senator for Culture, Ulrich Roloff-Momin, showed any intention of altering the exhibition, either before 20 July 1994 or subsequently.

While conservatives could not achieve the desired removal from the exhibition, they could omit communists from commemorative speeches, and play down their right to commemoration. Most significant in this regard was Kohl's 20 July speech in the Bendler Block. He stressed that 20 July 1944 was the zenith and end-point of resistance, rather than just one, rather dramatic representation of it. He split up the resistance into social and professional groups. By means of this classification, he was able to talk of 'workers' rather than communists or even social democrats. Kohl distinguished, moreover, between resistance worthy of 'respect', and resistance deserving of classification as 'exemplary', the latter depending upon the 'political-moral goal' (*TSP*, 21 July 1994). In doing so, he was drawing questionable lines into the present again. He was identifying the current political order with the visions of the 20 July conspirators, and implying that communism past and present, because it was inherently undemocratic, was of no relevance to this current order. Commemoration was to be reserved for those considered to be of relevance as historical forebears to the present. In choosing one resistance tradition over another, however, Kohl appeared to contradict his express commitment to democracy by imposing a subjective evaluation.

Some CDU politicians explicitly argued that communist resistance should be regarded purely as a historical phenomenon. Opening an exhibition on military resistance in the Berlin Office of the Defence Ministry on 19 July 1994, Volker Rühe distinguished between 'historical representation' and 'moral valuation' (*TSP*, 20 July 1994). Eberhard Diepgen, in his 20 July speech in the Bendler Block, distinguished between 'honouring' resistance and subjecting it to 'complete historical treatment' (*FAZ*, 21 July 1994). He went on to suggest that the Memorial Site for German Resistance be reserved exclusively for commemoration; the exhibition could be moved elsewhere. From a conservative standpoint this separation would have had several advantages. Firstly, the communist resistance would no longer be able to bask in the glory 'borrowed' from the location, which was primarily associated with Stauffenberg. Secondly, the integrative thrust of the exhibition would no longer be able to influence commemoration in the Bendler Block. The Bendler Block would, as in the 1950s and 1960s, be given over once more to remembering Stauffenberg. The other resistance groups, particularly the communists, could be quietly forgotten. With the exhibition removed, visitors to the Bendler Block would no longer be invited to reflect on the fact that the 20 July conspiracy was not the only expression of military resistance. Nor would their attention be drawn to other uncomfortable facts, such as the greater radicalism of the NKFD and BDO. In the event, commemoration and documentation were not separated. Rumours that the Federal government would assume responsibility for the exhibition and then hand it over to the German Historical Museum were finally dispelled when the head of Berlin's Senate Chancellery, Volker Kähne, categorically dismissed the suggestion that such a division was in any way planned (*taz*, 27 July 1994).

Other developments in 1994 revealed the political interest of traditional elites and the CDU/CSU. In 1992, Rühe announced his decision to set up the Berlin Office of the Defence Ministry in part of the Bendler Block. This was clearly an attempt to legitimize present defence and military policy by associating it with the ideals of the 20 July conspirators. It was also a symbolical statement to the effect that the *Bundeswehr* stood squarely in the tradition of those in the *Wehrmacht* who had been critical of Hitler. In 1994, Rühe tried to instrumentalize the resistance commemorations. For the first time ever, the German army, in the form of a guard battalion, took part in the 20 July ceremony in the Bendler Block. This had not been possible before 1990 because of the terms of the Berlin status. The planned presence of the *Bundeswehr* gave rise to much criticism both from members of the families associated with the July 1944 plot, and from Ralph Giordano. In an open letter to Army Inspector General Klaus Naumann, Giordano protested at what he termed the 'tradition lie' (*Traditionslüge*): the *Bundeswehr*, in other words, liked to present itself as heir to the July 1944 resistance tradition, yet still named some barracks after *Wehrmacht* generals associated with Nazism or Nazi atrocities (*taz*, 14 July 1994). There can be little doubt that Rühe was seeking to divert attention from right-wing radicalism and continuing adulation of the *Wehrmacht* within the *Bundeswehr*. This was all the more necessary at a time when the CDU was planning to deploy the *Bundeswehr* in out-of-area NATO operations for the first time in its history. The CDU gained legal support for its plans from the Federal Constitutional Court, which in a ruling of 12 July 1994 confirmed that the army could be used in both peace-keeping and peace-creating activities given parliamentary approval in each case. But the equally important *moral* legitimation was to be provided by the participation in the 20 July 1994 celebrations. The decision in 1999 to have a group of recruits swear an oath in the Bendler Block on 20 July, a ceremony disturbed by some colourful nude protesters bearing slogans such as 'Soldiers are murderers' (a quotation from the writer Kurt Tucholsky), was also a suggestive gesture. For can new recruits really be sure they are joining an army moulded entirely in the 'positive' image of resistance within the *Wehrmacht*?

Party politics played a part in the 20 July 1994 commemorations in other ways. According to the 'rotation' principle, it was the CDU's turn to hold the keynote address. The conservative 20 July Foundation extended an invitation to Helmut Kohl. Rumours circulated in the press that the SPD's candidate for Federal Chancellor, Rudolf Scharping, had asked to be included among the speakers and been rudely rebuffed by the CDU. The CDU denied vigorously that there had been such a request, and the SPD itself eventually admitted the falsity of the rumour. Nevertheless, the CDU was clearly not keen to share the central speech-making on such a significant occasion with the SPD. Nor did the CDU show any interest in passing over responsibility for the speech to the Federal President, a figure who traditionally transcends party politics. It can be said in defence of the CDU, however, that when plans were being drawn up for the 20 July commemoration, the office of Federal President was in the course of changing hands, and it was unclear whether the new incumbent would have time to write a speech. In the event, the new Federal President, Roman Herzog (CSU), did hold a reception on the evening of 20 July in Castle Bellevue. Party politics were certainly visible in Chancellor Kohl's speech. He stressed the anti-totalitarian consensus, indirectly devaluing communist resistance (*TSP*, 21 July 1994). He went on to imply that this consensus should extend to opposing the PDS. In warning against a possibly 'fateful development' whereby social and political elites 'stretch out their hands to extremists', Kohl made barely disguised reference to the political situation in Saxony-Anhalt. Here, a minority SPD government was dependent on the support of the PDS.

The role played by the resistance issue in German international diplomacy was also influenced by party politics. Indignant at being excluded from the 6 June D-Day celebrations, the CDU persuaded the Foreign Office to pressurize branches of the Goethe Institute throughout the world into organizing conspicuous events on 20 July. Of course the Foreign Office insisted that it was not exerting pressure, but only making a recommendation. The Goethe Institute's reaction was to point to its independence. Indignant too at the refusal of the Washington Holocaust Museum to add an annexe covering the history of the Federal Republic, the CDU pushed for an exhibition on German resistance to be shown in Washington. Eventually a venue was agreed on in the Library of Congress. Entitled 'Against Hitler: German Resistance to National Socialism 1933–1945', the exhibition was initiated among others by *Bundeswehr* Inspector General Klaus Naumann. The *Bundeswehr*-affiliated Office for Research into Military History played a role in its conception. It came in for heavy criticism in America because the emphasis was on military resistance, there was no mention of Pieck, Ulbricht or Honecker, and the exhibition appeared to criticize the British and Americans for failing to support German resistance (see *Washington Post*, 24 July 1994).

If all of this sounds as if the conservative west German political establishment uniformly pursued a policy of 'commemoration apartheid', this was not so. Renate Laurien (CDU), at the time President of Berlin's House of Representatives, explicitly resisted the 'privatization of a particular resistance' and stated that any *post hoc* evaluation of resistance 'does not do justice to the complexity of the historical and personal situation' of those involved (*TSP*, 18 July 1994). Roman Herzog (CSU) may have been speaking with his Federal President hat on when claiming in his Bellevue speech that 'no-one is going to lose any jewels from his crown by admitting that there were communists in the resistance', but the explicit reference to communism was striking all the same (*ARD* [*Tagesthemen*], 20 July 1994). Rita Süssmuth (CDU) asserted in a televised interview: 'Resistance doesn't become non-resistance simply because it was staged by communists' (*WDR* [*Morgenmagazin*], 20 July 1994). Even Kohl may not have been in favour of a total exclusion of communists from official memory. While he did not mention communists in his 20 July speech, he did at least commemorate a former member of the Red Front Fighters' League (*Rotfrontkämpferbund*), Georg Elser. It was therefore not always lip-service when CDU parliamentarians occasionally underlined the importance of commemorating all resistance. In 1996, CDU Minister President of Thuringia Bernhard Vogel expressly referred to communist resistance in the central, official Bendler Block speech – a significant development for the CDU (*DP*, 2 August 1996).

Nor did the families of those involved in the 20 July plot necessarily support exclusion, in respect of either the exhibition or the 20 July commemoration. According to Franz von Hammerstein, whose brothers were involved in the plot, Stauffenberg's father would never have accepted 'the kind of exclusion his son now proposes' (*taz*, 19 July 1994). Freya von Moltke insisted that the communists had paid the highest price of all in the resistance. She rejected the desire to omit them as 'outrageous', and likewise asserted that Franz von Stauffenberg's views did not correspond to those of his father (*BM*, 15 July 1994). In mid-July 1994, a group of concentration camp survivors and individuals with links to the Kreisau Circle, the 'Red Orchestra' and the 'White Rose' published an open letter protesting against attempts to exclude 'particular groups of German resistance' from the exhibition (*taz*, 14 July 1994). The Kreisau Initiative was also behind a declaration in support of inclusion signed among others by leading members of the SPD, B'90/Greens, FDP and even the CDU (*SPA*, 18 July 1994).

In a whole cluster of press statements, interviews, regional commemorative celebrations and speeches, the SPD also resisted any form of exclusion. In an interview, then Deputy SPD Party Leader Wolfgang Thierse criticized attempts by a 'conservative offensive' to create a harmonized picture of history, and insisted on the need for a 'rich, contradictory, multifaceted picture of resistance' (*BZ*, 18 July 1994). Hans Eichel, at the time SPD Minister President of Hesse, declared in a regional commemorative speech in Wiesbaden that the communists have a right 'to be recognized as equally valued resistance fighters against National Socialism' (*FAZ*, 20 July 1994). Annemarie Renger, SPD politician and chairwoman of the 'Central League of Democratic Resistance Organizations', referred to the communists in her speeches at Plötzensee (20 July) and in Berlin's Town Hall (19 July). In the latter speech, she explicitly extended the conceptual symbolism of 20 July to cover communists. Renger's inclusive speeches provided an important counterweight to Kohl's mainly exclusive approach on 20 July.

To these voices were added those of the clergy. Former GDR Bishop Albrecht Schönherr argued in a speech in Brandenburg against any exclusion of communism and social democracy from the picture of resistance (*TSP*, 18 July 1994). As for the historians, they were, like the politicians, divided, though these divisions by no means ran along the fault-line of west German versus east German, any more than the divisions between (or, in the case of the CDU, within) the political parties did. Some historians imagined dark conspiracies to be invading the public realm. Joachim Fest, a conservative historian and author of a book on 20 July which appeared in 1994, dismissed communist resistance as 'totalitarian', and warned against falling under the sway of the 'legend of anti-fascism' (*MM*, 12 July 1994). Conservative historians Klaus Hildebrand, Horst Möller and Lothar Gall shared Fest's view. Left-liberal historian Hans Mommsen, by contrast, objected to what he saw as the reduction of resistance to the biographical and moralistic, and to an apologetic view which had emerged in the wake of the renascence of totalitarian theory. Mommsen defended communist resistance, and expressed the fear that denying its legitimacy would serve to 'push aside the self-understanding of the former GDR inhabitants', based as it was on anti-fascism (*FR*, 14 July 1994). Left-wing historian Wolfgang Wippermann shared Mommsen's anxiety (*ND*, 2 June 1994).

Overall, the defence of communist resistance in the press outweighed the condemnation of it – much to the chagrin of conservative cultural thinker Frank Schirrmacher, whose pessimistic article 'Newest Germany: The Left triumphs in the Cultural Struggle' appeared in the *Frankfurter Allgemeine Zeitung* on 22 July 1994. The indefatigable Mommsen, who published an enormous number of articles on the theme of resistance in German newspapers in 1994, was also the driving force behind a more critical picture of the 20 July plotters in the media, a picture soon reproduced by journalists and editors. The central media projection of this critical picture was a direct response to conservative memory politics. After all, as SPD parliamentarians Walter Kolbow and Andreas von Bülow put it, if you focus on the motives of the communist resistance, then you also have to subject the military resistance to the same scrutiny (*PM*, 18 July 1994). So it was that the military and related civilian resistance around Stauffenberg came to be measured by the same criteria – political, semantic, moral and didactic – by which the communist resistance was being judged. The result was interesting: the 20 July conspirators performed as questionably as the communists on all counts. Historians had known this for some years; but never before had the press been so receptive to airing their views.

Politically, it was pointed out that the military officers, as political scientist Antonia Grunenberg put it, had 'no democratic background and no democratic goals' (*STZ*, 20 July 1994). Historian Nicolai Hammersen pointed to the scepticism of some in the national-conservative resistance towards parliamentarism, democracy and individualism (*JF*, 15 July 1994). The most extreme form of this criticism was expressed by the 'Anti-national Action League', a group of students who occupied the Memorial Site for German Resistance on 19 July 1994 in protest at the planned 20 July commemoration. In a statement, they argued that the 20 July conspirators had shared Hitler's national and expansionist goals, and that commemorating them today was part of a process of 're-nationalsocializing' German society (*taz*, 19 July 1994). That the views of the 20 July conspirators were not without elements of racist anti-bolshevism or anti-semitism constituted the biggest question-mark as to their moral credibility. As historian Christof Dipper pointed out, while Goerdeler reacting indignantly to Hitler's genocidal methods of solving the 'Jewish problem', he nevertheless still thought there was such a problem, and suggested the resettlement of undesirable Jews in Canada and South America (*Zeit*, 1 July 1994). Semantically, it was argued that the 20 July military conspirators had long been the servants of a dictatorship before they rebelled against it. While the NKFD might have collaborated with the Stalinist Soviets, the officers involved in the 20 July plot worked against Hitler from within the collaborative *Wehrmacht*. Both groups were compromised. As a corollary of these criticisms, the 'exemplary' value of the 20 July 1944 conspirators was questioned. Jens Gundlach stated unequivocally that 'the men of 20 July cannot be models for resistance in a democratic state' (*HAZ*, 20 July 1994).

The party-political wrangling and the more general to-ing and fro-ing of the resistance debate in 1994 had one quite positive effect: it wore away entrenched positions, especially in the CDU. The fact that the left could invalidate the distinctions made by the right by applying the same principles of evaluation revealed the pointlessness of these principles. Gradually, a tentative sense of consensus evolved that it was what the 20 July conspirators and the communists had in common that really mattered, namely their opposition to Hitler, not what separated them. 'Resistance is indivisible', claimed Wolfgang Scheffler of the Centre for Research into Anti-semitism in Berlin (*ND*, 2 June 1994). The sense of the need to acknowledge the primacy of uniting elements was enhanced by the growing awareness that united Germany was heir to two different resistance traditions which, somehow, ultimately, had to be welded. Such consensus is vital, because only it can shift the focus of commemoration from legitimization of a state or a party to the evocation of a united stand against threats to democracy. The success of the Memorial Site for German Resistance in resisting calls for the removal of communist resistance will help with the evolution of this consensus. In 1997, Steinbach again stood firm when Jochen Staadt and Klaus Schroeder of the 'Research Union SED State' (*Forschungsverbund SED-Staat*) dismissed the picture of communist resistance in the exhibition as an undesirable tribute to the SED. When Steinbach's team made some readjustments to the photographic representation of Ulbricht and Pieck in the exhibition in 1998, placing them in group photographs, the *Forschungsverbund* thought it had triumphed. They missed the point that these new photographs stress the integration of Pieck and Ulbricht into a movement, making condemnation of them as individuals harder to justify. They also failed to notice that the presentation of the communist and social democratic contribution to resistance in the exhibition was gradually extended over the 1997 and 1998 period.

Communism, anti-fascism and street names

Before 1990, Steinbach pioneered the integrative approach; after 1990, he committed himself to defending and extending it. But while the Memorial Site for German Resistance had to be protected against reduction, the situation in the former eastern Germany was quite different. Here, by contrast, a degree of reduction was essential, given that the GDR had overemphasized communist resistance. On 17 March 1994, a Commission set up to review street names in the centre of Berlin maintained in its concluding report that the new 'historical centre of the Federal Republic [. . .] must bear the stamp of the spirit of pluralism' (SfVuB 1994: 5). The GDR was, indeed, hardly a pluralistic state. Statues of and monuments to Marx, Lenin and Engels abounded, and in some towns and cities it seemed as if every second street had been named after communists, particularly those involved in resistance. GDR worthies such as former President Wilhelm Pieck (co-founder of the NKWD) and GDR Minister President Otto Grotewohl (persecuted and imprisoned by the Gestapo) were honoured in street names across the GDR. Over the ten years since 1990, statues of Lenin and Marx and other communist figures have been torn down, leaving bare plinths – such as that in Leipzig's Mariannepark on which a bust of Ernst Thälmann used to stand. Many of the communist street names in eastern Germany have been dropped. For the second time this century, there has been something of a transformation of street names. The first one occurred after 1945, when streets named after Nazis were largely purged. In contrast to the post-1945 changes, however, the post-1990 transformation has been less radical; its extent has been exaggerated by its opponents.

In a number of cases, communist street names have been replaced with the names that the streets had before the communist takeover of eastern Germany after the war. Thus in Berlin's Prenzlauer Berg, the Lenin Avenue was restored to Landsberger Avenue in 1992, while the Wilhelm Pieck Street was changed back to Tor Street (literally 'Gate Street'), a name it had borne from 1800 until 1951 (Gärtner *et al.* 1995: 289). In some instances, a return to previous names has meant a reintroduction of names taken from Prussian history, a history spurned in the

GDR (at least initially). In 1993, the Otto Grotewohl Street in central Berlin was given its old name back – Wilhelm Street, named after Frederick William the First of Prussia (1713–1740). Claims that eastern Germany's street-name landscape is in danger of being 're-Prussianized' are, however, overstated. There has, rather, been a modest return to Prussian and particularly Wilhelminian names, restoring a historical dimension absent from GDR street names. In other cases, communist names have been replaced with the names of non-communist political figures from the Weimar Republic, of members of the West German civil, clerical and military resistance canon, or SPD, CDU and FDP politicians from the history of the Federal Republic – or they have simply been replaced with the names of flowers and bushes, admittedly a rather questionable 'greening over' of history.

For the critics, such changes constitute what one book-title calls the 'west German Final Solution for anti-fascism in the former GDR' (Zorn 1994). But comparing these changes to the holocaust is even more questionable than comparing the GDR to the Third Reich. The necessary reduction in communist street names has enriched eastern Germany's street landscape, not impoverished it. Why, for instance, should the east Germans not be introduced to historical figures – including those from the history of West Germany (such as Willy Brandt) – of whom they were deprived under communism? Moreover, the frequent implication of critics that the west Germans are largely responsible for street-name changes in the eastern *Länder* is inaccurate. In accordance with Article 28 of the Basic Law, which guarantees the right to communal self-administration, it falls to local authorities (*Bezirke*) to make street-name changes. In the major east German cities, 'immigrant' west German politicians will have been involved in changes, but not in most smaller towns and villages. If some towns were over-zealous in eradicating anti-fascist street names, then this has much to do with an east German wish to make a clean break with the past – rightly or wrongly – or with an over-adaptive sense of political correctness.

It is true that the historic centre of Berlin (*Berlin Mitte*) is something of an exception in that Berlin's Senate Department for Transport was given a say in the renaming of the streets in central Berlin, and that it then set up an advisory commission consisting of, among others, west German historians (such as Arnulf Baring and Heinrich August Winkler). The commission's final report is not free of anti-communism, and the Senate Department did follow one or two of its recommendations (see SfVuB 1994). Thus Marx-Engels Square was renamed Castle Square in 1994. This was the name it had borne until 1951, when the bombed-out remains of Berlin's ugly Castle (*Schloß*) were removed in an anti-imperial gesture by the GDR. However, in a significant number of cases the recommendations of the commission have not been implemented. The commission suggested renaming the Niederkirchner Street, location of Berlin's House of Representatives, *Am Preußischen Landtag* ('At the Prussian Parliament'): this would have cut more patriotic dash than the name of KPD anti-Nazi activist Käthe Niederkirchner. But the suggestion did not meet with Senate approval; the House of Representatives is still located in a street dedicated to a member of the communist resistance.

While there has been a reduction in communist names, it would, then, be wrong to say they have been systematically expunged. Any visitor to the new *Länder* will still encounter numerous Karl Marx and Ernst Thälmann Streets. Erfurt, in fact, has two Ernst Thälmann and two Thälmann Streets. In Schwerin, streets named in the GDR after Karl Marx, Friedrich Engels, Karl Liebknecht (a communist leader killed in 1919), Johannes Becher and Erich Weinert (involved in the founding of the NKFD) were kept; in irritation at the fact that he still had to go to work in the Karl Marx Street, the Minister of the Interior in Mecklenburg Western Pomerania had the entrance to the Ministry shifted to the Wismar Street. That the names of figures from the communist anti-Nazi resistance often found it hard to hold their own against Stauffenberg, Bonhoeffer and Moltke, whose names have appeared on east German street names in many areas, does not mean they were all removed. Erfurt now has both Stauffenberg and Thälmann in its street hall of fame. This, surely, is in the interests of balance.

Nevertheless, there has been a particularly rabid onslaught on some GDR notables, particularly Pieck, whose name is now very hard to find. This can be put down to dubious divisions into 'good' communist resistance figures who saw the light and became opponents of state socialism, and 'bad' ones who held political office in the GDR and served the system until they retired or died, or until it collapsed. Thus while it is good that Erfurt now has a Stauffenberg Avenue, the fact that this has replaced the Wilhelm Pieck Avenue represents an application of the totalitarian theorem: Stauffenberg has been given the posthumous task of doing (albeit symbolically) to Pieck what he did not quite manage to do to Hitler. In an absurd debate over the renaming of a school in Berlin-Lichtenberg, those who wanted to name it after the communist resistance fighter Hans Coppi found themselves up against those who wanted to rename it after Robert Havemann, communist victim of the National Socialists who later became a critic of GDR socialism. Hans Coppi, so it was argued by some, was not as good a choice because he had not seen the error of his ways, unlike Havemann. Unfortunately, Coppi did not have much chance to do so: he was executed at Plötzensee in 1943. To argue that the only good communist is the one who deserted his former cause is to devalue communist resistance to Hitler. While the communists may not have recognized the faults of communism, they recognized those of Nazism much sooner than most involved in the 20 July plot.

A complaint often voiced is that the changes in the eastern street-name landscape have not been accompanied by appropriate adjustments in the western *Länder*. Thus it is argued, with some justification, that there are not enough streets dedicated to communists in the west. It is worth, however, highlighting a significant exception. The Memorial Site at Plötzensee in west Berlin, dedicated to the memory of the victims of judicial murder during the Third Reich, is situated on a small side-street named after Richard Hüttig, a communist who was beheaded by the Nazis on 14 June 1934 [Plate 3.1]. One would have expected it to be named after one of the 20 July conspirators executed at Plötzensee. Plötzensee's small exhibition, moreover, gives prominence to individual acts of resistance, including communist ones. For years West German commemorations of resistance, including commemorations on 20 July, often took place here as well as or instead of in the

Plate 3.1 The Plötzensee Memorial Site to the 'Victims of the Hitler Dictatorship between 1933 and 1945'.

Bendler Block. Thus in a sense Plötzensee symbolized an inclusive commemoration long absent from the Bendler Block commemoration.

It has also been argued that western Germany has not done enough to change the names of barracks and streets associated with Nazism or those who promoted its cause. This is in part true. The hypocrisy of Rühe's claims in 1993 and 1994 that today's *Bundeswehr* is moulded entirely in the tradition of 20 July 1944 was clear from the number of barracks still named after *Wehrmacht* generals at the time. But there have been some very positive developments since then. In May 2000, the *Bundeswehr* barracks in Rendsburg, named after *Wehrmacht* general Günther Rüdel in 1964, were renamed Sergeant Schmid Barracks. Rüdel, a judge, was an honorary member of the dreaded People's Court (*Volksgerichtshof*); Schmid, by contrast, was a *Wehrmacht* soldier who helped 250 Jewish inhabitants of the Wilna ghetto and was executed in April 1942. While Bavaria still has too many street names dedicated to figures associated with Nazism, here too there have been recent changes. For many years, both Regensburg and Rosenheim had a street named after Florian Seidl, a Nazi poet and author of an 'Ode to the Führer'. In 1993, the director of a home for the handicapped located on Florian Seidl Street in Regensburg drew attention to Seidl's racist ideas, which included support for euthanasia! The CSU majority in the town's parliament stubbornly resisted the SPD initiative for a change of name, arguing that, if the Seidl Street were to be renamed, then so should streets named after Brecht and Tucholsky, who had allegedly subscribed to a 'totalitarian ideology' (*SZ*, 21 October 1999). The CSU majority in Rosenheim blocked a parallel SPD action in 1997. But common sense has at last prevailed. When Regensburg decided in late 1999 to rename the street, Rosenheim, in February 2000, declared its intention to follow suit (*SZ*, 19–20 February 2000).

The most scandalous case in Catholic Bavaria is the town of Dachau, which is still refusing to rename the Colonel Hofmann Street – Hofmann was a cofounder of Dachau's local Nazi Party (*SZ*, 5 February 1999). Even worse, perhaps, is that no attempt has yet been made to reverse Dachau's policy of allocating names which seek to relativize German guilt. While some street names around the former concentration camp are dedicated to its victims (though not communists), many others such as Danziger Street, Silesia Street and the larger Sudetenland Street are dedicated to the lost German homelands and territories in the east [Plate 3.2]. Dachau was used as an expellee resettlement base after 1945 (see Chapter One). But the presence of such street names today implies the wish to play down the enormity of the crimes of Nazism, and to cast doubt on their singularity, by pointing the finger

Plate 3.2 The Silesia Street signpost near Dachau Memorial Site.

at the Czechs and Poles. It is hard not to associate the street-sign Annaberg Ring with the German *Freikorps* victory against the Poles in 1921. It is equally hard in the case of Gleiwitz Street not to be reminded of the National Socialist propaganda claim that the Poles started the war by attacking a German radio station. A number of streets near the concentration camp memorial site, moreover, are named after figures in the Germanic Nibelung saga. Such street names are an attempt at historical revisionism, and surely an insult to the camp victims.

Buchenwald: demontage or restoring the balance?

There was also a considerable need for a scaling down of the emphasis on communist resistance so typical of GDR concentration camp memorial sites. This was achieved, firstly, by a process of balancing out; members of the Christian and conservative resistance, neglected in GDR commemoration, were brought into the picture. In 1994, a group of youngsters took part in an archaeological dig to uncover the remains of Dietrich Bonhoeffer's cell in Buchenwald. Bonhoeffer, a theologian who opposed Hitler as early as 1933, was imprisoned here along with others implicated in the 20 July 1944 assassination plot. At Buchenwald Memorial Site, plans are under way to set up a 'Site of Remembrance to members of the 20 July Resistance Group'. On 9 April 1995, an exhibition on Hans von Dohnanyi, a member of the dissident military intelligence group around Hans Oster, opened at Sachsenhausen Memorial Site: Dohnanyi was executed here in early April 1945. The overemphasis on communist resistance has also been corrected by means of (usually judicious) excision. Thus Buchenwald Memorial Site has dispensed with the GDR's Ernst Thälmann memorial rooms. Thälmann was murdered in Buchenwald, a fact still documented in the exhibition. But he was not imprisoned there. The focus on his fate at the GDR Buchenwald Memorial Site was disproportionate.

Balance and reduction have been accompanied by a sorely necessary critical deconstruction of camp communism, particularly at Buchenwald Memorial Site (see Chapter One). The requirements here were different to those at the West German Memorial Site for German Resistance, where Steinbach had to *construct* a balanced view of communist resistance, given its previous absence or delegitimization in the West – the negative western correlative to East Germany's tendency to glorify it. To undermine the assumption of flawless moral ardour and selflessness upon which the GDR narrative of communist camp resistance was based, post-unification Buchenwald Memorial Site draws attention to the more dubious aspects of its role, particularly criticizing the German communists. Whereas the GDR interpreted the communist takeover of camp functionary positions as a stage in the victory of anti-fascism, the new Buchenwald exhibition and its accompanying catalogue suggest that this takeover implicated the communists in the racist camp hierarchy imposed by the SS (GB 1997: 148). We are informed that, for SS Camp Commandant Pister, the administrative and organizational efficiency of the communists was an essential factor in the successful running of the camp (GB 1997: 147–8). Information is also provided on the fact that the communists denounced, discriminated against and even arranged for the murder of those who opposed them, measures also used against communists who deviated from the party line (GB 1997: 103, 132, 146 and 213).

In setting about this critique, however, Buchenwald's new team – a mixture of east and west Germans – has swung the pendulum too much the other way by projecting too negative a picture of communist resistance. Buchenwald's communists may have spent some of their time collaborating and denouncing, but certainly not all of it. Without the communists, there would not have been the solidarity that saved the lives of German writer Ernst Wiechert and Spanish writer Jorge Semprun. The ability of the communists to organize not only benefited Pister. It enabled the *kapo* system to be taken out of the hands of the hated 'Greens' (criminal prisoners), and was a prerequisite for the orchestration of an extremely effective resistance. Without the vision and determination of the communists, there would have been little hope. In the new exhibition, these facts are not exactly overlooked, but they are trivialized. The few positive comments relating to communists are generally outweighed by negative remarks (GB 1997: 67, 132, 147–8). The west German totalitarianist theorem underlies implicit equations of National Socialist and communist interests. The exhibition makes scant reference to the basic conundrum that only a degree of cooperation with the SS created scope for resistance and protection, and that, on occasion, only murderous practice prevented the collapse of the structures which assured this scope. As a result, the exhibition appears to deny the fundamental opposition of the communists to National Socialism, and their right to a status as victims.

The over-negative portrayal of communism is achieved by means of imbalance. Thus we are informed that the communists bribed camp doctor Waldemar Hoven into killing Russian officer Grigori Kushni-Kushnarev 'who *ostensibly* spied for the Gestapo among Soviet POWs' (GB 1997: 103, my emphasis). Yet there is strong evidence that Kushni-Kushnarev was indeed a particularly dangerous spy whose denunciations led to the murder by the SS of Russian prisoners-of-war (e.g. Hackett 1995: 82–3, 238 and 269). We are told that a political prisoner denounced senior camp inmate Josef Ohles as a homosexual to the SS (GB 1997: 146); yet he may have been brought down when he fell out with Deputy Commandant Florstedt over a signature (Hackett 1995: 257). We are also told that senior camp inmate Fritz Wolff was denounced because of his homosexuality (GB 1997: 146). But no mention is made of the fact that he may have been an SS informer, that he abused the trust placed in him by camp anti-fascists, and that he collaborated with Polish fascists (Hackett 1995: 268). In a questionable omission, the exhibition fails to mention that Fritz Wolff was both unscrupulous and half-Jewish; it focuses instead on his (by implication positive) hostility to communism. Nor is the issue adequately addressed that there were Jews among the communists. No mention is made of the fact that there were also Jewish functionaries in Jewish blocks, that these functionaries could be corrupt (an example is Walter Rosenbaum, a 'Green' prisoner) and that, in the Jewish blocks, there were also power struggles between political prisoners and 'criminal' prisoners.

On balance, the GDR view of camp life has been effectively, but not always equitably deconstructed in post-1990 Buchenwald. Overemphasis in the GDR exhibition on camp communism has been ill-advisedly replaced by underemphasis in the new exhibition, with respect to both the Oath of Buchenwald, which is inadequately documented, and the role of the prisoners in liberating Buchenwald – although the concept of 'liberation from inside and outside' in the new exhibition is certainly nearer the truth than the notion of 'self-liberation'. In a sense, the problem is one of throwing out the baby with the bathwater. Deconstructing the GDR's view of camp communism has to mean removing its one-sidedness and its propagandistic aspects. But it should stop short of denigrating camp communism in line with outworn traditions of western anti-communism (for more discussion on the post-unification view of Buchenwald's communists, see Niven 2000: 164–9).

Oskar Schindler and Georg Elser

In the post-unification period, other resistance-related issues were brought into focus by the showing of Steven Spielberg's *Schindler's List* in the German cinemas as of March 1994. The film was an extraordinary success. By the fifteenth week of showing, it had been seen by some 5.7 million Germans. It took an American to broach the topic of an individual German industrialist's protection of Jews. There had been Germans, notably Artur Brauner and Hark Bohm, who had wanted to film the Schindler material. But plans had foundered on the uncooperative response of the Berlin Film Promotion Institute. West Germany had not incorporated Schindler, an industrialist who saved the lives of Jews who worked in his factory, into official resistance commemoration. Indeed he was a rather forgotten figure, in his home town of Frankfurt on Main, and in West Germany as a whole. Like Elser, he was an eccentric. Neglect of Schindler perhaps also had to do with the fact that, while West Germany felt it necessary to point to evidence of resistance in the army and civil administration between 1933 and 1945, it did not feel it necessary to do so in the case of industry. Industry, it seemed, was above suspicion. For decades, German industry in West Germany managed to clothe itself in a mantle of non-involvement in Nazism. Commemorating Schindler might even have proven counter-productive. Schindler was a Nazi Party member, a manufacturer of pots, pans and ammunition for the *Wehrmacht* and an 'employer' of forced labour; any focus on his act of resistance would therefore also have revealed the fact of his collaboration, however this was then evaluated. In East Germany, the facts of industrial collaboration, as well as of the use of forced and slave labour, were accepted truths. But they were also exploited for purposes of propagandistic anti-capitalism. Schindler was neglected in East Germany because he was proof that not all capitalists were heartless, and that collaboration could be a means of camouflaging resistance. Spielberg's film was so important because, in its ambivalence, it served to undermine traditions of either whitewashing or demonizing German industry.

There were attempts by some German politicians and critics to deny this inherent ambivalence. Thus it was argued that Schindler is the 'good German', while Amon Goeth is the 'bad German'. But the film does not support these absolute moral characterizations. In seeking to engage Jewish labour, Schindler would appear to have been profit-motivated, at least initially, and even his gradual evolution into something of a saint in the eyes of those he comes to protect seems to inspire in him embarrassment, not satisfaction. He remains ambivalent over long stretches of the film, in motive and moral standing. As for Goeth, he may be evil, but Spielberg takes time to explore his complex, muddled psyche, and thereby presents him as human. Overall, Spielberg's differentiated presentation of Schindler, and the questions this raised, were sensitively registered in the German press. As critic Raimund Neuß pointed out, the fact that Schindler was a Nazi fellow-traveller and profiteer as well as someone who helped Jews begs the question as to why no other fellow-travellers did anything to help (*KR*, 17 March 1994). Dirk Kurbjuweit maintained that 'Schindler unmasks one of those German illusions: you could do something, even as a drinker and *bon viveur*' (*FAZ*, 1 April 1994). Spielberg's Schindler, then, gave the lie to the claim that the industrialists' hands were tied, or that it needed a certain nobility of character to take the risks he did. Schirrmacher rightly points to Schindler's 'contradictoriness' as the essential message for German filmgoers (*FAZ*, 1 March 1994). With an uncanny sense of timing, Spielberg produced a film which to a degree preconditioned and certainly anticipated the more general resistance debate discussed earlier. For that debate too, while it was primarily about the need to preserve a balanced picture of the social and political spectrum of resistance, was also about whether those involved in resistance could be regarded as 'ideal'. The bottom line of 1994 was that purity of moral character and a soundly democratic political vision were not prerequisites for courage. This, in turn, served to undermine one of the pillars of self-exculpation in eastern and western Germany (for a longer discussion of the impact of *Schindler's List* in Germany, see Niven 1995).

Georg Elser was an equally lonely figure. He was evidence that you did not need to be part of an organization with 'access' to the Führer, in fact you did not even need help and support, to carry out an attempt on his life. Elser collected the parts for his bomb, constructed it, chose the location for it and then planted it all on his own. That former Chancellor Kohl mentioned him on 20 July 1994 may indicate that Kohl saw in him a determined visionary facing difficult odds. This was how Kohl tended to view himself. But whatever Kohl's motives, he may have helped to bring Elser to public attention in the 1990s. Certainly Brandauer helped to do so, with his excellent film *Georg Elser – An Individual from Germany* (1992). Most credit, however, must go to the Memorial Site for German Resistance, which showed an exhibition on Elser in 1997, and to Elser's home town of Königsbronn, where a memorial site dedicated to him was opened on 14 February 1998 (Steinbach and Tuchel 1998). In 1999, Dachau Memorial Site finally provided adequate documentation of Elser's imprisonment there. If Schindler gave the lie to the idea that you needed to be a saint to stage resistance, Elser gave the lie to the notion that the 'ordinary German' could do nothing. Elser was about as ordinary as you could get.

That the post-unification focus on Elser was difficult for some to digest became clear when, on 8 November 1999, Lothar Fritze, a part-time lecturer in history at the Hannah Arendt Institute in Dresden, published an article questioning the moral legitimacy of Elser's assassination attempt. Fritze also asserted that Elser had overstepped his powers of political judgement, and that his deed was characterized by 'grotesque indifference' towards the lives of others (*FR*, 8 November 1999). For while Elser's bomb had not killed Hitler, it had, unfortunately, killed a number of others. Yet so had Stauffenberg's. It did not occur to Fritze to accuse him of 'grotesque indifference'. This apparently quite superfluous attack did much damage to the reputation of the Hannah Arendt Institute. Founded in 1993, it was originally intended by Saxony's Minister of Culture Matthias Rößler (CDU) as a centre for research into the history of the GDR, but it has become one of post-unification's main centres for research into both National Socialism and the GDR. Prior to Fritze's expostulations, it had produced much solid research work and had by and large resisted the temptation to drift off into relativist historiography – despite the New Right sympathies of deputy director Uwe Backes. The presence of notable historians such as Saul Friedländer on the advisory committee helped to solidify its reputation. Now, at a stroke, Fritze plunged the Institute into a crisis of esteem.

Fritze, known for his right-wing views, was implying that Elser was little better than a left-wing terrorist. In denying him moral and political credibility, Fritze adopted the practice of exclusion outlined earlier. But he went further than discrediting Elser's motives. He appeared to deny him the right to the assassination attempt in the first place, and redefined it as murder. Fritze's criticisms derived, I would argue, from the wish to protect the German officers' caste from the critical light shed upon it by Elser's deed. Elser had attempted to kill Hitler in 1939. Stauffenberg's attempt came almost five years later. There were, admittedly, a number of blighted attempts on Hitler's life from within the military before Stauffenberg's. But the most notable of these were in 1943. Generals Halder and Witzleben had planned a coup in 1938, but called it off because of Hitler's success in gaining the Sudetenland by means of diplomacy, which meant that the immediate threat of war had been averted. When war started in 1939, the military did nothing to stop Hitler, in fact it did everything to support him: it invaded Poland. Elser, a few weeks after this invasion, tried to kill Hitler. Elser's deed throws the tardiness of the military resistance into relief. The cumulative and collective process which gave rise to the 20 July 1944 plot appears, from the perspective of Elser's timely and radical individualism, as a belated and rather diffident fumbling. This – as well as Elser's erstwhile links to the far left – may well have been the reason for Fritze's attempted demontage. Few have supported his views, and the Hannah Arendt Institute has not yet recovered from the indignation his comments caused.

The basis for consensus

The attempts by some in the CDU in 1994 to instrumentalize the memory of 20 July 1944 both for the 'remilitarization' of Germany's foreign policy and for an assault on the left ultimately failed. The present scaling down of Germany's army under SPD Defence Minister Rudolf Scharping – accompanied by discussion as to whether military service should be scrapped – will reduce it to a modest international and domestic task force. It will not be much of an army any more. These CDU attempts also seriously misfired because the *Bundeswehr* came under criticism for tolerating right-wing radical elements within its ranks. The problem of right-wing extremism in the army grew worse between 1995 and 1998. The assault on the left, which hinged on the symbolic comparison of 17 June 1953 with 20 July 1944, has proven to be demagogy, because while left-wing radicalism has not posed a consistent or extensive threat to German democracy since 1990, right-wing radicalism has. The recent escalation in right-wing violence on the part of young people largely socialized in united Germany, not the GDR, has disproved CDU claims that the problem is solely the legacy of anti-fascism's failure to confront German guilt for Nazism. It is also a symptom of the iniquities of unification – for which the CDU was responsible in large measure.

Anti-totalitarian principles cannot serve as a basis for agreement in Germany today. Totalitarianism is a conservative political construction, not a fact. It posits an equivalence of fascism and socialism. For this equation to function, the GDR must be made to appear much worse, with hindsight, than it actually was. This denigration cannot proceed without a concomitant denigration of former East German citizens. The anti-totalitarian view of the past thus not only distorts this past, it is also inherently anti-consensual, presupposing as it does the moral superiority of the west Germans. The anti-totalitarian model of reaction in the present is equally distortive and divisive, because it falsely presupposes that the main source of threat to German democracy comes in equal measure from the far left and the far right. The only workable basis for consensus is a commitment to the so-called *wehrhafte Demokratie*: a sense of the need to defend civil liberties, rather than a party-political viewpoint. It is here that a more inclusive, critical and objective picture of resistance to Nazism can be helpful. What united those who staged acts of resistance, whatever their political ideals or lack of them, or their other motives, was the awareness that Hitler had done away with these liberties. The more the individual resistance figures are brought into the picture – from Georg Elser to Ludwig Baumann and other *Wehrmacht* deserters, who were finally allowed to lay a wreath in the Bendler Block in 1999 – the more the Germans will understand what was possible and what *is* possible for the individual. The less 'noble' the resistance appears, the less possible it becomes for Germans to claim they lack the moral prerequisites.

At the time of writing, November 2000, it would seem that this consensus is developing, as political parties, unions, civil initiatives, writers and 'ordinary Germans' come together to ward off right-wing extremist violence by forming an 'alliance for democracy' (see Chapter Nine). As for the adherents of the totalitarian theorem, their hopes of cancelling out National Socialist crimes with reference to those of socialism were somewhat confounded in 1995, when official commemoration of 8 May based conciliation with all the former Allies by and large on a firm acknowledgement of German guilt for Nazism.

4   8 May 1945 in political discourse

'Germany 1945: at once redeemed and destroyed'
(subsection heading in a book on the Third Reich (Studt 1995))

Capitulation: defeat or liberation?

On 30 April 1945, Hitler committed suicide, and power passed to the new Reich President Grand Admiral Karl Dönitz. On 1 May 1945, Dönitz took up the reins of government in Flensburg. But after unsuccessful attempts 'to bargain terms through partial ceasefires in the west' (Burleigh 2000: 794), Germany capitulated. It was Chief of the Operations Staff of the High Command of the Armed Forces (OKW), Alfred Jodl, representing Dönitz, who signed the capitulation of the *Wehrmacht* to the Allies at Eisenhower's headquarters in Reims (France) on 7 May 1945. According to the terms, the war came to an end on 8 May at 23.01 CET. The Soviets, however, were unhappy at the fact that the capitulation had been signed in territory occupied by the Western Allies. They insisted on a repetition of the ceremony in Soviet-occupied east Berlin. So, shortly after midnight on 9 May, after the ceasefire had come into effect, Chief of Staff of the OKW Wilhelm Keitel was made to sign a second capitulation at the Red Army Headquarters in Berlin-Karlshorst. It is therefore open to debate which day should be identified as the day of capitulation. Throughout the years of the Cold War, the Soviets, on 9 May in East Berlin, symbolically re-enacted the Keitel capitulation, while celebrations in the West tended to take place on 7 and 8 May. The two acts of capitulation in May 1945 were evidence of a growing rift between the Western and Soviet Allies, and anticipated the divided memory of 8 May in West and East Germany. The subsequently separate sets of commemorations on different days – Americans, British and French here, Soviets there – implied that there had been two wars, and two sets of victors.

One thing, at least, *was* undisputed from the perspective of all the Allies: namely that the capitulation of Germany meant victory for them, and defeat for the Germans. For Germany, however – or, as of 1949, the two of them – the situation was highly ambivalent.

The subjective view of many Germans of capitulation was indeed one of defeat in war (*Niederlage*). For those who still supported Hitler up until the bitter end, this was certainly the case. It was also the case for those who, whatever their opinion of Hitler and his campaign, experienced the Allied victory as an essential staging-post in what they regarded as a sequence of injustices before and after the end of the war. One of these perceived injustices was the intense bombing of German cities, as of the raid on Hamburg on 24 July 1943. It was particularly the destruction of Dresden on the night of 13–14 February 1945 which caused bitterness. One of the most beautiful cities in the world, it was razed to the ground by British and American bombers for no apparent reason other than sheer destructiveness or, at best, to plunge the retreating Germans into chaos; 35,000 people died. For decades afterwards, misleading rumours circulated that the death toll was actually 200,000, even 400,000, and that the British had peppered fleeing civilians with bullets from low-flying aircraft (a myth only clearly dispelled recently [see Bergander 1998]). Dresden became a symbol of arbitrary Allied violence for many Germans, and a card which could be played in the mutual accusation game when the Allies began to uncover the extent of German war crimes.

A second perceived injustice was the fate of the Germans who, for generations, had lived in East Prussia (divided up after the war between Poland and the Soviet Union), the Sudetenland (returned to Czechoslovakia) and Silesia. As the Soviet army advanced in late 1944, hundreds of thousands of German civilians fled westwards; many of those unlucky enough to fall into the hands of Soviet soldiers were killed, while German women were frequently raped. In February 1945, Soviet submarines sank passenger ships carrying East Prussian fugitives: at least 15,000 people were killed. By the end of the war, some five million Germans had fled the eastern territories. The subsequent expulsion of further millions of Germans in the wake of ethnic clearances above all in Poland and Czechoslovakia – an expulsion tolerated by the Western Allies in the hope that it would end nationality conflicts within individual countries – meant that, by the end of 1950, some 8 million fugitives had found a new home in the FRG, about 16.5% of the total West German population (Benz 1995: 10). Another four million settled in the GDR (many then moving to the West). While these fugitives were gradually integrated and contributed to economic revival above all in the FRG, they remained bitter at their loss of homeland. This bitterness made inroads into West Germany's political culture, in which open resentment at the absorption of East Prussia and Pomerania into what became eastern bloc countries could be exploited in the Cold War. In this context, 8 May was associated with massive expulsion and territorial sacrifice.

Thirdly, there was the perceived injustice of occupation itself, in all its short-term measures and long-term effects. 8 May was understood by many as the start of a campaign of arbitrary 'victors' justice' (*Siegerjustiz*). This campaign, it was felt, was made manifest in the Nuremberg trials (1946), where leading German Nazis and Nazi institutions were subjected to Allied moral scrutiny. There was widespread indignation among Germans in the Soviet and Western occupation zones at internment and denazification procedures. They were viewed, as were a number of other Allied measures, as an attempt to attach a label of collective guilt to the Germans. A further, and perhaps the most keenly felt injustice was the division of

Germany. 8 May 1945 was the result of Allied collaboration, but it also marked the starting-point of a gradual drifting apart of the alliance, with the Western Allies strengthening their grip on the Western zones of occupation, and the Soviets strengthening theirs on the Eastern zone. On 21 September 1949, the Federal Republic of Germany came into existence; this was followed on 7 October by the establishment of the German Democratic Republic (for an overview of the events leading to division, see Thomaneck and Niven 2001: 11–30).

In all the above cases, the Germans felt little inclination to see things in perspective. Without the war waged by Hitler, there would have been no defeat and division. While the expulsion of Germans from their eastern homelands was in many respects unjust and on occasion murderous, it was but the final stage in a whole series of infinitely more inhumane population transfers carried out by the Germans under Hitler – not least of Jews and Poles in the course of the Nazi racial reorganization of Europe. Whatever one might think of the bombing of Dresden, it did represent a response to German aggression and the bombing of cities such as Coventry. German support of Hitler had unleashed a sequence of cause and effect. Politically, of course, it could be valuable to understand and represent capitulation as defeat. One could then point to the need to redress what were felt to be concomitant injustices committed by the over-zealous victors.

Not all Germans, however, saw things negatively. There was a sense in which capitulation represented liberation (*Befreiung*). Most of those people persecuted by Hitler, a not insignificant proportion of them Germans, had been liberated prior to May 1945, with the notable exception of those in hiding in Berlin (such as Jews who had gone 'underground'). Thus Auschwitz was liberated in January 1945, Buchenwald and Sachsenhausen in April. Nevertheless, the capitulation was in a sense the 'guarantee' that this liberation would be irrevocable. It was a symbolic end to the Third Reich's campaign of military and racial aggression. For those millions of Germans who had fought in Hitler's army, or held out on the home front, the capitulation was also a liberation, namely from the threat of death and destruction. Of course many may not have realized it at the time; the ideological diehards probably never did. But, with hindsight, most Germans came to understand the end of hostilities as in some ways a blessing. As the years passed, as West Germany and even, in its own, more modest way, East Germany emerged as economic and political forces to be reckoned with, new identities were established, careers constructed. The expression 'Zero Hour' (*Stunde Null*) was applied retroactively to 1945, suggesting that, at that time, a new era had begun.

Viewed from another perspective, however, liberation has always been a very problematic term. For Germans to claim that they were liberated in 1945 can have a ring of self-exoneration. The term can imply that National Socialism was something imposed on the Germans by external forces – as if they had had to survive in occupied territory, like the Czechs or the Poles during the war. It may imply that they were victims, of Hitler, his imperialism, an anonymous war-machine, or just fate. The term can thus obscure their role between 1939 and 1945 as perpetrators and collaborators. West German politicans tended towards such self-exculpatory readings. In East Germany, the situation was different, yet comparable. The SED encouraged its citizens to identify so closely with the Soviets that there was a danger of East Germans imagining they had always been against National Socialism. This was an almost self-congratulatory reading of liberation. As long as Germany was divided, moreover, the term was loaded with Cold War ballast. The official view in the GDR was that it was liberated, but that the FRG was a lackey of capitalist, indeed fascist imperialism. While West Germany was a more complicated case, as of 1955 a part of the official view was that the FRG was a free state, whereas the GDR was seen as a lackey of the Soviet empire. Blame was passed back and forth between the two states. Yet the term 'liberation' can have a self-critical potential, a potential discovered in the 1970s, largely in West Germany. To acknowledge there was a liberation can be to admit that there had previously been repression, and, arguably, to force oneself to confront one's own role in the Third Reich, or the role of one's parents or grandparents. It can be to admit that the Germans needed to be freed from National Socialism. They had done infinitely more to advance its cause than to rid themselves of it.

Tensions therefore exist not only between 'defeat' and 'liberation', but within the latter term. This chapter explores these tensions as they found expression in the political remembrance of 8 May in East and West Germany. It then examines the reception of 8 May in 1995, when the 50th anniversary of this date came round. 1995 was also the 50th anniversary of the liberation of Auschwitz and Buchenwald, and the bombing of Dresden. Remembering 8 May was therefore embedded in the wider context of what the Germans called the 'super-year of commemoration' (*Supergedenkjahr*), in analogy to the 'super-year of elections' in 1994. More importantly, 1995 saw the first significant commemoration of 8 May in united Germany, a significance enhanced by the fact that half a century had passed since capitulation. Given that the geopolitical parameters had changed substantially in 1990, the question was how Germany as one country would approach a commemorative occasion for long so bound up with the Cold War. The contention here, as in previous chapters, is that the approach was inclusive, connecting elements typical of West German with elements associated with East German remembrance, uniting Germany in commemoration with all Allies (instead of either just the Soviets or just the Western Allies), and encouraging a variety of narratives and memories alongside an official policy of remembering.

The GDR: identifying with the victors

In East Germany, 8 May was positively remembered in official political discourse every year from 1950 onwards. Until 1966, and then again in 1985, it was a national holiday. The SED made of it a pomp-laden day of national festivity, as well as one of German–Soviet brotherhood. The fraternization was justified with reference to the fact that the East Germans and Soviets were now 'on the same side'. It was also pointed out that many of those German communists committed to building socialism in the GDR had worked together with the Soviets in overcoming Hitler. Chief among these were, in GDR parlance, the 'activists of the first hour' such as Wilhelm Pieck and even Erich Honecker. Ulbricht had been the leading member of a group flown in to Germany from Moscow exile on 30 April 1945. Honecker, imprisoned in Brandenburg prison for almost ten years under the National Socialists, was set free by the Soviet 32nd Tank Regiment. In later years, he liked to relate how the liberated prisoners, reaching Berlin on 4 May 1945, had hung the flags of the anti-Hitler coalition from the façades of houses. In official narratives, the post-war alliance between the Soviet Union and the GDR was traced back to these joint efforts. It was underpinned symbolically by 8 May medal ceremonies. In preparation for the 10th anniversary of 8 May, the Politburo decided not just that Soviet Marshal Zhukov should be awarded the 'Patriotic Order of Merit in Gold' on 8 May 1955, but also that illegal German underground communist fighters against fascism, as well as leading post-war east German functionaries, should be awarded the 'Patriotic Order of Merit' (SAPMO 1955a). On 8 May 1965, Willi Stoph and Erich Honecker were awarded the 'Patriotic Order of Merit's Honorary Badge in Gold'. In 1985, spy-chief Markus Wolf got a medal for his contribution 'at the front'.

Such an understanding of the past was not without its element of truth. The liberation of Germany was indeed a goal that the German communists had worked towards, however significant or insignificant their contribution. They had resisted Hitler, worked against him in exile or from within Germany. East Germany was to a significant extent run by communists with considerable 'resistance credentials'. However, the state-wide hullabaloo on 8 May falsely implied that *all* East Germans had somehow taken part in this act of liberation. Through the representatives of German communism, by proxy as it were, they had shared in the 'victory of socialism over fascism'. At the very least, because East Germans were now by official decree good socialists, they were credited with having *wished* they had liberated themselves from fascism.

This was the implication behind all 8 May festivities in the GDR and behind the focus on German–Soviet friendship. For 8 May 1955, the Politburo planned people's festivals and military concerts all over the city. Large-scale cultural programmes, sporting events, dancing, and mini-Olympics were to be staged (SAPMO 1955a). In many of these events, the Soviets and East Germans worked closely together. The regular 8 May East German–Soviet commemoration of Soviet soldiers at the Berlin-Treptow Memorial conveyed the impression that these dead Russians had been brothers in combat. In 1985, the shoulder-to-shoulder retracing of the path of the Red Army in 1945 from the Oder to Berlin by Lenin Pioneers from the Soviet Union and East German Thälmann Pioneers and the Free German Youth (FDJ) suggested that the Germans had been accompanying the Red Army, in spirit if not in flesh. Again and again Russian soldiers and German communist 'activists of the first hour' came together on or around 8 May to conjure up the image of a collaborative anti-fascist German–Soviet front, often before an audience of Free German Youth youngsters. 8 May festivities were usually accompanied by mass new membership of the Society for German–Soviet Friendship. In May 1975 alone, 2,500 East Germans in Berlin-Pankow, and 4,200 in Berlin-Köpenick joined the Society.

Surely the most telling, awe-inspiring and yet tasteless manifestations of this collaborative image were the spectacular military parades in East Berlin. The parade in 1965, which angered the Western Allies because its flexing of military strength was believed to be in violation of the Berlin status, was a case in point. In front of 6,000 guests from all over the world, the Soviets displayed their new intercontinental missiles. But the real emphasis of the parade was on GDR–Soviet 'brotherhood in weapons' (*Waffenbrüderschaft*). The architecture, timing and composition of the 1965 parade was worked out in advance to the last detail by the SED, as is evident from the minutes of a March 1965 Politburo meeting. The length of the parade was to be 7,275 metres: the display of infantry was to extend over 360 metres, the display of motorized East German troops over 3,580 metres, and of Soviet motorized troops over 3,335 metres (SAPMO 1965). On the day, participating units came together from all over the city, paraded past Kosygin and Ulbricht, meandered through Berlin's *Lustgarten* and then through other parts of East Berlin, ecstatically greeted, apparently, by the populace (*SZ*, 10 May 1965). In 1965, celebrations in East Berlin continued for an astonishing four days.

This massive military fuss cast the East Germans, retrospectively, in the role of heroic liberators. It was easy for them to forget that they had played their part in a war of aggression and had had to be defeated. In the 1980s, the GDR peace movement and the Churches did begin to challenge the official reading. Thus in May 1985, during a ceremony in honour of pastor Dietrich Bonhoeffer in Weimar, Bishop Albrecht Schönherr reminded his listeners that Germans did not liberate themselves, and for the most part did not want to. Only a few Germans, said Bishop Werner Leich, could say they belonged to the 'front of the victors' (*SZ*, 7 May 1985). But the official dogma largely prevailed until the *Wende*. On another level, of course, the military pomp was a demonstration of power directed at the West. The official slant put on the parades was that it was necessary for the peace-loving GDR to frustrate the imperialist ambitions of capitalism by frightening off the potential aggressors in the West. This robust pacifism was well formulated on 9 May 1965 by Karl Eduard von Schnitzler on GDR television: 'Certain people in Bonn and Washington should sit up and take note: the peace-dove doesn't only have wings, which it spreads over the whole world. It also has claws, and is prepared to show them.' Given that the SED tended to portray West Germany as but a somewhat milder version of the Third Reich, it followed that what the East Germans and Soviets were working to prevent was an intrusion of fascism – just as German communists and the Red Army had worked together to overthrow Hitler. In the past and in the present, the East Germans were on the right side of history. Whether the GDR was a dove with claws, or more of a wolf in sheep's clothing, is open to question.

In the 1950s and 1960s, when the theme of unification under socialist auspices was still on the official 8 May agenda, official pronouncements could certainly be intrusive in tone. In a statement made on 8 May 1950, the GDR's National Front proclaimed: 'We swear on this fifth anniversary of liberation to use all our resources to complete the liberation of our fatherland by freeing West Germany' (quoted in *taz*, 27 April 1995). Admittedly these resources seemed to be more of the tactical and propagandistic kind. In its meeting of 29 March 1955, the GDR Politburo agreed for 8 May 1955 a 'political-ideological campaign' of press publications and meetings in West Germany. Leaflets produced by the Committee for German Unity on 'The Liberation from Fascism' were to be handed out at border-points. 'Discussions' were envisaged with West Germans spending their holidays in East German resorts, who would then, it was hoped, return home and help to 'bring down the Paris Treaties' in order that peaceful unification might be possible (SAPMO 1955a). As hopes of unification dwindled, official pronouncements on the subject of 8 May nevertheless retained a pugnacious quality. The class-struggle may have been over in the GDR, but the world-wide anti-capitalist struggle was not. Indeed this very struggle was an ideologically programmed component of international communism.

Hence 8 May celebrations in the GDR were always manifestations of struggle (*Kampf*). Industrial and agricultural combines across the GDR, as well as schools and organizations such as the FDJ or the Free German Trade Union, would months beforehand set out certain goals that had to be attained by 8 May. In the case of industry, this usually meant increased output, while the FDJ would embark on marathon 'memory' tours such as in 1985, when young East Germans walked from the river Oder to Berlin. They laid wreaths at Soviet graves along the way, held meetings at memorial sites, met Second World War heroes and – inevitably – activists of the first hour (reported by Joachim Herrmann, SAPMO 1985). Remembrance of the end of the war was enacted in the form of sporting events such as the international relay 'Commemoration', also in 1985. Such industrial hyperactivity and youthful athleticism were deadly serious attempts to generate a strong socialist state, a 'reliable bulwark of peace, democracy and progress' as Honecker put it in his 8 May 1975 address (*ND*, 9 May 1975). Admittedly such activity could seem absurd, as when East Berlin meat combines promised in honour of the 30th anniversary of 8 May to manufacture cheaper, better-tasting and more 'popular' meat and sausages.

The identificatory, self-congratulatory model of 8 May remembrance in the GDR is nicely encapsulated in an anecdote recounted by theatre director Adolf Dresen. Once, in a GDR cemetery, Dresen's young son came across a war memorial in honour of the 1914–1918 war dead. Dresen pointed out to him that there was also a Second World War, though for this war there was no monument. His son did not find this surprising. After all, the boy said, we won the Second World War side by side with the Soviet army. So who lost the war, then, his father asked? The Germans, the boy answered. And where are the Germans now? 'Over there', replied the son, pointing to West Germany (*TSP*, 7 May 1995).

West Germany: defeat or liberation?

What of 8 May in West Germany? The Adenauer government did in 1949–1950 reflect on the possibility of declaring it a 'day of national commemoration'. 8 May would have had the advantage of being both the day of capitulation and the day on which the Parliamentary Council had approved the Basic Treaty – cornerstone of the new democracy – in 1949 (Dubiel 1999: 52). A national holiday on 8

May would have encouraged an understanding that without capitulation there would have been no democratic rule of law. But the first West German government was largely unwilling to encourage this understanding. Had it done so, capitulation would have been officially stripped of its association with the ignominy of defeat and the injustices in turn associated with this defeat. There was rather the feeling in the fledgeling West Germany that 8 May should be a day of national mourning and complaint. Instead, 7 September was chosen as 'national day of commemoration'; this was the day in 1949 on which the Federal Parliament and Federal Council had come together for the first time. In 1954, 7 September was replaced by 17 June, in commemoration of the workers' uprising against the SED in East Germany. From this point on, West Germans were encouraged to reflect on repression in the GDR, rather than on the National Socialist repression for which Germans on both sides of the border bore responsibility.

The feeling that 8 May was really a day for complaint is well exemplified in an editorial by journalist Erich Dombrowski from 1955 (*FAZ*, 7 May 1955). According to Dombrowski, in May 1945 Germany had become 'a no man's land', 'an immeasurable graveyard', a 'yawning field of ruins'. There was a 'terrible confusion of disorientated millions who had lost their possessions, homes and places of work'. For Dombrowski, the defeat was worse than that under Napoleon. To have to bear 'inevitable defeat in the desperate struggle against a coalition of the whole world' was bad enough, but to this had been added 'shame and disgrace' when the victors sought to burden the Germans with a 'collective guilt' in order that they might be 'ostracized for all time'. To this 'mental aberration, hatred and revanchism' on the part of the victors, Dombrowski put down the genesis of the Morgenthau Plan, according to which Germany, had the plan been carried out, would have been transformed into a de-industrialized landscape. But the Germans, Dombrowski continued, thanks to their 'love of the soil and homeland', found the courage to rebuild Germany and peace in Europe. 'And so we began in all our privation and misery to find ourselves again, although we were bossed around in the vast military barracks of the occupying powers.' Memory of 8 May, concludes Dombrowski, 'this dark day of deepest humiliation', should spur the Germans on to act to fulfil the most immediate need: 'the reunification of the German people'.

Historian Michael Freund, writing in *Die Zeit* on 5 May 1955, ploughed a similar furrow to Dombrowski. He went further, however, blaming the Allies for liquidating 'a thousand years of European and German history', embodied in the 'German settlement of the areas beyond the Oder–Neiße line'. Germany as a historical entity had disappeared: 'all that remains is political formlessness, which began with the erosion of Germany as a state in May 1945'. All the elements typical of West German 8 May political discourse in the 1950s and 1960s were present in these two articles: self-pity, indignation at the Allies, a demonstrative sense of loss, and absence of sympathy for the victims of National Socialism, accompanied by self-satisfaction at having overcome the devastation of 1945 and built up a democratic and, economically, increasingly successful Federal Republic. The strident sense of injury was complemented by an equally strident call for unification, even for a restitution of Germany in its 1937 boundaries. The young West

Germany confidently sought rectification of perceived injustice, but rarely focused on the injustices caused under Hitler.

Throughout the Adenauer era (1949–1963), freedom was not the value attached to 8 May 1945. Instead, it was seen as marking the beginning of a slide into unfreedom, and it was this unfreedom from which first West Germany, then Germany as a whole needed to be liberated. An important stage in this 'liberation' was 5 May 1955, when, at twelve midday, occupation formally ended. West Germany largely gained its sovereignty. On the evening of 8 May, the Western European Union (WEU) was formed, with West Germany among the founding members. To crown it all, West Germany became a member of NATO on 9 May. The 10th anniversary of the capitulation was obscured by this series of new-won freedoms and rights of inclusion. When Adenauer read out a government state-ment on 6 May 1955, his text bristled with the word 'free'. 'We are a free and independent state', he proclaimed proudly', or 'we stand as a free people among free peoples'. At last West Germany had been liberated – from Allied interference. Adenauer wanted more. Turning to the East Germans, he said: 'You belong to us, and we belong to you. Our joy at our regained freedom will be a qualified one as long as you don't have this freedom. You can always rely on us, because together with the free world we will not rest until you too have regained your human rights and live peacefully with us in one state.' For Adenauer, West Germany's new-found flexibility strengthened its right to act as moral champion of the cause of *East* Germany for liberation – in this case from Soviet control. Interestingly, the declaration avoided explicitly using the word *Befreiung* except in reference to those Germans still languishing in POW camps: 'We will do everything so that they too soon experience the hour of liberation' (*SZ*, 6 May 1955). The 'liberation' of the POWs remained high on Adenauer's priority list.

That it was not necessary for Germans to reflect unduly on the part they played in the Third Reich was implied by Adenauer in the speech he gave in Paris to mark West Germany's entry into NATO. He claimed that the Germans had 'paid hard for the misdeeds that were committed in their name by corrupt and blind leaders. These sufferings have transformed and purified the German nation' (*SZ*, 10 May 1955). On this view, the leaders had committed the crimes, not the Germans as a whole; in any case, the Germans had undergone a painful purification, whereby it remained unclear whether their sufferings were caused by the misdeeds or by having been made to pay for them by the Allies.

As of 1955, 8 May was associated in the FRG with the attainment of sovereignty and Western integration, and with the injustice of continued division. This was also the case under the second West German Chancellor Ludwig Erhard (1963–1966), also CDU. By May 1965, the 10th anniversary of the Paris Treaties and the 20th of capitulation, prospects of unification had receded. The three Western Allies could not even manage a joint Germany Declaration stating their commitment to unification. The British and Americans sent separate, vaguely formulated decla-rations; de Gaulle remained silent. Erhard was disappointed. In a radio and television address to the nation on 7 May, he declared that, if the defeat of Hitler's Germany had meant the end to injustice and tyranny, then all of mankind would have good reason to regard 8 May as a 'day for commemorating liberation'. 'We all know how far from the truth this is' (*SZ*, 8–9 May 1965). Yet he also encouraged his listeners to look back critically: 'we recognize today much more clearly than at the time that the military collapse had been preceded by a spiritual and moral decay'. In a memorable speech at the German Trade and Industry Conference on 6 May 1965, Erhard warned the Germans against pushing the terrible time of dictatorship from their memory. He said that the memory of deeds, misdeeds and guilt would be with the Germans for generations, and that they would have to bear responsibility for their 'political fate' from one generation to the next, regardless of the degree of personal guilt. He also pointed out that attempts to cast off the past had led to a certain loss of corporate political identity and the emergence of economically motivated group egoisms (*FAZ*, 7 May 1965).

If Erhard had at least seen fit to turn to the nation on the eve of 8 May, first SPD Chancellor Willy Brandt (1969–1974) introduced the practice of holding an hour of official remembrance on 8 May in Federal Parliament. This was a controversial decision at the time: there was resistance from the CDU on the grounds that defeats are not something to celebrate (Reichel 1999: 234). But all parties took part in the hour, and did so in subsequent years. In his own speech, Brandt began by stating that the 'war started by Hitler made victims of millions of people, children, women and men, prisoners and soldiers of many nations [. . .] The agony of their deaths, and the sufferings which resulted from the war compel us not to forget the lessons of the past, and to see in the maintenance of peace the greatest goal of our political actions' (*SZ*, 9–10 May 1970). While West German politicians had always stressed commitment to peace, it was Brandt who located the source of this commitment unequivocally within the context of the suffering caused by the Third Reich. It was Brandt who unambiguously expressed the fact that the end of the war meant the end of this suffering, and liberation. While he used the term *Befreiung* in relation to other nations, not the Germans, stressing instead their 'personal and national distress' in 1945, his focus on the 'chance for a new beginning' implied liberation for the Germans too.

But the most striking aspect of Brandt's speech lay elsewhere. In 1970, he met East German Prime Minister Willi Stoph in Erfurt (19 March) and Kassel (21 May) for the first top-level government meetings between the two states. This ushered in the era of active cooperation between the FRG and GDR. Accordingly, Brandt's 8 May speech avoided remarks about the need to liberate the GDR and, after calling for 'respect for the achievements' of the East Germans, asserted the need for conciliation with the East as the necessary correlative to Adenauer's policy of conciliation with the West. This GDR-friendly line had psychological implications. It became less easy for West Germans to vent their spleen on the unliberated condition of the GDR. The result was a chance for a more self-critical stance, a greater sense of responsibility for the Third Reich, without which, after all, division would never have occurred.

On 6 May 1975, a milestone was reached. Federal President Walter Scheel (FDP) stated in his address that the Germans had been liberated (*befreit*) from the 'terrible yoke of war, murder, slavery and barbarism'. He added that the Germans should not forget that the liberation had come from outside, and that 'half the world had to be destroyed before Hitler could be pushed from the stage of world-history'. The weakness of Scheel's speech was that he defined National Socialism as a 'yoke' borne by the Germans. On the other hand, he did blame the Germans not just for not shaking it off, but also for allowing it to be imposed in the first place. Hitler was not an inevitable fate, 'he was elected'. Scheel even went so far as to claim that 'the German tragedy began not in 1945, but in 1933'. He also mentioned the Jews and the Sinti and Roma, a novelty in 8 May speeches: 'We allowed our rights, the rights of our neighbours to be trodden underfoot. In our name mass murder was committed, of Jews, Gypsies, the mentally ill, political prisoners and others' (*SZ*, 7–8 May 1975). While Scheel implied, in traditional West German fashion, that the Nazi perpetrators were distinct from the broad mass of Germans, he nevertheless accused the latter of being passive onlookers. This accusation was a comparatively bold step. It was, arguably, in part a response to recent acts of left-wing terrorism; Scheel explicitly condemned 'every form of extremism' in his speech. Only two weeks earlier, on 24 April 1975, six terrorists had laid siege to the West German embassy in Stockholm in an attempt to secure the release of far-left terrorists imprisoned in the FRG. It took left-wing radicalism to trigger, under the impression of the vulnerability of West German democracy, official recognition of the need to learn from German weakness and susceptibility under Hitler.

1985: a clash of memory paradigms

'No-one is exempt from history', Brandt said in his 8 May 1970 speech. 'Only if we don't forget can we again be proud to call ourselves Germans', said Scheel on 6 May 1975. This was the significance of the shift in 8 May commemoration in the 1970s – it was one towards integrating self-critical awareness of the Nazi past into West German self-understanding in the present, and one away from the vague, self-pitying and inculpatory tone of the 1950s and 1960s. When Chancellor Kohl came to power in 1982, and the CDU/FDP coalition took over the reins of government, an 'intellectual and moral change' (*geistig-moralische Wende*) was proclaimed. One aspect of this was a harsher tone towards the GDR and Soviet Union. By 1983, the Cold War had reached a new height, marked by the stationing of nuclear weapons. Under the influence of this threat, Kohl redirected the policy of reconciliation back towards a focus on the West. He was encouraged in this by a close personal relationship to Ronald Reagan, which replaced the more distant, even hostile one between Helmut Schmidt and Jimmy Carter. He also, in May 1985, sought to redefine the terms of reconciliation. Brandt's idea of reconciliation was based on humility and a sense of guilt – witness his falling to his knees at the monument for the Warsaw ghetto victims in 1970. Kohl's was based on an erasure of the difference between Germans and their victims, on, in other words, the exculpation of the Germans under Hitler.

Bitburg in the Palatinate is a town known for its beer. Since May 1985, it is also remembered as the site of a cemetery at which 2,000 people lie buried, most of them German soldiers, a handful – 48 in all – members of the *Waffen-SS*, an organization responsible for heinous crimes. Helmut Kohl and Ronald Reagan paid a visit to this cemetery on 5 May 1985. Following protests at their intention to do so, the visit was kept very short at ten minutes, and it was offset by an hour-long visit to a former concentration camp, Bergen-Belsen. Nevertheless, protest from America and within West Germany continued for weeks afterwards. The American Jewish Committee was indignant. 250,000 people demonstrated against Reagan in New York on 6 May, many of them war veterans. Within the FRG, the political left, intellectuals and the Central Council of the Jews in Germany slated Kohl and Reagan for constructing a symbolic act of reconciliation upon the graves of Nazi perpetrators, who were being recast as 'victims of war' (for more detailed accounts, see Maier 1988: 9–16, and Reichel 1999: 235–43).

That such a German–American gesture was possible was the result of Reagan's impassioned anti-communism. He seemed prepared to forgive the Germans for anything in the past just as long as they were friends *now*. Historical responsibility was sacrificed to the exigencies of the geopolitical moment. Reagan no doubt hoped that the more generous he was in conciliation, the more prepared the West Germans would be to support his Strategic Defense Initiative (SDI). Reagan's speech at the US air-force support base in Bitburg following on from the visit to the cemetery was an almost embarrassingly intense exoneration. While acknowledging the crimes of the SS, Reagan described the 'others buried at Bitburg' as 'ordinary soldiers in the German army'. In reference to a boy killed shortly before his 16th birthday, Reagan said there were 'thousands of such soldiers for whom National Socialism meant nothing other than the brutal end of a short life', and that 'at Bitburg today we commemorated the goodness and humanity which, never given the chance to develop, was liquidated 40 years ago'. Only God can look into the hearts of men, he claimed, elevating German soldiers above the scope of earthly justice. After a eulogy of German–American conciliation and partnership for peace – which he saw reproductively reflected in the 6,000 marriages between Germans and American soldiers in Bitburg – Reagan concluded with the warning 'that the battle for freedom is not over, because today part of the world is still in the darkness of totalitarianism' (*SZ*, 6 May 1985).

Reagan's speech depicted German *Wehrmacht* soldiers as hapless victims, and implied that their war against the Soviets had been part of an ongoing struggle which united Americans and West Germans. This implicit rehabilitation antici-pated the position of some conservative historians in the Historians' Dispute (*Historikerstreit*) in West Germany one year later. While historians such as Ernst Nolte spectacularly attempted to dismiss the holocaust as a panic reaction to bol-shevist atrocities, Andreas Hillgruber quietly set about portraying the *Wehrmacht* as an institution committed to protecting Western civilization against the ravages of Soviet communism (for an overview of the Historians' Dispute, see Evans 1989). The result of these interpretations and Reagan's speech was a reinforcement of the West German tendency to exculpate the *Wehrmacht* (see Chapter Six). Brandt's and Scheel's tentative thrust towards a more self-critical view of 8 May, it appeared, had been replaced by a vigorous indulgence in self-pity. But the SPD, in its turn, resisted this reactionary trend. Peter Glotz, presenting the key ideas of the

'Nuremberg Manifesto' in which the SPD stated its position on the issue of 8 May, accused the government of being 'incapable of formulating the historical and political significance of 8 May 1945 for the Germans in an appropriate manner'. The Manifesto stated that 8 May 1945 was, for most Germans, a day of relief, even liberation. It also described it as a day of mourning for the millions of those who died in, or were otherwise victims of the war, persecution, racial madness and expulsion. 'Then there is the shame at the crimes committed by Germans' (*SZ*, 2 May 1985). By and large, this statement situated liberation within the self-critical framework.

On 7 May, the SPD held a 'peace dialogue' in Nuremberg to which representatives of many international cities whose inhabitants had been the victims of destruction and persecution during the war were invited. While the 'all-victims-together' axiom shone through here in places, the focus was largely on the destructive impact of the war unleashed by the Germans. This emphasis was well planned. Sections of the SPD considered Reagan's anti-communism, the US intervention in Nicaragua and the 'Star Wars' project to be as dangerous to peace as anything the Soviets were doing. Lafontaine even expressed fear of an 'atomic Auschwitz'. The price of Kohl's conciliation with Reagan, in other words, was possibly too high. The SPD felt it necessary to locate 8 May remembrance firmly, and as an admonishment, within the memory of devastation caused by Germans during the Second World War. Willy Brandt made it clear that the terrible things which had happened under Hitler were 'committed not just in the German name, but also by Germans'. He warned against understanding history as tragic destiny: history is 'made, and we must face the responsibility that derives from this'. Deputy SPD chairman Johannes Rau maintained unequivocally that 8 May was a day 'of liberation, not one of collapse, a day of shame, a day of release, and a day of deep horror' (*SZ*, 8 May 1985).

For all this, it was a CDU member, Federal President Richard von Weizsäcker, who, in Federal Parliament on 8 May 1985, most powerfully advocated a humble understanding of the day. His memorable speech has been well analysed (Dubiel 1999: 207–16, and Kirsch 1999a: 96–122). What needs to be stressed here are the elements which made up its character as a conscious antithesis to the implications of Bitburg. For the Jews, Weizsäcker argued, memory is the source of faith in redemption, and of conciliation. In the case of the Germans, forgetting would both represent a possible affront to Jewish faith, and destroy the beginnings of conciliation. Memory, Weizsäcker reminded his listeners, is *er-innern*, literally 'internalizing'. In calling for such internalization, Weizsäcker individualized the responsibility for remembering. Rather than seeing conciliation as an external symbolic gesture, as represented by Kohl's and Reagan's visit to Bitburg, Weizsäcker understood it as a spiritual act, and as an enduring one: 'What we need is a memorial of thinking and feeling within ourselves' (*FAZ*, 9 May 1985). Whereas Kohl appeared to seek a form of conciliation that would bury the past, Weizsäcker spoke out for a form of conciliation that was dependent upon the memory of this past. Instead of seeking to eliminate differences between perpetrators and victims, as Kohl and Reagan had done, Weizsäcker made it clear that the Germans had a moral debt of memory towards the Jews.

Weizsäcker gave credence to the different and often negative personal experiences of the end of the war. But he also stressed that it was not this end which was the original cause of expulsion and loss of freedom (presumably a reference to the GDR); the cause was rather the start of the war, and of the rule of violence which led to this war. He also stressed that the end of the war must be set in relation to the fact that 8 May 1945 was the prerequisite for democracy and a new start: '8 May was a day of liberation. It freed us all from the inhumane system of the National Socialist rule of violence'. Weizsäcker was careful not to allow his use of liberation to resonate with any self-exculpatory implications. He distanced himself from Kohl's identification with the Americans at Bitburg by declaring that the Germans had no reason to take part in victory celebrations. '8 May is a day of remembrance.' There followed, in the style of a *memento mori*, a list of those who died during the Third Reich. Weizsäcker began his list with a generalized nod towards all those who died in the war and under National Socialist rule. He then referred to the six million Jews who had died in concentration and extermination camps, and, in a gesture of commemorative *Ostpolitik*, to the Soviets and Poles who were killed during the war. This was the real surprise: Weizsäcker mentioned the latter *before* referring to those Germans who died as soldiers, or in the course of bombing-raids or expulsion. It is true that Weizsäcker placed the Sinti and Roma, homosexual and mentally handicapped victims further down his list, but at least he mentioned them. Moreover, he firmly reminded his listeners that awareness of the need to practise a humane ethics in the present can be sharpened by remembering the fate of the handicapped under Hitler – another neglected group.

Weizsäcker thus resisted Kohl's attempt to set 8 May free of self-critical memory, and oriented German awareness towards their victims and their guilt, not least as passive onlookers. He stressed the need for memory-based conciliation, not just with Jews, but also with the Soviets. Of course the theme of division and unification was addressed, but in the context of a desire for peace across the military blocs. Weizsäcker argued for a sober, reflective, yet multi-dimensional view. Kohl had sought self-exculpatory identification with the Americans, in analogy to East Germany's identification with the Soviets. It remained to be seen whether Kohl's or Weizsäcker's model of 8 May remembrance would have the greatest long-term effect.

West Germany: a belated Ally?

As of 1990, the parameters for the political reception of 8 May 1945 changed significantly. The 'Two Plus Four' Treaty between the GDR, the FRG and the Allied powers on 12 September 1990 signalled the conferral of 'full sovereignty over internal and external affairs' upon a united Germany (von Münch 1991: 377). The Western Allies thus relinquished residual rights in the FRG, the Soviets their rights over the GDR. It was agreed that the Soviet army, so massively present in East Germany, would withdraw completely by 1994. Symbolically, at least, the 'Two Plus Four' Treaty represented the long-postponed post-war peace treaty. This was particularly so with regard to the Oder–Neiße line, which was now finally and irrevocably declared to be the eastern border of Germany, much to the chagrin of many former expellees. Unification in October 1990 brought the geopolitical impact of the rift between the Allies to an end. Germany, then, was now truly united and free of occupation.

There are those who would argue that these dramatic developments went to Kohl's head. In the years after unification, conservative west German politicians hardly missed an opportunity to condemn the GDR for its hypocritical identification with the Soviet liberators. Yet in 1995, it seemed as if Kohl was only too ready to identify with the Allies – not just with the Americans, as at Bitburg, nor just with the Soviets, à la GDR, but with *all* the Allies. In May, he embarked on an extensive, if rapid tour during which he took part in British end-of-war commemorations in London on 7 May 1995, French ones in Paris on 8 May, and Russian commemorations on 9 May. Indeed his participation suggested that Germany, now that it was united, had matured *post hoc* into one of the Allies, shedding its historical skin to slip into an altogether more distinguished one. The term 'role reversal' comes to mind. In appearing at the side of the Allies, Kohl seemed to imply that what was significant now was not the Allied liberation of Germany in 1945, but the end of varying degrees of occupation in 1990 and the acknowledgement of Germany as a moral and political equal. Kohl's critics complained of his lack of humility. In reference to the planned 8 May commemoration in Berlin, historian Klaus Naumann acidly observed that the CDU was planning 'One plus Four' celebrations. Instead of remembering 8 May in a purely national ceremony, the government, claimed Naumann, was cranking up the wheels of diplomacy to ensure all former victors would attend. Their function, as 'guarantors' of unification, would be to sanction and confirm Germany's new place in the European and global constellation (*Freitag*, 7 April 1995).

Naumann feared a kind of mega-conciliation ceremony, which he called 'Bitburg Part Two'. In the event, the official commemorative act on the evening of 8 May in the Berlin *Schauspielhaus* (a theatre) was rather low-key, but Naumann's fears were nevertheless borne out to a degree. Al Gore represented Bill Clinton, Victor Chernomyrdin represented Boris Yeltsin. John Major and François Mitterrand, however, attended in person. Given that the Russians had suffered more under Hitler than any other nation, their attendance was a significant reminder of German aggression and atrocities. But their presence did serve to sanction symbolically Germany's inclusion among a now reunited set of Allies. Obligingly, Chernomyrdin in his speech maintained that the division into victors and vanquished no longer applied, that Russia and Germany had embarked along the road of historical conciliation, and new perspectives of German–Russian cooperation had opened up (*TSP*, 9 May 1995). Given the heavily westernized nature of the official commemoration, it appeared to represent as much a tentative acceptance of Russia by the western league of democracies as an all-round act of conciliation with Germany. Things had changed since 1990. Russia looked to Germany for economic and political help, as well as – given the threat posed by planned NATO and EU eastern expansion to Russia's sense of security –

understanding. The ceremony in Berlin turned into a confirmation of Germany's central role in the restructuring of Europe.

Neither the Poles nor the Czechs were invited to Berlin, chiefly because they were political lightweights. They were not in a position to sanction anything. Indeed they were 'receiver' countries. Their role, in the eyes of many in the CDU, was to regard themselves as dependent on German support and aid. Both these countries were victims of National Socialism, rather than victors over it. Their presence would have swung the pendulum towards too strong a focus on German guilt. Besides, conservatives were still indignant at the irrevocable loss of the eastern territories following the confirmation of the Oder–Neiße line as Germany's eastern border in 1990. As for the Czechs, they were less prepared to put the memory of Nazi atrocities behind them, it seemed, than the Allies. Inviting the Czechs would, moreover, have drawn international attention to the scandal of the so-called *Junktim*, whereby the CDU–FDP government was only prepared to grant compensation to 17,000 Czech victims of National Socialism if the Czechs agreed to grant compensation to the Sudeten Germans.

To be fair, the problem of the neglect of the Poles and Czechs was to a degree rectified. After massive protest within Germany, particularly at the exclusion of the Poles, Kohl asked Parliamentary President Rita Süssmuth (CDU) to invite Poland – represented by Foreign Minister and former Auschwitz prisoner Bartoszewski – to a separate commemorative act on 28 April held jointly by the Federal Council and Federal government. This did something to allay the anger of the Poles. As for the Czechs, a top-level meeting between Czech President Havel and German Federal President Roman Herzog was hastily agreed at the beginning of May 1995, and Foreign Minister Klaus Kinkel (FDP) came under pressure, not least from within his own party, to review the *Junktim*. Germany's blushes were also saved somewhat by the Federal system. The *Länder* organized their own 8 May acts of remembrance. This gave the east German *Länder* and east German politicians the chance to demonstrate that sense of solidarity with eastern Europe inherited from the GDR. Brandenburg's Minister President Manfred Stolpe (SPD) attended a joint Polish–German commemoration in Zielona Gora on 6 May, where he explicitly stressed the contribution of Poles who had fought in Allied units, and highlighted the suffering and destruction visited on Poland by the Germans during the war (*TSP*, 7 May 1995). Another east German SPD Minister President, Reinhard Höppner, invited Poland, Hungary, the Czech Republic and even the Baltic States to Saxony-Anhalt's official act of remembrance on 7 May 1995. Höppner was one of the most vehement critics of Kohl's invitation politics, arguing that they created the inappropriate impression that 'Germany was on the side of the victors' (*TSP*, 8 April 1995).

It was not just Germany's new-found unity and sovereignty, nor its magnified importance, which put Kohl in victorious mood: it was also his understanding of his own and West Germany's role in bringing unification about. The conservative west German reading of unification is, commonly, that it represented the victory of western-style democracy and market capitalism over gerontocratic socialism. This reading overlooks the fact that the *Wende*, initially at least, was a call for more rights, but not necessarily for westernization or even western-style democracy. For the conservatives, West Germany appeared to have 'liberated' East Germany. 'Freedom and democracy on the other side of the former Iron Curtain', Kohl wrote in his 8 May 1995 declaration, 'could only be achieved [. . .] after the end of the communist dictatorship' (*TSP*, 6 May 1995). While this is true, by using the passive mood, Kohl plays down the role of the East Germans as actors in their own revolution. It was their protest in the autumn of 1989, not West Germany, which brought the SED to its knees and secured basic freedoms. Equations of 1945 with 1989–1990 are politically dubious because they suggest that the second act of liberation (or self-liberation, from the east German perspective) somehow cancels out the debt to the Allies created by the first. They also obliterate the essential distinction that, while the GDR was a result of Soviet occupation, National Socialism was a purely German product.

Thus it was also Kohl's view of himself as 'liberator' of the GDR that prompted him to seek a place among the former Allies. Even the SPD, when it took up government in 1998, continued the practice of playing down the role of the East Germans. The official state celebrations to mark the tenth anniversary of the fall of the Wall in November 1999 nearly took place without an east German speaker. Only after massive protests was Joachim Gauck invited to deliver a speech. In September 2000, immediately prior to the 10th anniversary of unification, Kohl launched an attack on the SPD's alleged failure to support the cause of German unity, particularly in 1989 and 1990. A petty party-political squabble ensued which conveyed the impression that the only forces whose role in the pre-unification period was worth discussing were the SPD and CDU.

The positive side of conciliation

There can be little doubt that, in 1995, Kohl was in many respects celebrating the end of the post-war era, rather than commemorating the end of the war. At last, Germany was equal among equals, perhaps even *primus inter pares*. In an interview on the German television channel SAT1, Kohl had claimed: 'We are number one in Europe. The leadership role is there, not because we are looking for it, it's just there' (reported in *FR*, 12 May 1995). It is debatable whether Kohl would have been able to make such a remark without the all-round conciliation in which he had just participated. He thus soon set about instrumentalizing it. But it would be wrong to imply that only Kohl had been interested in conciliation. It was Major who invited Kohl to London on 7 May, Mitterrand who invited him to Paris on 8 May: Kohl did not invite himself. It was even suggested by the media that Mitterrand had *wanted* to be invited to Germany on 8 May. Having invited Mitterrand, Kohl could hardly fail to invite the other former Allies. In 1995 there was a noticeably conciliatory tone towards Germany on the part of some countries on which it had inflicted great suffering. This was the result, in part, of an increasing readiness of these countries to acknowledge their own cooperation with National Socialism. In her Christmas address to the nation in 1994, Queen Beatrix asked the Dutch nation to stretch out a hand of friendship to the Germans: 'after repression comes liberation, but after liberation comes conciliation' (*Spiegel*, 21 January 1995). She also focused on the issue of collaboration, challenging assumptions that the Dutch had been united in opposition to Hitler (some 25,000 Dutch people had served in the SS). The Norwegians also acknowledged collaboration on 8 May 1995. The 1990s have been marked by revelations of collaboration, as well as of profiteering from the fate of the Jews, throughout Europe between 1939 and 1945. The recent trend towards the 'globalization' of remembrance, with several European countries introducing Holocaust Remembrance Days (including Britain), has much to do with an increasing awareness that connivance at or passive acceptance of Nazi criminality was a phenomenon not limited to Germans.

There is a certain logic, as well as historical fairness, in these developments. As European countries grow together and shape a common future, they discover a common past of the *wrong* kind of collaboration. It may be a psychological truism, but conceding past errors and failings creates a basis for mutual trust in the present. Without this there can be no united Europe. President Havel of the Czech Republic may be reluctant to grant rights of compensation or restitution to the Sudeten Germans, but he is in no doubt that their expulsion was carried out in a violent and unjust manner. On 8 May 1995, he asked the Czechs to find the strength to condemn all forms of injustice and atrocity inflicted on the Sudeten Germans after the war (*FAZ*, 9 May 1995). In January 1997, the German–Czech Declaration was signed, in which both countries acknowledged injustices committed during and after the war (see Hofhaensel 1999: 113–16). However, there were moments when the spirit of international conciliation in 1995 took on exonerative forms. President Mitterrand went too far when, in his 8 May speech, he defended the 'patriotism' and 'courage' of German soldiers during the Second World War. 'We are creating Europe, we love our fatherlands', he continued (*Welt*, 11 May 1995). The devastation of the Soviet Union by the *Wehrmacht* was hardly an act of patriotism worthy of emulation. Sadly, Mitterrand's speech was abused by conservative defenders of the *Wehrmacht* within Germany.

As far as the Jews are concerned, conciliation was also something they, to a degree at least, sought. The rebuilt Jewish Synagogue in Oranienburg Street in Berlin was opened on 8 May 1995. Work on the rebuilding had begun under Honecker, and it ended under Kohl – one of the few major GDR cultural projects to be continued by united Germany. It symbolized the reconstruction of Jewish life in Berlin, and German commitment to this reconstruction. But it was not a reconstruction based on forgetting: the ruins of the main synagogue remain, as a reminder of the destruction of Berlin's Jews (see Chapter Eight). That conciliation was not to proceed without remembering was confirmed in another way. On 15 May 1995, the leaders of the parliamentary parties in Federal Parliament took up the suggestion of Ignatz Bubis, then President of the Central Council of Jews in Germany, that a day of remembrance for the holocaust be introduced: this was to be 27 January (the day of the liberation of Auschwitz). At the beginning of June 1995, Kohl visited Israel and was very well received. Minister President Rabin described his visit as a 'milestone' in the development of German–Israeli relations (*FAZ*, 9 June 1995), and the Institute for European Studies at Jerusalem's Hebrew

University was renamed the Helmut-Kohl-Institute in honour of Kohl's contribution to the European Union and relations between Europe and Israel.

Moreover, while the official 8 May act in Berlin did foreground forward-looking conciliation, there were other moments when Kohl showed he had not forgotten why this conciliation was necessary. Kohl's handling of the theme of the Nazi past has always been somewhat cautious. Throughout his chancellorship, his commemorative speeches displayed a typical tendency to pin sole responsibility for the war on Hitler or the Nazi Party, while implicitly exonerating the broad mass of Germans. 1995 was no exception in this regard. But 1995 was significant in that his condemnation of Nazism and his sympathy for its victims were expressed with unusual clarity and vigour. In Moscow on 9 May 1995, he stressed the 'millionfold misery which Hitler's war brought to the Russians and the other peoples of the Soviet Union' (*STZ*, 10 May 1995). In a speech in Holland on 22 May, he said succinctly: 'the attack on Rotterdam was a crime, the occupation of Holland was a crime, the whole war unleashed by Hitler was a crime' (*Welt*, 23 May 1995). A day or two after the Holland speech, in the context of German–Czech negotiations on the issue of compensation for the Sudeten Germans, Kohl said: 'Only the incorrigible can dispute that the primary cause of the expulsion tragedy has to be sought in the Nazi takeover in 1933. Responsibility for the war of aggression in the east, first against the Poles and then the Soviet Union, is equally clear' (*FAZ*, 2 June 1995). Overall, Kohl's commitment to conciliation in 1995 was an awkward mixture of self-celebration, self-stylization as victor, brash self-confidence and moments of apparently genuine remorse and awareness with regard to Nazi crimes.

That conciliation in 1995 was based on ceremonies involving the four Allies, moreover, need not only be read negatively. These ceremonies were also a symbolical realization of the post-unification chance for Germans, in east and west, to acknowledge their indebtedness to *all* the Allies, rather than to some or only one of them. It was no longer possible to play off one set against the other. The very fact that the Russians were invited to Berlin represented a significant concession to their role in 1945 on the part of the CDU. In 1995, politicians of all parties took the opportunity to stress that 8 May had been a day of liberation. Helmut Kohl did so in his 8 May Declaration, as did the leader of the CSU, Edmund Stoiber, in his speech to mark the anniversary in Aschaffenburg (*BS*, 12 May 1995). The FDP presidency, in its 8 May Berlin Declaration, stated that 8 May means 'remembering the liberation from the Nazi dictatorship and from the most terrible war in the history of Europe' (*TSP*, 9 May 1995). An SPD statement declared that, on 8 May 1945, the 'millionfold murder and terrible repression [. . .] came to an end. For this reason, 8 May was a day of liberation from dictatorship and rule of violence' (*FR*, 4 May 1995). For the first time, such comments came across as expressions of thanks to *all* those countries responsible for bringing this liberation about.

Where has all the German suffering gone?

According to some surveys, the view that 8 May represented a liberation was also shared by the public at large. An Allensbach Institute survey of 2,000 Germans of all ages found that 64% associated 8 May with peace, 63% with a new start, 62% with a feeling of relief and 54% with the hope of a better future (*Welt*, 25 April 1995). According to the FORSA Institute, of 1,001 young people interviewed, 79% saw 8 May 1945 as a day of liberation (*Woche*, 5 May 1995). Germany's New Right warned against an overemphasis on the notion of liberation and pointed to the danger of German suffering being elided from the historical picture. It even instigated the publication of an appeal entitled '8 May 1945 – Against Forgetting' in which reference was made to the need to remember expulsion, Soviet repression and the division of Germany (*FAZ*, 7 April 1995). Among the 296 co-signatories were not only high-ranking conservative politicians, such as Alfred Dregger (CDU), but also the deputy heads of the extremist Republicans Ottmar Wallner and Ingeborg Seifert, former general state lawyer Alexander von Stahl (FDP) and even former SPD Defence Minister Hans Apel. In securing this range of signatures, Rainer Zitelmann (FDP) and Heimo Schwilk sought to create the impression that their protest was an inter-party, truly broad-ranging initiative from far right to, at least, centre-left.

This initiative was based on a false premise. It cannot be legitimately claimed that the Germans were in the course of forgetting their past pain. Indeed the east Germans had begun to rediscover their negative memories. When the GDR came to an end in 1990, its official 8 May dogma, namely that East Germany had been liberated by a kind of Soviet–German communist joint effort, also came to an end. With the legitimate discrediting of this aspect of anti-fascism, east Germans had to confront the fact that their parents or grandparents had not liberated themselves in 1945. On the other hand, surviving members of the war generation at last had a chance to express publicly feelings of personal grief and pain associated with the end of the war. The exclusive emphasis on 8 May 1945 as a day of liberation in East Germany represented a devaluation and silencing of negative personal experience. Particularly moving in 1995 were the ceremonies in Dresden and Potsdam in remembrance of the bombing of these cities in 1944 and 1945 respectively. The SED had instrumentalized the bombings for purposes of anti-Western propaganda. The GDR opposition movement sought by contrast to interpret the ruined Dresden *Frauenkirche* as a symbol of the need for peace between East and West. It was not until 1995 that public remembrance ceremonies acquired a self-critical note *and* allowed significant scope for mourning. Potsdam's Church superintendent Hans-Ulrich Schulz told the crowds gathered on 14 April 1995 that 'we made of the air a place for bombers, over Guernica and Rotterdam, Coventry and Leningrad'. Yet Schulz also spoke of the need for the town to allow itself to feel 'pain at its destroyed buildings'. Such pain, said Schulz, had for decades been regarded in the GDR with suspicion as 'an expression of reactionary German nationalism' (*Welt*, 15–16 April 1995).

Suffering endured after the war had not been forgotten either. This was clear from the mass media coverage in 1994 of the 50th anniversary of the beginnings of ethnic cleansing in eastern Europe. Series on German television in 1995 covered both the negative and positive impact of the Allied victory. For the first time, too, the issue of the rape of over a million German women by the advancing Red

Army in 1944–1945 was adequately presented in the media. In the GDR, the invitation to identify with the Soviet liberators had certainly not been accepted by all. Indeed for those women who had been raped, it represented a cynical invalidation of their agonies. During the *Wende*, east German writer Christoph Hein published a short story examining how one individual sought, with negative consequences, to elide her own memory of the rape of her grandmother in line with the official view of the Soviets as liberators (*ND*, 2–3 October 1989). Arguably, too, the end of the GDR made it possible for expellees living there to express their memories of expulsion without being accused of fascist revisionism. Equally, the final recognition of the Oder–Neiße line as Germany's eastern border in 1990, far from putting an end to memories of expulsion, set them free – potentially at least – from politicization.

A glance at official speeches from April and May 1995 reveals a widespread concern to acknowledge German pain. Thus Kohl stressed in his 8 May declaration the 'mourning of expellees and fugitives for the country of their childhood'. 8 May awakens 'manifold memories', for which 'there is no common denominator' (*TSP*, 6 May 1995). The FDP Berlin Declaration stated that calling 8 May 1945 a day of liberation does 'not exclude individual memory of and mourning over repression, suffering, expulsion and division' (*TSP*, 9 May 1995). The SPD pointed out that, despite liberation, the 'effects of the war continued, indeed for millions of expellees and prisoners the suffering and injustice continued in some cases up to the present day' (*FR*, 4 May 1995). On 25 April 1995, the Catholic Church issued a statement in which 8 May was defined as a day of liberation; but the statement also acknowledged that many hopes were dashed by division and the Cold War (*Welt*, 26 April 1995). In some statements and speeches, liberation was not mentioned first or given priority over personal pain. Edmund Stoiber (CSU) saw 8 May 1945 as characterized by a 'simultaneity of opposites', 'of joy and mourning, hope and despair, liberation and new enslavement, preservation and loss of homeland' (*BS*, 12 May 1995). According to a ZDF television survey, which came to a slightly different conclusion to the abovementioned surveys, 41% of Germans saw 8 May 1945 as both defeat and liberation (*Bild*, 13 April 1995).

Given that German pain was recognized, why did the New Right claim it was not? The New Right objected not just to the prioritization of liberation over pain, but also to any suggestion that both should be remembered in equal measure. It wished for a prioritization of pain. By incorrectly asserting that pain was not being acknowledged at all, it hoped to awaken more sympathy for this pain and shift the weight of remembrance more towards it. The New Right dismayed of a Germany that declined to draw political capital from indignation at past suffering. Kohl in his 8 May 1995 speech had implicitly identified the sufferings of Germans and Jews, perpetrator nation and victims, and his 1993 concept for the *Neue Wache* (see Chapter Eight) reflected in part the tone of Bitburg. But, when the chips were down, Kohl did acknowledge on the international stage the primacy of National Socialist atrocities, and he did not allow memories of German suffering to over-influence his foreign policy. He wanted conciliation, not confrontation. The New Right foregrounded German suffering, hoping to use it in the bid to create a less ashamed, more demanding and assertive Germany. Kohl's conciliation policy towards the Allies was felt by the New Right to stem from a shame-driven rather than a suffering-driven politics. Such a policy would lead, it was feared, to a strengthening of the already strong western and transatlantic alliance, and to further integration for united Germany, rather than its emancipation and self-determination. Seen from this perspective, Kohl's conciliation politics appear positively liberal and modest, aimed as they were at 'merely' making Germany the equal of the former Allies. The New Right's emphasis on German suffering was effectively a reactionary throwback to West German remembrance of 8 May under Adenauer. In the event, its protest crumbled. On 9 April 1995, Hans Apel withdrew his signature from the 'Against Forgetting' advertisement, and on 26 April the FDP signatories distanced themselves from the extreme right-wing signatories. Finally, on 28 April, an event planned by the New Right in Munich for 7 May which would have highlighted Allied injustice towards Germans was cancelled when Alfred Dregger, possibly under pressure from the CDU, withdrew his support.

Political and personal

The New Right reacted allergically to an inevitable, if gradual diminution in the political value of German pain after unification. Philosopher Jürgen Habermas has distinguished between the purely 'psychological' experience of 8 May 1945 and the political understanding that the date had acquired over time (Habermas 1995: 167). Right up to unification, West Germany's litanies of German pre- and post-1945 suffering served to draw attention to the wound of division. Now, this wound is closed. While German suffering has lost most of its political leverage, liberation has not, indeed a line seems to lead from 8 May 1945 to the present. Liberation, to quote Kohl, 'was necessary in order to create a state of law based on liberal values in Germany, and make possible peace and conciliation between peoples in Europe' (*TSP*, 6 May 1995). One could argue, then, that the consensus in 1995 attributed less political relevance to the experiences of bombing, rape, expulsion and socialist injustice than to those of liberation, democratization, unification and conciliation. The former are now largely historical; the latter represent a continuing process and commitment. But while these negative experiences may have been relegated somewhat to the *political* sidelines, they have not been devalued. There was a sense that they were as personally and historically important as the fact of liberation, *post hoc*, was politically and nationally important.

Indeed it seemed as if these experiences were being 'returned' to the individuals who endured them. As a result, they acquired nuanced biographical contours. Instead of a politicized victimization narrative, there were victims. It became possible, as President Herzog demonstrated in Dresden in reference to the bombing of the city, to remember such victims without seeking to cancel out National Socialist atrocities (*FAZ*, 14 February 1995). Of course there was still self-pity. But politicians insisted on the need to set this in context. During the Federal Parliament's commemorative ceremony at the end of April 1995, Rita Süssmuth stressed the connection between 1933 and 1945, the sequence of cause and effect. Without

National Socialism, there would have been no expulsion from the eastern territories (*TSP*, 29 April 1995). Moreover, perhaps the very depoliticization of German suffering could pave the way for pity and regret on the part of the Czechs and Poles. And is not self-pity but a substitute for the pity denied by others? It was the Polish Foreign Minister Bartoszewski who, in his speech in the German Parliament, pointed out that the unification of Germany and the fixing of its eastern boundaries meant that discussions about 'lost homelands' could now be conducted without fear of a threat to peace (*TSP*, 29 April 1995). In acknowledging the suffering of the German expellees in 1945, he demonstrated that the resolution of the border issue had made it easier to express regret at Polish injustice.

Certainly 1995 saw an upsurge of personal memory – on the part both of Germans and of their victims – the likes of which Germany had never witnessed. Of course the war generation was slowly dying out. The tribute to personal experience in 1995 therefore had a valedictory tone. It was an intense tribute indeed. Many books appeared anthologizing the diverse and complex manner in which the end of the war had been experienced by different people, ordinary and famous, Jews and Germans, soldiers in the *Wehrmacht*, but deserters too, German mothers and children in the Hitler Youth, communists and loyal Hitlerites. Attempts were made to compartmentalize these experiences. Thus one volume grouped the subjective narratives under 'The Military Collapse', 'Desertion at the Last Moment', 'Liberation from the Concentration Camp', 'End of the War and Imprisonment', 'After the Nights of Bombing', 'The Long Road West' and 'In the Service of the Russians and Americans' (Trampe 1995; other volumes include Bechtel 1997, Filmer and Schwan 1995, and Apel 1995). Such categories failed, however, to disperse the impression of disparate experience. These collections of memories resembled a post-modern kaleidoscope, yet surely reflected the truth. They undermined, for instance, black-and-white clichés about evil Russians and good Americans. They revealed that individuals who see 1945 in terms of liberation have their own particular day which they associate with this experience – usually before 8 May 1945, by which time Germany had largely been liberated. They revealed memories shot through with positive and negative elements. They revealed processes of shock, relief, loss, shame, guilt, disappointment and anger. Some people lay in hospital on 8 May 1945, oblivious to the world. Others were in American or Soviet POW camps. Jews emerged from hiding in the ruins of Berlin, freed at last from the double burden of isolation and bombing. Or, as in the case of Inge Deutschkron, free only for minutes before hiding once more to protect herself against the danger of being raped by the Russians.

Of all the cultural manifestations of this diversity, it was surely Volker Schlöndorff's film *The Ogre* (*Der Unhold*), after a novel by the French writer Michael Tournier, which was the most articulate and moving. It was shown in cinemas around Germany in 1996. Towards the end of the film, Russian tanks advance on an elite Nazi school where young Germans selected for their racial purity have been left in the hands of a rather simple French prisoner-of-war, Abel, played by John Malkovich. He tries to persuade them to flee, but is beaten to the ground as they prepare a senseless act of resistance. Riding around the forests of East Prussia,

Abel encounters different sets of people: concentration-camp prisoners on a death march (two prisoners are graphically shot by the accompanying SS), other French captives, now liberated, making their way home, and east European Germans fleeing from the Red Army. The film has its weaknesses, but these concluding scenes of dark, terrible and bewildering confusion are among the greatest in recent German cinema.

In conclusion

Commemoration in 1995, as suggested at the outset of this chapter, combined elements of East German and West German traditions of remembrance. On the negative side, Kohl's rather celebratory official style of conciliation echoed both the self-congratulatory tone of SED commemoration and the exculpatory 'handshake across graves' at Bitburg. The strong focus on liberation also recalled SED commemoration. In contrast to the latter, however, the nature of this focus was frequently self-critical, adopting the reflective tone of remembrance which had been developed by Willy Brandt and Richard von Weizsäcker in the 1970s and 1980s. Nor was the focus exclusive. Memory of German suffering, a West rather than an East German tradition, still played a significant part in remembrance. But – a new development – it was now largely depoliticized, opening up possibilities for a form of remembrance in which this suffering was important *as suffering*, rather than as a rhetorical weapon in the Cold War. A further new development was that, while acts of conciliation in both West and East Germany, in the interest of the Cold War, had been predominantly one-sided, in 1995 they were more international, generally less strained, and achieved in the name of a new European order of peace. Some critics have seen in this emphasis on peace an unexpected triumph of the GDR's model of remembrance. There is limited validity in this point of view. United Germany's concept of peace, unlike that typical of GDR antifascism, appears entirely sincere and non-combative; besides, the rhetoric of peace also played a part in West German remembrance before 1990. Generally, then, the 'integrated' model of memory in 1995 can be welcomed, with reservations. If there were nevertheless doubts as to Germany's continued willingness to confront its role during the Third Reich, these were surely dispelled one year later. 1996 saw the third debate on the National Socialist past in as many years, and it was triggered by a single person – Daniel Jonah Goldhagen.

5 Daniel Jonah Goldhagen and Victor Klemperer

'The book is a deliberate provocation – I consider this a neutral judgment.'

(Fritz Stern 1996: 128)

'Goldhagen's book is [. . .] an offensive book and this in two senses: it arouses indignation and provokes.'

(Herbert Jäger 1997: 85)

Success

In early 1996, Daniel Jonah Goldhagen's doctoral thesis was published in the USA under the title *Hitler's Willing Executioners: Ordinary Germans and the Holocaust* (Goldhagen 1996a). The book, built on the generalizing hypothesis that the vast majority of Germans during the Third Reich shared Hitler's paranoic hatred of Jews, became a bestseller. By spring 1997, sales had topped 350,000 in the United States. The German translation of the book, published in early August 1996, had sold 180,000 copies by March 1997. It soared to the top of the bestseller list, relegating Chancellor Kohl's *I wanted German Unity* (*Ich wollte Deutschlands Einheit*) to third place (*Spiegel*, 16 December 1996). This was an astonishing achievement for a young scholar. What made it even more astonishing was that the book was for the most part dismissed by historians. They protested at the use of what were perceived to be dubious marketing techniques by Goldhagen and his publishers, who had supposedly hoodwinked the public into believing that the book broke radically with traditional holocaust studies. The press, for its part, was blamed for broadcasting this claim to the world at large: the helpless public had fallen victim to sensationalist media hype. Critics of the book in the USA put down its success to its 'implicit political agenda', an agenda which confirmed American anti-German prejudice while glorifying the American democratic and moral tradition. Goldhagen was charged with peddling an emotive, prejudice-driven Zionism. In Germany, there was a considerable degree of helplessness as German historians struggled to explain the positive impact of a 'bad book' on the German public. When Goldhagen toured Germany in September 1996, he was hailed as a star. Was it his handsomeness? The fact that, for some, he looked like Tom Hanks? Was it his engagingly polite, well-educated and discrete manner? His suave, well-dressed appearance? Was his popularity linked to German masochism? A reaction against the commemorative rituals of 1995, which for some at least represented the drawing of a line under the past? With not a little arrogance, most German historians dismissed the notion that Goldhagen's appeal might be connected to any substantive merits in his arguments. They argued that the ordinary Germans of today were too naive to understand the holocaust as it really had been: hence their enthusiasm for Goldhagen's 'fantasy version'.

One striking feature of the critical rejection of Goldhagen's book in Germany was that it did not follow the predictable political patterns. In contrast to the 'Crimes of the *Wehrmacht*' exhibition (Chapter Six), which was largely viewed positively by left-liberal historians, the SPD and Greens, and negatively by the CDU and CSU, Goldhagen's book was criticized by all political parties and by historians right across the political spectrum. In fact, left-liberal historians were so indignant at the book that the New Right by and large sat quietly back and allowed them to do the work of demontage. This degree of consensus made the public support for Goldhagen seem almost defiant, ill-disciplined. Again in contrast to the 'Crimes of the *Wehrmacht*' exhibition, there were no verbal or physical altercations when Goldhagen toured German cities – with the notable exception of a few scuffles in the scramble for tickets. During podium discussions in August 1996 in German cities, the dividing line was not just between German historians and Goldhagen. Goldhagen enjoyed the noticeable support of audiences. The general public demonstrated irritation at the objections of its own historians. While in each discussion Goldhagen appeared to modify his position, he never really did. By contrast, German historians were forced, in some frustration, to take their public and its support for Goldhagen more seriously. The 1996 Goldhagen debate, I believe, was marked by an intriguing discrepancy between public and historiographical memory. It also led in the public realm to a greater awareness of the holocaust and of the extent of German involvement.

Holocaust historiography and Goldhagen's book

Before outlining the central tenets of Goldhagen's book, we must first look briefly at the history of previous research into the holocaust. The chain of events which led to the holocaust, the Nazi genocide of European Jews which resulted in 6 million deaths, has long been and still is a subject of intense debate. Generally speaking, two schools of historiographical thought have evolved over the past decades. The first, which emerged in the late 1960s and has been called the 'intentionalist' school, argues that the primal cause of the genocide was Hitler himself (Dawidowicz 1975 and Fleming 1984). There is disagreement as to when Hitler developed genocidal intentions, and as to when these intentions became hard and fast plans (for an overview of contrasting opinions, see Browning 2000: 26–34). Intentionalists have also presented a range of possible dates for the issuing of the Führer order to exterminate Europe's Jews. Thus it could have been when Hitler attacked Poland, or just before he attacked the Soviet Union in June 1941; it could have been at the height of the success of Operation Barbarossa; or it could have been in late autumn 1941, in frustration perhaps at the stagnation of the eastern front. But intentionalists are unanimous in their conviction that, without Hitler and without his explicit order, there would have been no holocaust. They point to evidence of his rabid hatred of Jews, and indications of his wish to exterminate them, in some of his earliest writings and speeches from the time of the Weimar Republic (1918–1933), and in a few of his major speeches during the Third Reich itself (such as his *Reichstag* speech of 30 January 1939). For many intentionalists, the socially discriminatory measures against Jews introduced by Hitler after 1933 are the precursors to genocide, perhaps even carefully conceived stages in a masterplan directed towards ultimate annihilation.

In the late 1970s and 1980s, a second school of thought came to the fore which took issue with the intentionalist line of argument. This school, known as 'functionalism' or 'structuralism', did not deny the influence of Hitler altogether, but it did see it as less prominent. Thus German historian Martin Broszat argued that, while Hitler certainly strove to clear Germany of Jews, he was less specific about what was to happen to them subsequently; Jews were deported eastwards, and Nazi officials in the occupied eastern territories were then left with the conundrum of what to do with them (Broszat 1979). Functionalists have pointed to the manner in which solutions to the 'Jewish problem' spiralled gradually towards destruction, a process Hans Mommsen has defined as 'cumulative radicalization' (see, for instance, *Zeit*, 30 August 1996). This process might be defined as follows. Firstly, in the course of the massive population transfers that took place as the Nazis sought to Germanize parts of eastern Europe, Jews were rounded up, deported and ghettoized in Poland. But ghettos soon became overcrowded. In 1940, the second stage of the process, drastic plans were developed according to which the Jews would have been transported *en masse* to Madagascar (the so-called Madagascar Project). When these plans collapsed, the ghettos became a more long-term feature of Nazi policy, and attempts were made to turn them into economically self-sustaining units (see Aly and Heim 1991). This, the third stage, resulted in a barbarous and often murderous exploitation of human resources. After Hitler's campaign against the Soviet Union had got bogged down in the autumn of 1941, and prospects of deporting Jews further east had waned, mass-murder on an unprecedented scale represented the fourth stage in the radicalization. The extermination of Jews at annihilation camps and elsewhere in eastern Europe was worked out in all its grisly details at the Wannsee Conference in Berlin in early 1942.

Functionalists have emphasized the initiative taken by civil and military German authorities in occupied eastern Europe, even claiming that, in some towns, Jewish pogroms were organized without orders from above and without Hitler's knowledge. The general consensus of the functionalists, however, is that such initiative was not, or at least not generally, murderous from the start. The holocaust was rather the response of the Nazis to their failure to realize other, essentially non-genocidal solutions to the 'Jewish problem'. Somewhat pointedly, Browning has asserted that the intentionalist approach believes the Final Solution to have been like the Manhattan Project, while the functionalist approach assumes it to have been like Chernobyl – the unintended 'by-product of a dysfunctional system' (Browning 2000: 1). But the difference between the schools may not be so great, given that many (but not all) functionalists would admit to the existence of a Hitler order, and some intentionalists would admit to the importance of circumstance and local initiative. Recently, in fact, the schools of intentionalism and functionalism have begun to merge, or at least overlap. Saul Friedländer has developed a 'moderate intentionalism', Browning a 'moderate functionalism' (Bartov 2000b: 5). Philippe Burrin has argued for a 'conditional intentionalism', whereby Hitler intended to launch the holocaust only if he got caught in a war on all fronts (Browning 2000: 26–7). Ultimately, the debate seems to focus on whether the holocaust was more a 'function' of the dead-end situation into which the Nazi occupying forces had manoeuvred themselves, or more the result of a long-held 'intention' harboured by Adolf Hitler (for a good overview of the intentionalist–functionalist debate, see Marrus 1993).

Goldhagen, at first glance, is an intentionalist. He believes that Hitler planned the genocide, and that this plan in essence came into operation when Hitler launched his assault on the Soviet Union (Goldhagen 1996a: 148ff.). What distinguishes Goldhagen's work from that of others in the field of holocaust studies is, firstly, his belief that Hitler's intention was the logical conclusion of an exceptionally virulent tradition of anti-semitism inherent within German history and the German people from the Middle Ages. This tradition he describes as an '"eliminationist" variant' (Goldhagen 1996a: 23), and he has no hesitation in defining it as a 'dominant cultural thread' (Goldhagen 1996a: 47). In the second and third chapters of his book, he examines the form taken by this 'eliminationist anti-semitism' in pre-1933 German history, particularly the 19th century. Turning to National Socialism, Goldhagen argues that it represented a reinforcement of this historically well-rooted 'cultural cognitive model of Jews' (Goldhagen 1996a: 88), or an unshackling of the 'Germans' pre-existing, pent-up antisemitism' (Goldhagen 1996a: 443). In a second departure from established holocaust research, he contends that the vast majority of Germans 'subscribed to the underlying Nazi model of Jews' (Goldhagen 1996a: 87). Far from simply following orders, those who carried through Hitler's murderous plans, from the various Nazi officials at state and local level down to the killers, were responding to the same historical tradition of potentially genocidal hatred as Hitler himself.

In the central sections of his book, Goldhagen sets out to demonstrate the exterminationist anti-semitic motivation of three, in his view, exemplary sets of killers: the police battalions, those who ran Jewish work-camps, and those who oversaw death-marches in the final stages of the war. He devotes particular attention to the members of Police Battalion 101, responsible for atrocities in Poland and Russia, and comes to the conclusion that they had killed Jews because they wanted to: after all, they had been given the chance *not* to take part in the killings, and had largely turned it down. Jewish work-camps such as Lipowa or the Airport Camp in Lublin had been run according to Goldhagen not primarily to extract labour from the Jews, but to make them suffer and die. Goldhagen also sees evidence of the wilful nature of killing in the behaviour of the SS guards who had accompanied the prisoners on their march in summer 1944 from Helmbrechts to Prachatice after Helmbrechts had to be evacuated (Helmbrechts was a satellite camp of

Flossenbürg). Despite the fact that Himmler had explicitly forbidden the killing of any more Jews during such evacuations (Goldhagen 1996a: 356), many of the Jewish women from Helmbrechts were liquidated on the trek. Goldhagen is at pains to argue that the killers were typical. To support this view, he argues that Police Battalion 101 was made up of men who represented a cross-section of German society (Goldhagen 1996a: 205–11). These were 'ordinary Germans', only one third of whom were members of the National Socialist Party, and thus in the main not brainwashed by party ideology. 'What these *ordinary* Germans did', wrote Goldhagen of the police battalions, 'also could have been expected of other *ordinary* Germans' (Goldhagen 1996a: 402).

In other words, as Goldhagen himself puts it, anti-semitism not only moved 'many thousands of "ordinary" Germans' to slaughter Jews, but would also 'have moved millions more, had they been appropriately positioned' (Goldhagen 1996a: 9). *Hitler's Willing Executioners* was new, or at least provocative, because it went beyond a personal intentionalism (Hitler's) to posit the existence of an historical and indeed a national genocidal intentionalism. With a generalizing force untypical of holocaust research over the last three decades, he broadened the concept of intentionalism to breaking point.

The outcome of German history?

The following section provides an overview of the objections to Goldhagen's ideas as they were expressed by both German and non-German historians and critics in the German media. Most, indeed all, of these objections had also been expressed in the American and British media, and subsequently found their way in more detailed form into serious academic publications in the USA and Great Britain (see Birn 1997, Evans 1997 and Finkelstein 1997). Objections in the German press were thus of a piece with the international historiographical response. That German newspapers were keen to publish the critical comments of non-German as well as German historians was almost certainly the result of the wish to ward off any suspicion that criticism of Goldhagen's book might be a purely German phenomenon and, therefore, a national defensive reflex.

The most vehemently opposed aspect of the book was Goldhagen's belief in the existence of a long-standing historical tradition of eliminationist anti-semitism in Germany before the advent of the Third Reich. Historian Arnulf Baring dismissed this in a ZDF podium discussion with Goldhagen as an 'historical lie' (*JA*, 19 September 1996). In a public discussion with Goldhagen in Hamburg, the director of the Topography of Terror in Berlin, Reinhard Rürup, objected that the author had argued as if there had been no enlightenment in Germany, no liberalism and no Jewish emancipation. He pointed out that Jews wanted to settle in Germany prior to 1914, and that with good reason. Moreover, it was the Jews who brought German culture to fruition (*BaZ*, 6 September 1996). Historian Eberhard Jäckel, for whom Goldhagen's study was 'simply bad', complained that Goldhagen had totally failed to incorporate historical research into his account, research which had revealed continuities and discontinuities in German anti-semitism since 1878, and a downfall of anti-semitic parties between 1903 and 1914 (*Zeit*, 17 May 1996). That Goldhagen had ignored evidence of changing degrees of and fluctuations in anti-semitism was made clear by Olaf Blaschke. In a close analysis of Catholic approaches to 'the Jewish question' in 19th century Germany, Blaschke demonstrated that these had been varied; proposals had ranged from complete assimilation to total and partial segregation, expulsion and sporadic ideas of genocide (Blaschke 1998: 63–90). Goldhagen, in other words, was making things too easy in suggesting that German anti-semitism was inherently annihilatory, quite apart from overlooking evidence of positive views on the Jews. Another complaint was that he had failed to support his claim that German anti-semitism was essentially different to that elsewhere. Historian Hans-Ulrich Wehler argued that anti-semitism in the pre-1933 period was an international phenomenon, and that it would not be easy to decide whether German, Russian, French or Austrian anti-semitism was its most dangerous expression (*Zeit*, 24 May 1996). Some believed there were even grounds for arguing that German anti-semitism had been *less* virulent in international comparison. After all, there had been no Dreyfus affair in Germany; there had been no pogroms, in contrast to Russia. Indeed, as German Jewish historian Michael Wolffsohn pointed out, large numbers of eastern European Jews fled to the more tolerant USA and Germany to escape anti-Jewish pogroms at the end of the 19th century (*BM*, 24 April 1996). Persuasively, literary critic Frank Schirrmacher argued that Goldhagen had understood historical processes as driven by a gigantic software program, generating, as its final product, the holocaust (*FAZ*, 15 April 1996). Schirrmacher accused Goldhagen of a 'remythification of the holocaust'. Historian Norbert Frei found Goldhagen's thesis 'monocausal' (*SZ*, 13–14 April 1996), a charge echoed by Austrian historian Walter Manoschek, who believed it to be 'one-dimensional and certainly untenable in its determinism' (*profil*, 29 April 1996).

While Goldhagen argued for the importance of individual responsibility, his book did appear to imply that the Germans were the helpless playthings of a national project, the bits and bytes of an all-powerful computer software, to continue Schirrmacher's analogy, rather than their own agents. National Socialism, Hitler, the SS, the individual killers – all came across as tools of the self-realizing programme of destructive anti-semitism underpinning the course of German history. This had significant, if unintended exculpatory implications. Effectively, as Hans-Ulrich Wehler argued, Goldhagen had created an 'abstruse new variant' of the German special historical path (*Sonderweg*) (Wehler 1996: 200). Wehler had been instrumental in developing the idea that German history in the 19th century was marked by a '"feudalization of the German bourgeoisie" into aristocratic modes of behaviour' (Evans 1997: 13). This view identified a certain backward authoritarianism as one key reason for the development of Nazism. Now, Goldhagen was arguing that it was eliminationist anti-semitism that had given a unique and particular shape to German history. A key figure in opposing revisionist versions of the German past during the Historians' Dispute, Wehler criticized Goldhagen because he saw in his book a danger of the 'ethnicization of the debate on National Socialism'. Wehler believed Goldhagen's arguments to have been inspired by a scheme of thinking comparable to that behind Nazi ideology, with the difference that, in Goldhagen's view, it was the Germans who were the 'accursed people' and the incarnation of evil, rather than the Jews (Wehler 1996: 200). His monolithic reading, critics felt, flew in the face of the attempts by German and other historians to uncover the complexities of the process which had led to the genocide. It also, rather depressingly, suggested that Germans were stuck with their predisposition towards eliminating Jews – this fifty years on after supposed democratization, at least in the west (although, as we shall see, Goldhagen took a surprisingly positive view of West Germany).

Most holocaust historians, including German historians, share the view that German anti-semitism can explain neither Hitler's rise to power, nor – on its own – the holocaust. Hitler's success in 1933, it is generally argued, had much more to do with economic recession and Hitler's promises of national revival; indeed Hitler had come to reduce anti-semitic propaganda in the course of the Weimar Republic, focusing instead on anti-Marxist rhetoric (which remained a central element of his anti-semitic rhetoric after 1933). After coming to power, Hitler introduced anti-semitic measures which led to discrimination against Jews, but many historians are unconvinced that these measures found broad-based popular backing. Certainly the lack of protest against them cannot simply be read as indicating consent. Leading Hitler expert Ian Kershaw writes in his book *The Hitler Myth* that anti-semitism was 'of only secondary importance in cementing the bonds between Führer and people' (Kershaw 1987: 250), and that the 'Jewish question' retained only a relatively low level of importance among the mass of 'ordinary' and 'non-organized' Germans (Kershaw 1987: 252).

The Nazis, of course, did not hesitate to present what were in effect carefully orchestrated acts of anti-semitism as expressions of spontaneous popular will. A good example of this is the *Reichskristallnacht* pogrom of 9–10 November 1938, during which several hundred Jewish synagogues were burnt down, and thousands of Jewish businesses and homes looted and destroyed; 100 Jews were killed, and the Gestapo subsequently incarcerated at least 30,000 Jews in concentration camps. The pogrom was largely the work of the Nazi Party, the SS and the SA; but Goebbels's propaganda machine made the German people responsible, an effective way of concealing the real cause. There was a degree of civilian participation, not least in Berlin, and much passive bystanding. But there were also examples of German civilian protest and resistance; in some small villages, according to German historian Hermann Graml, 'virtually the whole population confronted [. . .] NS functionaries who wanted to launch the pogrom' (Graml 1998: 35). Graml contends that 'larger sections of the population outside of the NSDAP and SA' played no part in initializing the pogroms (Graml 1998: 34). Goldhagen's view is rather that the pogrom was a national enterprise (Goldhagen 1996a: 140–1). In the ZDF podium discussion with Goldhagen, Arnulf Baring took Goldhagen to task for describing the pogrom as a kind of 'popular festival' and surmised that Goldhagen had 'no idea' of the real mood in Germany at the time (*JA*, 19 September 1996).

The irritation at Goldhagen's rather monolithic and drastic view of German anti-semitism both before and after 1933 was certainly understandable. Not just because it was undifferentiated, but also because of its implications for historiography. Goldhagen was seeking to provide a single and conclusive key to the problem of the holocaust: it emerged from a popular eliminationist ethos. If this view were to gain in currency, then holocaust studies would become redundant. Future discussions as to what else apart from anti-semitism led to the holocaust would become pointless. Debates as to when Hitler gave the order would also be senseless, because circumstances would no longer be of importance. Investigations into the extent of anti-semitism in the Third Reich and degrees of German collusion would also become redundant, indeed even frivolous or revisionist. Goldhagen seemed to want to sever the intricate intellectual cabling of previous holocaust research at one stroke.

To be fair to Goldhagen, he repeatedly insisted he had been misunderstood. Firstly, he claimed that there was no reference in his book to 'an unchangeable anti-semitic German national character': 'it is rather a matter of political culture, whose development I explain historically'. Secondly, 'I also do not claim the holocaust was inevitable; without Hitler and the Nazi accession to power, there would certainly have been no holocaust' (*BddB*, 7 May 1996). While his protest appeared sincere, his claims were not borne out by his book. Terms such as a 'powerful subterranean anti-Jewish animus', used by Goldhagen in reference to 19th century Germany, seemed to describe something altogether more sinister than a political culture (Goldhagen 1996a: 73). In his book, Hitler and his movement came across as executors of a 'pre-existing genocidal potential' (Goldhagen 1996a: 126).

Why were the orders carried out?

Given that they believed Goldhagen to have overstated the extent of anti-semitism amongst 'ordinary' Germans during the Third Reich, it was only logical that German historians would also take issue with his contention that it was anti-semitism which had driven many Germans to murder Jews. Doyen of German historians Hans Mommsen argued in contrast to Goldhagen for a multicausal explanation of the holocaust (*Zeit*, 30 August 1996). Norbert Frei maintained that 'anti-semitism is only one, and not an adequate explanation for the holocaust' (*FR*, 9 September 1996). Hanno Loewy believed Goldhagen's monocausal theory to be, essentially, a tautology: 'the Germans murdered the Jews because they wanted to murder the Jews' (*FR*, 15 June 1996). An article by Hannes Heer on Goldhagen was even titled 'The Great Tautology' (*taz*, 4 September 1996). Loewy and Heer implied that it is obvious that anti-semitism played a major role, but that, taken on its own, it did not, or did not always, possess a destructive force. At all levels of responsibility for the holocaust, from the bureaucrat sitting at his desk down to the individual killer, motivation was more complex, a mixture of racist ideology, obedience to authority, careerist zeal, opportunism, frustration, even moral blindness and perhaps, on occasion, fear. Christopher Browning had illustrated this complexity particularly well in his study of a group of direct perpetrators, Police

Battalion 101 (Browning 1992a), a group also analysed by Goldhagen. Browning highlighted motivational factors such as situational and peer pressure (factors summarily dismissed by Goldhagen [Goldhagen 1996a: 383–6]). Again and again critics of Goldhagen's book pointed out that the police battalions in eastern Europe had also murdered Poles and Slavs, not just Jews. Anti-semitism was clearly not, or not just, the motivation there. Indeed why did the National Socialists also liquidate Sinti and Roma? Why had they instituted a euthanasia programme *before* the systematic murder of Jews? What also undermined Goldhagen's argument was the fact that a number of men from Luxemburg also took part in 101's murderous enterprise (see Browning 1996). Indeed non-Germans, not least Ukrainians and Latvians, also took part in killing Jews (Heil 1996: 246).

Goldhagen's arguments appear to founder, ultimately, on their apparently most persuasive aspect: the issue of voluntarism. If, as Goldhagen writes, police battalion members had the option to say 'no' to the killing, then those who did say 'no' are as relevant as those who did not. He did not address this issue adequately, presumably because the existence of refusal would indicate that a number of Germans were not genocidally anti-semitic, perhaps not anti-semitic at all. But let us assume, for a moment, that Goldhagen is right, and that Germans at the time were uniformly anti-semitic. In that case, the men who refused can only have done so because they found the orders unacceptable *despite* their anti-semitism. It was not genocidal in character. This then makes us wonder if the anti-semitism of those who agreed to the killings was not equally non-genocidal. Could it even be that they agreed for a number of reasons that had nothing to do with anti-semitism? If so, what was the relative influence of these? Browning came to the conclusion that 'the existence of a small minority of non-shooters suggests the existence of an even larger group of accommodators drawn from the indifferent majority of German society, who did not share the regime's ideological priorities but despite initial reluctance and lack of enthusiasm became killers' (Browning 1996: 92). With reference to Helmbrechts, another of Goldhagen's voluntaristic examples, Hannes Heer pointed out that, while Himmler had indeed ordered that the Jews not be killed during marches, this order did not repeal an earlier one according to which prisoners unable to walk, or those who tried to flee, were to be killed (*taz*, 4 September 1996). As for Goldhagen's third example, Jewish labour camps, Bettina Birn convincingly refuted his argument that these camps were designed not to extract labour, but to make the Jews suffer gratuitously. Rather the Nazis wanted to get as much out of the Jews as they could before they killed them. Moreover, as Birn pointed out, apparently senseless cruelty was also inflicted on Soviet POWs, or Russian women, or 'gays' and 'people wearing glasses', not just on Jews (Birn 1997: 204).

It would seem that Goldhagen proceeded selectively in trying to underpin his theory of eliminationist anti-semitism. American political scientist Finkelstein took issue with his use of documentation relating to post-war trials of Police Battalion 101. Goldhagen, Finkelstein claimed, had chosen to omit what he adjudged to be the self-exculpatory testimony of battalion members. Yet he was quite prepared to garner evidence of brutality from the 'gratuitously self-incriminating testimony of the police battalions' (Finkelstein 1997: 74). As Finkelstein quite rightly implies, if the accused were prepared to incriminate themselves, then surely it was overhasty to say the least to assume that passages where they defended their conduct were *per se* self-exculpatory. In his book, Goldhagen cited from an eye-witness report relating how Major Trapp of Police Battalion 101 had cried during the first mass shooting of Poles in Talcyn in September 1942. Goldhagen claimed that the report does not give us reason to believe that Trapp 'became agitated and unsettled' after the killing of Jews (Goldhagen 1996a: 240). Yet Browning pointed out in a newspaper article that there is evidence that Trapp cried before and during the murder of Jews in Józefów (*Zeit*, 19 April 1996). Bettina Birn accused Goldhagen of tendentiously dismissing expressions of shame and disapproval on the part of battalion members in the trial records as mere visceral disgust. She also charged him with arguing from the particular to the general: Goldhagen had treated the fact that the wife of one of the members attended a killing as evidence that the men shared the experience of atrocities with their loved ones (Birn 1997: 199).

German historians tended to avoid such precise scrutiny of Goldhagen's methods, perhaps for fear of being accused of defensive nit-picking. Birn, Browning and Finkelstein did the work for them. Most impressive in this regard is Finkelstein, particularly his table of what he called 'tacit admissions, minimizations and misrepresentations' in Goldhagen's book (Finkelstein 1997: 62). Yet it was Birn's criticisms which angered Goldhagen the most. In May 1997, he threatened her with legal action unless she retract her critical comments, something she refused to do (*TSP*, 9 October 1997). Following Goldhagen's threat of litigation, the Canadian Jewish Congress approached Birn's employer, the Canadian Department of Justice, requesting her withdrawal from a book which took issue with Goldhagen's theories (Finkelstein and Birn 1998a). She also became the target of allegations of anti-semitism, and the Canadian Minister of Justice had a formal investigation conducted. Birn was exonerated. Goldhagen's treatment of his critics set an alarming precedent, as well as undermining the credibility of his arguments.

'The Germans', collective guilt and the unhistorical

Journalists and historians in Germany vigorously objected to Goldhagen's use throughout his study of the term 'the Germans'. Goldhagen's response was to argue that it was acceptable practice to talk about the French in Algeria or the Americans in Vietnam. Why not, then, of the Germans in Poland and the Soviet Union (Goldhagen 1997b: 232)? It should indeed be acceptable to write 'the Germans in Poland'. But Goldhagen's use of 'the Germans' was more programmatic. His prose bristled with the phrase. Sometimes, the narrative or analysis seemed to shift towards a liturgy of accusation, with 'the Germans' not so much a term of description, as one of condemnation. Moreover, Goldhagen tended to use 'the Germans' where he really meant a specific set of Germans, be these Nazi Party members, battalion members or concentration camp guard staff. In writing of the 'Germans' measures' against the Jews during the *Reichskristallnacht*, Goldhagen implied that the whole nation was involved; phrases such as 'the Germans' slaughter of Jews' were left uncontextualized (Goldhagen 1996a: 140 and 283). At one point, Goldhagen wrote that members of Police Battalion 65 crammed Jews into freight-cars 'in the typical German manner of these years', as if all Germans were in the habit of doing this (Goldhagen 1996a: 198). Of course Goldhagen's point was that all Germans were *potential* murderers or freight-car crammers. The Germans who actually did the murdering or cramming were executors of a national will. In this sense, as Goldhagen argued, the perpetrators were 'Germans first, and SS men, policemen, or camp guards second' (Goldhagen 1996a: 7). But this hierarchization eliminated differences between those who killed and those who did not. Execution became arbitrary, killers interchangeable with non-killers.

Because Goldhagen argued from the particular to the general, editor of *Die Zeit* Robert Leicht suspected him of seeking to pass judgement on all Germans (*Zeit*, 6 September 1996). CSU politician Peter Gauweiler described Goldhagen as the 'judge of a whole people' (*Bayernkurier*, 12 October 1996). On this view, Goldhagen's book was a moral indictment, prosecution and sentencing of the mass of 'ordinary' Germans during the Third Reich, indeed German history as a whole. Certainly Goldhagen supported his interpretation with all the rhetorical passion of a state prosecutor. He also deployed it with some intellectual aggression, verbally shooting down other interpretations. The accused's motive was, he insisted, simply a desire to eliminate Jews. Circumstantial pressures, conditioning through war, even equally terrible motives such as sheer callousness or unthinking, unfeeling obedience, were not taken seriously by Goldhagen. What emerged was a vehemently and murderously anti-semitic monomaniac, 'the German', whom Goldhagen believed one must approach with anthropological distance and detachment, discarding any assumption of the '"normalcy" of the German people' or their 'similarity to our ideal images of ourselves' (Goldhagen 1996a: 31).

German historians and critics rejected Goldhagen's book as an attempt to revive the collective guilt thesis of the late 1940s and 1950s (see Schirrmacher [*FAZ*, 15 April 1996], Marion Gräfin Dönhoff [*Zeit*, 6 September 1996] and Johannes Willms [*SZ*, 15 October 1996]). Even Foreign Minister Klaus Kinkel felt moved to repudiate Goldhagen's argument. In a speech delivered in Washington in commemoration of the 51st anniversary of the end of the war and delivered to a full gathering of the American Jewish Committee, Kinkel said: 'Guilt is always personal, not collective and not inheritable' (*SZ*, 9 May 1996). These complaints were understandable. Goldhagen's attribution to the Germans of collective genocidal urges did little justice to the complex relationship between the broad mass of Germans and anti-semitism in the Third Reich. It reduced active and passive resistance to a footnote. Worse, perhaps, was the apparent reduction of history to a function of stereotypic national psychopathology. Indeed it was in some respects a profoundly anti-historiographical book, preferring to place an almost Manichean, and certainly teleological, gloss on events.

A gullible public?

Given these weaknesses, given the fact, moreover, that the German public's attention had been drawn to them long before the book appeared in German translation, it was surprising that it refused to side with its own historians. In fact when today's 'ordinary Germans' entered the auditoria at the podium discussions in September 1996, they were determined to support Goldhagen *against* their historians. Journalist Elisabeth Bauschmid reported that, wherever these discussions took place, whether in Hamburg, Berlin, Aschaffenburg, Frankfurt or Munich, the public was on Goldhagen's side, 'ready to defend him [. . .] with boos and applause' (*SZ*, 12 September 1996). Negative explanations for this public disobedience were quickly to hand; so were positive ones. Both have to be taken seriously.

To begin with the negative ones. CSU politician Peter Gauweiler, not known for mincing his words, argued that the real executioner was Goldhagen. He also believed that the 'sucking-up' which Goldhagen ostensibly enjoyed was symptomatic of an 'irrational trait in the German character'. 'It is the done thing, between a glass of prosecco and a mouthful of quail breast, to react to Goldhagen's insults with delight' (*Bayernkurier*, 9 October 1996). Gauweiler thought he could identify a penchant for a trendy indulgence in frissons of masochism. Other conservative politicians pointed to a sado-masochistic symbiosis between Goldhagen and the public. On this view, many Germans were willingly exposing themselves to verbal flagellation in order to expiate a sense of guilt induced in them by the moralizing left.

Perhaps it was even more complicated than that. In a much-discussed footnote to his book, Goldhagen claimed that the Germans in the west of the country had changed after 1945, largely overcoming their anti-semitism: 'that absurd beliefs can rapidly dissipate is well known' (Goldhagen 1996a: 594). In interviews prior to and during his visit to Germany in 1996, Goldhagen reiterated this point (see, for instance, Goldhagen 1996c: 13). There appeared to be a contradiction here. How could eliminationist anti-semitism, inherent as it was to the German national psyche, itself be largely eliminated in such a short space of time? In his speech in receipt of the *Blätter* Democracy Prize in Bonn on 10 March 1997, Goldhagen eulogized both West Germany's post-war evolution into a model democracy, and the rewriting of national history to take account of German responsibility for the holocaust. He explicitly put these developments down to the impact of internationalization, a term he understood to mean westernization and Americanization (Goldhagen 1997a). Goldhagen's eulogy of West Germany was thus, indirectly, a eulogy of the Western Allies, and particularly the USA. At no point did he address developments in the GDR, or the impact of revisionism on the FRG. Nothing, it seemed, was to detract from the impression of an astonishing transformation at the hands of the USA.

Goldhagen even went so far as to suggest that the current German model of national history construction should be internationalized (Goldhagen 1997a: 80). Thus Germany was as much of a positive role model now as it had been a negative role model in the past. Goldhagen counterbalanced his extreme criminalization of the German population during the Third Reich with an equally extreme elevation of the German population in the present. This may have had a significant psychological effect on Goldhagen's German audience. The more the German population felt it was being praised in the here and now, the more, surely, it would be prepared to berate itself for Germany's national past – arguably the goal Goldhagen sought to achieve. By presenting American and western ideals as the necessary precondition for Germany's moral transformation, moreover, Goldhagen gave these the status of a religion, of which today's Germans would need to continue partaking if they wished to preserve their ethical health. This religion had Catholic undertones. By 'confessing' their past national sins in a spirit of enlightened self-condemnation, today's Germans could gain absolution. Thus mass self-condemnation in 1996 was followed by Goldhagen's paean of praise to contemporary Germany in 1997. Perhaps, then, for the broad public, Goldhagen was offering a form of secularized redemption, acting more like a priest than a judge. Frank Schirrmacher even described him somewhat cynically as a 'miracle-healer' (*FAZ*, 13 September 1996). Certainly he was binding his German readers into a panegyric of the USA, helping to counteract anti-American trends in post-unification German political culture.

Goldhagen's rich name lent itself to religious interpretations. Here, it seemed, was a second Daniel in a second lion's den. In organizing what were indeed often tribunal-like podium discussions in which leading German historians did their utmost to discredit his book, the media unintentionally made him into a kind of martyr figure. In the face of sometimes agitated and emotionalized criticism, Goldhagen's gently persistent and unflappable defence of his book made him seem somehow stoical, blessed with a higher wisdom. It is putting it strongly, but in a sense the public flocked to him as if he were a latterday Jesus. And he thanked it by playing it off against his critics, pointing to his cult following in answer to their carping. In 1997, he published in Germany a selection of letters written to him by his German readers, most of them positive. In his afterword, he praised his German readers for their perspicacity in 'seeing through' the 'condemnations of my book and my person' and not allowing themselves to be discouraged from forming their own opinions 'by the opinion leaders and some established historians' (Goldhagen 1997b: 228). That Goldhagen knew how to turn public opinion to his advantage, even to shape it, is undeniable.

Nor can it be denied that the simplicity of Goldhagen's argument, driven home in his book with a sledgehammer style, may have been one of the reasons for its appeal. Some German historians feared, not unreasonably, that interest in and patience with more differentiated and intricate explanatory models would decrease in the same measure in which Goldhagen's model of 'holocaust made easy' caught the public imagination. Even worse, historians given to more differentiated understandings would perhaps be classified as revisionist, as seeking to undermine plain, incontrovertible truths and play down German guilt. Left-wing and liberal historians in the 1980s had resisted attempts by Ernst Nolte to relativize the singularity of the holocaust. Now, they felt bound to resist Goldhagen's attempts to singularize its cause. In both cases their interest was in doing justice to the complexity and in resisting ideological misreadings of history. But to the general public it appeared they had 'switched sides'.

In podium discussions on German television, Hans Mommsen could be observed going various shades of red in response to groans from the audience every time he attempted to complicate the picture. The public, he lamented, wanted 'a historical myth of evil' (*FR*, 21 September 1996). One might argue that the 'remythification' identified by Schirrmacher in Goldhagen's book was an adapted understanding of the holocaust, adapted to the needs of a modern public. Like other west Europeans, perhaps even more so, west Germans – and, increasingly, east Germans – have been brought up on the stark, over-simplified images of Hollywood. This could partly explain the understanding response to Goldhagen's argument that Germans killed Jews principally out of an inherent anti-semitic bloodlust. This projection of an internalized evil just waiting for its opportunity to emerge reminds one of the concept behind the *Alien* films. It has also been argued that Goldhagen's gruesome, blood-curdling descriptions of German atrocities, leaving nothing to the imagination, were inspired by the over-literal horror of Hollywood. Hans Mommsen, in reference to these descriptions, feared that 'opening Pandora's Box to penetrate the atavistic dimension to the historical would be to foster a radical collapse of cultural values' (*FR*, 21 September 1996). This was overstated, but Mommsen felt duty-bound to resist what he believed to be the German public's susceptibility to the exhibitionistic.

A discriminating public?

If the German public itself is to be believed, then its interest in Goldhagen lay not in gullibility or over-schematic thinking, but in an altogether more positive impulse. A reader of the weekly *Die Zeit*, Maria Mischkowsky, wrote in a letter to the newspaper: 'The self-confident rebuttal of the American book by the critics is frightening' (*Zeit*, 23 August 1996). A glance at the readers' letters collated by Goldhagen reveals a similar indignation. Thus we read that the podium discussions were conducted like tribunals (Goldhagen 1997b: 21, 29); that German historians had misunderstood and misrepresented Goldhagen's book (Goldhagen 1997b: 15, 37, 55, 162); that their comments were a cause for shame and anger (Goldhagen 1997b: 25, 29, 41); that the book when it appeared 'enlightened' readers as to the value of Goldhagen's ideas and the misunderstandings of critics (Goldhagen 1997b: 15, 37, 41); that ordinary Germans were omitted from the discussions (Goldhagen 1997b: 33); and that contemporary recognized specialist historiography is too clean and abstract (Goldhagen 1997b: 47). On this evidence, the German public was positive towards Goldhagen because it wanted to give him a chance, not because of uncritical adulation. It protested in this way against what critic Rainer Lingenthal called 'the premature demontage of the Goldhagen book'. According to Lingenthal, the pre-publication discussions had sought to 'deprive the public of the right of decision' (*WP*, 8 August 1996). Seen in this light, the historians and journalists who rejected the book were behaving in an undemocratic and censorious manner. In contrast, it was the public which appeared to be upholding values of fair play and freedom of opinion.

The German public felt it had learned something from Goldhagen. Dietrich Giffhorn wrote in a reader's letter that 'Goldhagen is right: the perpetrators were quite normal people, "people like you and I"' (*Zeit*, 23 August 1996). This was a typical reaction, one which can only be understood within the context of the political culture of both the GDR and the 'old' FRG. In West Germany, the tendency had been to attribute Nazi crimes to the SS and other elite organizations. That 'ordinary' Germans might also have been involved did not enter the picture. As former east German civil rights' movement veteran Wolfgang Ullmann put it, in the FRG the belief was that anti-semitic crimes had been committed 'in the name of Germans', not by them (*Freitag*, 16 August 1996). In the same article, Ullmann pointed out that, in East Germany, anti-semitism had been understood as a class-related problem and therefore analysed in terms of class-war theory. A volume of articles on Goldhagen's book from 1997 argued that West German left-wing intellectuals also embedded their critique of anti-semitism within a Marxist critique of materialism (Küntzel *et al.* 1997). In other words, both Germanys had seen the holocaust in terms which put it at arm's length. By blaming the holocaust on certain elite organizations (which no longer existed) or elite class interests (which were now overcome), it was possible to imply that anti-semitism had never been a grass-roots problem, and to disclaim responsibility. Atrocities were attributed to individuals in the grip of fanatical ideologies. Goldhagen's view that such atrocities could also be committed as a matter of course by 'ordinary Germans' was received with a sense of shock by the general public. One reader, Stefanie Weidemann, described the impact of the book as follows: 'The awareness that it was not "beasts", but people who committed these atrocities for explainable reasons means that we lose the distance to them that we built up by denying their humanity' (*Zeit*, 23 August 1996).

It has to be said that the main schools of historical research into the holocaust, intentionalism and functionalism, can, in their more extreme variants, serve to exculpate the Germans. The more Hitler appears as the key to the holocaust, the more not only those involved in planning and implementing the genocide, but also the German people as a whole appear as hapless tools in his monstrous project. Functionalism, for its part, can construct a view of the holocaust as something so infinitely contingent upon such a diverse range of circumstances that human responsibility becomes diffuse; even worse, actors in the holocaust come across as victims of their own helplessness, and the element of anti-semitic volition is minimized. In the wake of the Goldhagen debate, Hans Mommsen, presumably in reaction to Goldhagen's essentialist version of intentionalism, himself gave expression to a radicalized functionalism in which Hitler appeared as someone 'driven' by circumstances into killing the Jews. This exonerated Hitler. Mommsen was rebuked by colleagues for his remarks (see *JW*, 6 December 1996). Fragments of the intentionalist–functionalist debate will have filtered down to the German public in 1996, and if it reacted cautiously, then this was not necessarily a bad thing. That the public preferred Goldhagen's reading to those of other historians can, moreover, be put down to its greater political relevance in the present. It could be understood as a warning against underestimating the virulence and impact of anti-semitism, and against conceiving of it as a prejudice characteristic only of specific individuals or groups. The circumstances examined by functionalists would probably not reoccur, at least not in the same combination. Nor would a second Hitler take over Germany. But anti-semitism could re-emerge, as attacks on synagogues in post-unification Germany appeared to indicate.

Neither in Germany's political culture, nor in international holocaust historiography had there been much interest in those at the end of the killing chain, the killers themselves and their immediate victims. Browning's study of Police Battalion 101 was an exception (Browning 1992a). If Goldhagen did achieve something as a historian, then it was by virtue of his focus on direct perpetration, and on those killings of Jews which happened outside of the extermination and concentration camps. This focus, and his stress on the 'ordinariness' of the killers, counteracted the tendency of the functionalists to present the holocaust in terms of abstract, elite bureaucracies and technocrats. As Jan Philipp Reemtsma argued in a newspaper interview, Goldhagen helped to draw attention to anti-semitism as a factor within the 'community of the people' (*News*, 7 November 1996). In a sense, perhaps, Goldhagen returned the holocaust to the Germans both as individual actors and as a collective, and reminded them of their responsibility in the past, present and future. Moreover, because he graphically described the acts of murder, he removed the atrocities from the cool analytical prose of much historiography and restored to them something of their original horror. Goldhagen may have exploited the techniques of Hollywood, but his style was also influenced by modern war journalism and photography, precisely those means which have done so much to alert the world to the horrors in the former Yugoslavia and elsewhere.

The public response also helped to counteract the regrettable tendency on the part of some, largely conservative commentators in Germany to discredit Goldhagen's arguments by discrediting his motives. Arnulf Baring, in the ZDF podium discussion, suggested that Goldhagen had written out of rage and moral indignation, rather than out of an objective spirit of enquiry (*JA*, 19 September 1996). Gauweiler's remark that the 'economic yield' from the book must have been over a million marks came close to stereotyping Goldhagen as a money-greedy Jew (*Bayernkurier*, 9 October 1996). In the press, Goldhagen's name was occasionally parodied, notably as 'Daniel J. Goldhafgenuch', translatable as Daniel J. Gold-have-enough. Gauweiler also accused Goldhagen of inverse racism. The generally liberal Gräfin Dönhoff was concerned lest Goldhagen's book should 'revive' anti-semitism. She thereby blamed Goldhagen rather than the Germans for any anti-Jewish feelings that might emerge (*Zeit*, 6 September 1996). Clichéd prejudices about Jews and anti-semitic reactions were flanked by attempts to play down collective responsibility for anti-semitism in the Third Reich. In the ZDF podium discussion, Erich Mende (FDP) denied the existence of anti-semitism in the army before 1936, while Baring maintained that the deportation of Jews was witnessed only by a 'few' (*JA*, 19 September 1996). If Goldhagen overdid the degree of anti-semitism or German compliance, this was underdoing it.

Reactions to the book on the part of the New Right were predictably negative. The New Right had been seeking to uncover the 'modern' and progressive aspects of National Socialism as a means of creating a homogeneously positive history (Zitelmann and Prinz 1991). Goldhagen emphasized the destructiveness of the holocaust as the central, indeed all-determining feature of the Third Reich. Totalitarian theorems generally took a blow when the book was published, not just because of Goldhagen's stress on the singularity of the holocaust, but also because he rejected any division into 'them' and 'us'. Moreover, the implicitly pro-American agenda in his book was anathema to a New Right determined that united Germany should slip its 'over-westernized' moorings and find a more independent sense of political direction. Goldhagen's stress on the importance of Americanization for Germany, which he brought out so strongly when awarded the *Blätter* Democracy Prize in 1997, was certainly one reason why Jürgen Habermas, Germany's leading left-liberal philosopher, delivered the encomium. Goldhagen could be instrumentalized, whatever the excesses of his argument, to ward off the New Right's wayward dreams of a new, self-confident Germany.

A lesson to be learnt?

Interestingly, while historians were largely sceptical of Goldhagen's book, psycho-analysts, sociologists and social scientists reacted more positively. They admired its interest in the relationship between authority and will, between social codes and personal morality, and between political and subjective motivations. Historians had objected that Goldhagen was not justified in expecting moral choices of men who, in his interpretation, had been driven by rabid anti-semitism. Psychoanalyist Christoph Biermann rejected this objection, arguing that madness and intact eth-ical responsibility can coexist, as two sides of a dichotomy. Inspired by Goldhagen, Biermann called for a 'theory of the subjectivity between good and evil, and of the anthropological conflict structure between *conditio humana* and *inhumana*' (*JA*, 12 December 1996). To a degree, the abovementioned objection by historians mir-rored their long-standing assumption that men following orders cannot be said to possess freedom of moral choice. Jan Philipp Reemtsma, sociologist and one of Goldhagen's strongest supporters in Germany, argued that 'there appears to be something like an involuntary consensus between a mentality that insists on the dis-avowal of freedom and morality, and historiography' (Reemtsma 1997: 40). Now, Goldhagen had shown that the men did have a choice to turn down orders. Moreover, despite his apparently deterministic understanding of anti-semitism, he assumed the existence of a counter-impulse which was largely not heeded, open-ing up an area for investigation within an apparent contradiction.

If Goldhagen's sociological approach was potentially fruitful for historiography, so, perhaps was his indignant tone. Historian Norbert Frei compared the impact of Goldhagen's book to that of the American TV series *Holocaust*, thus more than implying that it was essentially a piece of fiction which had nevertheless made people think about the Nazi past (*SD*, 25 February 1997). In contrast to Frei, one might argue that Goldhagen had not so much fictionalized the holocaust as adapted techniques generally associated with fiction, such as descriptive metaphor and narrative, to the requirements of a new, more popular form of historiography. In a book on the opposition of German historians to Goldhagen, Fred Kautz expressed the suspicion that the reason they disliked Goldhagen's book had more to do with them than with Goldhagen. Kautz argued that Hans Mommsen, Eberhard Jäckel and Hans-Ulrich Wehler were shaped by their experience as members of the 'flak-helper' generation: those Germans who grew up in the Third Reich but were too young to serve at the front. Given their 'tainted' roots, Kautz contended, these historians developed analytical methods and prose styles which enabled them to distance themselves from too direct a confrontation with the horrors of the Third Reich. In Kautz's opinion, this explained the dry and over-rationalized tone of German historiography, which these men had helped to set. 'By means of technical mastery, emotional abstinence and abstract language they distanced themselves from them [their roots, BN]' (Kautz 1998: 74). If Kautz is right, then Goldhagen's evocative depiction of killings, his visceral language, struck at the core of German historiographical self-understanding.

One should perhaps be sceptical of Kautz's theory of 'tainted' roots. While he was right to argue that German holocaust historiography was marked by a stylistic and analytical coolness, this was surely the result of a genuine fear of appearing voyeuristic. The problem with too much coolness, however, is that the holocaust may lose its force and power as a moral warning. Such coolness may even imply an unintended wish to exculpate. One of the few German historians to reflect on the need for a less detached approach was Johannes Willms. Willms pointed out that historians, in line with the premise of 'strict scientific analysis', had focused on the empirically verifiable preconditions of history. 'In other words: they focused largely on the facts of the matter.' But in so doing they had failed to take language, as a form of mediation, seriously enough. They overlooked the adage that 'it is not the deeds which shock people, but the words which describe these deeds' (*SZ*, 15 October 1996). Willms acknowledged that the success of Goldhagen's book lay in its language, and in the moral thrust of his argumentation.

However, if the 61st Historians' Convention in Munich at the end of September 1996 was anything to go by, the last thing the majority of German historians wanted was to conduct a fundamental discussion on the relationship in historiographical writing between the subject of analysis and the moral and linguistic terms in which this analysis is conveyed. Indeed they appeared reluctant to discuss the holocaust at all. There was no official section on Goldhagen. The programme treated participants to sections on the coins of Asia Minor and recent agrarian history, but not to a single section on the Third Reich. Instead, there were six sections on the GDR (in comparison to one in Leipzig two years earlier), and none on the Federal Republic. The format of this programme implied at best that German historians felt more research work needed to be done on the GDR than on National Socialism, at worst that East German history was being shoved into the foreground to play down both the crimes of National Socialism, and West Germany's weaknesses in dealing with the legacy of Hitler. Some historians may even have felt that the Nazi past was now off the agenda. The Fischer publishing-house did organize a podium discussion on 20 September outside the official programme, where most participants denied the greater historiographical relevance of Goldhagen's study.

It is true that historians were on occasion prepared to acknowledge useful aspects of the book. Hans-Ulrich Wehler argued that the role of the 40 or so police battalions in the holocaust had not been as closely examined as that of the SS brigades and mobile killing squads (*Einsatzgruppen*). Goldhagen (and Browning) had addressed a deficit. Wehler also pointed to the necessity for research into Jewish work-camps and the death-marches (*Zeit*, 24 May 1996). Hans Mommsen may not have agreed with Goldhagen's estimation of how many people were actually involved in killing Jews, but he acknowledged that Goldhagen had drawn attention to the fact that the holocaust had been implemented by a 'shockingly large number of people' (*Zeit*, 30 August 1996). Goldhagen's book, as historian Ulrich Herbert argued, had triggered an important public discussion on the extent of the hatred of Jews (*Zeit*, 14 June 1996). But such acknowledgements were usually embedded in severe criticism. Besides, this praise was restricted to areas of research. There was little praise of Goldhagen's application of methods inspired, according to Ingrid Gilcher-Holtey, by recent developments in cultural sociology (*Zeit*, 7 June 1996), and only a little more for the plasticity of his prose. When the style was acknowledged, it was because it made the material more accessible to a, by implication, intellectually undiscriminating public. This was damning with faint praise.

According to Herbert Jäger, had it not been for the impact of the Goldhagen controversy, the events of the National Socialist period would have been erased once and for all by the commemorations in 1995 (Jäger 1997: 85). This may be overstated; as we saw in the previous chapter, these commemorations could be read in a variety of ways. But 1995 certainly represented for some politicians and historians, and for some members of the general public, a symbolic act of closure. The effect of the Goldhagen debate was to counteract the will to forget, ensuring that the post-unification trend towards a more intense preoccupation with the Nazi past was not impeded. Indeed through the discussion surrounding Goldhagen's book, many Germans appeared to 'rediscover' the holocaust. Not that the holocaust had not been a subject of public interest before this. The Auschwitz trials in Frankfurt in the early Sixties and the showing of the American television series *Holocaust* in West Germany in 1979 created waves of interest, as did the showing of *Schindler's List* in 1994 (see Chapter Three). But it was the Goldhagen debate, along with the 'Crimes of the *Wehrmacht*' exhibition and the discussions surrounding the Holocaust Memorial (Chapter Eight), which firmly anchored the holocaust in German public memory. Of course we cannot know for sure whether sections of the public swallowed Goldhagen's over-simplified view of the role of anti-semitism, or responded to his style with purely aesthetic feelings of horror. We cannot know how many Germans entered into a mysterious ritual of penitence. My own impression from readers' letters, however, is that many, thanks to Goldhagen, simply gained in terms of general awareness of the horrors of the holocaust and German involvement. In the case of historians, it is difficult to know when rejections of Goldhagen were based on serious concern for a loss of complexity, and when they were driven by a reluctance to confront the critical implications of his very concrete historiography. Certainly politicians on the right, and some conservative historians, were angry that an American Jew had damaged hopes of a new self-confidence based on burying the National Socialist past.

Goldhagen and Klemperer

The discussion of Goldhagen's book was to a degree accompanied by discussion of the diaries of Victor Klemperer, which were published in 1995. The diaries covered the period 1933 to 1941 (Klemperer 1995a) and 1942 to 1945 (Klemperer 1995b). Klemperer was a German Jew who, because he was married to an 'Aryan' German, was not deported and lived through the Third Reich in Dresden. His diaries provided a picture of the increasing discrimination against and exclusion of Germany's Jews under Hitler. Omer Bartov has argued that Klemperer's diaries represent examples of 'everyday history' (*Alltagsgeschichte*), a historiographical tradition harking back to the 1970s and 1980s which 'attempts to understand individuals rather than systems, to see ideology in context rather than as an abstract entity'. In contrast to previous examples of such history, however, Klemperer's diaries are 'written from the perspective of the victim, who was simultaneously an insider, a patriotic, conservative, well-educated and Christian German, who was declared a Jew by the regime' (Bartov 2000c: 177). Bartov dismisses Goldhagen's descriptions of atrocities as 'voyeuristic fantasies', but he nevertheless also accredits Goldhagen with having expanded the bounds of the *Alltagsgeschichte* tradition by focusing on the victims and seeking to elicit empathy for them (Bartov 2000c: 178). This view ran counter to the impression created by some German historians that Goldhagen's study was an erratic block. He had perhaps redirected what German historians, notably in the Bavaria Project, had started.

Goldhagen's study and Klemperer's diaries are comparable and complementary. Both described a reality which had hitherto been rather overlooked, Goldhagen the killings outside of the concentration and extermination camps, Klemperer the possibility of Jewish survival within the borders of the Reich. Both depicted the impact of anti-semitism on actual human beings. Goldhagen's study depicted explicitly the suffering of the victims and endeavoured to enter the mind-set of the perpetrators; Klemperer's diaries opened up an avenue into the minds of the victims, but also explored the mentality of the German persecutors. Goldhagen focused on 'ordinary Germans' at the killing front, Klemperer described 'ordinary Germans' at the home front. But this is as far as any comparison can go. For while Goldhagen's 'ordinary Germans' were always anti-semitic, Klemperer's were not. Klemperer's multi-layered picture of German attitudes to Hitler and the Jews appeared to bear out the results of the Bavaria Project, which had also come to the conclusion that it would misguided to assume a uniform behaviour pattern on the part of 'ordinary Germans' under Hitler.

Klemperer felt himself to be a German. His initial conviction was that the National Socialists were in some way un-German, while he, imbued with an appreciation of high German culture, was the real German, a 'German "nationalist"'

(Klemperer 1995a: 210) or a 'German European' (Klemperer 1995a: 220). Against the background of what Klemperer adjudged to be the historical integration of Jews into Germany, he regarded National Socialist anti-semitism as a form of mad extremism, and it is clear that he hated every form of perceived extremism, be this bolshevism or even Zionism (Klemperer 1995b: 77). Initially, too, he understood the lack of resistance against Hitler as a symptom of cowardice among the Germans (Klemperer 1995a: 245). Over time, especially with increasing isolation, the onset of war, the deportation of Jews and the rumours of what was happening in Auschwitz and elsewhere in the east, Klemperer became more sceptical. In a much-quoted entry of 23 June 1942, he wrote that he could no longer believe National Socialism to be quite so un-German (Klemperer 1995b: 140). Reviewing the course of German–Jewish history, he concluded that he had known too little about the setbacks to the history of emancipation and about precursors to Hitler's racist thinking (Klemperer 1995b: 56). Given his experience under Hitler, given too his self-imposed reading of works by National Socialist thinkers such as Alfred Rosenberg, this pessimistic shift in opinion was not surprising.

Yet negative thinking never consistently overcame positive thinking, resulting in some ambivalence. On a tolerable day, Klemperer might stress the liberal traditions in Germany. This enabled him to construct a view of German history central to which were those very values which led to the integration of the Jews. It also enabled him to understand the Germans as heirs to a concept of Germanness not based on blood or intolerance. On a bad day, he leaned more towards seeing in the Germans heirs to a tradition of racism and aggression which he had underestimated. Many factors could lead to a tolerable or a bad day. One of them, a central one, was whether or not Klemperer had had to bear, on a particular day, the brunt of open anti-semitism, or whether he had experienced an act of solidarity from 'Aryan' Germans. A recurrent phrase in the diaries is *vox populi*. Klemperer was constantly on the search for the 'mood of the people', towards the war, towards Hitler, and, not least, towards the Jews. He never managed to find this 'mood'. At one point, admittedly still before the outbreak of war on 22 January 1939, he wrote: 'no-one, either within or outside the country, can truly assess the mood of the mass of the people' (Klemperer 1995a: 459).

His diaries shed light on the reasons for his uncertainty. He experienced brutal anti-semitism, and counter-examples of solidarity, kindness, even apparent philo-semitism. On one notable occasion, 5 October 1942, he witnessed the negative and the positive sides of the 'Aryans' almost simultaneously. Out cycling in Dresden, he was overtaken by two members of the Hitler Youth, who laughed at him. A moment later a young worker passed him, coming from the opposite direction. He smiled at Klemperer, saying: 'Don't let that bother you' (Klemperer 1995b: 252). Particularly after the introduction of the compulsory Yellow Star for all Jews in September 1941, a measure which severely curtailed Klemperer's freedom of movement, he sensitively registered examples and counter-examples. On 26 July 1942, noted by Klemperer the following day, another worker on a bicycle called out to him: 'You Jewish scoundrel!' (Klemperer 1995b: 186). Yet on 24 September 1942 Klemperer was struck by the 'demonstrative [. . .] politeness' of a group of workers, a gesture which, Klemperer wrote, could be dangerous for the latter (Klemperer 1995b: 249). He described the torture of being stared at when wearing the Yellow Star (Klemperer 1995b: 117). On 17 August 1943, he noted how he was insulted by 'well-dressed, intelligent-looking boys of eleven or twelve', who called out: 'Finish him off, the old Jew' (Klemperer 1995b: 420). Yet on another occasion, 19 July 1943, an old man approached him and shook his hand, saying in reference to the Yellow Star that he 'condemns this ostracization of a race, as many others do too'. 'Which voice will dominate and win out?' Klemperer asked himself somewhat helplessly (Klemperer 1995b: 406).

Klemperer experienced gratuitous physical violence from the Gestapo, gratuitous verbal violence from 'ordinary' Germans, and equally as many expressions of support. Reading Klemperer, one can only come to the conclusion that monolithic interpretations of mood and history are *post hoc* over-simplifications, indeed falsifications. In this context, Klemperer's diaries do not corroborate Goldhagen's view of German history or Germans. Nor, however, do they corroborate the view of those who believe there to have been a deep divide between the Germans and the Nazis. From the diaries, it emerges that some Germans were anti-semitic regardless of whether they were Nazis in any formal sense. But there were also examples of non-anti-semitic members of the Nazi Party, and even of polite members of the Gestapo (who were nevertheless generally brutal). To complicate matters, there were examples of Jews with prejudices against East European Jewry – including Klemperer himself. One might even be entitled to ask whether those who insulted Klemperer were not so much anti-semitic as simply bad-tempered, unstable individuals who felt they could publicly vent their spleen on Jews because Jews were a legalized target for abuse. Conversely, it can be argued that Klemperer's projection of a now abusive, now supportive German population is unreliable, to a degree at least. It is possible that he played down evidence of anti-semitism in order to reduce somewhat his feelings of fear and despair. It would be difficult to refute either of these arguments. German reactions to Jews remain impossible to stereotype.

It was thus legitimate for critics of Goldhagen's book to draw attention to the fact that Klemperer's diaries provided a much less cut-and-dried picture, or even that they 'disproved' Goldhagen's thesis. The first-hand, autobiographical account was set against the historiographical. As Hanno Loewy rightly pointed out, even those who gave Goldhagen's book serious consideration did not fail to refer to Klemperer, 'who in 1941, after all, is surprised how many Germans react to his Yellow Star with shame' (*FR*, 15 June 1996). Journalist Volker Ullrich cited Klemperer as proof of the need to be sceptical about the 'image of a society utterly infected by National Socialism, even during the years of dictatorship' (*Zeit*, 12 April 1996). But there were times when critics ran the risk of instrumentalizing Klemperer in their campaign against Goldhagen, and even of misrepresenting Klemperer in an apologist manner. Norbert Frei claimed that Goldhagen had 'failed to register' the reality captured in all its detail by Klemperer, who had noted more 'gestures of friendliness' and 'shame' than negative responses when he started to wear the Yellow Star (*SZ*, 13–14 April 1996). This was an unbalanced reading.

In a review of Klemperer's diaries, Ekkehart Krippendorff even claimed that Klemperer was 'unable to detect any evidence of anti-semitism' in his day-to-day life, and that Klemperer's view of the Germans was 'nearer to the truth' than that of historians such as Goldhagen (*Freitag*, 14 June 1996). It was precisely this review, among others, which prompted former GDR historian Kurt Pätzold to protest against the tendency to use Klemperer's diaries as proof 'that the Germans were not so anti-semitic after all'. The dead Klemperer, Pätzold remarked, was being declared the victor over the living Daniel Jonah Goldhagen (*JW*, 13–14 July 1996).

However, some of those who sounded such warnings themselves instrumentalized Klemperer, in this instance in *defence* of Goldhagen. A case in point is Jan Philipp Reemtsma. The gist of Reemtsma's argument was that Goldhagen had demonstrated the true extent to which the Germans had supported Hitler's anti-semitism; they had supported it despite the fact that it would not have been to their personal disadvantage had they not done. Reemtsma also believed German anti-semitism to have been distinct from that in other countries because the developing idea of nationhood in Germany was strongly linked to the notion of a homogeneous community of blood relations. Reemtsma interpolated into his article select quotations from Klemperer's diaries which, taken on their own, appear to prove that Hitler and the 'ordinary Germans' formed a perfect team. Reemtsma makes only one (immediately qualified) reference to a counter-example in the diaries of German solidarity towards Jews (*SZ*, 24–5 August 1996). Subsequent to the Goldhagen debate, a book of essays edited by Hannes Heer was published which, by and large, also focused on the negative dimension to Klemperer's portrayal of the German treatment of Jews (Heer 1997).

The reception of Goldhagen's book did not signal the beginning of the instrumentalization of Klemperer. As Stuart Taberner has shown, Martin Walser's 1995 eulogy to Klemperer displayed all the hallmarks of the interpretation subsequently imposed by Goldhagen's critics (Taberner 1999). Walser read the diaries as evidence of the strength of the German–Jewish symbiosis. He played off Gershom Scholem's 'experience of growing anti-semitism' in pre-holocaust Germany against Klemperer's belief that anti-semitism had been overcome not least through assimilation (Walser 1996: 33). Scholem's view was adjudged by Walser to be *post hoc*, Klemperer's to be historically judicious. Retrospective assessments of German–Jewish relations often turn on the holocaust axis. Goldhagen argued inductively, concluding from the atrocity of Auschwitz a long-term and generalized genocidal will; he then rewrote history to prove the thesis. Walser, by contrast – quoting Golo Mann – understood the holocaust rather as a consequence of the 'mother of all catastrophes', namely the First World War and its aftermath (Walser 1996: 34). This also involved a degree of historical rewriting, and exculpated the Germans (who appeared, implicitly, as the victims of the Versailles Treaty). By defining the holocaust as the outcome of a historical hitch, Walser sought to lend weight to his belief that it was a development which ran counter to the historical evolution of a German–Jewish symbiosis. Moreover, embodied in survivors such as Klemperer, as well as those Germans who showed solidarity towards him, this symbiosis bypassed Auschwitz and continued in the post-war period. By declaring anti-semitism to be the determining force in all German relations with Jews not just during, but long before the Third Reich, Goldhagen effectively denied that there had been any degree of symbiosis between Germans and Jews. He overemphasized the negative, while Walser underemphasized it.

The negative and the positive

Klemperer's ambivalent portrayal of German attitudes towards Jews and his ambivalence towards his own sense of Germanness are misrepresented by Walser and a number of critics. It is important to separate out what Klemperer actually wrote from how it has been interpreted, because his ambivalence surely comes closer to the truth than Goldhagen's monolithic view. Before 1933, and even after 1933, there were both negative and positive elements in German–Jewish relations. The inclusive model of memory, Germany's post-unification memory paradigm, must reflect on both of these elements; Klemperer's diaries will support this process. It is however undeniable that, in political and social terms, the negative elements increasingly outweighed the positive after 1933. That not all Germans were anti-semitic during the Third Reich, that some showed courage and kindness towards Jews, was in itself not enough to prevent the systematic demolition of Jewish life in Germany and Europe by the National Socialists. Jews were driven into exile, incarcerated, deprived of rights and property, deported and murdered. The ultimate expression of this demolition was Auschwitz. As for the positive, it was marginalized, continuing to manifest itself only secretly, sporadically and at the level of individual acts of courage and kindness. To place too much emphasis on the positive retrospectively would be to portray the Third Reich in an unacceptably revisionist light. Of course today's Germans and the rapidly increasing Jewish community can and should look back to positive aspects of German–Jewish relations, certainly before 1933, and even between 1933 and 1945, as a point of orientation. But remembering these positive aspects should never serve to counterbalance the negative impression left by the holocaust. This is why it is important for present-day Germans to read Goldhagen's book, despite its weaknesses. It is a stark reminder that, while a few Germans were showing solidarity towards an increasingly isolated Klemperer, others were orchestrating and indulging in mass murder behind the front; not just the SS or specially trained killing units, but also 'ordinary Germans' in police battalions, even, as we shall see in the next chapter, 'ordinary soldiers' in Hitler's army – the *Wehrmacht*.

6   The crimes of the *Wehrmacht*

'Endless queues outside an exhibition in Munich's Town Hall. Picasso? The death mask of Tut'ankhamun? King Ludwig's collection of chamois-beard hat decorations? Nothing of the sort. Instead, a sober, depressing chronicle of horrors called 'War of Annihilation – Crimes of the *Wehrmacht* between 1941 and 1944'. Seldom has a contemporary-history exhibition made such an impact on so many people [. . .].'

(Benedikt Erenz, *Zeit*, 11 April 1997)

Interest and controversy

Early in 1995, the privately run Hamburg Institute for Social Research (HIS) launched an exhibition in Hamburg entitled '200 Days and 1 Century: Violence and Destructiveness as reflected in the Year 1945'. It drew attention to the Janus face of 1945, not only focusing on the liberation of Auschwitz, the extensions to the Soviet GULAG system and the bombing of Hiroshima, but also pointing to revolutionary developments in international law and politics, notably the Nuremberg trials and the establishment of the United Nations (HIS 1995). By way of an adjunct to this exhibition, the HIS presented a separate exhibition as of March 1995 in the Kampnagel Factory. Called 'War of Annihilation – Crimes of the *Wehrmacht* between 1941 and 1944', it explored the theme of *Wehrmacht* involvement in acts of killing in eastern Europe which did not fall within the framework of regular warfare. The Hamburg Institute was totally surprised by the impact of this spin-off exhibition, which was far greater than that of the '200 Days' exhibition. About 5,000 people saw the 'Crimes of the *Wehrmacht*' exhibition in Hamburg, 6,000 when it was shown in Regensburg in 1996, and 4,200 when it travelled to Nuremberg in the same year. Showings in Austria in Linz and Klagenfurt (1996) attracted some 25,600 visitors. But the real breakthrough came in Munich in 1997, where 90,000 people streamed into the exhibition. In Frankfurt, numbers reached 100,000. By the time the exhibition had to be withdrawn from circulation in late 1999 to enable the HIS to correct inaccuracies, 900,000 people had seen it in 32 towns and cities in Germany and Austria. If one adds to this the hundreds of thousands who attended events organized as part of the various accompanying programmes, and considers the intense media coverage, it would not be inaccurate to talk of mass interest and of a nationally significant exhibition.

The exhibition also provoked intense controversy, which, given the fact that it travelled from venue to venue, soon took on an almost ritualized quality. The stereotypic pattern of reactions was as follows. The Greens, SPD and FDP – the latter with reservations – supported and were often partly responsible for organizing the showing of the exhibition; the CSU and CDU were generally against it. Particularly following the CSU's campaign of hostility towards the exhibition in Munich in 1997, the extreme right-wing felt emboldened to orchestrate vehement protest. This in turn provoked anti-neo-Nazi demonstrations on the part of the left and far-left. Many ordinary citizens also took part in demonstrations against neo-Nazism. The negative high-point of every showing of the exhibition, for the police, the politicians, the judiciary, the media and, not least, the population of towns and cities, was the clash of extreme right-wing and left-wing demonstrators. Thankfully, the number of anti-exhibition demonstrators in Munich was not exceeded subsequently, while the number of visitors to the exhibition remained high. Controversy also flared in the columns of national and regional newspapers. Outside and inside the exhibition, there were heated discussions, between old and young, and between members of the war generation itself as they debated contrasting memories. Some feared the exhibition would tear up the fabric of society, setting grandchildren against their grandparents, sons and daughters against their parents, or stir up the 'old' animosity between Jews, Russians and Germans. What good could come, they asked, of an exhibition which split the generations? Was Germany not polarized enough, on the west–east axis? The expressed fear of divisiveness often camouflaged a dubious wish to preserve a holistic view of the *Wehrmacht* as a purely military organization. Yet despite all party-political debate, street-fighting, angry demonstrating outside the exhibition and remonstrations within, the showing of the exhibition had a profoundly positive effect. Indeed these conflicts may have enhanced this effect. It was an effect of enlightenment. Long-held illusions were shattered. Once again, these were illusions based on an exclusive picture, in this case of a 'clean' *Wehrmacht*.

The message of the exhibition

On 6 April 1941, the German forces, together with Italian, Hungarian and Bulgarian troops, attacked Yugoslavia and Greece; within about two weeks, both countries had capitulated. Two months later, on 22 June 1941, Hitler ordered the invasion of the Soviet Union (Operation Barbarossa). According to the exhibition, the war in the Balkans and Soviet Union was planned and conducted not as a 'normal' war between two enemy armies, but as one of annihilation against Jews, prisoners-of-war and the civilian population which resulted in millions of deaths (HIS 1996: 7). This ideologically driven campaign, moreover, was not solely the responsibility of Hitler's anti-bolshevism and anti-semitism; nor were those who did the killing always taken from outside the ranks of the regular army. The exhibition showed a series of orders dating from 1941 issued either by or with the collusion of the *Wehrmacht's* leaders demonstrating the express intention of these leaders to involve the army in the annihilation campaign. These include a guideline issued by *Wehrmacht* High Command on 19 May 1941 which stressed the need for 'ruthless and energetic measures against bolshevist agitators, partisans, saboteurs, Jews and complete elimination of all active and passive resistance' (HIS 1996: 179). They also include the notorious Commissar Order ('Guidelines for the Treatment of Political Commissars') of 6 June 1941, which claimed that the political commissars of the Red Army are 'authors of barbarously Asiatic methods of combat' and are to be 'disposed of by gunshot immediately' (HIS 1996: 179). To illustrate *Wehrmacht* involvement at all levels and in all types of crime, the exhibition focused on three telling examples: the treatment of partisans in Serbia, the conduct of the 6th Army on its way to Stalingrad, and the three-year occupation of the Ukraine. To render this involvement shockingly visible, the exhibition featured hundreds of gruesome photographs. But it also included text boards with excerpts from testimony given in trials (for instance in Minsk in 1945), letters from the front and other documents. One soldier almost joyfully proclaimed in a letter home: 'Today we set a new record! This morning in Belgrade we shot 122 communists and Jews' (HIS 1996: 36).

The generally accepted truth is that it was largely the SS, not least in the form of its mobile killing squads (*Einsatzgruppen*), as well as units of the Security Police and SD which did the bulk of the killing behind the front. The exhibition did not call this into question, but it did draw attention to widespread *Wehrmacht* participation. The boundary between hugely exaggerated acts of reprisal in the face of genuine civilian resistance and acts of gratuitous anti-bolshevist and anti-semitic terror was often a fluid one. Following sporadic partisan attacks on *Wehrmacht* positions in Kraljevo (Serbia), the 717th Infantry Division rounded up and shot 300 hundred 'communists, nationalists, democrats and Jews'. It then gathered together all male inhabitants of Kraljevo aged between 14 and 60 years of age, and indulged in a veritable orgy of killing. 1,736 men were shot – as well as 19 'communist women' (HIS 1996: 50). Often any mantle of rationality in *Wehrmacht* responses to 'problem situations' was so thin as to be little more than a flimsy excuse for a killing spree. In a transit POW Camp or DULAG in Bobruisk, the *Wehrmacht* was faced in late 1941 with the difficulty that the capacity of the camp was overstretched. Its solution was to set fire – on 7 November, the anniversary of the socialist revolution – to the prisoners' huts. Some 4,000 Soviet prisoners were either burned to death or shot by machine-guns as they tried to flee the flames. Generally, the *Wehrmacht*-run POW camps were sites of mass killing, notably of political commissars, or of death through hunger and epidemics. Of 5.7 million Soviet prisoners, 3.3 million died in *Wehrmacht*-run POW camps (HIS 1996: 126). According to Hannes Heer, one of the exhibition's creators and its most active proponent, the number of Jews killed 'directly or indirectly' by the *Wehrmacht* can be put at 1 to 1.5 million, the number of civilians killed in collaboration with the SS and police units in the campaign against 'partisans' at about 7 million (*RZ*, 16 July 1998).

Direct involvement in atrocities was complemented by indirect involvement, as when the *Wehrmacht* provided organizational support to help the SS and SD carry out killings. This was probably the most widespread and institutionalized form of involvement. The exhibition featured photographs and textual commentaries providing examples of collaboration. Thus the *Wehrmacht* collaborated with Himmler's

Einsatzgruppen in selecting political commissars and, as of 24 July 1941, other 'politically unacceptable and suspicious elements' for liquidation; 500,000 people were killed in this way (HIS 1996: 130). The ghetto in Minsk, the biggest in occupied Russia (100,000 people), was subjected to a series of massacres in 1941, 1942 and 1943 in which at least 73,000 people were murdered (HIS 1996: 120). The massacres were the responsibility of the SD and Security Police. But the *Wehrmacht* cordoned off the ghetto and supplied the killers with lorries (HIS 1996: 120). In the ravine of Babi Yar near Kiev, one of the most terrible of all crimes against humanity during the Second World War was committed by the SS on 29 and 30 September 1941: according to its own records, it killed 33,771 Jews. The *Wehrmacht* town commandant in Kiev discussed and planned this barbarous act with the perpetrators. As in many newly conquered Soviet towns, *Wehrmacht* and SS and SD worked together to facilitate acts of killing (HIS 1996: 78).

Post-war images of the *Wehrmacht* in West Germany

The exhibition styled itself as a demythologization. Its opening section illustrated the uncritical, indeed heroic view of the *Wehrmacht* in post-war West German film, popular literature and magazines. There can be little doubt that this view had also for a long time been the norm in West Germany's political culture. According to historian Wolfram Wette, when the *Bundeswehr* was founded in 1955, a 'generally positive image of the *Wehrmacht* was already firmly established in West German society'. Wette identified various stages in the creation of this image: firstly, the self-exculpatory tract written by German generals in autumn 1945 and their 'future-oriented' defence strategy at the Nuremberg trials; secondly, the Himmerod Declaration of October 1950 in which former *Wehrmacht* generals called for the public rehabilitation of *Wehrmacht* soldiers; and, thirdly, the testimonies to the honour of the *Wehrmacht* given by Konrad Adenauer in 1951 and 1952, as well as by NATO Supreme Commander Dwight Eisenhower (Wette 1998: 129ff.).

As the Cold War escalated in the course of the 1950s, the Western Allies needed West German military support. Adenauer, however, made it clear to them that he would not agree to the planned establishment of a European Army with West German participation as long as German soldiers languished in Allied prisons or faced trial (Streim 1995: 575). The increasingly lenient attitude of the Allies encouraged the Federal government to pass two amnesty laws of 31 December 1949 and 17 July 1954. These laws benefited SA, SS and Nazi Party functionaries who had been sentenced or were due to stand trial (Frei 1996: 52), but they also benefited members of the *Wehrmacht* who had committed crimes. Generally, the Federal Republic was particularly dilatory about prosecuting crimes committed by the *Wehrmacht*; the situation in the GDR appears to have been little better (Streim 1995). Thus it was that the positive image it enjoyed was never seriously challenged. In 1955, it was not regarded as morally problematic to invite former *Wehrmacht* generals to help with building up the *Bundeswehr*. On the contrary, the spirit of ideological anti-communism they brought with them was welcome. To be fair to the *Bundeswehr*, recruitment to the officers' caste was made dependent on the expression of a positive attitude to the July

1944 plotters such as Stauffenberg (see Chapter Three). But many officers never-theless regarded Stauffenberg as a traitor. Names of barracks for the West German army were chosen from a list of First World War generals drawn up by Hitler him-self for the *Wehrmacht* in 1937 as part of the ideological preparation for the Second World War. Some barracks were even named after Second World War commanders such as Eduard Dietl. Only in a few cases were barracks given the names of indi-viduals involved in the 20 July 1944 plot.

On 1 July 1965, CDU Defence Minister Kai-Uwe von Hassel issued the first *Bundeswehr* Decree on Tradition (*Traditionserlaß*). Without mentioning the word *Wehrmacht*, it distinguished between the broad mass of 'solid and heroic soldiers' and those 'few' individuals who had committed crimes (Wette 1998: 134). Hassel also emphasized the importance of the 20 July conspiracy. But there was no state-ment on the *Wehrmacht* as an institution. Debates on atomic armament policies sensitized the public to military issues in the 1980s, and a second Decree on Tradition was issued by SPD Defence Minister Hans Apel on 20 September 1982. Apel's Decree also failed to use the word *Wehrmacht*. It admitted that parts of the armed forces under Hitler had incurred guilt through their involvement with National Socialism, and stated that a system of injustice such as the Third Reich cannot provide a basis for tradition. But the word Apel used for this involvement was 'caught-up in' (*verstrickt*), suggesting a certain helplessness, as if the *Wehrmacht* had been a fly caught in Hitler's web; and he also claimed that many soldiers had been 'abused' by Hitler. He was careful not to say that the *Wehrmacht* cannot pro-vide a basis for tradition; nor did he mention crimes.

This step was taken on 17 November 1995 when CDU Defence Minister Volker Rühe made the following declaration at the 35th *Bundeswehr* Commanders' Conference in Munich: 'As an organization of the Third Reich, the *Wehrmacht*, at the level of its military leaders, and with certain parts of its troops and soldiers was caught up in the crimes of National Socialism.' 'As an institution', Rühe continued, 'it therefore cannot form the basis of a tradition.' Rather it was above all the 'lib-eral values of German history' which formed this basis, as well as the actions of 'the women and men of German resistance against Hitler' (quoted in *Zeit*, 1 December 1995). Rühe's remarks demonstrated a shift in the official view of the *Wehrmacht*. But many on the left found this shift too tenuous and objected to exon-erative formulations. Thus Rühe had used the formulation also used by Apel, 'caught up in' crimes. Moreover, in his speech he had referred to the exemplary role of some soldiers at the front. In contrast to the exhibition, Rühe was not pre-pared to break fundamentally with the 'two-wars' theory, according to which the *Wehrmacht* had fought a decent, indeed honourable war, largely distinct from the one the SS had waged behind the front.

This theory was one of the essential exculpatory pillars in post-war under-standings of the *Wehrmacht*. It made it possible to conceive of the Second World War in terms of 'them' (chiefly the SS or SD) and the 'ordinary soldier'. A similar division sustained the second of these pillars. Blame for the war was lodged with Hitler and other prominent National Socialist leaders, while the *Wehrmacht* was seen as a helpless tool, its soldiers as pawns. Indeed the consensus was that these soldiers were no less victims of Hitler's imperialism than the Red Army soldiers they were forced to fight against. The disastrous defeat at Stalingrad symbolized this self-understanding. Such divisions were, initially at least, necessary. In encouraging such a view, Adenauer bound the majority of Germans to his politics, and that meant to democracy and western integration (for Adenauer's political handling of the Nazi past, see Frei 1996). But it was also a problematic division. It resulted in millions of Germans conceiving of the fault-line between perpetrator and victim as running not between Germans and those they attacked and massacred, but between Hitler, or the SS, and the 'mass' of ordinary German soldiers. If they did conceive of the fault-line in international terms, then it was to blame the Red Army for alleged violations of the military code during the war, or the Soviets, Poles and Czechs for murdering and expelling Germans immediately before and after the end of the war.

This view was a standard feature of the official commemorative calendar and the rhetoric of remembrance in West Germany. Sabine Moller has appropriately termed this lumping together of Germans with the victims of National Socialism 'de-concretization' (Moller 1998). In 1984, the People's League for German War Graves Maintenance (*Volksbund Deutsche Kriegsgräberfürsorge*), an organization responsible for tending German war graves, suggested constructing a national memorial in honour of the German war-dead. The list of victims to be honoured was to begin with the 4.3 million dead German soldiers. The victims of Germany's civilian population, some 500,000 of whom had been killed in bombing-raids, were to follow. Those killed by the National Socialists on racial, religious or political grounds were only to feature third on the list (Moller 1998: 17). This more or less mirrored the order of victims in the text of the necrologue read out each year in November on the occasion of the Day of National Mourning (*Volkstrauertag*). When, in 1993, Chancellor Kohl suggested dedicating Schinkel's *Neue Wache* to the 'victims of war and the rule of violence', he was continuing this tradition of blurring the distinctions between dead German soldiers, dead Red Army soldiers, dead Jews, dead Sinti and dead communists (for a more general discussion of this tradition, see Chapter Eight).

In the context of the Cold War, moreover, it became normal in West Germany to argue that the *Wehrmacht*, in its attempt to hold back the 'red tide' in 1944, had been protecting the west and its civilized values against the more primitive culture of bolshevism. It had, in other words, been fighting against the right enemy, but for the wrong cause, namely National Socialism. Former soldiers were invited to believe that the *Wehrmacht*'s battle against the advancing Soviets had anticipated the post-war conflict between East and West. The *Wehrmacht* was even hailed as a forebear. This sympathetic view of the *Wehrmacht*'s stubborn retreat in the east was supported by historian Andreas Hillgruber in the 1980s (Hillgruber 1986). It was not only the political culture of West Germany which encouraged such exculpatory views. In indignation at the 'Crimes of the *Wehrmacht*' exhibition, the war generation would point to statements by Winston Churchill, Liddell Hart and other non-Germans confirming the soldierly honour of the *Wehrmacht*. Or they would quote Ronald Reagan, who, when advised not to join Helmut Kohl in an act of commemoration in 1985 at Bitburg (see Chapter Four), replied: 'I think there's nothing wrong with visiting that cemetery where those young men are victims of Nazism also, even though they were fighting in the German uniform, drafted into service to carry out the hateful wishes of the Nazis. They were victims, just as surely as the victims in the concentration camps' (Hartmann 1986: 240). Remarks such as these made self-exculpation all too easy – especially when they came from the highest political representative of a former enemy.

There were attempts by historians to present a less positive picture of the *Wehrmacht*. In 1964, historian Hans-Adolf Jacobsen produced a report for the Frankfurt Auschwitz trials revealing that the notorious Commissar Order was in essence formulated by *Wehrmacht* High Command itself, rather than 'imposed' by Hitler. In 1969, historian Manfred Messerschmidt demonstrated that *Wehrmacht* soldiers had been prepared for the ideological and genocidal war against communists and Jews since 1933; they had as it were been mentally sworn in to Hitler's plans for annihilation (Messerschmidt 1969). Christian Streit's groundbreaking dissertation proved the responsibility of the *Wehrmacht* for the mass murder of Soviet POWs (Streit 1978). But his study earned him little recognition; on the contrary, he was unable to obtain an academic post and became a schoolteacher. In the 1980s, *Wehrmacht* military justice attracted critical attention, notably from Messerschmidt and Fritz Wüllner. The issue of the holocaust took somewhat longer to move into focus as a *Wehrmacht*-related problem. In 1981, Helmut Krausnick and Hans-Heinrich Wilhelm produced a study which pointed to the support role of the *Wehrmacht* in the slaughter of Jews by the Gestapo, Criminal Police and SD (Krausnick and Wilhelm 1981). In the mid-1990s, the young Austrian historian Walter Manoschek examined the connection between the taking and killing of hostages, and the holocaust (Manoschek 1993). Manoschek subsequently edited a volume documenting *Wehrmacht* racial criminality (Manoschek 1996).

But there was for a long time a certain reluctance to integrate this awareness into the major standard narratives of the Second World War. Omer Bartov, an expert on the *Wehrmacht*, has pointed out that the multi-volume series 'The German Empire and the Second World War', edited by the *Bundeswehr*-affiliated Office for Research into Military History (MGFA), 'almost completely fails to mention the holocaust' (Bartov 1995: 610–11). The policy within the MGFA of providing a framework for the production of individual studies which revealed *Wehrmacht* complicity (notably by Manfred Messerschmidt), while not incorporating these micro-narratives into the grand narrative, demonstrated a conflict of interest. The source of this conflict of interest can be located in the clash between the claims of objective historiography on the one hand, and the claims of what one might term the 'prevalent image' on the other: the image of the *Wehrmacht*, in other words, within West Germany's social and political culture. As Bartov has pointed out, critical publications were greeted by the media and public 'with expressions of astonishment and disbelief, horror and rage' (Bartov 2000c: 168).

Despite the historians, then, the popular and political image of the *Wehrmacht* in West Germany remained largely uncritical. In many ways, too, the *Wehrmacht* remained a model for the *Bundeswehr*, which was partly built on a questionable view of the *Wehrmacht* soldier as a skilled craftsman, transcending politics and ideology, yet equipped with the right anti-bolshevist instincts; hard in battle, yet fair; loyal, yet – as the July 1944 plotters became more of an ideal for the *Bundeswehr* – not indiscriminately obedient; active and engaged, yet in some respects the passive victim. This was an inherently contradictory image that was just waiting to be blown apart.

Post-war images of the *Wehrmacht* in East Germany

Former *Wehrmacht* soldiers also contributed to the rebuilding of the army in the GDR, although not to the same extent as in the FRG. Of the 17,500 officers in the National People's Army (NVA) at the time it was set up in 1956, only about 500 had served in the *Wehrmacht*. But quite a number of these played a central role in running the NVA. NVA soldiers, moreover, wore uniforms which, in cut and colour, were not dissimilar to the *Wehrmacht* uniform. This was justified by the SED with reference to the need to rescue the 'symbol of military and patriotic honour' from 'German imperialism and fascism'.

In 1957, however, a ruling by the GDR Politburo led to the gradual removal of former *Wehrmacht* officers from active service, a radical measure without parallel in the more dilatory FRG. In East Germany's political culture, it was also generally the case that the crimes of the *Wehrmacht* were not hushed up to the same degree as in West Germany. GDR historian Kurt Finker has pointed out that an obligatory GDR school textbook for history from 1958 drew the attention of pupils to the fact that 'many soldiers in the Nazi *Wehrmacht* stole property from the inhabitants of the occupied territories', and that 'the execution commands of *Wehrmacht*, SS and SD waged a war of destruction' (*ND*, 30 January 1998). Finker admitted, however, that the remilitarization in the GDR and the escalation of the Cold War went hand in hand with a tendency to lose sight of issues of *Wehrmacht* criminality. What Finker did not say is that there was also a tendency in the GDR to present the *Wehrmacht* as a victim; terms such as 'Nazi *Wehrmacht*' implied an abuse of the army by fascism, and exculpated the individual soldier, even the army itself. Given that the GDR was, by official ordination, anti-fascist, the former *Wehrmacht* soldiers were invited to imagine that they had now swapped sides from the 'wrong' one to the 'right' one, a view which hardly encouraged self-critical reflection. Moreover, while *Wehrmacht* history in the West was often reduced to the story of Stauffenberg, in the East there was much official focus on the National Committee for a Free Germany, an anti-Hitler organization set up by *Wehrmacht* POWs in Soviet imprisonment (see Chapter Three). *Wehrmacht* soldiers converted to the cause of opposing Hitler were an ideal in both the FRG and the GDR.

When shown in Potsdam (1995) and Erfurt (1996), the 'Crimes of the *Wehrmacht*' exhibition attracted little attention. This was put down by some to the fact that the east Germans were better acquainted with the history of *Wehrmacht* crimes. The exhibition was accordingly declared to be of relevance only for 'west' Germans. But numbers of exhibition visitors in the west were also fairly low prior to Munich, which marked the beginning of the mass interest. Moreover, when the exhibition was shown in Dresden in January and February 1998, it attracted 54,000 people –

44,000 more than in Potsdam and Erfurt together. Jens Hommel, who organized the showing of the exhibition in Dresden, said it had hit an 'east German nerve' (*SächZ*, 2 March 1998). Interestingly, Hommel's organization, an adjunct of the Heinrich Böll Foundation, had arranged for a number of exhibits to be added demonstrating that the reception of the *Wehrmacht* in the GDR was no less problematic than it had been in the FRG. These exhibits included the post-war memoirs of Wilhelm Adam, a 6th Army Adjutant turned opponent of Hitler, and pamphlets such as Wolfgang Scheyer's 'Codeword – Free Germany', which focused on the National Committee for a Free Germany.

Despite these additions, the argument that the message of the exhibition was not new for east Germans remained a staple feature of its reception in the east. Vice-President of Saxony's Regional Parliament, Heiner Sandig (CDU), claimed that it was a 'typically west German exhibition' and 'out of place' in the east because the problem in the GDR was that it had not been possible to suggest that there were those in the *Wehrmacht* who might *not* have been criminals. Dresden town councillor Andreas Grapatin (CDU) remarked: 'we don't need any west German communists to tell us things about the *Wehrmacht* which the East German communists drummed into us for 40 years' (*Welt*, 22 January 1998). During the debate on whether to show the exhibition in Dresden's Regional Parliament, Volker Schumpff (CDU) argued that 'we didn't take to the streets in 1989 so that communist lies about history can be disseminated today in a democratic parliament' (*FPC*, 4 March 1997). The suggestion here was that the reputation of the *Wehrmacht* had been sullied by communist demonization, a demonization which the exhibition was adjudged to be reinforcing. It was, in other words, this demonization that the eastern *Länder* should be coming to terms with, not the crimes of the *Wehrmacht*. One suspects the CDU of using this argument in the interests of inculpating socialism and exculpating traditional elites, a time-honoured west German practice. But there were those in the SPD with similar views, such as Thomas Mädler, a member of the Dresden Regional Parliament, who claimed that his father, an officer in the *Wehrmacht*, had talked openly about its role under Hitler. For Mädler, the debate about the exhibition was also a 'west German discussion' (*SächZ*, 23 January 1998). On balance, it will have been the case that the GDR faced the issue of *Wehrmacht* crime more, though only somewhat more, than the FRG.

The voice of the camera

With the collapse of communism in 1990, there was no longer any East Germany to blame West Germany for continuing in the imperialist footsteps of the *Wehrmacht*. With the end of any real threat from eastern Europe, the need to adapt *Wehrmacht* history to the Cold War exigencies of western anti-communism likewise fell away. National confrontation with the crimes of the *Wehrmacht* became possible. It became possible, also, to see Soviet Russia as what, between 1941 and 1944, it undoubtedly had been – a victim of Hitler, and of the *Wehrmacht*. The return of war and of atrocities to Yugoslavia in the 1990s, and the decision to deploy the West German army in logistical support of NATO troops in Bosnia in September

1995, caused many Germans to look back anxiously to the role played by the *Wehrmacht* in Yugoslavia, and to ask whether the *Bundeswehr* really was a different army, and whether the deployment in support of NATO was morally acceptable. All these developments prepared the ground for the massive and enduring impact of the *Wehrmacht* exhibition. Equally, the Goldhagen debate in 1996, which also focused on the crimes of 'ordinary Germans', created a climate in which the exhibition could be received as it was. Yet it may not have had the effect it did had it not chosen a particular medium of representation: the photograph. In an article on the exhibition, historian Gerhard Paul argued that the exhibition had succeeded where historical research on the *Wehrmacht* had failed. 'It needed the medium of photography', he wrote, 'characterized as it is by the aura of the objective and concrete, to make a wider public aware of the crimes of the *Wehrmacht* and to trigger dialogue across the generations about the responsibility of the individual' (*KN*, 7 January 1999).

Generally, we conceive of armies at war in terms of advancing or retreating soldiers, soldiers in battle, soldiers dying or wounded, and soldiers in victory or defeat. This is a functional, yet at the same time epic image. It is also a heroic and sometimes tragic one. In the post-war period, Germans will have had such an image of the *Wehrmacht*, an image reinforced by the soldiers themselves, who returned home and told of the devastating effect of the Russian winters, of inadequate clothing, hunger and brutal treatment at the hands of the Russians. This tragic view of Hitler's war in the east was recently underpinned in clichéd images by the conservative film-maker Josef Vilsmaier in his feature film *Stalingrad* (1992). The 'Crimes of the *Wehrmacht*' exhibition broke radically with this view. It adopted a perspective which showed those commonly thought of as victims, namely the German soldiers, as killers – not of enemy soldiers, but of civilians, not in action at the front, but in firing squads. In hundreds of photographs, the various stages in the killing of Jews, communists and others arrested as 'partisans' or in the course of grotesque reprisal actions were graphically illustrated. These victims, the real victims, were shown as they awaited or lined up for execution. They were shown being shot or hanged. They were shown lying in mass-graves, or dangling from balconies, trees, telegraph poles and makeshift gallows. In other photographs, their bodies lay in haphazard piles, or strewn across the ground, cast away like spent matches. Soldiers could be seen arresting civilians, accompanying them to their execution, looking on as the victims dug their own graves, or standing by as preparations for killing got under way. Soldiers were seen cocking their rifles, shooting into crumpling bodies, and placing nooses around necks. Worst of all, there were photographs of soldiers gazing listlessly and indifferently at dead bodies; on occasion, they were smiling. Many photographs suggested that killing was mechanical; some suggested it was a source of satisfaction, even pleasure.

The exhibition impressed on the viewer, in a similar manner to Goldhagen's study (see Chapter Five), the importance of understanding that the campaign of destruction extended well beyond the gates of the SS-run annihilation camps. It extended to the 'killing fields' of occupied Russia (Heer 1995: 57). Even more shockingly, perhaps, it involved the *Wehrmacht*. The 'Crimes of the *Wehrmacht*' exhibition understood the war in the east not in terms of battles or of territorial gains and losses, but in terms of inhumanity. Thus the subsections of the exhibition were titled 'Jew-torturing', 'Gallows', 'Death Zones', 'Shots in the Neck', 'Imprisonment' and 'Deportation'. These killings had nothing functional, but appeared gratuitous. They were not epic, but heinous and cynical. Not tragic, but senseless. In a way, the photographs were more shocking than the films shot by the Allies on liberating the concentration camps. For here were photographs taken *immediately before, during* and *after* acts of murder. They showed victims in direct and visible relation to their perpetrators, unlike the typical photographs of the dead in Bergen-Belsen.

Had the exhibition relied merely on text to convey its message, it would not have had the same effect. Most of the photographs had never been shown before; many were taken from east European archives only accessible since 1990. An aura of suddenly discovered criminal and judicial evidence adhered to them. The juxtaposition of hundreds of similar photographs may have resulted in an impression of repetition. But this repetition was not merely a rhetorical device or an aesthetic element, as some claimed. More importantly, it also served as evidence of widespread involvement in a murderous norm. In a recent study, Cornelia Brink examined the phenomenon of the iconization of concentration camp photographs. She argued that religious icons point beyond what is depicted and 'symbolize the heavenly realm', and that concentration camp photographs have a comparable symbolic power (Brink 1998: 235). In their case, of course, this power is negative: the unseen atrocities fall within the implicit framework of reference of each photograph. The photographs of dead bodies in the 'Crimes of the *Wehrmacht*' exhibition had a similar metonymic dimension.

In the modern technical age, photography and film enjoy the reputation of authenticity, turning hearsay into fact. The sources for the photographs in the exhibition were often not precisely specified, their locations left vague, their immediate event context unclear. Yet this weakness could not deflate the power of the images. Even when it became clear, as we shall see later, that a number of the photographs did not show what the exhibitors thought they showed, the public streamed into the exhibition. Many felt irritated by questions as to the reliability of the photographs, arguing that it did not matter whether some of them showed Jews bathing, or Finnish soldiers, or victims of the Soviets: others still showed *Wehrmacht* crimes. And even those that did not showed a similar kind of crime to that committed by the *Wehrmacht*. So the captions may have been wrong, some crimes even assigned to the wrong perpetrators, or the wrong location, but the photographs retained their exemplary character.

The photographs in the exhibition were also effective because – a truism – photographs access the emotions very directly. Visitors to the exhibition would peer at the often very small photographs, absorbing the visual, but hardly registering the text. The textual, to a degree, became redundant, because the photographs appeared to capture the essential moments in an unchanging sequence of arrest, preparation for execution, killing and body disposal. What mattered were the mechanics of annihilation. One serious charge against the exhibition was that it dissolved issues of context. Those executed came across in each case as absolute victims, the German executors as cruel perpetrators; nothing was 'said' in the images, often not in the text either, about why any given civilian or group of civilians had been arrested, or why they were being killed. After all, critics protested, there had been partisans, and it had been legitimate to take measures against them. Nothing was said, moreover, about the motives of the German soldiers. There were also complaints that the photographs were 'suggestive'. To a degree, they were. In those cases where it was not clear from the photographs who had actually done the killings, the visitor would nevertheless automatically imagine the cause of death to be an act of killing by the *Wehrmacht*. Viewers were invited to 'supply' the perpetrator.

Last but not least, the photographs in the 'Crimes of the *Wehrmacht*' exhibition were forceful because of what they implied about the photographer, and because the visitor to the exhibition was enjoined to share in the photographer's perspective. German soldiers, as of 1942, were forbidden from taking such photographs. That they still took them could be interpreted as a courageous gathering of evidence for posterity. But, equally, it could be construed as the expression of voyeuristic enjoyment, even pride. After all, such photographs were often sent home as trophies. Certainly the photographers were, quite literally, looking on. They were visually participating as much as those soldiers who could be seen standing around as captives were hanged or shot by others. The visitor had cause to reflect that the photographer observes, registers, knows, indeed objectifies his knowledge, but does not intervene. He comes to symbolize the position of those many German soldiers who observed crimes, or knew of them, yet did not protest. The perspective in the exhibition was that of the onlooker from *within* the ranks of the German army. It raised questions as to the moral complicity of those who did not murder, but witnessed brutality.

Towards the centre of public discourse

Journalist Theo Sommer maintained that the photographs had 'disposed once and for all of the myth that the *Wehrmacht* had remained an unassailable repository of decency, chivalry and honourable conduct in Hitler's empire of evil' (*Zeit*, 28 February 1997). Myths can only be disposed of if the process of enlightenment reaches deep into society. In this case, it certainly did. Thanks to the exhibition, the topic of *Wehrmacht* criminality moved, ineluctably, to the centre of public discourse.

Nearly a million people saw the 'Crimes of the *Wehrmacht*' exhibition. The spontaneous, informal, often heated discussions it triggered were counterbalanced by more formalized podium discussions. Many televised or taped interviews with former *Wehrmacht* soldiers were conducted. When the exhibition was shown in Vienna, Ruth Beckermann approached members of the older generation as they studied the photographs, asked if they had been in the *Wehrmacht* and, if so, if they had witnessed or known of atrocities (Beckermann 1998). But interviews were not restricted to the war generation. Social scientist Gabriele Rosenthal and her team, at the behest of the HIS, interviewed 131 people who had seen the exhibition in

Berlin, Potsdam and Stuttgart. Many of these belonged to other generations, such as the 'flak helper generation' (born between 1922 and 1929), the 'white generation' (men born between 1930 and 1939, who were neither in the *Wehrmacht* nor, subsequently, in the *Bundeswehr*), or generations born during and after the war (HIS 1998a). Countless interviews were conducted by the media, again by approaching people visiting the exhibition. Other, more collective forms of discourse were encouraged, not least by teachers, who accompanied groups of schoolchildren to the exhibition and, later, coordinated the articulation of responses back in the classroom. A frequent practice was to organize discussions between schoolchildren and those who had lived through the Second World War either as *Wehrmacht* soldiers or as citizens of the countries occupied by the *Wehrmacht*. Thus in Hamelin, during the showing of the exhibition in Hanover, a 79-year-old former *Wehrmacht* soldier related to schoolchildren how he witnessed executions near Shitomir (*DWZ*, 18 December 1998). When the exhibition was shown in Frankfurt, the Sigmund Freud Institute organized 'jour-fixe groups' every Friday, where some 30 to 35 participants of all age-groups would discuss their responses and experiences, under the guidance of a psychologist, in plenary session. The letters' pages of newspapers offered a vehicle for people throughout Germany to articulate their views, even to debate them. One critic of the exhibition, Günter Lichtenwalter, engaged in an exchange of letters with supporters in the Constance newspaper *Südkurier* in 1997–1998.

The psychological, sociological, media and public interest in such forms of articulation reflected a trend which even penetrated individual families. One girl showed her grandfather pictures from the exhibition catalogue; he reacted by talking to her for the first time about his war experiences, which included sharing a room with a man who had had to 'shoot 100 Jews a day' (*AN*, 5 May 1998). The exhibition triggered a response in members of *every* generation in Germany. It seemed that the self-delusion not just of the *Wehrmacht* generation had been shaken to the core, but also of generations not directly involved. For some, it was as if a taboo had been lifted on the asking of questions repressed for years, even decades. The following paragraphs examine the response to the exhibition as it was articulated in readers' letters and interviews. Most of the letters quoted were written to the *Saarbrücker Zeitung*, which proved a particularly rich source; they are, however, typical of responses around Germany.

Turning our attention first to the war generation, a perhaps surprisingly high number of soldiers was prepared to admit having witnessed crimes. In a study of the reception of the exhibition, Heer pointed out that comments by former soldiers in the visitors' books were often affirmative: 'It was true!', 'That's how it was! I was there!', 'Alas, this is how it was', 'The pictures are not lying – all of this happened!' (Heer 1999b: 138). Heer was right to remark that letters from former soldiers reproduced in newspapers were usually dismissive of the message of the exhibition, but there were exceptions. Heinz Battis, who fought in Russia, reported on crimes he had witnessed (*SBZ*, 18 February 1999). In Minsk, he recalled, he saw a German soldier kill an exhausted Russian prisoner simply because he was too weak to walk; and in a Russian village, the soldier walking next to him, on seeing a curious old woman stick her head out of a window, had casually thrown a hand-grenade at her. Another former soldier related how he witnessed the killing of 127 Italian forced labourers by officers (*MA*, 8 July 1995). Ruth Beckermann's interviewees, mostly Austrians, confirmed the crimes. One man claimed he had witnessed the very atrocities shown on some of the exhibition photographs (Beckermann 1998: 70). For some soldiers, it was often a relief to be able to talk freely. That they had been unable to tell their families and friends about the crimes they witnessed had to do with their sense of shame, the fact that their immediate environment generally did not want to know, and a fear of being branded a *Nestbeschmutzer* (someone who fouls his own nest). After all, their memories collided with the positive post-war images of the *Wehrmacht*.

Sadly, few of the soldiers who participated directly in such crimes were prepared to admit they had done so. Mostly, moreover, former soldiers were indignant at the exhibition. Not that they denied there had been crimes. The tendency was rather to place them firmly at the door of the SS and SD. Where *Wehrmacht* crimes were admitted, these were regarded as exceptions. Most former soldiers denied that they had been involved in, witnessed or even heard of *Wehrmacht* crimes. Instead, examples of enemy inhumanity were provided. Peter Koch described in a letter how Soviet planes bombarded a clearly marked hospital convoy, which was then attacked by partisans (*SBZ*, 17 February 1999). Josef Nonninger related how partisans mutilated and then killed soldiers who were going on leave (*SBZ*, 18 March 1999). Others related tales of Russian brutalities in POW camps, pointing to a Soviet predilection for cutting off genitals, or pouring water over German soldiers who froze into ice-blocks in seconds. By contrast, the *Wehrmacht* was presented as gentlemanly and honourable. According to Wilfried Backes, when the commander of his division heard that the English intended to bomb German positions in a Belgian village, he proposed surrendering rather than risk the life of the civilian population (*SBZ*, 24 March 1999). If such letters are to be believed, the German soldiers were not only the true gentlemen, they were also the true victims. Paul Baltes described how he was called up at the age of 18 in February 1945, captured in May, subjected to three POW camps, beaten, robbed, kicked, shaved from head to foot, carted off to Central Russia, put to work in a labour camp where he had to dig peat, and sent home in November 1945 reduced to a skeleton and suffering from dysentery and scabies. 'Was I a victim or perhaps a "criminal" in this *Wehrmacht?*' he asked pointedly (*SBZ*, 20–21 February 1999).

The striking thing about these criticisms is that they were based on the assumption that the exhibition sought to brandmark all members of the *Wehrmacht* as criminals. Particular exception was taken by former front soldiers to the exhibition's title, which, they felt, implied that the whole *Wehrmacht* was implicated in crimes. Would it not be better, they suggested, to rename it 'Crimes *in the Wehrmacht*', or 'Crimes of *individual Wehrmacht* units and soldiers'? These suggestions were often made against the background of the term '*Wehrmacht* exhibition', a term generally applied in the press, but studiously avoided by the HIS itself. This misnomer, used partly in provocation, and partly for ease of reference, did indeed imply that the exhibition was about the whole history of the *Wehrmacht*. Again and again Hannes

Heer insisted that it had not been the intention to pass generalized judgement. The introduction to the catalogue stressed this very point (HIS 1996: 7). During the showing in Stuttgart, the HIS did become involved in a 'percent debate'. Newspaper reports claimed that Hannes Heer had estimated the degree of *Wehrmacht* involvement in crime in the east at 70% or even 80% (see *FR*, 11 September 1995). In doing so, however, they misquoted him, interpreting the contents of a letter he read out at a press conference of 8 September 1995 as representing his own opinion (Nedelmann 1999: 238). At the same conference, he had made it clear that it was not possible at a distance of fifty years to draw up meaningful statistics. For all the focus on crime, the exhibition did not inculpate all *Wehrmacht* soldiers. Why, then, did front soldiers feel that a representation of part of the truth about the *Wehrmacht* was intended as a blanket condemnation?

As stated earlier, after the war most soldiers remembered their experience on the eastern front as one of privation, at best as one of courage and tenacity; any awareness that the *Wehrmacht* had committed crimes was suppressed. In the case of quite a number of former soldiers, the sudden emergence in the public arena of pictures of these crimes also brought to the surface their dormant feelings of guilt, if not for involvement in crime, then for knowing about it and turning a blind eye. Once released, this long-repressed guilt was so strong that it threatened to engulf the self-image as victim or honourable soldier. Straining under the impact of their own self-reproach and unwilling to admit or deal with the problem, many former front soldiers tricked themselves into believing that the blame was coming from outside, namely from the exhibition. They sought to project this blame back onto the trigger and, in delegitimizing the exhibition as biased, rid themselves of what feelings it had unleashed. But there was another possible reason for their anger, and here one would have to agree that the exhibition did generalize. Its underlying implication was, namely, that the war waged by the *Wehrmacht* was in all respects a 'war of annihilation'. Even those soldiers simply doing their duty at the front and not involved in crimes were in a sense guilty, because they had helped to advance this front, thus paving the way for the murderous killing units which followed behind. Without the territorial gains, there would have been no 'second' war against the civilian population. Indeed the war itself was arguably a crime, a war of aggression, started without warning and fought without mercy. It was therefore not correct to talk of two wars, one 'decent' and one 'criminal'. In this context, concepts such as fighting for the fatherland, courage, good-soldierly conduct and nobility in battle become meaningless as moral counterweights. What made the exhibition so painful for the war generation was the devaluation of their personal view of the war. This personal view may have been a *post hoc* construction, but in many cases individual soldiers will have simply done their duty as soldiers, no more, no less. To realize that this in itself was dishonourable was a shock.

This also explains why soldiers who had fought in the west, a campaign only briefly touched on in the exhibition, also felt their honour was being besmirched. By most accounts, the war in the west was conducted without the same rapacity as that in the east. But both campaigns were part of the same war, and served to uphold the same regime and its policies. Without doubt the exhibition undermined the belief of many surviving soldiers that they had been fighting not for Hitler, but for some transcendental ideal of fatherland. The *Wehrmacht* had, it now seemed, not been holding back the red tide; it had been helping to mass-murder human beings in a racist campaign. This, in turn, cast loyalty to army leaders and adherence to their orders in a problematic light. Loyalty came across, suddenly, as a betrayal of the real 'fatherland' – the conscience within. In showing soldiers killing helpless civilians, the exhibition raised the question as to why they had not refused to do so. Prior to this, many Germans had thought of moral rebellion as something one could only reasonably have expected from higher echelons of the army. Since Goldhagen's book and the 'Crimes of the *Wehrmacht*' exhibition, many Germans are dismayed that it was not more typical of ordinary soldiers.

The relocation of the notion of fatherland from within the tradition of protective anti-communism to within the conscience, in line with international human rights, is a shift which has led to the redefinition of military honour. It was with some confusion that former loyal front soldiers followed the first moves towards the rehabilitation of *Wehrmacht* deserters in the late 1990s. Not only had an exhibition morally censured them for their loyalty; now those who had disobeyed orders or deserted were being regarded with sympathy. In a reader's letter, one Fritz Leitermann protested: 'A normal people honours its soldiers as defenders of the fatherland' (*SK*, 22 October 1997). Post-1990 Germany, for many former soldiers, is not normal. The tenor of many soldiers' letters is that they feel dishonoured in the country for which they once fought. They accused the exhibition of 'generalized denigration' (*pauschale Verunglimpfung*). The abovementioned shift in the definition of honour has, perhaps, led some younger Germans to be unfair to the *Wehrmacht* generation, which was much more obedience-conscious than today's generations, and corrupted by Nazi propaganda. But there were those in the *Wehrmacht* who were aware of human rights, who refused to carry out inhumane orders, and who complained to their superior officers when they witnessed such orders being carried out. Thus Helmut Winkelmann related how his father consistently reported SS and *Wehrmacht* crimes; he was not disciplined in any way for doing this (*SBZ*, 18 February 1999). Even those who were ideologically blinded by anti-bolshevism could possess a conscience. Fritz Krause related that he believed Goebbels's propaganda about bolshevist subhumans until he 'experienced the inhumanities of war at the eastern front day in, day out' (*FR*, 11 March 1997). The message here, as with Goldhagen's study, was that racism did not preclude the evolution of a sense of conscience.

It was not just the former soldiers who felt dishonoured. Many of their wives also wrote to protest against the exhibition. Erika Groß recounted how, during the war, she had received a letter informing her that her husband 'had fallen on the field of honour, for nation and fatherland'. Over the course of fifty years she had told her daughter and her grandchildren of their good father and grandfather. 'Now our good men are being branded murderers and criminals' (*SBZ*, 31 March 1999). Another woman, Erika Franz, related that her husband had written to his parents of the welcome German soldiers received in Hungary; the Hungarians had 'rolled out whole barrels of wine' in celebration (*SBZ*, 20–21 February 1999).

Children, too, felt called upon to defend their fathers. Inge Schiffmann related how her father, in letters from the front, had asked her mother to send any food she could get hold of. He 'distributed it all to starving Russian children' (*SBZ*, 17 February 1999). Images of the *Wehrmacht* soldiers as heroes, victims and gentlemen were passed down from one generation to the next. Children also struggled to protect these images in the light of an exhibition which, while not directly invalidating subjective experience or memory, was clearly felt to be questioning its relevance in the overall context of a 'war of annihilation'.

Yet not all members of the 'second' generation reacted defensively. Some reacted angrily towards their fathers, or towards the Nazi system in which they were embroiled. Some sought in the exhibition answers to questions they had asked as children, or explanations for photographs they had seen, but not understood. Helga Flohr related that her father, a *Wehrmacht* soldier, possessed an album with photographs of burning towns and synagogues, as well as of victims of hangings. The exhibition provided her with a chance to procure answers to questions she could not ask her father or his comrades (*SBZ*, 22 March 1999). One woman interviewed by the HIS told how, during the war, a school-mate had brought photographs of hangings to show to the class. The images caused her sleepless nights, but she had been unable to talk about such matters to her father (HIS 1998a: 121–2). She told the interviewer she was glad others could now see the kind of photographs which had caused her distress. Another interviewee related that his father had witnessed atrocities and had possessed pictures of prisoners and civilians, but never talked about his experiences (HIS 1998a: 104). Faced with the silence of their families, children were unable to process the images, and repressed them. The exhibition released memories of these images and enabled them to be put in context. Some felt they were able to understand their fathers better, even if they could never know how they came to have the photographs, or what they actually did during the war. In one or two extraordinary cases of chance encounter, children discovered their own fathers on the photographs. Thus Annegrit Eichhorn identified her father in one of the photographs showing hangings of supposed partisans in Minsk in October 1941. He looks on as another soldier places a noose around a woman's neck (HIS 1996: 145).

Head of the Central Council of the Jews in Germany, Ignatz Bubis, expressed the hope that 'many young people would see the exhibition in order to understand how dehumanized' the 1933–1945 period was (HIS 1998b: 163). Statistics prove that the two groups best represented among those who saw the exhibition throughout Germany were the war generation itself, and young people of between 15 and 25 years of age. Of the 52,000 who saw the exhibition in Bremen, 20,000 fell into this younger category (*BA*, 9 July 1997); the percentage of young people amongst the 21,535 who had seen the exhibition in Bonn by the end of October 1998 was a very high 45% (*GA*, 30 October 1998). Most of the 16,500 who attended the exhibition in Constance were either young people or members of the war generation itself (*SK*, 20 November 1997). For some younger people, the motivation was to find out more about the kind of war their grandfathers were involved in. For others, the interest was more one of general interest in a dimension to national history which, despite the long-standing general presence of National Socialism on various subject curricula at school, was not one they had confronted in the classroom. Of course many were simply taken along by their teachers, but reactions were rarely indifferent. 'I find it difficult to express what I feel', said 18-year-old Willi Heinrich after seeing the exhibition in Koblenz. He acknowledged that he had been informed about National Socialism at school, but then added: 'these photos of tortured people and these mountains of bodies – that's something else!' (*RZ*, 16 July 1998). West German schools had in most cases, if at all, only tentatively broached the subject of *Wehrmacht* involvement in crimes. The 'Crimes of the *Wehrmacht*' exhibition changed this fundamentally.

Some 18 million German soldiers had served in the *Wehrmacht*. In bringing the extent of the army's criminal involvement to public attention, the exhibition triggered a process of coming to terms with the past within the 'ordinary family'. Intense inter-generational dialogue on issues of complicity was also an aspect of public, not just private discourse. Karl-Heinz Faßmann, who worked in the exhibition office in Bonn, saw in this a cathartic function: 'complete strangers talked to one another, young people with older people and the other way round, former *Wehrmacht* soldiers with other former *Wehrmacht* soldiers'. Bonn's town archivist Manfred von Rey described the exhibition as a 'communicative field the likes of which I've never experienced' (*GA*, 30 October 1998). During a discussion on the exhibition in Aachen, historian Norbert Frei welcomed the nationwide discussion and the dialogue between the generations. Frei maintained that the older generation at last felt the need to confront the findings of historical research, 'and the younger generation is ready to listen' (*AAZ*, 25 April 1998). It was this dialogue which ensured that the impact of the exhibition was, ultimately, more cohesive than divisive.

What helped to make the dialogue possible was the relative lack of judgementalism on the part of the younger generation. That this generation was ready to listen did not mean it was eager to act as judge and jury. Many simply wanted to know the truth. While some children and grandchildren indiscriminately defended or condemned their parents or grandparents, most assessed them more fairly: critically, but without moral superiority; with disappointment at their subjective failings, but with an awareness of the brutalizing effects of the times. There was often a sense that *Wehrmacht* soldiers had been both perpetrators and victims, victims not of Hitler, but of their own susceptibility, weakness or cowardice. Hannes Heer has pointed out that the first generation to ask the question 'Father, where were you?' was the 1968 generation. But this generation, according to Heer, had formulated this question as a self-righteous accusation. 'We can handle things differently today', Heer continued. 'Only if we can supplement the question "Father, where were you?" with the question "On which side would *I* have stood? How would *I* have reacted?" will we be able to bring this war to an end once and for all' (HIS 1998b: 113). The shift from a self-righteous to a more judicious, even self-critical assessment of the role of others was one identified by many commentators in their analyses of the effects of the exhibition. One newspaper reported that the important question for the 250 classes of schoolchildren that had seen the exhibition in Marburg was the personal one of 'How would I have behaved?' (*OP*, 7

October 1997). They examined the strength of their own moral reserves. The exhibition certainly helped to contribute to a generational change in perspective. For younger Germans today, the National Socialist past is not so much a source of personal shame, as, increasingly, a reminder of the importance of taking moral responsibility in the present and future. This development will concern us again in the context of the Martin Walser debate (Chapter Seven).

Political reception: the mainstream parties

The 'Crimes of the *Wehrmacht*' exhibition was not in any way 'imposed' on the towns or cities in which it was shown. The cost of acquiring the exhibition was at least 30,000 marks (Nedelmann 1999: 233). Local funding was required to meet these costs, and a considerable degree of organization needed to find an appropriate venue and set up an accompanying programme. From the very beginning, various institutions, foundations and committees clubbed together to meet these preconditions. Thus in Stuttgart, the local branch of the German League of Unions got together with the New Union of Judges to organize a showing. Other collaborative ventures included those between the East–West Society and the Town Culture Office in Freiburg, and between the City Department of Culture, the Region of Hesse and the Fritz Bauer Institute in Frankfurt. Local party branches of the Greens, often together with the SPD, mobilized support for the exhibition and arranged both funding and a venue felt to be 'appropriate' to its national importance. SPD politicians sometimes acted as patrons to the exhibition. In Aachen, the SPD and Greens were among the organizers, as well as the local branch of the trade unions and the Peace Prize Union. In contrast to this, the CDU, CSU and Republicans consistently sought to block any kind of official support for the exhibition. They resisted attempts to grant permission for showings in representative buildings such as town halls, hindered the allocation of town or state funding, and refused to speak at or even attend opening ceremonies (a notable exception is Georg Lewandowski, CDU mayor of Kassel, who gave the opening address in Kassel's Documenta Hall in 1998). They also organized 'alternative' events or exhibitions designed to counteract the impact of the 'Crimes of the *Wehrmacht*' exhibition, and issued an unending stream of statements rejecting it. CDU or CSU politicians who saw its merits were left stranded by local party branches. A case in point was Sven Thanheiser in Munich. The Munich CSU threatened to expel him from the party, and he was eventually demoted from his position as supervisor of Munich's Zoo in March 1997.

It might seem strange that events over fifty years ago should have preoccupied local party politics to this degree. But of course many of the CDU's voters are members of the older generation, who, the CDU presumably thought, would be against the exhibition. The SPD and Greens felt they should represent the views of their voting clientele, relatively speaking from the younger age-groups. These are very rough distinctions, but in large measure valid. The question is why such representation was understood to be the responsibility of political parties. There were enough organizations of former war veterans, enough pacifist youth organizations, to voice the views of the different generations. The political squabbles surrounding the exhibition can be explained by the fact that a certain understanding of history implicitly underpinned political positions in the present. Broadly speaking, the CDU saw itself as the party which had engineered German unification and established Germany as a leading and respected actor on the international stage. Germany's involvement in the eastward expansion of the EU and NATO, and the deployment of the *Bundeswehr* in out-of-area operations, reflected this new, self-confident role. It was legitimated historically with reference, self-contradictorily, to the image of the 'clean' German *Wehrmacht*, and the military resistance against Hitler. The position of the SPD, while not one of principled objection to this more 'expansive' German role, and while it seemed to shift more in favour of it throughout the 1990s, was more cautious. The SPD, and particularly the Greens, doubted that the *Bundeswehr* really had broken with a certain adulation of the *Wehrmacht*. They were alarmed at increasing instances of right-wing radicalism, use of Nazi insignia and celebration of gratuitous violence in the *Bundeswehr*. Some within the SPD distinguished between an acceptable 'peace-keeping role' for the *Bundeswehr*, and an unacceptable one of 'peace-making', which would bring the army too close to fighting in a war. There was a greater awareness here of the negative dimension to German military history, and of the need to avoid any scenario which might smack of a 'repetition' of the Second World War – a possibility which emerged with the bombing of Serbia by NATO. Those further to the left, including many in the PDS, suspected united Germany of attempting a 'remilitarization' of Germany's foreign policy. For the moderate left, a focus on *Wehrmacht* crimes would serve as a warning in the present; for the more radical left, it might even prevent the intended expanded role for the *Bundeswehr*.

Images of the *Wehrmacht* were thus of great relevance in the present. Given that the exhibition presented a critical view, it was bound to draw political flak from the CSU and CDU, and support from the left. Once caught up in the maelstrom of politics, it was equally inevitable that the right would seek to discredit the exhibition by declaring it to be left-wing propaganda, and the left to discredit criticism of the exhibition as right-wing propaganda. The HIS, angered by the charge that the exhibition was 'political' rather than historical, contributed to the politicization of the debate by dismissing all criticism regardless of its source and substance as right-wing carping. The politicization became increasingly vituperative and was often conducted *ad hominem*. Most notorious in this respect was CSU politician Peter Gauweiler, who sent a letter to over 300,000 Munich households pleading with people not to go to the exhibition, and insisting that Heer, as an active communist, was not a reliable judge of the *Wehrmacht*. He also claimed that Heer had been sentenced for a number of crimes including committing serious bodily harm. Heer succeeded in having a temporary injunction issued by Hamburg's Regional Court forbidding Gauweiler from repeating this assertion. The truth was that Heer had been sentenced to a small fine for resisting arrest during a demonstration against Emperor Hirohito in 1971, but had never physically assaulted anyone (*SZ*, 19 March 97). Besides, he had long since left the communist party. Surprisingly, the left made little of the fact that Peter Gauweiler's uncle, Nazi functionary Helmut

Gauweiler, had been responsible for producing a volume of anti-semitic propaganda photos during the war (*Focus*, 14 April 1997). Green Party leader in Munich, Bernd Schreyer, claimed that the Munich CSU was 'degenerating more and more under the rod of jacket-pocket Mussolini Gauweiler into a heap of brown salon fascists', evidence that the left could give as good as it gets; two CSU members promptly started a legal action against him (*SZ*, 16 May 1997).

It has to be said that the rejective attitude of the CDU to the exhibition was based on the weaker position. Roland Koch, CDU Parliamentary Party Leader in Hesse at the time, dismissed it as 'completely one-sided and undifferentiated' in its portrayal of *Wehrmacht* soldiers (*GIA*, 3 June 1995), while Erika Steinbach (CDU Frankfurt) described it as an 'exhibition with blinkers on' (*FR*, 10 March 1997). This charge was founded on what was perceived to be the unacceptable absence of references to the fact that many, indeed most soldiers had not committed crimes against the civilian population. Jan Philipp Reemtsma, head of the HIS, rightly wondered why the constant insistence that not all soldiers had been involved in inhumanities did not yield to the common recognition that *too many* had been involved. Could it be, he surmised, because there is an interest in resisting the implication that, if it had been so many, it could have been all (HIS 1998b: 157)? Certainly the CDU's fear was that the focus on crimes would lead to a shift towards a more critical view of the *Wehrmacht*. By imputing to the exhibition's organizers a defamatory intention, the CDU sought to persuade the general public that the image it projected was insulting, tendentious and wilful. On this view, images were being strategically deployed as a means to various ends, be this the criminalization of the *Wehrmacht*, driving a wedge between the generations, or indirectly undermining the reputation of the *Bundeswehr*. The general public was encouraged by the CDU and CSU to understand the exhibition as little more than communist slander, directed against German history and present democracy. In the CSU newspaper *Bayernkurier*, journalist Florian Stumfall even accused the left of initiating a 'moral campaign of annihilation' against the German people (22 February 1997).

In the eyes of the CDU, the exhibition was also one-sided because it 'left out' the history of *Wehrmacht* involvement in the July 1944 plot. The leader of the CDU in Frankfurt's City Council, Bernhard Mihm, noted with indignation that '20 July 1944, one of the proudest dates in German history, is not a theme in the exhibition' (*SZ*, 8–9 March 1997). The CDU feared that the exhibition would serve to undermine identification of the *Wehrmacht* with German resistance (see Chapter Three). I know of no corresponding concern in the CDU that the presentation of the *Wehrmacht* mainly in terms of resistance in the Berlin Memorial Site for German Resistance might lead to an underestimation of the extent and significance of *Wehrmacht* crime. The CDU's position was, therefore, not free of hypocrisy. The CDU, itself apparently so concerned about instrumentalization, sought to deploy the 16-year-old MGFA exhibition 'Rebellion of Conscience', which takes military resistance to Hitler as its main theme (and grossly overgeneralizes its extent), as a kind of counter-exhibition. Thus in Bremen in 1997, where the SPD and CDU were in coalition, the CDU only conceded to the showing of the 'Crimes of the

Wehrmacht' exhibition in Bremen's Town Hall on condition that the 'Rebellion of Conscience' exhibition also be shown there – which it duly was. Frankfurt's CDU pursued a similar tactic: the 'Rebellion of Conscience' exhibition was opened early in 1998, a few months after the Frankfurt showing of the 'Crimes of the *Wehrmacht*' exhibition. Historian Hans Mommsen was due to make a speech at the opening ceremony of the 'Rebellion of Conscience' exhibition, but the invitation was withdrawn after his objection that 'it is simply absurd to want to set one exhibition against another' (*Presse*, 24 January 1998).

Concessions to the CDU in Bremen also led to the placing of a board outside the 'Crimes of the *Wehrmacht*' exhibition stating *inter alia* that the majority of *Wehrmacht* soldiers were not involved in atrocities and that the 'individual soldier had no chance of preventing Hitler's war of annihilation'. The 'important chapter of resistance against Hitler' was also mentioned (*FAZ*, 4 March 1997). This went further than the board in Munich Town Hall, which had stated that the exhibition was not intended as a general condemnation of all soldiers. That the CDU's concept of counterbalancing was tendentious became clear when Ignatz Bubis suggested providing a permanent home for the exhibition alongside the Memorial Site for German Resistance in Berlin. The SPD greeted this idea, particularly Wolfgang Thierse, who thought the two exhibitions could relativize one another and create a 'rounded picture' of history (*Bild*, 27 March 1997). But Berlin's CDU reacted as if Bubis and Thierse had uttered a profanity. The point here is that, while there has long been acknowledgement of and a good exhibition on German resistance, this is not true in the case of *Wehrmacht* crimes. The argument that the 'negative' exhibition should be placed alongside the 'positive' one can be defended; such a juxtaposition could serve to counteract long-standing illusions about the *Wehrmacht* which the focus on military resistance helped to sustain. To reject this argument, while suggesting that a 'positive' exhibition should be set alongside the 'negative' one, is to reveal a questionable wish to stifle critical tones and protect idealized images. The Ministry of Defence, whose Berlin Office is right next to the Memorial Site for German Resistance, also rejected Bubis's idea. According to its understanding, the *Bundeswehr* must be linked to positive figures such as Stauffenberg, not seen in relation to any of the generals described in the 'Crimes of the *Wehrmacht*' exhibition. Yet today's soldiers could learn as much, if not more from an example *not* to follow as from one to follow. Although Rühe forbade *Bundeswehr* soldiers to get involved in public discussions on the exhibition or attend it in uniform, some local *Bundeswehr* officers nevertheless passed a partly positive judgement on the exhibition, and some *Bundeswehr* units did attend. Aachen's *Bundeswehr* Town Commandant sent 14 groups of soldiers in uniform to see the exhibition in Aachen, and was criticized from within the *Bundeswehr* for doing so (*AN*, 26 May 1998).

It remains to be seen when, if, and where the new 'Crimes of the *Wehrmacht*' exhibition will find a permanent home. Potsdam did not want to provide this home any more than Berlin did; in April 1997, its town councillors voted against the idea by 22 to 18. The CDU and FDP felt that Potsdam should be associated in the public realm with the finer points of Prussian history, Prussian virtues and military resistance against Hitler, whereas Hannes Heer saw Potsdam as the symbolic locus of Hitler's co-option of Prussian military tradition for his own purposes on the Day of Potsdam on 21 March 1933 (*FAZ*, 4 April 1997). Both views are tenable, as are the contrasting views of the *Wehrmacht*. Only the realization that one truth does not rule out another will put an end to opposition to providing the exhibition with a home.

Political reception: extremist groups

While parties wrangled in parliaments about the exhibition, the Young National Democrats – a scion of the NPD – and militant groups of anti-fascists, particularly the *Autonome*, fought it out on the streets. The high-point of these battles was in Munich on 1 March 1997, when 5,000 extreme right-wing demonstrators who had been bussed in from all over Germany faced 10,000 left-wing demonstrators near the Town Hall. If the extreme right-wing protestors demonstrated peacefully, then it was only because the police had gone to the trouble of disarming them in advance of their iron bars, gas pistols, knuckle-dusters and nail-studded boards. The more violent left-wing demonstrators pelted the young skinheads with stones, bottles, eggs and tomatoes. The police made arrests. These scenes were repeated, on a smaller scale but with disturbing regularity, in Dresden, Marburg, Kassel, Kiel, Cologne, Bonn and Hanover. Part of the responsibility must lie with the courts. In most towns where the exhibition was being shown, the police banned demonstrations for fear of public safety; this ban would then be upheld by the local Administrative Court. But, following the inevitable appeal, the Higher Administrative Court generally overturned the ban shortly before the demonstrations were due to take place, plunging town populations, police and politicians into panic.

It was as if the period of history described in the exhibition were being re-enacted. The extreme right marched in orderly, military-style formations through the streets, while the masked *Autonome* launched small-group attacks from side-streets, like latter-day partisans. But fears of a neo-Nazi escalation proved unfounded. After Munich, the extreme right was unable to muster many supporters for its protests. In Hanover in December 1998, 150 NPD supporters faced 2,500 left-wing and 100 extreme left-wing protesters. About 2,500 policemen were needed to keep the 150 and the 100 apart. By now, it was the extreme left that had to be disarmed of metal chains, knives, tear-gas canisters and slings. The violence was not restricted to clashes between demonstrators, however. The extreme right launched a bomb-attack on the exhibition in Saarbrücken in 1998, damaging part of it. In June 1996, the notorious right-wing extremist Manfred Roeder and an associate sprayed the words 'Lie' and 'Agitation' (*Hetze*) over a number of exhibits in Erfurt. Not to be outdone, the extreme left in May 1999 vandalized the house and car of Rüdiger Proske, a (Social Democratic) critic of the exhibition, in Hamburg-Bergstedt. In the same month, an anonymous anti-fascist group set fire to three buses in Schenefeld belonging to a bus-company which had driven NPD demonstrators to a protest against the exhibition in Kiel in January 1999. Here was the physically violent correlative to the verbal intensity of political debate; the exhibition was either literally or verbally attacked, its critics likewise.

It may have been the case that the extreme right-wing protest against the exhibition was what first drew it to public attention. In Munich, it became a gesture of anti-neo-Nazism and of commitment to democracy to go to the exhibition. Interest gathered its own momentum after Munich, but in Munich it can be causally linked to the violence – and seen as a reaction to Peter Gauweiler's aforementioned letter to 300,000 Munich households advising them to keep away from the exhibition, as sure a way of attracting interest as any (Kulturreferat 1998: 165–8). Clearly, the extreme right-wing, committed as it is to a glorification of German military tradition and driven by an aggressive nationalism, was bound to react angrily to an exhibition which cast a critical light on this tradition. But to a degree the CDU, and particularly the CSU, must take blame for not distancing themselves enough from the NPD. When Peter Gauweiler (CSU) laid a wreath on the grave of the Unknown Soldier in Munich in protest at the 'Crimes of the *Wehrmacht*' exhibition, he was hailed by the NPD as a hero. Similar NPD praise followed his much-publicized remarks in a Schwabing fish-restaurant, where he insisted that Reemtsma would be better advised to put together an exhibition on the victims of smoking (Reemtsma's father had been a cigarette-manufacturer) (*tz*, 20 February 1997). The CSU did not rebuke Gauweiler. Anti-exhibition cooperation between the NPD and the CDU, as in Stuttgart, conveyed the impression that there was no political distance between these two parties. At times, it seemed the CSU and CDU not only believed it necessary to foreground resistance and the decency of the ordinary soldier, but also tended towards the total heroization of the *Wehrmacht* typical of the far right. That the far left appropriated the exhibition in its protest against the *Bundeswehr* was also problematic. Arguably, the SPD and Greens could have done more to distinguish their position of scepticism towards certain kinds of *Bundeswehr* deployment more clearly from the total opposition to the *Bundeswehr* characteristic of the far left. Both the CSU/CDU and SPD/Greens were guilty, moreover, of not taking into account the possible effect that the political radicalization of the debate and the mutual mud-slinging among politicians would have on the far right and far left. Radicalized tones can lead to radicalist violence.

The search for parliamentary consensus

But the political interest in the 'Crimes of the *Wehrmacht*' exhibition should not only be seen negatively. The SPD and Greens, sometimes together with the FDP and PDS, did succeed in ensuring that the exhibition was shown in central, representative political buildings. It started its journey in a converted factory in Hamburg, and travelled to venues such as the Old Town Hall in Potsdam and Trade Union Buildings in Stuttgart and Erfurt before reaching its first truly 'political' building, the Town Hall in Munich (1997). This was the third attempt to organize a showing in a town hall; attempts in Nuremberg and Regensburg had foundered on the rock of CSU resistance. The exhibition was subsequently shown in the Town Hall in Bremen and Hanover (1997). Attempts to organize showings in the Regional Parliaments of Hesse and Baden-Wurttemberg failed, but the exhibition was shown in Schleswig-Holstein's Regional Parliament in Kiel in 1999. Gradually, the sense that the theme of the exhibition was central to Germany's political and historical culture could be given appropriate symbolic expression. It is perhaps unfortunate that the exhibition was not shown in the Federal Parliament. PDS members of parliament Heinrich Graf von Einsiedel and Gerhard Zwerenz had spearheaded a proposal that it be displayed in the foyer, but the Speaker of Federal Parliament Rita Süssmuth (CDU) turned this down. Nevertheless, the subject of the exhibition was debated in Federal Parliament in a quite extraordinary plenary session on 13 March 1997, a session now considered to be one of the highpoints of post-1990 parliamentary debate in Germany.

What was extraordinary about this session was the personal, emotional, even tearful tone of the contributions. Several parliamentarians took the chance to recount family histories. Otto Schily (SPD) talked of his uncle, an air force pilot who, towards the end of the war, had chosen to die in a hail of bullets from low-flying enemy aircraft – in despair at Nazi crimes. Schily also talked of his eldest brother, who volunteered for the front after an unsuccessful attempt to flee Germany; and of his father, an opponent of Hitler who was nevertheless indignant at not being called up because of his membership in an anthroposophical society (Thiele 1997: 181). Schily then referred to his wife's father, Jewish partisan Jindrich Chajmovic, who had fought against the *Wehrmacht*. Of those he had mentioned, Schily concluded, only Chajmovic had put his life at risk for 'a just cause' (Thiele 1997: 182). Christa Nickels (B'90/Greens) told of her belated discovery from a photograph that her father was a member of a Death's Head Unit (Thiele 1997: 192–3), Freimut Duve (SPD) of the deportation of his Jewish grandmother (Thiele 1997: 190), and Erika Steinbach (CDU) both of her grandfather's death after a period of concentration camp imprisonment, and of her great-uncle's death due to the NS euthanasia programme (Thiele 1997: 191). Gerhard Zwerenz (PDS) and Alfred Dregger (CDU) put their cases for and against the exhibition from the respective positions of Second World War deserter and duty-conscious infantryman. Here, at the very centre of politics, the same personal and inter-generational exchanges took place as had taken place wherever the exhibition was shown. Complexities were rendered visible. Thus Steinbach, a vehement opponent of the exhibition, had a family which had been persecuted by the Nazis, and Nickels, a supporter, expressed deep understanding for the sufferings of the perpetrators. Alfred Dregger, an intransigent upholder of *Wehrmacht* honour for decades, even agreed to 'examine the criticism made of me' (Thiele 1997: 193). In the sometimes tearful atmosphere of personal revelation, the various motions for and against the exhibition were not very fully discussed. For one session, Federal Parliament favoured narrative and even group therapy over debate.

Unfortunately, the tolerant tone of the debate was not carried over into the subsequent small-group sessions. It was unlikely that the CDU would agree to the showing of the exhibition in German Parliament, but there was still hope that it would be possible to draw up an all-party statement on the role of the *Wehrmacht*.

Freimut Duve (SPD) attempted to negotiate a compromise. Finally, he formulated a text which stated that it was 'above all the leadership of the criminal German Nazi regime, which included parts of the leadership of the *Wehrmacht*, that was responsible for millions of Second World War victims and for the act of genocide' (*SZ*, 18 April 1997). But the CDU found this too hard on the *Wehrmacht*, while the Greens found it too soft. On 24 April 1997, the CDU, CSU and FDP used their parliamentary majority to push through a three-party motion repudiating 'any one-sided or generalized condemnation of members of the *Wehrmacht*', and declining support for the exhibition on the grounds that it is 'not the job of Parliament to judge or evaluate private initiatives' (Thiele 1997: 222). The motion also reiterated the conservative view that the Second World War was 'one of the most terrible tragedies of German and European history' to which 'millions of German soldiers and civilians had also fallen victim'. Responsibility for this war was placed squarely with the 'criminal regime of National Socialism'. But the motion did, albeit rather too briefly, concede *Wehrmacht* participation in criminality – *before* the standard exculpation of most *Wehrmacht* soldiers and the obligatory reference to resistance.

In a sense, there were two debates here. The first had to do with the exhibition's exclusive focus on crime, the second with how the parties themselves saw the *Wehrmacht*. Whenever the debate swayed towards the second of these issues, it appeared that politicians genuinely wanted to find an inter-party consensus which would, if not depoliticize this chapter of history, then at least distil an essence of agreement on how it should be viewed. Such agreement was reached in 1998 in Lower Saxony's Regional Parliament. All political parties underwrote a statement which welcomed the exhibition to Hanover's Town Hall, while pointing to the importance of resistance to Hitler and condemning attempts to relativize Nazi crimes (*BraunZ*, 13 November 1998). In Hamburg in 1999, the CDU, Greens and SPD agreed on a motion which emphasized that the exhibition was 'important for enlightenment', but included the term 'caught up in' to describe the relationship between the *Wehrmacht* and Nazi crimes (*Welt*, 20 May 1999). These formulations were bland and awkward, but at least the CDU appeared willing to acknowledge a degree of *Wehrmacht* criminality. For its part, the SPD was willing to accept that resistance could be mentioned alongside criminality without playing the latter down. Against the background of these statements, all parties in Hamburg and Hanover were able to welcome the exhibition, even if the CDU still felt it vastly overstated the crimes. This agreement was important, because it signified the first step amidst all the political wrangling towards a new staple in the political culture of memory: a mutually acceptable ambivalence.

In other ways, too, the debates had a significant impact on the political and legal realm. The shift in perceptions encouraged by the exhibition helped the cause of those surviving deserters from the *Wehrmacht* who were seeking moral and legal rehabilitation. Deserters and other victims of Nazi military justice such as Ludwig Baumann, Gerhard Zwerenz and Willi Jünemann often spoke at events accompanying the showing of the exhibition. In Marburg in October 1997, a Memorial to the Unknown Deserter was erected near the site of the exhibition, though it was subsequently removed because it had been put up without permission (*GIA*, 18 October 1997). The exhibition also helped to create a climate of public and media sensitivity to the issue of benefits for perpetrators. The North German Television *Panorama* programme reported in early 1997 that some German war criminals were still in receipt of special war pensions. This revelation caused such waves of indignation that some local authorities moved to cancel these, and the SPD and Greens called for the exclusion of 'perpetrators' from war pension schemes (*BN*, 1 February 1997).

The impact of criticism

On 4 November 1999, Jan Philipp Reemtsma called a press conference and announced that the HIS intended to withdraw the 'Crimes of the *Wehrmacht*' exhibition from circulation and, over a three-month period, allow it to be scrutinized by an independent commission. A new exhibition would then be designed on the basis of its recommendations. This commission consisted among others of Omer Bartov, Christian Streit and Manfred Messerschmidt (historians), Cornelia Brink (an expert on holocaust iconography), Friedrich Kahlenberg (Federal Archive President) and Reinhard Rürup (the former director of the Topography of Terror). Reemtsma admitted that errors had been made in the choice and presentation of photographic material (*SZ*, 5 November 1999). He also maintained that the HIS had 'defined the parameters for its research too narrowly' (*ND*, 5 November 1999). Reemtsma regretted that, as a result of criticism, the exhibition had suffered a huge 'loss of credibility', a loss which could not be overcome by making small changes. The withdrawal of the exhibition was something of a surprise: plans to show it in Braunschweig (as of 11 November 1999) and New York (as of 2 December) had to be abandoned. There had been no indication that the HIS would suddenly cave in to criticism after having withstood it for over four years. But Reemtsma, clearly, had become alarmed at the recent incursion of criticism into serious academic publications (*FAZ*, 5 November 1999). Two of these publications, indeed the most important, were by foreign historians, Bogdan Musial (a Pole) and Christián Ungváry (a Hungarian). Reemtsma recognized that criticism from outside Germany, on the surface at least, appeared objective, in contrast to the politicized criticisms from conservative German historians. It was being taken seriously and widely publicized by all German newspapers, even those hitherto supportive of the exhibition. That Heer had instigated legal proceedings against Musial (and other critics) Reemtsma publicly regretted (*SZ*, 5 November 1999). Presumably, Reemtsma feared that international criticisms would cast a shadow over the showing in New York, the exhibition's first foreign venue outside German-speaking countries. Presumably he was also confident that allowing the criticisms to be investigated by a highly professional team of academics from outside the HIS would benefit the Institute. In the event, he was right. The commission came to the conclusion that the HIS had not manipulated material, a charge which had been repeatedly levelled against it.

The objections raised by Musial and Ungváry – whose views were subsequently heard by the commission – were hardly new. But they furnished their criticism with a mass of evidence and statistics. Musial's criticisms, published in the prestigious *Vierteljahreshefte für Zeitgeschichte* (*Quarterly Journal for Contemporary History*), were based on the discovery that at least 11, and possibly as many as 31 photographs out of 801 in the catalogue showed victims not of *Wehrmacht* crimes, but of murderous actions carried out by the NKVD, the Soviet secret police. Surprised by the rapid advance of the Germans, the NKVD in Poland and the Ukraine had had no time to organize the transport of tens of thousands of prisoners, and so resorted to slaughtering them. Jews, Ukrainians and Poles deemed hostile to Soviet interests were massacred, for instance in the citadel in the Polish village of Zloczów (Musial 1999: 567ff.). The advancing Germans came upon these bodies and exhumed them. In support of his thesis, Musial pointed out that, in one or two of the photographs, Germans could be seen holding handkerchiefs over their noses, a clear indication that the victims had been dead for a while, not recently shot by the *Wehrmacht* (Musial 1999: 564). Musial's implicit contention was that Heer and his team may have fallen for Soviet propaganda. The Soviets, on finding photographs of killings on German POWs, sent them to the 'Special State Commission for Establishing and Investigating the Crimes of the German Fascist Invaders', which promptly attributed the depicted atrocities to the *Wehrmacht* even in cases where the NKVD had been responsible. Moreover, because Heer's team had not recognized that some photographs showed NKVD crimes, they had not understood why such photographs had been taken in the first place – namely for exploitation by the Goebbels propaganda machine (Musial 1999: 586). Had they referred to other sources and archives, as Musial had, these and other mistakes could have been avoided.

Musial also pointed out that photographs of burning villages – examples of which were also to be seen in the exhibition – may show villages set on fire by the Soviets, not the *Wehrmacht*. He concluded his article by stating his intention to investigate the many 'errors, weaknesses, false captions, manipulations, distortions or inconsistencies' in the exhibition (Musial 1999: 590). His criticism was taken up and reinforced by Ungváry (Ungváry 1999). Thus Ungváry also believed some photographs to show NKVD victims, such as those taken in Tarnopol: these could not show crimes committed by the *Wehrmacht*, as the HIS claimed, because the *Wehrmacht* was never in Tarnopol (Ungváry 1999: 588). He pointed out that several photographs showed Hungarian and Finnish soldiers, recognizable by their caps, shoulder-straps and the lapels on their uniforms, and that some photographs showed SD or SS members, or Soviet auxiliaries, with the *Wehrmacht* not in evidence. His most telling criticism was that the organizers had used photographs of the same scene taken from different angles at different points in the catalogue, sometimes providing them with different captions (Ungváry 1999: 594, note 43). Thus photograph 9 on page 187 of the exhibition catalogue and photograph 84 on page 196 show the same hangings from contrasting perspectives; in one case, the caption is 'Unknown Location: Soviet Union or Poland', while in the other it reads 'Unknown Location: Soviet Union. Propaganda Company Photo' (HIS 1996). Ungváry came to the conclusion that only 333 of the photographs in the catalogue might actually show crimes; of these, he argued, only 80 show crimes which could be allocated to *Wehrmacht* soldiers (Ungváry 1999: 593–4).

This was a harsh judgement. The HIS was able to defend itself against some charges. It pointed out that the *Wehrmacht* and SS had used auxiliary troops of non-Germans to do their dirty work; that while the SS and SD had often done the killing, the *Wehrmacht* was indirectly involved; and that those photographs which did not portray crimes nevertheless set the scene in the sense that they showed the exceptionally destructive context of the war in the east. As regards the false attributions, the HIS could not convincingly counter the claim that it had not cross-checked in different archives. The use of photographs showing the same scene from different perspectives with different captions was at best sloppy – contradictions could have been avoided by closer comparison of the exhibition's photographs – and at worst indeed manipulative, in the sense of trying to make a little material go a long way. Close examination of the photographs in the catalogue, moreover, reveals examples of photomontage. Thus on page 73, the heads of the figures in the foreground of photograph 2 are clearly too large for the bodies, while the body shown in photograph 68 on page 209 appears to have three legs (HIS 1996). The use of such photos does not necessarily demonstrate trickery (though it might). But it does prove that the HIS handled its sources less than critically.

To be fair to the HIS, the incorrect attribution of photographs is a common occurrence. One of the most notorious of all photographs of German atrocities shows a man pointing his rifle towards a woman, who, with her back to him, protectively clasps her child to her breast as if expecting to be shot. It has been shown in exhibitions around Germany, and features in permanent exhibitions in Sachsenhausen and the Memorial Site for German Resistance. Another version of this photograph, showing a group of figures huddled in front of the woman on the far right of the picture, is also in circulation. It can be seen in the exhibition on *Wehrmacht* justice in Torgau (see Chapter Two), and seems to indicate that the soldier may have been shooting *past* the woman, not at her. The soldier has been variously identified as a *Wehrmacht* soldier (e.g. Goldhagen 1996a: 407), a member of the police battalions and a member of the *Einsatzgruppen*. The location is variously given as the Ukraine, Ravensbrück, Finland, the Black Sea and Poland (see Sojka 1998: 289–93). Given the secrecy with which many photographs of such acts were taken, given that the photographers often did not write the date, event and location on the back, given the often convoluted route by which photographs came to be in an archive, precise attribution is difficult. Much remains guesswork, not least for the archives. Because of such problems, cross-checking becomes essential. Few historians have been inclined to go to so much trouble. As the director of the Koblenz Federal Archive Friedrich Kahlenberg pointed out, photographs as a form of historical evidence have never been handled with the greatest of care by historians generally (*KSA*, 30 October 1999). It seems, too, that photographs have often been understood and used illustratively: this is the way it *could* have happened. The HIS may to a degree have opted for a similar approach. Because its thesis was controversial, and because this thesis was so dependent on photographic material, the reliability of the photographs as precise documentary evidence was an important issue for the critics. Their criticisms have highlighted the need to apply much more precise methods of sourcing when using such material.

In further defence of the HIS, it must be said that the criticisms by foreign historians may have been more political than at first appeared to be the case, and therefore somewhat exaggerated and pointed. Musial, a former activist in the Polish *solidarnosc* movement, has made communist crime his research theme. He has pursued this theme with a vigour which may have prejudiced his judgement. While he was right to identify false attributions in the exhibition, his motive may have been, in part, the wish to present the NKVD as the 'greater' criminal, and certainly as the 'original' criminal whose savagery was then 'imitated' by the German invaders. A review of his recent book (Musial 2000) points to this very tendency, and to arguably tasteless passages in which Musial implies that the Jews may have been in part responsible for the pogroms unleashed against them (*Spiegel*, 7 August 2000). Musial's views will be music to the ears of those conservative German historians keen to relativize the crime of the holocaust with reference to those of bolshevism.

Certainly right-wing historians in Germany, not least at Munich's Institute for Contemporary History, were quick to applaud Musial's criticisms and to deploy them against the exhibition. A key figure in this instrumentalization was the Institute's director, Horst Möller, one of the editors of the journal in which Musial's article appeared (a journal produced under the auspices of the Institute for Contemporary History). Möller, not without reason, is regarded as a supporter of relativist theories. Thus on 4 June 2000 he delivered a public encomium for historian Ernst Nolte on the occasion of the latter's receipt of the Konrad Adenauer Prize in Munich. As we saw (Chapter Four), it was Nolte who first seriously argued for interpreting the holocaust as a reaction to bolshevist atrocities. Möller has recently published a volume *The Red Holocaust* (Möller 1999) which explores similar anti-communist themes to those advanced in *The Black Book of Communism* (Courtois *et al.* 1998). Möller was therefore quick to recognize the relativist potential inherent in Musial's and Ungváry's criticisms, and to use these in an attempted delegitimation of the exhibition as left-wing propaganda. In an interview which appeared shortly before Reemtsma's withdrawal of the exhibition, Möller claimed that it was intended not as a serious work of research, but as 'agitation', and suggested that the HIS had used 'hammer-home' methods similar to those approved of by Adolf Hitler (*Focus*, 25 October 1999). Ungváry, a military historian, is also not without right-wing sympathies: he sought to exculpate the broad mass of *Wehrmacht* soldiers, views quoted by deeply conservative German newspapers (see, for instance, *JF*, 24 October 1997).

There is something of an 'institutional war' being waged here between the HIS and the Institute for Contemporary History. This latter Institute has done and still does much to promote and undertake good, critical research into National Socialism. But, under Möller's directorship, it seems that the strong conservative tendencies within the Institute are becoming stronger. Certainly the editorial committee for the Institute's journal is dominated by conservative historians. After Möller's Nolte encomium, the SPD's Minister for Education and Science, Edelgard

Bulmahn, described the Institute for Contemporary History as 'calcified' (*Focus*, 24 July 2000). By contrast, the left-leaning HIS has enhanced its public profile over the last five years, not least as a result of the exhibition (despite the criticism) and of a number of groundbreaking monographs into National Socialism – notably by Christian Gerlach (2000a and 2000b) – which have appeared in its publishing house. Not surprisingly, members of the Institute for Contemporary History have attempted to stigmatize the HIS as 'communist' or at least 'far-left' in order to discredit it. This criticism has focused largely on Hannes Heer. But while Heer once had communist associations, the HIS's membership – and the exhibition team – are politically more diverse. The remit of the HIS is to investigate the theory and history of violence across all political systems. The exhibition '200 Days and 1 Century' of 1995, which explored violence in 1945 by Germany, the USA and the Soviets, demonstrated that the HIS could be as critical of communism as of liberal capitalism. Attempts have also been made, more in the far-right-wing press, to discredit Reemtsma, who uses money he inherited from his father's cigarette company fortune to fund the HIS, as a 'salon bolshevist', or to suggest that the 'Crimes of the *Wehrmacht*' exhibition resulted from his bad conscience (his father, it has been claimed, may have collaborated with the Nazis). Reemtsma is certainly too subtle a thinker to be categorized as 'far-left'.

As it turned out, Reemtsma's withdrawal of the exhibition and convocation of an independent commission proved an effective reaction to the criticisms, whatever their provenance and motive. The commission published its bulky 86-page report in November 2000. In its conclusions (Bartov *et al.* 2000: 75–6), it stated that the 'Crimes of the *Wehrmacht*' exhibition was necessary and valuable, and may continue to make an essential contribution to the development of the historical-political culture in Germany – provided certain changes are made. The criticisms of the exhibition, according to the report's conclusions, were in part valid; it did contain some errors of attribution, was imprecise in its use of material, and did make too many generalized and suggestive statements. But the commission was not of the opinion that the Institute had faked material, either photographic or textual, and stressed that the false attributions were symptomatic of a general historiographical lack of sensitivity in dealing with visual documentary sources. The commission was in no doubt that the exhibition's research team had worked seriously and responsibly, and also in no doubt that the basic thesis of the exhibition was correct, namely that the *Wehrmacht* was not merely 'caught up in crime' in eastern Europe, but had in part led and supported this criminal campaign. The commission thus recommended that the exhibition be corrected of errors in both photographs and text, adapted somewhat to include the perspective of the victims, generally overhauled to meet the requirements of historiographical methodology and rigour, and reshown.

This was a disappointment to those, such as Möller, who had hoped the moratorium – which had been extended from three months to a year – would turn out to be permanent. It was a disappointment too, surely, for Musial and Ungváry. The commission had examined their complaints carefully, and taken issue with most of them. All in all, only 20 photographs out of the 1,433, the commission found, definitely had no place in the exhibition (Bartov *et al.* 2000: 70). The commission's most serious charge was directed against the HIS for the manner in which it had dealt with its critics, namely by taking legal action against them (Bartov *et al.* 2000: 75–6). In August 2000, Reemtsma had more or less ejected Heer from the HIS. The HIS has remained tight-lipped over the reasons. Personal differences between Reemtsma and Heer may explain Heer's departure, as may disagreements as to the possible extent of changes to the exhibition. One other reason may be that Heer had to go because a scapegoat was needed. But it was Heer who, to judge at least from press reports, was most vigorous in his pursuit of litigation against Musial and others. Undoubtedly his failure to restrict himself to defending the exhibition by conventional means, namely through serious academic argument (of which he is very capable), gave rise to the impression that the HIS had run out of such arguments. By removing Heer, who had already had to step down as the head of the exhibition in November 1999, Reemtsma appeared to acknowledge the error of litigation. With Heer gone, moreover, the constant objections from the right that the exhibition had been entrusted to a 'communist' or a 'non-historian' will come to an end (Heer had completed his first university state exam in literary studies and in history, but had been prevented from completing the second because of his connections to the German Communist Party).

Conclusion

We still await the 'new' 'Crimes of the *Wehrmacht*' exhibition. When the exhibition does re-enter the public realm, then it will presumably do so considerably improved, at least in terms of accuracy and rigour. It will thus come armed with stronger support for its argumentation. This is important, because it will undoubtedly be scrutinized as much as its predecessor. It is to be hoped, however, that it will not be so top-heavy with academic baggage as to lose its emotional force, and that it will be able to sustain and even build on the generally enlightening impact of its predecessor. Certainly it can be said of the 'old' exhibition that it triggered a discussion which served to place *Wehrmacht* criminality, at institutional and individual level, firmly within the centre of political, cultural and social discourse in Germany. Interestingly, while the main tenor of public reactions to both the exhibition and Goldhagen's findings was one of interest and shock, there were more dissenting voices in the case of the exhibition. The reason is that Goldhagen's killers were not drafted soldiers. Surviving members of the *Wehrmacht* did not feel they had to defend their personal honour against Goldhagen, but they did feel they had to defend it against an exhibition, which, as we saw, was felt to be criminalizing an entire army. The exhibition also triggered more political debate than Goldhagen's book because of conservative fears that the criticism of the *Wehrmacht* would result in distaste for the idea of an expanded international role for the *Bundeswehr*. But in the final analysis, the politicians did seek to transcend politicization in a most memorable parliamentary debate; it remains for the historians to follow suit.

7 The Walser–Bubis debate

'The majority of Germans living today bear no guilt for Auschwitz. But of course they have a particular responsibility to ensure that something like the holocaust, like Auschwitz, never happens again.'

(Roman Herzog, *FAZ*, 21 January 1999)

Mediation or trust?

It will have been hard for Germans not to have taken notice between 1990 and 1998 of the debates relating to the National Socialist past. They were closely followed by the media, indeed the media were one of the main actors in these debates, which, as this book sets out to demonstrate, accompanied and indeed symptomized the post-unification shift towards a less blinkered understanding of the Third Reich. Thus historians and journalists in German newspapers had begun to debate Goldhagen's book before it had even been published in German translation, drawing public attention to it. Debates between Goldhagen and German historians were televised, and in part organized by television networks. There were countless news bulletins on the 'Crimes of the *Wehrmacht*' exhibition. Western German Radio (WDR) even based a crime thriller in the popular *Scene of the Crime* (*Tatort*) series around the exhibition; it was broadcast in June 1998. A flood of television programmes accompanied the 50th anniversary of 8 May 1945. The German television media to this day provide a wide range of programmes not just on the theme of coming to terms with National Socialism, but on the Third Reich itself. Indeed hardly a day passes without a programme on the period. The week's television programme at the time of writing will serve as an example. Thus on 28 October 2000, between 10 p.m. and midnight, the private channel VOX showed two hours of colour film of the Second World War. This was just one sequence in a series – *The Colour of War* – which VOX has been sharing with SAT1. On 30 October 2000, at 11 p.m., WDR ran a programme entitled 'Monaco under the Swastika', while on 1 November, the third part of the series *Holokaust* (whose makers rejected the usual spelling *Holocaust* as too 'anglicized') was shown at peak viewing time, 9 p.m., on Germany's ZDF (Second German Television Channel).

There is, of course, a potential danger in such coverage, whatever its contribution to awareness and discussion. Some fear that a high number of newspaper reports and especially television programmes on the Third Reich might breed an indifference to the theme, or even irritation. A quite different concern is that National Socialism may become a kind of visual fetish. Viewers might switch on merely to indulge in frissons of horror as images of the Führer at party rallies, or of the Second World War and its atrocities, pass over their television screens. On 28 October 2000, VOX followed up film-footage of the war with a sex-film. Viewers were taken from images of destruction to those of soft pornography. One might therefore suspect some television programmers of carefully planning the evening viewing so that a contrastive range of visual stimuli is provided. Some cynics have remarked that Hitler's greatest success was his conquest of the post-war German media. That images of the war and the holocaust, however they are presented, might be read by some misguided individuals as emblems of Hitler's 'achievements' cannot be excluded. Moreover, the tendency of *Spiegel TV* (VOX and SAT1) to set such images to music, usually of the dark and sinister variety, moves them into the sphere of epic film. They are encased in sound, rather than critically explored. A further danger is the creation of a foreshortened understanding of German history, which appears to consist only of the Third Reich and, by way of redemptive contrast, liberation and post-war democracy. One looks in vain, usually, for programmes on other periods in German history on German television networks.

Similarly ambivalent is the role of politics in managing memory of National Socialism. Regular commemoration of anniversaries linked to events and developments in the Third Reich was an important feature of post-1945 political culture in both East and West Germany. Without the speechmaking and the wreath-laying year after year at Bergen-Belsen or Buchenwald, for instance, Germans on both sides of the German–German border might have felt even less inclined to recall the horrors of Nazism. Some speeches, such as Richard von Weizsäcker's in 1985 to mark the end of the war, triggered productive processes of reflection on the Nazi past. Sometimes even a gesture had a profound impact. When Willy Brandt fell to his knees at the Warsaw Ghetto Memorial in December 1970, he paved the way for a more self-critical memory. Since unification, politicians continue to be the most frequently represented speakers at major commemorative occasions, as exemplified by the 20 July 1994 and certainly the 8 May 1995 acts of remembrance (see Chapters Three and Four). The downside of this political memory management, however, is that memory can become the tool of international, domestic and party politics, as we saw in the earlier chapters of this book. The second and equally significant problem is that the general public, to a degree, becomes inclined to leave matters of remembering up to the politicians. Commemoration is delegated to the political establishment. The same might apply to memorials. As we shall see in Chapter Eight, one of the objections to the planned Holocaust Memorial in Berlin is that it might encourage Germans to imagine that a memorial is now doing the job of remembering, and that they can therefore go about their daily business without having to reflect on the holocaust.

These fears, however, should not be overstated. For one thing, as we saw in previous chapters, politicians have over recent years to a degree sought to transcend party politics and reach a basic consensus on how aspects of the Third Reich should be viewed. For another, in the course of the 1990s, the German public has itself begun to take an active interest in National Socialism. The success of *Schindler's List*, Goldhagen's book or the 'Crimes of the *Wehrmacht*' exhibition was primarily a public success, to a degree indeed one which flew in the face of the scepticism of many historians and politicians. In 1995, the Germans did not just follow the central or regional political acts of 8 May commemoration, they also set about exploring the histories of their own towns and villages at the end of the war. It is thus no longer the case that memory of National Socialism is entirely managed by politics, the media and memorials. Precisely this shift towards active public memory has led to a degree of reflection on the issue of finding a balance between mediation and trust. How much mediation should there be? What should its nature be? How much can the Germans be trusted to remember without such mediation? These questions became particularly acute following a speech given by the German writer Martin Walser on 11 October 1998 in Frankfurt. His speech caused much indignation because it appeared to suggest that the left and perhaps even the Jews were manipulating media discourse on the Nazi past for their own self-interested ends, such as imposing on the Germans a crippling sense of national guilt and preventing a return to 'normality' and self-confidence. But Walser's speech did not, as some feared it might, damage the image of the media, or discourage the latter from focusing on National Socialism. What it did do, perhaps contrary to Walser's intentions, was to support the shift referred to above: it was understood that individual Germans must take more responsibility for memory, and that they must be given 'space' to do so.

The speech

First to Walser's speech, given in the Frankfurt *Paulskirche* on receipt of the 1998 Peace Prize of the German Book Trade. The University of Tübingen's Section for Rhetoric designated it 'speech of the year' in December 1998. There is no doubt that the speech is a rhetorical masterpiece. Attempts to interpret it came to radically different understandings of its message. For fellow-author Monika Maron, it was as if Walser had given two speeches (*Zeit*, 19 November 1998). What follows is therefore a cautious attempt to distil the essence of what lies behind the speech's play with irony and ambivalence.

At the outset of his speech, Walser informs his listeners that his first impulse had been to write a speech in praise of the finer things in life. However, he had then realized that a critical speech would be expected of him, and that he would have to defend his 'potpourri of the beautiful' (Walser 1999: 8) by making excuses for his inability to be critical. He confesses that he tends to look away when television presents the world as intolerable: 'I wouldn't be able to get through the day, and certainly not the night, without looking away and diverting my thoughts' (Walser 1999: 8). He rejects the idea that all the things which happen in the world need to be atoned for, and expresses his distaste at the fact that a West German who spied for the GDR, Rainer Rupp, is still serving a prison sentence (he has since been released). Observing himself adopting a critical tone after all, he notes that certain intellectual activities predispose those engaged in them towards the role of 'guardians of conscience', a role he admits he himself has performed, albeit always under the proviso of 'saying to yourself what you say to others' – in other words, it is important to avoid conveying the impression that one knows any better than those one criticizes (Walser 1999: 9–10).

Walser goes on to illustrate why he is sceptical of this role of 'guardian' adopted by intellectuals. He cites the example of a 'really important thinker' who, in 1992, had suggested that the apparently indulgent reaction of Rostock's inhabitants and Bonn's politicians towards anti-foreigner violence in Rostock was evidence of a deep-rooted 'moral-political degeneration'. Walser also cites the example of an 'equally significant writer' who had opined a few years earlier that, while guests in any Salzburg restaurant might look decent enough, they are probably dreaming of extermination and gas-chambers (Walser 1999: 10). In neither case does Walser name names. It is clear, however, that the 'thinker' is Habermas; Walser quotes from a newspaper article by the latter (*Zeit*, 11 December 1992). Critics were divided as to whether the 'writer' was Thomas Bernhard or Peter Handke, but subsequent research revealed it to be Bernhard (see Kirsch 1999b: 324, and, for the original Bernhard comment on Salzburg, Dreissinger 1992: 111). Similarly, Walser does not name the intellectuals who, he claims, had rejected German unification with reference to Auschwitz, but one of these is probably Günter Grass (Walser 1999: 12). Finally, Walser cites the example of a 'smart intellectual' who had objected to the fact that Auschwitz had played no part in Walser's recent novel set during the Third Reich, *A Gushing Fountain* (*Ein springender Brunnen*, Walser 1998). Press reports on Walser's speech tended to assume this was a reference to either literary critic Helmuth Karasek or Marcel Reich-Ranicki.

For Walser, those who make such comments may be seeking to wound others or indeed themselves; they may also be seeking to place themselves on a par with the victims of Nazism. In contrast to this, Walser tells us, he has never felt he could leave the ranks of the accused (Walser 1999: 11). Walser's citations are also designed to point up the use of direct or implicit references to National Socialism in support of a given position. This position, as Walser understands it, might be a critical stance towards the CDU, the wish to condemn provincial Austria or a negative stance on unification. Walser sees in such references acts of instrumentalization 'for present ends' (Walser 1999: 12). He insists that it is not appropriate to use Auschwitz – a metonym for National Socialist atrocities as a whole – as a 'means of intimidation' or a 'moral cudgel' (*Moralkeule*). He also warns against ritualized memory: 'whatever results from such ritualization has the character of lip-service' (Walser 1999: 13). Walser then criticizes plans to build a Holocaust Memorial in Berlin (see Chapter Eight), dismissing any such memorial as a 'monumentalization of disgrace' (Walser 1999: 13). For Walser, the Holocaust Memorial exemplifies what happens when people feel responsible for the conscience of others. The result is a 'banality of good' (Walser 1999: 13). Walser continues his speech by exploring briefly the view of conscience expressed in the writings of Martin Heidegger and Friedrich Wilhelm Hegel, and in Heinrich von

Kleist's play *The Prince of Homburg* (*Der Prinz von Homburg*). He enlists these writers in support of his own belief that any publicly expressed or publicly elicited show of conscience may well be false. Conscience is a matter for the individual: 'each of us is alone with his or her conscience' (Walser 1999: 14). Walser extends this principle to the literary writer, arguing that the author is answerable only to himself, and only by means of such self-answerability can his writing be of interest to others. With an almost comic twist, Walser concludes his speech by asking Federal President Herzog to amnesty Rainer Rupp (Walser 1999: 16).

As indicated, Walser's speech is rich in sophisticated self-irony. The speech is informed, in line with the principle 'say to yourself what you say to others', by the spirit of inner monologue. It makes liberal use of the conditional tense and is frequently couched in qualifications. Thus Walser not only states that he looks away from the 'constant presentation of our disgrace', meaning, presumably, media images of the holocaust. He also goes on to say that he is 'almost glad' when he 'believes' he 'is able to detect' that commemoration is 'often no longer' the motive for this constant presentation, but rather the 'instrumentalization of our disgrace for present ends' (Walser 1999: 12). This is a very self-conscious style. It implies that Walser mistrusts his motives for identifying such instrumentalization, and wishes to communicate this self-doubt to the audience. That way he can avoid coming across as a moral authority. Yet his professed belief is that one cannot make public appearances without wanting to become such an authority. To prove his point, he introduces into his self-conscious manner a note of insincerity. The longer the speech goes on, the more assertive Walser becomes, expressing opinions as assuredly as the 'really important thinker' and 'equally significant writer' ostensibly do. His request that Rainer Rupp be amnestied, however playful, is as much a piece of political meddling as Habermas's remarks on Rostock. The speech is a carefully constructed demonstration that, if you put an intellectual on a rostrum, he will be seized by a kind of moral power-hunger. The only answer for the author is to return to the text, where he or she can write self-reflexively.

The ultimate irony of the speech, then, was its advocacy before the assembled political elite – and millions of television viewers – of the withdrawal of the writer from any role as public conscience. This advocacy echoed the position adopted by literary critic Frank Schirrmacher during the 'Literature Debate' (*Literaturstreit*) of the early 1990s, which centred on whether or not authors should continue to write literature that is politically engaged. Criticisms of GDR writers such as Christa Wolf for supposedly supporting a corrupt socialism in her texts soon broadened into an all-out attack on *littérature engagée* in both Germanys. Schirrmacher and Ulrich Greiner thought the time of writers as 'conscience of the nation' had come to an end. After all, Germany was now united, and the political battles of the Cold War had been decided in favour of western values. Writers, therefore, should be getting down to the task of producing 'pure' literature. Walser, for whom Schirrmacher delivered an encomium at the prize-giving ceremony in Frankfurt in 1998, appeared in his speech to adopt a similar stance. Yet Walser was not necessarily advocating literary quietism. He was, rather, calling for an end to any function for the author which went beyond writing literature. This is a position which has been echoed by other German writers, such as Christoph Hein, a former GDR author. Germany is now a nation, but it is also post-national. With the 'wound' of division closed, and the iniquities of socialism and the Cold War overcome, writers have in a sense been 'liberated' from the task of intervening in political affairs. But this need not mean their literature becomes apolitical.

Instrumentalization

Walser's speech contained little that he had not expressed elsewhere (for his thoughts on conscience, for instance, see *Spiegel*, 7 November 1994), and it was hardly shocking. It was also, surely, in some respects correct. There is an instrumentalization of the holocaust. It may even be that Walser's speech was intended as a critical counterpoint to an example of such an instrumentalization during the Peace Prize ceremony of the previous year. On 19 October 1997, Turkish writer Yasar Kemal received the Peace Prize of the German Book Trade. Günter Grass delivered the encomium. He provoked an albeit short-lived storm of indignation when he implicitly compared German Minister of the Interior Manfred Kanther's asylum politics, and particularly the incarceration of fugitives from Turkey, Algeria and Nigeria due to be expelled from Germany, to Hitler's deportation of Jews. 'It is the case that we are all passive witnesses of yet another, this time democratically legitimated act of barbarism', he asserted. Grass also condemned the delivery of German tanks to Turkey, on the grounds that the Turks could be expected to use these against the Kurds. 'We were and are co-perpetrators', he added, again conjuring up memories of the Third Reich (*FAZ*, 20 October 1997). With all due respect to the moral and political problems posed by delivering weapons to Turkey and by the weaknesses of the German asylum system, Grass's statements represented exactly the kind of instrumentalization of the Nazi past which Walser criticized one year later. Both the CDU and SPD took issue with Grass's speech, seeing in it, in the words of Ulrich Klose (SPD) a 'piece of intellectual polemics'. Peter Hintze, CDU party spokesman, claimed that the speech marked the 'intellectual nadir of a writer who has once and for all forfeited his right to a place among the ranks of serious writers' (*SZ*, 21 October 1997). Even Ignatz Bubis was displeased with Grass's comparisons with the Third Reich: 'this way of handling the negative experiences of recent German history is something I'm not comfortable with' (*SZ*, 27 October 1997). Walser's point was also borne out in December 1998, when Cologne's Cardinal Joachim Meisner compared use of the abortion pill RU 486 with that of Cyclon B in the annihilation camps. SPD Federal Minister for the Family Christine Bergmann called his remarks 'irresponsible', and the Protestant Church condemned the comparison sharply (*SZ*, 10 December 1998).

But it is one thing to warn against instrumentalization, and quite another to imply, as Walser does, that this instrumentalization has utterly corrupted the public realm. Walser provides no examples of what might be considered a judicious handling of the holocaust theme in the public realm, although there are certainly many examples. Moreover, his examples of instrumentalization are taken from thinkers – notably Habermas – generally ranked on the left, or at least thought of as 'critical'.

He does not provide a single illustration of right-wing instrumentalization, although this would also not have been hard. It has long been standard practice for the right to instrumentalize atrocities or injustices committed against Germans in a bid to play down the significance and singularity of the holocaust. The right, in other words, espouses a variety of the victimization theory. It is quite possibly because Walser sympathizes with this theory that he fails to criticize it. Indeed in his speech he extends the existing one to embrace today's Germans. While the right believes Germans in the past to be victims, not least of the Soviets, Walser sees today's Germans as victims of a left-wing conspiracy of *Vergangenheitsbewältigung* – a conspiracy designed to keep them in a self-condemnatory state of mind, thus preventing the emergence of any positive national feeling, so hated by the left. For Walser, the holocaust has become so bound up with left-wing manipulation, the baby so much a part of the bathwater, that it would not be unreasonable to assume he would like to see the theme dropped from the public agenda. With the holocaust off this agenda, national pride would regenerate, enabling the Germans to act with the assertiveness Walser appears to miss.

In Walser's speech, the bogeyman of left-wing instrumentalization is understood to have replaced fascism as the greatest danger in the present. This view is underpinned by Walser's use of terminology generally reserved for descriptions of the far right. It was historian Heinrich August Winkler who used the term 'negative nationalism' in respect of the Holocaust Memorial. Walser quotes this term (Walser 1999: 13). It implies that the real nationalist terror comes from the left, and consists in the constant immersion of Germans in a sense of shame for their past as a source of national cohesion. Walser applies the term 'custodian of conscience' (*Gewissenswart*) to those critics who feel responsible for telling an author how he should write (Walser 1999: 15). This evokes the Nazi term 'block leader' (*Blockwart*). He also describes such critics as 'opinion soldiers' who use a 'moral pistol' to force writers into 'the opinion service' (*Meinungsdienst* evokes the Nazi Workers' League, or *Reichsarbeitsdienst*). In the discussions surrounding the planned Holocaust Memorial, Walser writes, later generations will find evidence of 'the damage done by people who feel responsible for the consciences of others' (Walser 1999: 13). When Walser claims that he 'looks away' from images of Auschwitz, then of course he knows 'looking away' is associated with German behaviour during the Third Reich. Today's Germans, he implies, are being left as a result of the pressure of the media with no alternative but to indulge in a comparable act of looking away. It is the source of this pressure which is to blame, not the Germans for looking away.

Walser's speech is thus built on a deeply tendentious equation of left-wing management of memory of the holocaust with the tyranny of National Socialism. In line with this equation, Walser presents conscience not just as the proper repository for memory, but also as the site of moral resistance against the tyrannical left. His understanding of conscience is thoroughly combative. In refusing to kow-tow to left-wing demands for feelings of guilt, the individual acts out a 'protest of conscience'. It might be taking things too far, but it is hard when reading Walser's speech not to think of resistance to National Socialism, which was also based on such a sense of conscience. In this way, the 'Stauffenberg' tradition of conscience is redirected against the left. In the final analysis, Walser advocates a kind of moral strike, in that the population at large is encouraged to turn a deaf ear to those public figures who point to the need to reflect in shame on the National Socialist past. For Walser, the Germans are now a normal people. Because he understands references to the holocaust in the public realm as designed to kindle inappropriate feelings of guilt, he is able to imply that it is the people who make such references who are abnormal. These references may even be the very source of the problem they seek to combat. Elsewhere, Walser has argued that the social taboo imposed on the national by the left – a reaction to the holocaust – plays into the hands of the far right. Aggressive nationalism has become attractive to young people because it appears to constitute an effective form of protest against the establishment (see, for instance, Walser's article in *Spiegel*, 28 June 1993).

Redefinitions

When Walser had finished his speech on 11 October 1998, the audience stood up to applaud him. Only Bubis and his wife remained sitting, stony-faced, refusing to applaud. A day later Bubis accused Walser of 'intellectual arson' (*FAZ*, 13 October 1998). He also compared his remarks with those of extremist right-wing figures such as Gerhard Frey (the man behind the German People's Union) and Franz Schönhuber (former head of the Republicans). The reason for Bubis's indignation was, firstly, Walser's use of the term 'instrumentalization'. Bubis was convinced that this was a reference to the claims of former forced labourers, who had been compelled to work for German firms during the war and were now seeking compensation (see Bubis's letter to Klaus von Dohnanyi, *FAZ*, 16 November 1998). Secondly, Bubis was convinced that Walser was preaching a philosophy of 'looking away' from National Socialist crimes – of, in other words, refusing to confront these. Bubis's criticisms were in one respect unfounded. In an interview on ARD television on 6 December 1998, and on other occasions, Walser denied he had meant forced labourers. In support of Bubis, several commentators argued that Walser had not provided examples of what he meant by instrumentalization. Reemtsma, for instance, maintained that, because of this omission, 'everyone could understand Walser' to mean forced labourers (*SZ*, 24 November 1998). But Walser had provided examples, as we saw above. Moreover, his examples were principally of instrumentalizations by *Germans*, not German Jews, and certainly not by victims of Nazism, Jewish or otherwise, or their legal and political representatives in the present. The distinction is important. Had Walser been suggesting that Jews or other victims of Nazism instrumentalized the holocaust, then he could legitimately have been accused of tactlessness, revisionism, even anti-semitism.

There is one possible exception, however: Walser's reference to a 'smart intellectual' in his speech (Walser 1999: 12). While this would appear to fit literary critic Helmuth Karasek better than Polish Jew Reich-Ranicki, it was the latter who had most vigorously complained at the non-treatment of Auschwitz in Walser's novel

A Gushing Fountain (Walser 1998). It may even be the case that Reich-Ranicki's complaint triggered the *Paulskirche* speech, which defended the right of the author to write as he or she sees fits. Generally, Walser appears to see himself and other leading writers as victims of Reich-Ranicki's never-ending criticisms of contemporary German literature. In an interview three weeks prior to the speech, Walser described those authors criticized by Reich-Ranicki as 'victims', Reich-Ranicki as 'the perpetrator'. 'Every author he treats in this manner could say to him: in our relationship, Mr. Reich-Ranicki, you are the German and I am the Jew' (*SZ*, 19–20 September 1998). This was an intriguing role-reversal. If Bubis's instinct told him that Walser's speech was not sympathetic to Jewish suffering under Hitler, then this may have been because it was informed by an undertone of sympathy towards non-Jewish Germans. Walser seemed to imply that the Jewish victims of the holocaust have been 'replaced' by German victims of subsequent attempts to instrumentalize it. Constant and, for Walser, inappropriate comparisons between today's problems and National Socialism are preventing the Germans from living in harmony with themselves. In a televised conversation organized by Frank Schirrmacher in an attempt to bring about a reconciliation between Bubis and Walser, Walser made it quite explicit that he regarded Bubis's very presence in Rostock after the racial attack in 1992 as a form of such illicit comparison: 'I saw your indignant, shocked face on television, illuminated by the light from the burning houses [. . .] When you turn up, then the connection to 1933 is immediately established' (*FAZ*, 14 December 1998). In the light of this remark, and the general sense of victimization which informed Walser's speech, Bubis's suspicion that Walser's indignation was also addressed at the Central Council of the Jews in Germany was not totally unreasonable.

Reich-Ranicki himself defended Walser against the charge of anti-semitism (*FAZ*, 12 December 1998). But while it may not be anti-semitic, Walser's speech suggests a reversal of roles which has serious implications. By seeing in present-day references to the holocaust an unfair moral condemnation of today's Germans, Walser makes the left, the Jews and indeed anyone else who makes such references into targets of legitimate criticism. German–Jewish relations in post-war West Germany had been based on the assumption that the Germans had a moral debt to the Jews. Walser's dig at Reich-Ranicki and the tone of his speech suggested that this debt, given German normality in the present, no longer obtains. The moral playing-field for Germans and Jews, in other words, is now a level one. This, in turn, implies that any continuing Jewish claims on German moral guilt or shame are self-righteous acts of victimization. Kai Köhler has called this the 'inversion of the perpetrator–victim relation' (Köhler 1999: 78). Walser's use of the term 'disgrace' (*Schande*) for the holocaust in his speech reflects this inversion. Disgrace is something attached by the outside; it does not derive from within. In a seminal 19th century drama by Friedrich Hebbel, *Maria Magdalena* (1844), *Schande* is identified as a stigma inflicted by oppressive social convention. It does not represent the violation of any 'true' value. In a not dissimilar fashion, Walser understands current references to the holocaust, essentially, as part of an agenda-driven attempt to stigmatize today's Germans and prevent legitimate feelings of 'normality'.

Hamburg's former mayor, Klaus von Dohnanyi, subsequently applied Walser's 'level playing-field' principle to the Third Reich. In an article which prompted almost as much media discussion as Walser's speech, Dohnanyi wrote: 'Jewish citizens in Germany must, of course, also ask themselves if they would have behaved any more courageously than most other Germans did if, after 1933, "only" the handicapped, homosexuals or Roma had been dragged off for annihilation. Everyone should try to answer this question honestly, for herself or himself' (*FAZ*, 14 November 1998). In other words, the right to criticize or to expect shame is no longer an unconditional right deriving from Jewish agony, but is made dependent on an act of moral self-estimation. After criticism from Jan Philipp Reemtsma, Dohnanyi redirected his comments more towards today's Germans, who, he claimed, should ask themselves how they would have reacted before 'judging Germans for looking on during the Third Reich' (*FAZ*, 30 November 1998). He insisted that this principle also applied to the British, American and French. But the damage was done. Israeli historian Saul Friedländer said he understood Dohnanyi to mean that Jews would have been as indifferent or as bad as the Germans had they not been the victims, and that Dohnanyi was effectively saying to Bubis 'don't get morally so inflated, you're no better' (*SZ*, 24 November 1998). Dohnanyi's argument rendered historical constellations arbitrary. Today's Jewish citizens, he implied, must restrain themselves from criticizing Germans, because Jewish victims might not have been victims. As for the Germans, they need feel no shame, because the victims might have looked on as well – had they not been the victims. Without doubt, Dohnanyi made the most startlingly clumsy contribution to the whole debate.

Both Walser and Dohnanyi introduced into German discussions on the past a new relativism. Behind the Historians' Dispute of 1986 and *The Black Book of Communism* (Courtois *et al.* 1998) was a dynamic of comparison: if the Stalinists murdered 30 or 40 million people, and Hitler between 6 and 10 million, then Hitler's atrocities were neither unique nor the worst, at least numerically. While such comparison may or may not, in itself, be valid, it functions as a mechanism of self-exculpation. To this end, it is the past of other countries and systems that is instrumentalized. The comments by Walser and Dohnanyi broadened the scope of the comparative approach, which was now to be applied to those judging the past, as well as to the past itself, to those involved in the discourse, as well as to the object of discourse. If Auschwitz, according to conservative historians, had to be understood in the light of the GULAGs, it also, Dohnanyi implied, had to be assessed in the light of general human fallibility, which potentially afflicted not just the perpetrator, but the victim; not just the judged, but the judge. Of course Dohnanyi knew that no Jew could prove to himself or others that he would have acted differently to Germans. Making criticism dependent on moral infallibility effectively precludes it.

It cannot be denied that Walser's interpretation of public rituals of remembering as left-wing instrumentalization, and Dohnanyi's moral disqualification of Jewish criticism of the Germans represented a disturbing development. Walser is interested in the arguments of the New Right, but had never moved as far to the right as this. Dohnanyi is a prominent SPD politician. It may be that Walser, a member of the 'flak-helper' generation which grew up under Hitler but was too young to see active service, felt threatened by the interest in the 1990s in uncovering the true extent of perpetration and responsibility for National Socialist crimes. His attempt to stigmatize this interest as a left-wing campaign would then be a defensive reaction, similar to that of those who dismissed the 'Crimes of the *Wehrmacht*' exhibition as left-wing propaganda (see Chapter Six). Dohnanyi, as the son of a member of the anti-Hitler resistance, may also have been rebelling against this focus on perpetration. Anti-Nazi resistance had been in the foreground of public memory in 1994 (Chapter Three), but as of 1996 it was the crimes of the Third Reich which preoccupied the general public. There were other examples of unfortunate lapses on the part of some generally considered liberals. Rudolf Augstein, editor of the generally left-of-centre *Der Spiegel*, published an article on 30 November 1998 suggesting that the Holocaust Memorial was being forced on the Germans, and more or less blaming this imposition on the New York press and on the lawyers representing the interests of victims of Nazism. Augstein not only apportioned blame for victimizing the Germans; he placed any subsequent blame for anti-semitism at the door of Jewish and pro-Jewish interest groups. Augstein's argument is an extension of Walser's and Dohnanyi's. If the Jews are acting without moral right and in self-interest, then anger towards them becomes the moral right and healthy self-interest of the Germans.

Encouraging the neo-Nazis

The effect of Walser's speech, according to some, has been to make ideas generally associated with the far right socially and politically more acceptable. Certainly this is how the far right itself evaluated his contribution. It greeted the speech ecstatically, publishing excerpts in journals such as *Der Neue Republikaner* (December 1998). Walser was hailed as one of its own. Thus in the *National-Journal* on 28 October 1998, his statement that Auschwitz is not suitable as a moral cudgel was set beside a claim by right-wing extremist Günter Deckert that the ruling elite in Germany has always used the 'Auschwitz cudgel to kill off every attempt at a nationally minded politics'. Walser was presented in the far right-wing press as 'He who breaks with taboos' (Thorsten Thaler in *JF*, 6 April 1996). In a speech at Duisburg University, Walser claimed that he had received thousands of letters which showed that Germans had experienced his speech as 'liberating, liberating for their conscience' (*FAZ*, 28 November 1998). The word Walser used here was *Befreiung*, a term normally associated with the liberation from Hitler on 8 May 1945 (see Chapter Four). In similar vein, the notorious right-wing radical Manfred Roeder described Walser's speech as 'the beginning of the liberation of Germany' (Dietzsch *et al.* 1999: 82). Here again, it is those who insist on the need to come to terms with the past who are seen as today's oppressors. The far right, convinced of growing popular support for their ideas thanks to Walser, began to polemicize against Bubis and other German Jews with more than the usual venom and dismissiveness. Roeder called Bubis a 'guard-dog'. In several far right-wing newspapers Bubis was accused of persecution and materialism. Even respectable publications included interviews, letters or editorials of distinctly aggressive tone (for a good selection of such pieces, see Dietzsch *et al.* 1999: 102–8).

1998 saw a rise in anti-semitism. Berlin's police had registered 90 anti-semitic criminal acts by October – as many as in the whole of 1997 (*Freitag*, 22 December 1998). The grave of Heinz Galinski, erstwhile head of the Central Council of the Jews in Germany, was violated in September and again in December. On 28 October, a group of people pulled a pig over Alexander Square in Berlin. On its back, they had painted a Star of David, in blue, and the word BUBIS, in red. A journalist who contacted the police to inquire about the incident was told that the pig was in good health; the paint had not harmed its skin in any way (*SZ*, 28 October 1998). The authorities, the journalist reported, were considering taking legal action on the grounds of cruelty to animals. Bubis complained, as did Michel Friedman (CDU politician and current Vice-President of the Central Council of the Jews in Germany), of an increase in the number of threatening letters he was receiving. He noted too that these letters were no longer always anonymous. Julius Schoeps, head of the Moses Mendelssohn Centre for European-Jewish Studies in Potsdam, stated that some 17 Jewish cemeteries a week were being vandalized. He concluded: 'The debate triggered by Walser is dangerous for Germany' (*SZ*, 28 October 1998). Heinz Galinski's daughter Evelyn, in connection with the attack on her father's grave in December, claimed that 'the intellectual arsonists and desk-perpetrators are responsible for the fact that a climate has arisen in which such a deed is possible'. Walser's reaction was to say that, if he was being connected with this attack in any way, 'then there's no alternative for me but to emigrate' (*SZ*, 22 December 1998). This was a clear indication that Walser felt the roles in the Third Reich had been reversed: he indirectly compared Galinski's daughter to Nazi persecutors.

The worrying series of anti-semitic attacks has continued, reaching a new peak in the months of September and October 2000. A group of Jews narrowly escaped being blown up in Düsseldorf, while synagogues in Berlin-Kreuzberg, Düsseldorf, Halle and Essen were damaged by vandalism. Turning over and besmirching Jewish gravestones is still a regular practice. This might seem to corroborate Bubis's pessimistic statement shortly before his death on 13 August 1999 that he had 'achieved almost nothing' as Head of the Central Council of the Jews (*SZ*, 15 September 1999). It was his conviction that, not least because of Walser's speech, Jewish warnings about disturbing trends in present-day Germany, or calls for compensation, were now perceived as self-interested and exploitative. Indeed in the new climate of insistence on German normality, Jews had become an irritating reminder of the holocaust. After he died, German politicians emphasized his contribution both to the reconstruction of Jewish life and to Jewish–German conciliation in the Federal Republic. But his decision to be buried in Israel prompted some such as writer Maxim Biller to argue that, whatever his previous German–Jewish patriotism, he had ultimately decided 'to become a Jew again' (*SZ*,

23 August 1999). It is an unfortunate irony, perhaps, that Walser, for whom the German–Jewish symbiosis is so important (see Chapter Five), may have damaged relations between Germans and Jews. The new Head of the Central Council of the Jews in Germany, Paul Spiegel, has certainly blamed worsening relations on Walser. On several occasions in the autumn and winter of 2000, Spiegel pointed to a phenomenon he described as 'Walserism', a desire among some intellectuals to 'shake off history' (*SZ*, 17 April 2000). In October 2000, he protested against the intention of Halle's Town Council to honour Walser with a prize ('The Fearless Word'). 'Walser has provided neo-Nazis and right-wing radicals with ammunition for their arguments', he claimed (*SZ*, 6 October 2000). The recent celebrations of the 50th anniversary of the founding of the Central Council of the Jews in Germany should have been a hopeful occasion. But Paul Spiegel expressed doubt that there had ever been such a thing as a German–Jewish symbiosis: in reality there was a 'one-sided, ill-fated love' (*SZ*, 22 September 2000). Without the recent anti-semitic attacks, it is doubtful Spiegel would have felt quite so negative.

Guilt, shame and disgrace

In the discussion with Walser organized by Schirrmacher, Bubis retracted his accusation that Walser was an 'intellectual arsonist' (*FAZ*, 14 December 1998). Instead, he used the term 'intellectual father' to describe Walser's relationship to those who had felt 'liberated' by his speech. A retraction is not an apology (which is why Walser rejected it). And Bubis clearly still felt that Walser, while perhaps not an anti-semite, had sympathy for Germans who wished to draw a line under the past (*Schlußstrich*). There can be no doubt that Walser's theory of repressive *Vergangenheitsbewältigung* legitimates verbal, if not physical, anger towards the left and, in the second instance, the Jews. Those readers who understood his speech as such a legitimation were not misinterpreting it. Nor were they wrong to understand Walser's concept of conscience as they did. Walser's speech does present conscience as a safe haven to which the individual can withdraw to have his or her peace of mind (in fact Walser used this term – *Seelenfrieden* – in the above-mentioned discussion with Bubis). Many of those readers who, as Walser put it, experienced his speech as 'liberating' only did so because they felt Walser was freeing them of the necessity to reflect on Auschwitz. Conscience, in the words of historian Micha Brumlik, was to function as a place where the preoccupation with the Nazi past could be 'permanently disposed of' (*taz*, 15 October 1998). Yet not all who reacted positively to Walser's Frankfurt speech did so for questionable reasons. As already pointed out, the speech was wrapped in layers of irony. Underneath these layers is Walser's distaste for public forms of commemoration and his defensive view of conscience. Nevertheless, his apparently vague and ambivalent use of terms and concepts allowed for a more responsible and productive pattern of reception. Indeed this pattern of reception, I would argue, proved stronger than the negative one.

The productive pattern was characterized, firstly, by serious reflection on the issue of public references to the holocaust. As we saw, Walser's complaint that the public realm had fallen victim to an instrumentalization of the Nazi past was highly generalized, but not in specific cases unfounded. While this complaint was, on occasion, objectively discussed in editorials and in readers' letters to the press, it was more the question of ritual which prompted a high level of intelligent and fruitful discussion. Walser's use of the terms 'exercise of duty' and 'lip-service' in his speech (Walser 1999: 13) highlighted the danger of such rituals becoming purely routine, mechanical and even insincere. Acts of commemoration, from public speeches to the laying of wreaths and the building of memorials, can function as substitutes for active reflection. Thus while rituals are desirable, ritualization is not. Given the plethora of such acts in today's Germany, some express anxiety that people might start to suffer, as historian Johannes Willms put it, from 'commemoration fatigue' (*SZ*, 11 November 1998). In the course of the discussion of Walser's speech, it became clear that young people – not just older ones – also felt 'liberated'. One young German, Mareike Ilsemann, wrote in a reader's letter that Walser had 'spoken for many young Germans, not just for me' (*Zeit*, 10 December 1998). This suggests the existence of an irrational sense of guilt in many youngsters. Such a sense of guilt derives in part from the disastrous post-war process of displacement, whereby guilt for National Socialism was not acknowledged by the generations responsible, but 'passed down' to their children, who in many cases passed it on to their children. But it may also reflect a certain heavy-handedness on the part of the education system. Ilsemann went on to relate how her teacher in 1985 had read out to 11-year-old children an eye-witness report of atrocities by SS men who delighted in throwing 'Russian babies against a house until their brains stuck to the wall'. Young children can hardly be expected to process these images. Finally, a feeling of guilt may stem from an accusatory tone in public rituals.

For Walser, as his novel *A Gushing Fountain* appears to demonstrate, guilt is a category which does not apply in equal measure to all who lived through the Third Reich. Guilt-focused rituals obliterate discrepancies between contrasting degrees of involvement and moral complicity, and obscure the fact that there was resistance, even innocence. In the case of Germans born after 1945, it elides essential differences between generations. If young people react with a mixture of bad conscience and resentment to public acts of remembrance, then it is perhaps because they feel unfairly compelled to do penance for crimes they never committed. This then begs the question as to what the moral tone of public remembrance should be. Walser conceived of the collective relation of Germans to the holocaust in terms of disgrace. But this term earned him much criticism. Thomas Assheuer took him to task for it, arguing rightly that disgrace could be understood as something which 'simply happens to you or to a people' and that it does not allow for moral responsibility (*Zeit*, 12 November 1998). In a speech in Duisburg, Walser replied by arguing that shame is bound to an individual's particular experience, while 'disgrace is the term for the whole historical burden' (*FAZ*, 28 November 1998). This suggests that Walser would privatize both guilt, leaving it to the individual perpetrators, and shame, which he would leave to those who wish to feel unreasonably bad about their country. As Aleida Assmann has suggested, such privatization would free up the public realm for 'national self-esteem' and 'honour' (Assmann and Frevert 1999: 95).

The terms 'disgrace' and 'guilt' may make sense in the context of the very different biographies of Walser and Bubis. Walser, afflicted by a subconscious persecution complex typical of Germans of his generation, responded to his affliction by seeking to distance himself from the holocaust by calling it a 'disgrace'. Bubis, a holocaust survivor, preferred to talk of German 'guilt', principally because of his experiences. For Bubis, Walser's use of the word 'disgrace' was an unacceptable way of not saying 'crimes' (*FAZ*, 16 December 1998). But the general consensus in the German media was that neither the concept of 'disgrace' nor that of 'guilt' is appropriate to commemoration in the present. Some preferred the term 'shame'. Much depended on whether shame was understood purely as a quality deriving from direct involvement in National Socialism, or as a collective inheritance of subsequent generations. For Assheuer, shame is appropriate because it implies an ethical relation; you can be ashamed by being born into a collective without being guilty yourself (*Zeit*, 12 November 1998). Others preferred to argue that a 'new language' needed to be found.

Responsibility and conscience

The highly personalized verbal battle between Bubis and Walser was based on their strong sense of who they were and what they wanted or did not want. Others preferred to see the issue of memory in terms of questions as yet unanswered. In his November 1998 speech in commemoration of the *Reichskristallnacht* pogrom, Federal President Herzog expressed uncertainty as to 'whether we have already found the correct way to prepare coming generations' for the 'fundamental necessity' of preventing a recurrence of National Socialism (Schirrmacher 1999: 114). Herzog had no answers. On Holocaust Remembrance Day on 27 January 1999, he turned directly to young people: 'We need you as active participants in debate. We need your questions, which are probably quite different to ours, we need your way of looking at things, your way of arguing, your interest' (*FAZ*, 28 January 1999). Herzog's appeal to youth was taken up by many others, who felt that the 'old men' Bubis, Dohnanyi and Walser were caught up in an embittered, solipsistic generational wrangle. Wolfram Schütte lamented the 'public silence of younger people' (*FR*, 9 December 1998). 'A new generation, those who were born later, is now called upon to find new answers to old questions, to formulate anxieties, to measure out in their turn the shadows cast by a past that will never disappear', wrote Johannes Willms (*SZ*, 8 December 1998).

There was a sense here that the function of public ritual was changing with the gradual erosion of any experiential or causal link between an event over fifty years ago and today's Germans. To admit of the need to involve the public in the reformulation of such ritual, as Herzog did, is to admit that public commemoration must be drawn into the democratic process. It cannot simply be imposed, but must evolve to reflect changing generations. The Walser debate thus helped to open up public ritual for renegotiation. If there was a tentative idea of what form the new 'language' should take, then it was expressed in terms of 'responsibility'. 'Not guilt, but responsibility', said Rita Süssmuth (CDU), must shape German conduct (*FR*, 24 December 1998). 'Our legacy is called responsibility', claimed Roman Herzog (*FAZ*, 28 January 1999). Not for the past, he added, but the future. The new discourse, then, would relate to the past in terms not of a retrospective sense of guilt, but of a forward-looking sense of democratic duty. It is here, in this nexus between reflecting on the National Socialist past and the notion of responsibility, that the public and private converge. Collective responsibility for democratic and humane standards can only be maintained if each of the individuals in the collective seeks to uphold these standards. Thus while Walser sought to reduce ritual in the public realm, his speech was understood by some as a call for a 'readjustment' of ritual to embrace the concept of responsibility.

The most productive outcome of the discussion surrounding Walser's Frankfurt speech was the view that public and private should be conceived of in terms not of opposites, or dichotomies, but of interaction. 'People born later do not remember – they are reminded', wrote Robert Leicht (*Zeit*, 3 December 1998). But how can factual knowledge be transformed into personal consciousness, he asked? Federal President Herzog advocated increasing the number of local projects to uncover traces of the National Socialist past. The more concrete the preoccupation with this past, he suggested, the more people would become personally engaged in reflecting on the moral issues of crime and suffering. He called this 'an exercise in empathy' (*FAZ*, 28 January 1999). Recent years have seen the construction of a number of local holocaust memorials in Germany which do not 'impose' an interpretation on the viewer, but invite interpretation, even participation (see Young 1993: 27–48). The 'active' memorial breaks down divisions between public and private. Herzog broke down these divisions when he directly appealed to today's younger generation. The combination of the historiographical and the aesthetic at former concentration camps (see Chapter One) also represents such a dissolution: the viewer must 'make sense' of this combination. The interaction of public and private was thus, to a degree, already under way.

Some critics took issue with Walser's self-referential concept of conscience, arguing that conscience needed to be bound into a public system of memory coordinates which stimulated it. Konrad Schuller, while recognizing the value of the autonomous conscience, pointed out that it cannot reliably limit the influence of pressure and propaganda on the majority (*FAZ*, 1 December 1998). Stefan Reinecke feared that Walser's notion of conscience represented a continuation of the 'fatal German tradition of unpolitical individualism' (*taz*, 28 November 1998). Fears that, left to conscience, memory of the Third Reich would simply evaporate, were surely valid. But, equally, it was understood that people, in the words of Manfred Fuhrmann, needed to do their own 'spiritual work' (Schirrmacher 1999: 303). Ultimately, moreover, only if the conscience feels called upon to convert the 'message' of public ritual into individual action does this ritual have any valuable purpose. 'Knowledge can strengthen conscience; but only the individual can exercise control over his or her own conscience', wrote Rita Süssmuth (*FR*, 24 December 1998).

The value of dispute

Bubis and Walser may have fallen out, but the impact of Walser's Frankfurt speech on German–Jewish relations was not only negative. German Jews born after the war proved to be as sceptical of public ritual as many younger Germans. Salomon Korn, a representative of the Central Council of the Jews in Germany, wrote in reference to such ritual of a 'jargon of *Betroffenheit* conveyed through cliché-ridden expressions' (*FAZ*, 1 December 1998). The German term *Betroffenheit* suggests an automatic and unreflective sense of dismay, which can be turned on or off at will. German-Jewish writer Rafael Seligmann also pointed to a culture of *Betroffenheit* which 'robbed living Jews of their freedom of action' (*Welt*, 21 November 1998). Hungarian Jew György Konrád, President of the German Writers' Union, took issue with the 'all too frequent mentioning of Auschwitz, because then, together with all the other images of horror, it becomes a media platitude' (*Zeit*, 22 December 1998). Two central ideas emerge here: firstly, that the Germans might for a long time have simply repeated well-worn expressions of regret rather than actually felt regret; and secondly, that German Jews, afraid lest they provoke the Germans into renewed acts of anti-semitism, had been reluctant to criticize this culture of superficial *Betroffenheit*. The assumption was that, as long as the Germans were committed to expressions of moral shock, however routine, they would at least not harm the Jews. The silence of German Jews in post-war Germany was thus conditioned by fear. Seligmann has even referred in this connection to a 'ghetto of fear'. There thus existed a mutual dependence between ritualized German memory and passive Jewish acceptance of this ritual. Seligmann greeted the emotionalized debate between Bubis and Walser because it showed that this role-playing in German–Jewish relations had become intolerable: 'we need an open debate' (*Welt*, 21 November 1998). For Seligmann, Jews and Germans now, at last, have a chance to argue about how the memory of the murdered might best be preserved.

In the relationship between Germans and Jews, then, as well as in that between public and private, a new interaction was needed. This had to mean that Germans could criticize Jews, and vice versa, without such criticisms immediately being construed as evidence of anti-semitism or of a campaign of 'blaming' the Germans. Historically, too, it was felt that today's Jews must be prepared to review critically the degree to which some Jews had cooperated with National Socialism as *kapos* in concentration camps, or in other ways. Thus György Konrád declared: 'among the Jews, I know, there were not only victims, but perpetrators [. . .] I therefore think that being strict towards ourselves, as well as forgiving towards others is a golden rule of ethics which the Jews too must respect' (*Zeit*, 22 December 1998). When Dohnanyi called on Jews to be strict towards themselves, he appeared to be doing so in a dubious attempt to undermine their right to criticize Germans. But when Jews begin to explore the issue of Jewish complicity, and in consequence decide in favour of a more forgiving attitude towards Germans, this has nothing dubious about it. Walser's principle of 'say to yourself what you would say to others', as a basis for German–Jewish relations, is valuable, but only if it is voluntarily adopted by Jews, not under rhetorical enforcement. In the course of the Walser–Bubis debate, there were Jews who criticized Bubis for some of his remarks. Michael Wolffsohn, historian at the *Bundeswehr* University in Munich, argued that Bubis, in describing Walser as an 'intellectual arsonist', had provided an example of exactly the kind of moral cudgel to which Walser had referred in his speech (*FAZ*, 18 October 1998). He even called for Bubis's resignation. French-Jewish intellectual Alain Finkielkraut resisted Bubis's suggestion that Walser was latently anti-semitic because he felt it to represent an act of verbal terrorism; it did not allow for counter-arguments (*Welt*, 20 February 1999). Wolffsohn and Finkielkraut clearly did not feel that the holocaust gave Jews an unqualified right to the moral condemnation of Germans.

Normalization

Older Jews such as Bubis saw in Walser's remarks, and in the comments of his supporters, an act of 'coming out', whereby the mask of political correctness was removed, revealing the untamed beast of anti-semitism. They feared the excision of the holocaust from public memory, a flourishing of aggressive nationalism, and renewed discrimination against Jews. For them, Walser's speech encouraged 'negative' normalization, in the sense of a return to a past norm of persecuting minorities. But when Rafael Seligmann described the Walser–Bubis debate as 'a chance on the road to normalization' (*Welt*, 21 November 1998), he understood the latter term more positively. Younger Jews, more trusting of German democracy and able to acknowledge that today's Germans cannot be made guilty for the holocaust, were prepared to accept that complaints about ritualization were not all motivated by a desire to bury the past. And they were glad at the chance of greater openness. If Germans feel they can criticize forms of memory or even the Jews without being accused of anti-semitism, and if Jews can criticize Germans without fear of giving rise to anti-semitism, then 'normal' dialogue will be possible, and resentments deriving from the suppression of true opinion overcome.

While such hopes of 'positive' normalization may still be premature, it must be pointed out that anti-semitism in today's Germany, at least in its violent form, is not typical. It is still the behaviour of a minority, mostly young people, and to a considerable extent east Germans. It is part of a general protest against foreigners on the part of people unable to come to terms with social and economic problems. It is also symptomatic of a Europe-wide trend. There have been recent attacks on French synagogues as well as German ones. Moreover, some recent attacks in Germany on Jewish synagogues may well have been staged by non-Germans protesting at Israel's Palestine politics. In the long term, moreover, more open debate between Germans and Jews might serve to reduce what violent anti-semitism there is. Jewish property is often the target of aggression because some young Germans feel the Jews are somehow 'sacrosanct', so that aggression towards them still represents a violation of the strongest taboo.

Walser's speech was given but a matter of days after the shift of government from CDU/FDP to SPD/Greens in the national elections of 27 September 1998.

Pessimists have diagnosed an unsettling parallelism between Walser's conservative vision of a renationalized public realm freed of memory of the holocaust, and the supposed *Neue Unbefangenheit* of the new left. This term implies a certain rough-and-ready, shoulder-shrugging brashness of tone in dealing with the Nazi past. This, it is argued, derives from the fact that the new government's members are too young to have any personal experience of the Nazi period, in contrast to many members of the previous government, including Kohl himself. Because they do not feel responsible, they do not feel 'inhibited' by the Nazi past. The left-wing Berlin Republic, therefore, may become more nationalistic than the old right-wing Bonn Republic was. It is true that, in an interview, Schröder agreed with Walser's diagnosis of ritualization, and insisted that his generation and subsequent generations with no personal memory of the Third Reich should be 'able to walk around without guilt complexes' (*Zeit*, 4 February 1999). But while the SPD today may be more relaxed about the Third Reich, it is also so thoroughly Europeanized as to be immune to any interest in nationalism. The normality of the SPD's Berlin Republic is solidly, even matter-of-factly democratic. Schröder is a pragmatist, not so much uninterested in National Socialism as keen to deploy the lessons learnt from it: 'it's our job to shape present and past in such a way that the past cannot be repeated' (*SZ*, 9 November 1998). Nor need a less fraught attitude to National Socialism be such a bad thing. A more interest-free atmosphere, in contrast to the revisionism of Kohl, can allow for a pluralist discourse on the past. The new normality of the Berlin Republic, accordingly, is not one of the absence of the holocaust, but of its continued presence, indeed magnified presence, in a multiplicity of perspectives. It is a normality, moreover, which is characterized by a greater stress on the issue of responsibility and personal conscience (for a wider discussion of the topics of this final section, see Chapter Nine).

8 The Holocaust Memorial

'No memorial can give adequate expression to an unparalleled crime and an unimaginable occurrence in German history. The fact that the memorial is built will be more important than the form it takes. To do something which it is not really possible to do successfully – that's the huge quandary we're faced with.'
(Norbert Lammerts (CDU), during a debate in Federal Parliament, 25 June 1999)

The master-debate

In his October 1998 Frankfurt speech, Walser had referred to the Holocaust Memorial planned for Berlin as the 'monumentalization of shame' (Walser 1999: 13). He believed that any such memorial would represent the institutionalization of negative moral emotion and the raising of historical guilt to a state creed, forever blocking attempts by Germans to derive strength and orientation from a history that had more to it than National Socialism. The discussion of Walser's speech in the media often revolved around the Holocaust Memorial. Walser supporters saw in the memorial a prime example of that 'moral cudgel' of which Walser had spoken. Bubis supporters defended it as the legitimate, indeed necessary manifestation of Germany's intention to face the crimes of the holocaust. As a result of the Walser–Bubis debate, support for the memorial became associated with those who wanted to remember the holocaust, criticism of it with those who wanted to forget. This, in turn, meant that SPD Chancellor Gerhard Schröder, initially against the idea of a memorial, felt obliged to support it. The Bubis–Walser debate impacted on the memorial plans in another way. The new government, or at least State Minister for Culture Michael Naumann, favoured a shift away from the idea of a 'pure' memorial towards a combination of memorial and documentation centre. The SPD and Green parliamentarians, having no personal experience of Nazism, were aware that young people could not commemorate without first being informed of what it was they were supposed to be commemorating. But the general agreement that commemoration should be less abstract and symbolic, more 'concrete', was also a result of the intense discussion of Walser's speech.

The Walser–Bubis debate was just one of the many influences to which the Holocaust Memorial project has been subject. The project was initiated by, among others, West German television journalist Lea Rosh and historian Eberhard Jäckel in 1988. Initial plans to build this memorial at a site in West Berlin were dropped when, following the fall of the Wall in 1989, a more central area became available. With unification, and with the involvement of the German government, the project took on a national significance. Indeed views on the memorial became something of a yardstick for the role that intellectuals, politicians and the public at large were prepared to allocate to holocaust remembrance in defining national consciousness in united Germany. Concern at the re-emergence of totalitarianist theories in the early 1990s strengthened the commitment of Rosh and Jäckel to the memorial, which, they hoped, would anchor the anti-semitic genocide at the centre of historical awareness. Initially, Helmut Kohl threw his weight behind plans for a different kind of memorial. In 1992 and 1993, he oversaw the transformation of the *Neue Wache* in the former East Berlin into a central memorial to all victims of war and totalitarian regimes. However, when Ignatz Bubis, Head of the Central Council of the Jews in Germany at the time, objected to the fact that the *Neue Wache* appeared to elevate German suffering above that of Jews, Kohl reacted by promising that the Jews would get their 'own' memorial. By and large, he remained committed to fulfilling his promise. In 1996, the impact of Goldhagen's *Hitler's Willing Executioners* (see Chapter Five), with its focus on the supposedly unique nature of German anti-semitism, did much to help the memorial's cause. So did the 'Crimes of the *Wehrmacht*' exhibition, which enhanced awareness that the holocaust was an integral, indeed central component of the war in the east, not something completely separate (see Chapter Six). Yet the exhibition also made it clear that there was a need to remember the Soviet POWs and all those killed as so-called 'partisans'. Sinti and Roma critics of the planned Holocaust Memorial felt bound to point out that it was too exclusive in its focus. With the German parliament's move to Berlin in 1999, discussions as to what the character of the new 'Berlin Republic' should be also influenced responses to the idea of a Holocaust Memorial.

While the shifts and twists in the memorial's planning were conditioned by other debates, it also influenced these. Would the general public's initial interest in Goldhagen's book have been as great without the increased sensitivity to issues of anti-semitism generated by the memorial's supporters? Would his book have been so resisted by conservative German historians had they not felt it was grist to the mill of those who wished, in the view of such historians, to reduce German history by means of a memorial to a baleful tale of exterminating Jews? It was a sense of the need to counteract this tale which led to the enthusiastic reception of Victor Klemperer's diaries with their defiant emphasis on German–Jewish symbiosis and their 'message' that survival had been possible (see Chapter Five). Yet, equally, these diaries themselves told another baleful tale, namely that the Germans, in persecuting the Jews, had destroyed part of themselves; a symbiosis implies a degree of fusion. When James Young, an American scholar and expert on representations of the holocaust, said in 1997 that any Holocaust Memorial should reflect a sense of emptiness and loss, this notion resonated throughout the press and influenced future concepts for the memorial's form and purpose.

The history of the memorial debate is confusing, and in portraying it one runs the risk of becoming enmeshed in its contradictions. Thus the project was started by Germans who wished to remember the victims of the holocaust; yet more and more it also became a memorial for Jews who wished to remember these victims. The memorial is designed, loosely speaking, as a gesture of regret and penance; yet, increasingly, suspicions have been voiced that today's Germans are wanting to snuggle up to the victims of their fathers or grandfathers. It is to be a memorial to the most terrible atrocity, yet in being such it excludes and may play down other atrocities. Some critics suspect that the most important thing is who the memorial is *not* dedicated to. Germans, in other words, want to remember the murdered Jews so that they can continue to overlook the murdered Gypsies and homosexuals, and do not have to overcome continuing prejudices against these. The memorial aims to establish shame and mourning as a constituent of national identity; yet it may be misread by some, such as neo-Nazis, as a tribute to Hitler's elimination of a third of the world's Jews. It could give memory of the holocaust a central status; yet, equally, it could detract from regional centres of memory. It could focus attention on the holocaust, yet at the same time 'put the lid on it'. Much depends on the perspective, but there is an ambivalence at the heart of the matter nevertheless.

In the course of the thrashing out of these conflicting views in the public realm, it became a truism for politicians and intellectuals to argue that the memorial was not as important as the debate surrounding it. Indeed this discussion was itself a kind of memorial. One 1,200-page compendium of articles on the subject appeared under the title *The Memorial Debate – The Memorial? (Der Denkmalstreit – das Denkmal?* [Heimrod *et al.* 1999]). The debate was influenced by the usual right–left dichotomy so typical of debates on the National Socialist past in Germany. Thus Eberhard Diepgen, Berlin's CDU mayor, spearheaded right-wing resistance to turning Berlin into a 'centre of regret', while Berlin's SPD was more supportive of the memorial. Yet Schröder was also lukewarm. Thus attitudes cannot always be classified in accordance with this right–left dichotomy. They transcended party politics to a degree, running along the fault-lines of generation difference, family background or even simply diversity of personal opinion. Given the ambivalence described above, being against the memorial did not necessarily mean being against a commemorative focus on the holocaust. Equally, support for it could stem from a certain wish to get an unpleasant theme over and done with. The inherent ambivalence also explains changes of opinion. Walter Jens and Günter Grass, initially for the Holocaust Memorial, became increasingly sceptical; Wolfgang Thierse (SPD) warmed to the idea after initial scepticism, as did Naumann. In the CDU, Kohl championed the idea, first for diplomatic reasons, then with genuine passion, creating tensions between himself and Diepgen. In the by and large intelligent debate on the memorial in the German Federal Parliament in June 1999, while the CDU position was sceptical and that of the SPD supportive, this was only broadly speaking the case. To a degree, the holocaust as a subject of memory had been freed from the constraints of party-political discourse.

In the following, I shall provide an overview of the history of central memorials in both Germanys, in order to set the development of the idea for a Holocaust

Memorial in context. I shall also trace the development of local memorials to Germany's murdered Jews, particularly in Berlin. Leading on from this, I will examine the history of the Holocaust Memorial, tracing its key stages and the key arguments and counter-arguments which accompanied its conceptual evolution. In the course of the past ten years, the memorial debate has broadened into a fundamental, principled discussion on all possible tensions within holocaust memory. There have been debates on the relationship between art and the holocaust, commemorative art and historiography, commemoration and enlightenment, memorials and urban space, artificially created and supposedly authentic sites of memory, the positive and negative within history, and shame-based and pride-based national identity. The contention is that this debate has served to enhance understanding of the holocaust in the public realm, and it has certainly also helped to shift discussion onto the meta-level referred to in the previous chapter. Unlike some, I do not believe that the Germans are now so caught up in discussing how best to remember that they may actually forget to do the remembering. The discussion is generally driven by a sincere concern for establishing the most appropriate form of bridge between past crime and present reflection.

The *Neue Wache*

Pre-unification West Germany had a small central memorial. It was dedicated to the 'victims of wars and the rule of violence', and took the form of a bronze plaque outside the Academic Art Museum in Bonn's *Hofgarten*. While the dedication referred to those who had died in the two world wars and under National Socialist rule, it was kept vague enough to encompass the victims of post-1945 Stalinism. Indeed when Federal President Lübke inaugurated the memorial in 1964, he did so on the eve of 17 June, the day on which West Germany pointedly remembered the victims of the 1953 uprising in the GDR. He also explicitly stated that the memorial was in honour of these victims. The Federal Memorial of Honour, as it was pompously called, was thus founded on an equation of National Socialism and Stalinism, and served as a political tool in the Cold War. It implied that those who had fallen in the Second World War, or died in Allied bombing-raids, were as much victims as those persecuted and murdered by the Nazis. This all-victims-together narrative could even include the National Socialist perpetrators themselves – especially after 1980, when the Federal Memorial was moved to Bonn's North Cemetery. Here, soldiers and the civilian dead of both wars, Soviet forced labourers and members of the *Waffen*-SS lie buried.

However, this still rather modest memorial did not completely satisfy political needs. On 6 May 1981, Helmut Schmidt called for 'a memorial for those who lost their lives as a result of the failings and the crimes of the Third Reich, be this in the prisons or concentration camps, in the homeland during the bombing war, or at the fronts of the Second World War' (Moller 1998: 15). While this call was based on the typical all-victims-together model, others began to demand a more explicit dedication to the German soldiers who, as erstwhile Parliamentary President Richard Stücklen put it, 'lie buried in unknown graves in the east or at some other point of the compass' (Moller 1998: 15). Stücklen's idea found most drastic expression in an aide-mémoire published on 8 May 1983 by the People's League for German War Graves Maintenance. This aide-mémoire envisaged a 40,000 square-metre monument laden with Christian symbolism and dedicated exclusively to the German dead of both world wars (Reichel 1999: 203). There was no thought here for the millions of Jews murdered in the course of the holocaust, most of whom were also without graves. Chancellor Kohl supported calls for a more weighty national memorial in November 1983 on the People's Day of Mourning (*Volkstrauertag*), a day given over to mourning the German war-dead. In addition to making the usual vague references to the victims of both world wars and of the rule of violence, Kohl also mentioned the victims of 'racial madness'. But he quickly followed this up with a reference to the victims of resistance, expulsion and division, and even of terrorism (*FAZ*, 12 November 1983). He thus reinforced both the all-victims-together and the totalitarianist paradigm. In March 1985, the Federal Cabinet decided to launch a competition for a grander central memorial site along these lines, but no cross-party agreement could be reached, and the idea was dropped on 13 March 1986.

In the meantime, Richard von Weizsäcker had given his famous 8 May 1985 speech in which he also listed the victims of the war, but reversed the hierarchy, mentioning first the Jews, next the Russians and Poles, and only then the Germans (see Chapter Four). The SPD had wanted to make this hierarchy the operative basis for the text of the Federal Memorial, but the CDU resisted. In 1992, two years after unification and without parliamentary consultation, Chancellor Kohl declared his intention to make a building known as the *Neue Wache* in Berlin united Germany's national memorial to 'the victims of war and the rule of violence'. Kohl's purpose was not only to put an end to calls for a more differentiated approach to the issue of victimhood. In the GDR, the *Neue Wache* had been the site of East Germany's central memorial. In replacing this with his own memorial, Kohl sought to oust East German traditions of commemoration, in line with the general imposition of things western on the new *Länder*.

The *Neue Wache* was built between 1816 and 1818 by Karl Friedrich Schinkel. As one commentator has pointed out, it 'had already been used by three different German governments and their leaders to chart the course of their respective memorial politics' (Wiedmer 1999: 116). In 1930, the *Reichswehr* Ministry entrusted Heinrich Tessenow with the task of reconfiguring the building as a memorial to the fallen of the First World War. Tessenow came up with the idea of placing inside it an altar-like black block of granite with a golden wreath of oak-leaves upon it. After coming to power, the National Socialists hung an oak cross at the back of the *Neue Wache* and continued to use it as a memorial site to the war-dead. It was destroyed by a bomb-attack in February 1945. In the GDR, the *Neue Wache* was reconstructed and used as of 1960 as a memorial to the 'victims of fascism and militarism' (Reichel 1999: 202). As of 1969, it was fitted out with an 'eternal flame', with the GDR state insignia, and with two urns containing, respectively, the ashes of an unknown resistance fighter from a concentration camp, and of an unknown soldier who had died in the Second World War. According to Ute

Frevert, the SED felt uncomfortable with this equation of victims, and in official pronouncements tended to stress more the importance of resistance fighters (Assmann and Frevert 1999: 165–6). Nevertheless, the *Neue Wache* did represent the eradication of differences between those who had fought for the Third Reich and those who had been persecuted by it, in parallel to the Federal Memorial. A further parallel was the use of symbolism to encourage an exclusive interpretation of the open dedication. Those who died as a result of racism, the 'passive' rather than active (communist) victims, had no urn in the *Neue Wache*. Jews were excluded. Like the Federal Memorial, the *Neue Wache* was a piece of Cold War propaganda. While the FRG's memorial practice subsumed Nazism under totalitarianism, the GDR's subsumed it under fascism, militarism and 'monopolistic capitalism'.

The *Neue Wache* was Kohl's symbolic affirmation of the triumph of West Germany's historical self-understanding over East Germany's. In Kohl's view, the Germans were the victims not of the barbarous extremes of capitalism, but of a tradition of dictatorship which had found expression in National Socialism and socialism. Now, this had given way to a tradition of liberal and democratic capitalism. The irony of this, of course, was that Kohl's decision to bypass Federal Parliament in realizing his new concept was no less dictatorial than the cultural politics of the SED. His insistence on placing at the heart of the revamped *Neue Wache* a massive blow-up of Käthe Kollwitz's *Pieta*, which shows a mother grieving over her dead son, effectively resulted in a renewed exclusion of the Jews [Plate 8.1]. The Maria-like figure and pose are quintessentially Christian. Kollwitz's sculpture, moreover, was inspired by the loss of her son at the front in the First World War.

Plate 8.1 Inside the *Neue Wache* memorial in Berlin.

The sculpture's frame of reference narrows down the applicability of the open dedication, so that it effectively extends only to soldiers. That this was intended is borne out by Kohl's statement that it was a question of 'our country's dignity' to have a memorial to the fallen 'as other countries do' (Wise 1998: 145). In choosing a perspective of maternal loss, Kohl encouraged an undifferentiated view of war. For a mother, a son who dies in war is always a victim, regardless of which side he fought on, or for what cause. At least the maternal perspective draws attention to female suffering in war. But this suffering is then abused for purposes of engendering uncritical sympathy for the war-dead.

This memorial triggered much indignation. Historian Reinhard Koselleck, in reference to the *Neue Wache*'s dedication, pointed out that the German term *Opfer* means both victim and sacrifice. The suffering of the victims of conquest and murder is placed on a par with the active and voluntary *sacrificium* of the soldier (*FAZ*, 8 April 1993). Bubis saw in the dedication a 'levelling down of the victims' (*TSP*, 11 July 1993), while Jerzy Kanal of the Berlin Jewish Community objected to the equation of victims and perpetrators (*Spiegel*, 4 October 1993). A few weeks before the opening of the *Neue Wache*, State Minister Anton Pfeifer (CDU) and Ignatz Bubis came to an agreement that two plaques would be mounted at the entrance. One would provide an overview of the history of the building, the second a necrologue along the lines of Weizsäcker's 8 May 1985 speech (Moller 1998: 56). Bubis made his attendance at the opening ceremony dependent on this latter change. It would be fair to say that he allowed himself to be duped. The second plaque encourages the visitor to understand war as a natural catastrophe removed from the sphere of human responsibility, rather like an earthquake. In this way, everyone can be declared a victim. After a vague commemorative gesture towards 'the peoples who have suffered through war' and 'their citizens who were persecuted and lost their lives', the plaque makes reference to the fallen of the two world wars, and to the 'innocent' people who lost their lives not just in war, but 'in the homeland', 'in captivity' and 'when being driven out of their homeland' (for the whole text, see Reichel 1999: 208). There then follow references to the murdered Jews and Sinti and Roma, and to all those murdered on the grounds of race, homosexuality or 'sickness and weakness' (a reference to euthanasia victims). That all these groups are mentioned, and that they feature higher on the list than those who died in the resistance, is to be welcomed. Nevertheless, the *Neue Wache* necrologue is in the first instance a tribute to those Germans who died at the front, in bombing raids, or when fleeing the eastern territories before and after 8 May 1945. Weizsäcker's necrologue was in the first instance a tribute to dead Jews, Russians and Poles. The *Neue Wache* allocates to the Jews the status of second-class victims, and, in good anticommunist tradition, fails to mention Russians and Poles.

The House of History in Bonn

If the *Neue Wache* was to be united Germany's central war memorial, Bonn's House of History, opened on 14 June 1994, was to be one of united Germany's main historical museums, alongside the German Historical Museum in Berlin. As already discussed in Chapter Two, it presents post-1945 German history in terms of the superiority of West Germany over East Germany. Just as significantly, it portrays West Germany as the state which successfully reconnected to the liberal and parliamentary traditions of pre-1933 Germany. As in the *Neue Wache*, National Socialism, war and its effects are presented as natural catastrophes, with the Germans as their main victims. The significance of the holocaust is played down. All of this is not surprising, perhaps, given that conservative historians such as Horst Möller, Klaus Hildebrand, Michael Stürmer and Andreas Hillgruber played a leading role in the conception of the House of History, plans for which date back to the 1980s (Berger 1997: 206).

On entering the exhibition, the visitor is confronted with film footage showing Germans fleeing towards the west. A text board informs us that, as a result of the war started by Germany in 1939, millions of people throughout Europe were driven out of their homes. The film of German fugitives encourages the visitor to imagine that these were the prime victims of this process of displacement, not the Jews or Poles. To the right of this video installation, pictures of liberated concentration camps can be seen. The liberated inmates on some pictures appear in reasonable health. What suffering they have endured, we infer, is over. In contrast, the suffering of the expellees, expressed as it is in terms of movement, comes across as long-drawn-out, indeed enduring. To the left, information is provided on the fate of German POWs, many of whom, we are told, died in eastern, but also western camps. After this, visitors approach a kind of black box, its contents closed off from the surrounding exhibition. In this box, a video film reels off the names of concentration camp victims. The cubicle also shows images of the persecution of Jews, of Auschwitz, and of piles of shoes and corpses. Information on the Third Reich is provided on the outside of the box, but discreetly, tucked away in side-pockets. One row of pockets supplies information on dictatorship, one on the 'mills of death' and one on resistance. There is one picture of camp victims outside the cubicle, on an opposite wall, but in the form of an Allied poster accusing the Germans at large of responsibility: 'This disgraceful act: your guilt'.

Such organization of material invites the visitor to understand the holocaust, and the process of anti-semitic discrimination which preceded it, as something hidden from the broad mass of Germans. All that was immediately visible to them, it is implied, was the post-1945 accusation of collective guilt, the validity of which is implicitly undermined by the 'concealed holocaust' symbolism of the black box. In this way, the exhibition serves to exculpate the Germans and inculpate the Allies. Moreover, by placing the theme of the holocaust in a black box which can be easily bypassed or even overlooked by visitors, the designers of the exhibition imply that knowledge of the holocaust is not essential for an understanding of post-1945 German history. A black box invites comparison with the black box in an aeroplane, the device that might provide a clue to what made it break down. By association, then, the holocaust is presented as an unfortunate technical hitch, thus detaching it from the flow and shape of Germany's history before, after and even during the Third Reich.

The *Neue Wache* and the Bonn House of History – at best – play down the holocaust and make second-class victims of the Jews, attaching prime victim status to non-Jewish Germans. In defence of these two national centres of memory, one might argue that nations usually commemorate, in the first instance, their own dead. To expect the Germans to do differently may well be hypocritical. Where, one might ask, are the American monuments to the victims of Hiroshima, or the British ones to the victims of Amritsar? That historical museums distort national history to make it appear better than it really was, or play down the negative episodes, is hardly an exclusively German trait. Having said that, the holocaust remains a unique atrocity, and Jews were victims not of battle, but of calculated genocide. Moreover, given that both post-war Germanys were founded, on paper at least, in conscious opposition to National Socialism – on anti-fascism here, liberal democracy there – awareness of the destructiveness of the holocaust, of German perpetration and complicity, *should* have been central to their picture of history. This was not the case in East Germany, nor, always, in West Germany, where coming to terms with the past was long understood in terms of compensation, even of unjust claims and charges, not in terms of shame and penance. It was almost as if, in clinging to their self-understanding as victims, the Germans sought to avoid confronting the facts of perpetration.

The 1980s in West Germany were marked by a developing awareness of German crime during the war. But this was also the decade when conservative historians attempted to play down the severity of these atrocities by pointing to the crimes of other nations, notably the Soviets. Unification in 1990 led to calls for an end to the supposed preoccupation with the aberrations of German history, and, in total contrast, to calls for Germany to at last take full and unmitigated national responsibility for the crimes of the holocaust. The *Neue Wache* and the House of History seemed to indicate that the conservative camp had been successful in its bid to preserve an image of the Germans as victims, and to play down the issue of German perpetration. But by 1994, three projects were either completed or under way in Berlin which gave greater weight in the public realm to the significance of the holocaust, drawing attention to German perpetrators and their victims. The House of the Wannsee Conference Memorial Site, opened in 1992, documents the bureaucratic planning of the genocide. The Topography of Terror, currently under construction, also focuses on perpetration, while the planned Holocaust Memorial places its emphasis on the victims. In the course of the 1990s, moreover, a series of significant local memorials to the Jews and other Nazi victims were built. Such projects have helped to foster a process of disaggregation, countering the undifferentiated all-victims-together paradigm. As German perpetrators moved more into the frame of memory, questions had to be asked as to the role of 'ordinary' Germans in the Third Reich, who now appeared as upholders of a criminal regime. As Jewish victims moved into focus, so it became harder to see Germans as the prime victims, indeed as victims at all. A critical, and self-critical, readjustment of perspective became necessary.

Topography of Terror

The Topography of Terror is a site, a foundation and an exhibition. The site, known as the *Prinz-Albrecht-Gelände*, formerly housed the Gestapo (Prinz-Albrecht Street 8), the SS (Hotel Prinz Albrecht) and the SD (Prinz-Albrecht Palace). In 1992, becoming fully independent in April 1995, a foundation supported by the Federal Parliament and Berlin was set up to oversee the transformation of this site into a documentation centre. The centre, to be built to a unique design by the Swiss architect Peter Zumthor, is in the course of being erected. Building costs turned out to be higher than estimated, having shot from 38 to 79 million DM by June 2000. This problem, and the fact that Zumthor's complicated construction requires a special kind of concrete which can only be cast at a certain temperature, have led to long delays. A visitor to the site today will see what looks like a deserted building-site, and it is likely to remain deserted until Zumthor, Berlin's Building Senate and the construction firm find a solution to the financial problems.

The problems plaguing the site are perhaps symptomatic of a long-standing reluctance to preserve the traces of perpetration. Under the National Socialists, especially after the conglomeration of the Gestapo, Criminal Police and SD into the Reich Security Main Office (RSHA) in 1939, the *Prinz-Albrecht-Gelände* was the coordination centre of terror throughout Germany and the entire area occupied by Hitler's troops. It was here that the activities of the notorious *Einsatzgruppen*, known for their brutal massacres in Poland and the Soviet Union, were planned. Here, too, the parameters were marked out for the genocide against Jews and Sinti and Roma. The *Prinz-Albrecht-Gelände* was also the location of a Gestapo prison in which, particularly, some members of the group involved in planning the 20 July 1944 plot (see Chapter Three) were interrogated, tortured and killed. But it was primarily a 'place of the perpetrators' (Rürup 1997: 7). After the war, the ruins of the bomb-damaged buildings were torn down, the final traces being removed in 1962–1963. The centre of the SS state had been, as it were, flattened to the ground. Neglect of the area was made easier by the fact that the Berlin Wall ran through it. There were plans to use it as a helicopter port, or run a street across it, before it was used in the early 1970s by a firm which processed building rubble. It was also used as an autodrome.

In 1983, after historians and Berlin's SPD had drawn attention to the historical importance of the site, a competition was started up to find an appropriate form of memorialization. But there was a danger of trivialization. The competition guide-lines suggested that what was more important was placing any such reminder of Nazi atrocities within a leafy green environment: Berlin-Kreuzberg, the terms stated, needed a park and playgrounds (Heimrod *et al.* 1999: 38). In his foreword, Richard von Weizsäcker, at the time mayor of Berlin, wrote that the history of National Socialism as reflected in the site should be palpable not as a unique, iso-lated event, but as the 'unspeakably tragic and horrific apogee of a totalitarianism which, as a political and social phenomemon, was by no means overcome in 1945'. The history of the site was to act as an 'emblem and a matrix of other possible or current crimes' (Heimrod *et al.* 1999: 37). In good West German tradition, the Nazi past was to function as a mirror for reflecting Soviet and GDR repression. The problem here was not just the totalitarian equation, but its use as a means of deflecting blame and responsibility.

The first prize was awarded to Nikolaus Lang and Jürgen Wenzel, who proposed covering the area in sheets of cast-iron, on which the contents of several thousand documents relating to persecution by the Nazis were to be imprinted. In addition, chestnut trees were to be planted on the site. Reactions were largely negative. While quite a number in Berlin's CDU opposed any kind of reference to perpetration, objections from politically more neutral quarters were based on a genuine concern that Lang and Wenzel's design would not adequately enhance awareness of the site's history. It was felt that, while the design did integrate documentation, it also aestheticized it; setting this documentation in the ground, moreover, would result in people walking over it rather than stopping to read it. Nor was the shade of chestnut trees likely to trigger critical reflection. On 20 November 1984, the Berlin Senate decided against the prize-winning design, and plans for memorialization were temporarily shelved. Archaeological digs in the mid-1980s, and a successful provisional exhibition installed in time for the 750th anniversary of Berlin in 1987, paved the way for a policy of trace-preservation and documentation such as pursued at the former concentration camp sites. In March 1990, after much prevarication, a specialist commission set up by the Berlin Senate advocated against an aesthetic representation of the site's history and recommended a concentration on the 'expressive force of the historical site in its present form' (Heimrod *et al.* 1999: 65). Hence Zumthor won a prize for an exhibition centre, not a memorial.

As it happens, Zumthor's planned steel-rod construction is so striking architecturally that, while its internal purpose will be one of documentation, its external appearance will stimulate an emotional response to the immediate physical and historical environment. It is therefore not entirely functional in the sense of being subservient to its contents; it also has the character of a memorial. The discussion about the relative merits of aesthetics and documentation as triggers to reflection anticipated later debates relating to the Holocaust Memorial. The Topography of Terror is also important because it was originally considered by Lea Rosh and Eberhard Jäckel as a possible site for the Holocaust Memorial. But it was rightly argued that the Jews were not the only victims of the murderous plans hatched at the *Prinz-Albrecht-Gelände*. It was also pointed out that a memorial to the victims would detract from the perpetrators at a location where the intellectual barbarity of these men should be in the foreground. This was not to argue against empathy for the victims, or to play down the impact of murderous planning. But it was felt that this particular site must stand in primary associative relation to the fact of this planning. In this way, it could be understood that atrocities emerged from the bureaucratic heart of Berlin and the Third Reich, wherever they subsequently took place. In March 1990, the specialist commission also explicitly rejected the idea of a memorial to the murdered Jews being erected on the site (Heimrod *et al.* 1999: 65–6).

The cold-hearted planning, over breakfast, of the mass murder of Jews is now documented at the House of the Wannsee Conference Memorial Site. The planning of organized massacres in the east is also now documented, and is to be more fully documented, at the Topography of Terror. These exhibitions are the necessary correlatives to Goldhagen's *Hitler's Willing Executioners* and the 'Crimes of the *Wehrmacht*' exhibition (see Chapters Five and Six). Taken together, all four convey the impression that criminality was a cohesive element in the Third Reich, linking politics, bureaucracy, the SS, the army and the 'ordinary' German soldier and reservist. Building a Holocaust Memorial specifically on the *Prinz-Albrecht-Gelände* would, perhaps, have worked against this agenda of enhancing awareness of the true extent of responsibility. It might have misled some to associate the murder of Jews exclusively with certain organizations and bureaucrats. The 'ordinary Germans' who carried out the orders would have been implicitly exonerated. By contrast, erecting a Holocaust Memorial outside the *Reichstag*, as Rosh rightly pointed out when she rejected this suggestion, would have been to unfairly accuse *all* Germans of involvement in the holocaust.

Local memorials to the Jews

On the other side of the coin showing perpetration is victimhood. Accordingly, in the 1980s and especially the 1990s, a significant number of sites of Jewish suffering, or sites associated with the starting-point for this suffering, have been given a place in the memorial topography of Berlin. Memorials to the murdered Jews had been erected in West Germany and West Berlin before this; East Germany, too, had its few memorials. But Jewish suffering was often presented in a rather idealized or over-symbolic form. An example of idealization is Hans Wimmer's over-dimensional figure dedicated to the victims of the concentration camps, which was unveiled near the Frankfurt *Paulskirche* in 1964. A good example of vague symbolical gesturing might be Corrado Cagli's 86 intertwined triangles of chrome, nickel and steel in memory of the suffering of Göttingen's Jews, erected in 1973 over a pattern resembling the Star of David. Memorials could also be tendentious. One of the earliest memorials to the victims of the concentration camps, erected in 1964 at Ohlsdorf cemetery in Hamburg, bore the inscription 'injustice brought us death'; there was no reference to the fact that Germans were responsible for this injustice [Plate 8.2]. At the same cemetery, in questionable counterpoint, those killed in Allied bombing raids on Hamburg are symbolized by a crown of thorns. Their deaths are transfigured into an act of martyrdom.

In Berlin itself, the first official memorial to commemorate an aspect of the destroyed Jewish community was erected at the site of a former Jewish synagogue on Munich Street in 1963. Ironically, this synagogue was one of those not ransacked or destroyed during the *Reichskristallnacht* pogrom of 9–10 November 1938; it was torn down in 1956. It was not until 1988 that an additional plaque was mounted which registered this fact. The tearing down of ruined or 'obsolete' synagogues was a not uncommon occurrence in post-war Germany, in both states. In 1967, two memorials were erected on Wittenberg Square and Kaiser Wilhelm Square respectively. They listed the concentration camps under the rubric 'Places

Plate 8.2 Memorial to concentration camp victims at Ohlsdorf Cemetery in Hamburg. The inscription reads 'Injustice brought us death. To those who live: recognize your duty'.

of terror that we must never forget'. The virtue of these memorials is that they stand in busy, bustling parts of Berlin; they are not tucked away at some remote site. They were designed in conscious opposition to the 'Memorial for the Expelled Ethnic Germans' on the Mehringdamm. This latter memorial, finally removed in 1972, listed those cities now 'lost' to the Poles or Soviets, such as Danzig and Königsberg. It had been erected in 1952, long before most memorials to the victims of Nazism – a symptom of the fact that the immediate post-war commemorative sympathies of many Germans were with the German expellees (see Chapter One). The 'Places of terror' memorials were a necessary counterpoint, even if they now also seem somewhat over-didactic, more of a list of commandments than an evocation of suffering or an appeal to conscience.

The changes in West and even East Berlin's memorial landscape in the late 1980s and 1990s were multi-dimensional. Firstly, the suffering of Berlin's Jews, specifically, moved more into focus. Secondly, this suffering was presented in terms not just of its most extreme form and end-point – the annihilation camps – but also of its point of departure, namely Berlin's deportation centres and railway stations. Thirdly, the language of memorials changed. While memorials up until then had seemed to absorb the object of commemoration, there was now a move towards consciously projecting the task of commemoration onto the observer, and connecting the suffering of Jews with the issue of German responsibility. The passive concept of suffering was complemented by an active one; suffering, after all, had been inflicted, not just endured. Fourthly, memorials became less static, less detached, more visible and integrated. They were not just something people visited, but they were visited on people, so conspicuous or even omnipresent could they be. Yet in contrast to this, fifthly, some memorials to the Jews became less material, even non-material, evoking the horror of destruction, and drawing attention to the 'holes' left behind in Berlin, in its culture, society and history. Sixthly, Berlin's various city councils became more involved in commissioning memorials to the Jews, instead of leaving everything to grass-roots initiatives, the League of Human Rights or even Jews themselves. Finally, memorial debates came into vogue. There had always been debates in West Germany about memorials. But they acquired a new quality in the 1990s, a sign that shifts in commemorative topography were having an impact.

More than 50,000 Jews were deported between October 1941 and February 1945 from the station in the pretty Berlin village of Grunewald. In 1987, the Berlin Senate started up a competition to find a suitable memorial, and in 1991 the prize-winning memorial by Karol Broniatowski and Ralf Sroka – set into a slope below the station – was unveiled. It shows the negative impressions left by human figures, which have, as it were, been 'scooped' out of a block of white concrete. Echoes of bodies, ribs or fingers, intrude on the empty spaces. This is a monument of absence. When I was there, schoolboys tried to fit themselves into the bigger spaces, to 'fill' the gaps; into some holes, coca-cola cans and chocolate-bar wrappers had been tossed. The memorial does not appear to suffer under such 'abuse'. Indeed it invites reflection on what has gone, and what Germans might evasively try to put in its place. A few yards further on, there is another memorial, called 'Platform 17'. It was designed by the architectural team of Hirsch, Lorch and Wandel and dates from 1993, supplementing a plaque mounted in 1987. Long rows of rusted-metal strips run along both sides of the deserted railway-line, showing in chronological order the dates of the transportations, the number deported and the destination. This too is a memorial of emptiness, of almost eerie silence (for a fuller discussion, see ZAM 1993). Volkmar Haase's twisted staircase on the Putlitz Bridge, unveiled in 1987, also commemorates the deportation of Berlin's Jews, in this instance from Putlitz railway station. It resembles a crushed accordion, the melody stopped in mid-note [Plate 8.3]. As a staircase leading to nothingness, it stresses, as do the Grunewald memorials, that the sequence of events leading to annihilation began in Berlin, not in Auschwitz. At the former site of the Moabit synagogue, where Jews were forced to gather in preparation for deportation, a sculpture of rusted steel by Theseus Bappert, Peter Herbrich and Jürgen Wenzel was unveiled in 1988. It is in the form of a railway carriage; inside

Plate 8.3 Volkmar Haase's memorial to Berlin's deported Jews on the Putlitz Bridge in Berlin.

it, represented in stone, are huddled deportees. Synagogues were not just damaged or destroyed, they were also used as the starting point of the holocaust. In 1985, in East Berlin, a statue by Willi Lammert to Berlin's 56,000 murdered Jews was placed near the site of a former Jewish old-folks' home, also used as a pre-deportation gathering point.

Particularly interesting is the inversion in some of these memorials. A memorial might be thought of as a thing of substance. Yet the tangled staircase is really a non-staircase, the railway platform a non-platform, the scooped-out spaces non-figures. It is what you do *not* see, perhaps, that is the memorial. There are similar examples. Micha Ullmann's memorial on Bebel Square commemorating the notorious 10 May 1933 book-burning is not above ground, but below it, sunken. It shows empty shelves. It is a non-library. Karl Biedermann's memorial commemorating the Jewish contribution to German culture on Koppen Square was dedicated in 1996, but it resulted from a competition held in the GDR. It shows a table and chairs – one overturned as if someone had left in haste [Plate 8.4]. It is

a non-room, without walls, an image of permanently self-repeating, hurried departure. Then there is Christian Boltanski's 'The Missing House' of 1990 on the
Greater Hamburg Street. The house, whose former inhabitants, including Jews, are
named on plaques on the walls of the neighbouring houses, is no longer there.

In a sense, these are non-memorials, analagous to what James Young has called
counter-monuments (Young 1993: 27f.). The crowning example is Daniel
Libeskind's spectacular Jewish Museum, the result of a competition started in
1988–1989 [Plate 8.5]. It was designed as an extension to the Berlin Museum for
City History, and completed in 1997 (for a history of this extension, see Wiedmer
1999: 120–40). Since 1997, the building has been open to the public and proven an
enormous attraction – without exhibits. The exhibition is still under construction.
Libeskind's building, a zig-zag form inspired by the Star of David, is constructed
around what he calls 'voids', vertical shafts of open space intersected by corridors
along which visitors walk from one room to the next. These voids are 'the embodiment of absence' (Libeskind 1998: 10). One of them, the Holocaust Tower,
Libeskind describes as a 'voided void' because emptiness has as it were been taken
and materialized as a building (Libeskind 1999: 30). The Jewish Museum is one
vast symbolical text. Its lines and design features link it to the German–Jewish
historical, cultural and physical landscape of Berlin. Again and again Libeskind
returns to the idea of the expression of the absent. Not surprisingly, perhaps,
given that his design was partly inspired by Arnold Schoenberg's uncompleted
opera *Moses and Aaron*, which 'ends' with Moses uttering the wish to find a word

Plate 8.4 Karl Biedermann's memorial in Berlin in honour of the Jewish contribution to
German culture.

Plate 8.5 The Garden of Exile at the Jewish Museum in Berlin.

which eludes him (Libeskind 1998: 8). The opera thus seems to peter out with an expression of the unfound. Libeskind called his whole edifice 'Between the Lines'. It is here, in the gaps, that the truth is revealed or, at least, can be sought.

The whole building is accordingly organized around the centres of absence – German–Jewish history as loss. The exhibition to be housed here will cover the history of Jews in Germany and Berlin from earliest times to the present. There is more than a suspicion that politicians such as CDU mayor of Berlin Diepgen would like to use this extensive coverage as a means of minimalizing the historical significance of the holocaust. 'Persecution and genocide are not the last word. Upon the collapse, so barbarically enforced, follows the reconstruction, which is now coming into blossom' (Diepgen 1998: 4). The 'reconstruction' refers to the fact that Berlin's, indeed Germany's Jewish community has grown considerably since unification. Libeskind also understands the building as an embodiment of hope, as does its director Michael Blumenthal, who has repeatedly stated that Jews were not just the victims of discrimination, but, before 1933 at least, enjoyed acceptance and esteem. However, the Jewish Museum's picture of developments in the past and future, and of any German–Jewish symbiosis, will be ruptured by the voids. The holocaust is inscribed into the building and cannot be written out. The voids will undermine any impression of a seamless route from past to present, or of overriding harmony. The Jewish Museum will thus represent a true interpenetration of memorial and documentation, as will the final version of the Holocaust Memorial (see below).

The challenge of emptiness in the museum and in other memorials to Jews is complex. For whose loss are we talking about? The New Synagogue on Oranienburg Street in Berlin, opened in 1995, has been reconstructed around its *unreconstructed* heartpiece: the former synagogue itself. This enshrined ruin will serve Berlin's Jews as an expression of their sense of loss. But the Libeskind Museum reflects a loss for both Jews and Germans. The National Socialists, in making a racial distinction between Germans and Jews, sought to tear apart what had, to a degree at least, been intertwined. Their persecution of Jews, resulting in emigration or murder, brought a sudden end to the enormous contribution made by Jews to German history, culture and society. While this act of destruction represented an inestimable loss, there is certainly a danger of Germans feeling sorry for themselves as a result of it, as if they had been persecuted, rather than the Jews. Yet, on the other hand, the sense that Germans destroyed the richness of their own culture along with the Jews can open the way to mourning the latter. The memorials described above, moreover, address loss on all levels – not least the loss of Jewish lives, the nothingness into which the Germans sent them out or allowed them to be sent out. Emptiness poses the question as to who did the emptying.

Finally in this section, we should consider two other recent Berlin memorials to Jewish victims which pose this question by means of what one might term an 'integrative' model of memory. The first is the Mirror Wall in Berlin-Steglitz, completed in June 1995. Positioned near the site of a former synagogue on the busy Hermann Ehlers Square, it is the work of Wolfgang Göschel, Joachim von Rosenberg and Hans-Norbert Burkert, and consists of a massive rectangular reflecting wall. On both sides, the names of some 1,700 Jews from Steglitz and elsewhere in Berlin – taken from Gestapo transport lists – have been inscribed. The memorial, although it resulted from a competition started under the auspices of the local District Council, was controversial (see Seferens 1995). An alliance of local CDU, FDP and Republican politicians opposed its construction on various counts. Thus it was argued that post-reunification Germany should not be erecting new walls, that the wall would be besmirched with graffiti, that it was unsightly, too big, and too negative in tone, failing to register the German–Jewish symbiosis in Steglitz prior to 1933. Related arguments accompanied discussion of the central Holocaust Memorial. Ultimately, Wolfgang Nagel (SPD), Berlin's Building Senator, stepped in to push plans for the memorial through more or less by decree.

The mirroring technique is effective because it overcomes the spatial division between viewer and memorial. The viewer sees not just the names of the deported and dead, but his or her own reflection, which merges with these. As a result, various relations are symbolically highlighted. It is impossible to contemplate the names of the Jews without reflecting on the Germans who deported and killed them, or indeed on those passive bystanders among the Germans who 'looked on' as the visitor now looks upon his or her own reflection. In throwing back the visitor's reflection, the memorial passes back responsibility for remembering, and for doing what can be done to ensure that the present and future are a safer place for Jews and other minorities. In more positive vein, the memorial also features two contrasting pictures of the destroyed and rebuilt New Synagogue, setting the holocaust in relation to a reconstructed Jewish community. Unfortunately, because of CDU opposition, a text by Richard Chaim Schneider linking Third Reich racism to post-1990 racist attacks was replaced with the rather vague question 'and today?'. Schneider was understandably furious at this excision (see R. C. Schneider 1997: 132–8). The plea to remember the past when assessing the present has been considerably weakened.

The second integrative memorial is 'Places of Remembering', which has attracted particular analytical attention (see Wiedmer 1999: 103–15, and Kunstamt Schöneberg *et al.* 1994). Completed in 1993, it resulted from an idea developed by Renate Stih and Frieder Schnock. It consists not of 'one' memorial, but of 80 signs distributed throughout the Bavarian Quarter of western Berlin. The signs are attached mostly to lamp-posts or street-signposts. They are double-sided, on one side a pictorial symbol, on the other a short text, often referring to National Socialist anti-semitic rulings, or taken from letters or accounts by persecuted Jews. In many cases, there is an antithetical relationship between picture and text. Thus a sequence of musical notes is paired with a text stating that Jews 'are excluded from singing clubs', while a picture of a cat is combined with a text stating that Jews may no longer keep pets. There is a rupture, in a structuralist sense, between *signifiant* and *signifié*. Cat does not mean cat, it means no cats; musical notes do not mean music, but no music; benches not a place to sit down, but a place not to sit down. There is also a discrepancy between the function of a conventional street-sign system and the function of these signs. For they do not tell you how to get somewhere, or what to do, or what the function of a particular building is, but tell you where Jews were not allowed to go, what they were not allowed to do, where their presence was not wanted. Markers of rights, privileges and possession, which we take for granted, have become markers of deprivation, discrimination and dispossession. Markers of direction and location have become markers of restriction and dislocation. There could hardly be a more effective method of conveying to the inhabitants of the Bavarian Quarter what it meant to be a Jew under National Socialist rule. The effect is enhanced by the fact that the texts are kept in the present tense, lending them a disturbing sense of immediacy.

The uniqueness of this multi-sign memorial lies primarily in its focus, which is not on the destruction of synagogues and deportation, but on the gradual erosion of civil liberties for Jews. It traces the beginnings of the process which led to the holocaust back to the discriminatory social, political and legal measures introduced between 1933 and 1941. It implies that this discrimination was immediately visible, quite public, as visible and public as these signs are now. The signs tell today's Germans what yesterday's Germans saw, knew and passively accepted. Thus the memorial addresses both the discrimination of Jews and the tolerance of this discrimination. Interwoven into the quarter as a whole, it forces today's Germans to remember this fact as they go about their daily lives. In one case, a sign showing a loaf of bread, accompanied by a notice restricting Jewish shopping hours to an absurd minimum, is posted outside a supermarket. It must be difficult to shop here without reflecting on this sign [Plate 8.6]. The past ruptures the present.

Plate 8.6 One of the 80 signs in 'Places of Remembering', a memorial to the Jews in the Bavaria Quarter of Berlin. The sign shows a loaf of bread. On the back is written 'Jews in Berlin may only buy food in the afternoon between four and five o'clock. 4.7.1940'.

The central Holocaust Memorial in Berlin: issues of identity

By the mid-1990s, then, Germany had a generalizing central memorial to the victims of war and the rule of violence in Berlin, and a holocaust-marginalizing House of History in Bonn. By contrast, it had, in the form of the Topography of Terror, what was developing into a central site for reflecting on German perpetration in Berlin. It had, also in contrast, several significant new local memorials to Jewish victims, particularly in Berlin. It was in the process of acquiring a Jewish Museum, and had a rebuilt New Synagogue and a Centrum Judaicum. What it did not have was a central Holocaust Memorial to all those European Jews who had died in the holocaust. This omission will soon be overcome. Construction of Peter Eisenman's Holocaust Memorial on the site of the former Reich Ministries' gardens will be completed in 2004. As indicated at the outset of this chapter, every aspect of the project has been controversial. In the following I shall refrain from giving a blow-by-blow account of its twisted history (for such an account, see Reichel 1999: 209–17; Wiedmer 1999: 140–64; and Wise 1998: 145–54). Instead, I will examine the main areas of debate, which focused on the following questions. Which function would a central memorial to the Jews fulfil? Should not other victims of National Socialism also feature on the memorial? Where in Berlin should this memorial be placed? What form should it take? Should it just be a memorial? These fundamental what-who-where-how questions have not been answered in any consensual way. But there have been significant compromises. The final result will reflect these, and it will reflect a learning process.

In its first public appeal on 30 January 1989 calling for the erection of a memorial to the millions of murdered Jews, the citizens' action group 'Perspective for Berlin' (*Perspektive Berlin*) called it a 'disgrace' that, in the country of the perpetrators, and half a century after the holocaust, there was still no national memorial to these victims (*FR*, 30 January 1989). In April 1994, the Circle for Promoting the Construction of a Memorial to Europe's Murdered Jews (*Förderkreis*), the Berlin Senate and the central Federal government published details of a competition to find an appropriate memorial design. That they had come together to launch this competition showed, so the guidelines stated, that Germany was fully committed to 'facing the truth and not allowing it to be forgotten', to 'honouring the murdered Jews of Europe', to 'remembering them in mourning and shame', and to 'accepting the burden of German history'. A further aim was 'to point the way towards a new chapter in human co-existence, in which injustice against minorities will no longer be permissible' (Heimrod *et al.* 1999: 177). The memorial, then, was to be multi-functional. It would serve as a visible symbol of Germany's 'second guilt' (Giordano) in not coming to terms adequately with the Nazi past. It would force confrontation with the primary guilt of Auschwitz and German history. Finally, it would serve as a signpost to an ideal Germany of tolerance towards minorities, strengthening democracy in the present, as well as recalling the effects of its abandonment in the past.

According to the original appeal, 'the construction of this memorial is an obligation for all Germans in East and West' (*FR*, 30 January 1989). The list of signatories featured prominent West and East Germans. Among the former were, in addition to Lea Rosh and Eberhard Jäckel, writers Günter Grass and Walter Jens, legal expert Heinrich Hanover and television journalist Klaus Bednarz; among the latter were authors Volker Braun, Christoph Hein, Heiner Müller and Christa Wolf. From the beginning, the project for the memorial was to be an *all-German* project. Following the rejection of the *Prinz-Albrecht-Gelände* as a possible site, interest switched to a plot south of the Brandenburg Gate. Once the site of the Reich Ministries' gardens, this plot was also not far from the former location of Hitler's new Reich Chancellery. As mentioned earlier, it had become available after the fall of the Wall, which used to run through it. It therefore appeared to symbolize perfectly the vicissitudes of Germany's two repressive pasts; the 1994 competition guidelines even drew attention to this 'double past'. But, effectively, the Holocaust Memorial, when built, will have eradicated any traces or memory of the Wall at this site. It will seem as if the holocaust has emerged from the depths, asserting its singularity and primacy in German 20th century history, declaring the iniquities of the GDR and the Cold War to be secondary. As long as the Wall stood, guilt for the holocaust could be passed back and forth between the two states. Now that it has gone, historical responsibility must be shared. It is fitting that the symbol and instrument of division should make way for a memorial to a common past which became entangled in the propaganda of the Cold War.

Helmut Dubiel has argued that liberal western societies derived their claims to legitimacy from references to totalitarian societies in the east (Dubiel 1999: 291). For Dubiel, the changes in 1989 have ended this form of legitimation, which has been replaced by a post-totalitarian form; western nations are gradually turning away from 'triumphalist demonstrations' of their own national history (Dubiel 1999: 292). Dubiel believes that national history can no longer provide a positive source of orientation in the present. Rather, nations are beginning to make negative events in their national history a point of orientation. History becomes important not as something to emulate, but as something to avoid repeating. The *difference* between past and present becomes the measure of progress. In Dubiel's opinion, such developments are typical particularly of Spain, where a re-evaluation of the *conquista* is under way, but also of Germany. It seems to me that, by focusing commemorative attention on the common past of atrocities, the Holocaust Memorial will help to overcome strategies of guilt avoidance, one of which is the totalitarianist paradigm. What started out as an West–East project became, on reunification, a project for uniting east and west on the basis of a national, unrelativized, unmitigated acceptance of the significance of the holocaust for Germans past and present. Certainly one does need to be cautious. As we saw in Chapter Two, the totalitarianist paradigm enjoyed a renaissance in the early 1990s, as the west found that it could berate the east without fear of contradiction now that communism had collapsed. To a degree, this paradigm has been given concrete expression in the 'Berlin Wall Memorial' to the 'victims of communist violence' in the Bernauer Street. But the Holocaust Memorial will surely be more significant than any other memorial projects along the line of the former Berlin Wall. The huge media prominence it has enjoyed will be matched, when building is completed, by its size and symbolic power.

The Holocaust Memorial has also been interpreted as exemplifying a post-national development in Germany because it would be a symbol of respect for universal human rights and for a European order based on peace. At the moment of its national reconstitution, in other words, Germany must define its identity through a visible commitment to the universal or transnational. Both Aleida Assmann and Jürgen Habermas have understood the memorial in these terms. Assmann has argued that a nation which once crossed its borders in every direction, traumatizing its neighbours, must recompose its identity by taking into account the national memories of other countries, particularly those of its victims (*taz*, 20 March 1996). Habermas, within the context of an article on the planned memorial, claimed that the universalism of the democratic constitutional state was reshaping national consciousness. While stressing multi-perspectival historical awareness, Habermas believes that the holocaust must function as a 'monitor' for any assessment of which parts of history are suitable for the generation of German identity (*Zeit*, 31 March 1999). Memory of Auschwitz, as Habermas wrote in a letter of 1998 to Peter Eisenman (according to whose design the Holocaust Memorial is to be built), is 'a constitutive feature of the ethico-political self-understanding of the citizens of the Federal Republic' (Heimrod *et al.* 1999: 1185).

Never would a local memorial to the murdered Jews have inspired such reflections on German post-unification identity. From the moment the idea of a national memorial was mooted, it was discussed in terms of identity construction. This has to do with the centrality of the Holocaust Memorial, physically and functionally. Supporters of the memorial such as Habermas argued that a central memorial implies the need for an axial role for the holocaust in modern German consciousness. Conservative opponents have argued, predictably, that such a role is inappropriate. Firstly, they said, it would result in a 'trivialization' of Stalinism; indeed some conservatives see the focus on the holocaust as a strategy deployed by the left to avoid confronting the crimes of socialism. Secondly, it would found German identity on the utterly negative. Historian Heinrich August Winkler has described such a 'fixation on the holocaust' in terms of 'negative nationalism' (*Spiegel*, 24 August 1998). Cultural critic Karl-Heinz Bohrer even wrote sarcastically of a new 'foundation myth' (*SZ*, 16 December 1998), Walser of the 'monumentalization of shame' (Walser 1999: 13). Building post-unification identity on the holocaust, it is argued, is reductionist, perverse and self-inhibiting. Rudolf Augstein suspected that the Holocaust Memorial was directed 'against the new Germany being formed in Berlin' (*Spiegel*, 30 November 1998). In other words, its purpose was not to encourage Germans to reflect on the holocaust, but to block any sense that Germany might be a 'normal country'. Normal nations, Augstein and Walser imply, base their identity on positive achievements. Thus the German–Jewish symbiosis or the success of reunification should be a point of orientation, not the catastrophic holocaust.

Winkler's concept of negative nationalism, however, may mean more than feeling 'bad' about the past. It could also mean feeling good about feeling bad. That Germans should derive masochistic pleasure from a memorial to Jewish victims is problematic indeed. A contrasting fear, especially among German Jews, is that Germans may seek to salve their historical conscience by identifying with these victims. Henryk Broder remarked acidly that the 'murdered Jews to whom the memorial is supposed to be dedicated can rest easy in the knowledge that they have made a substantial contribution to the new German culture of conscience' (*Spiegel*, 17 April 1995). Richard Chaim Schneider, who lost his family in the holocaust, was furious at Lea Rosh for her adoption of the fate of the murdered Jews: 'I refuse her the right to want to climb into the same boat as me' and 'to cuddle up to today's Jews' (R. C. Schneider 1997: 138). Rosh has made some excellent television programmes on the holocaust, but she does appear to style herself as a Jew, an unfortunate fact which has given rise to fears that the memorial might even act as a kind of transformer by means of which Germans can metamorphose into Jews.

Moral self-condemnation, especially in a generation which bears no guilt for the holocaust, would be an inappropriate way of reacting to it. It would block true empathy and reflection. By contrast, over-identification with the victims is inappropriate because it would lead to a loss of any sense that the Germans had been perpetrators. It cannot be ruled out, moreover, that the memorial may be proudly interpreted by some Germans as a symbol of German achievements in coming to terms with the past. Connected to this is the anxiety that national shame might be 'absorbed' by the memorial while the Germans go shamelessly about the work of economically conquering eastern Europe. This fear was expressed by journalist Eike Geisel: 'from the ashes of the murdered, a fabric has been made which the new nationalism can use to clothe itself with a good conscience' (*TSP*, 6 January 1995). Thus one might ask whether the objections of Walser and Augstein are based on a false premise, namely that negative nationalism is necessarily inhibiting. The more the Germans ruefully acknowledge the wrongs of the national past, the more some of them, at least, may believe they have earned the right to a certain assertiveness in the present. There are also those who believe that the Holocaust Memorial may actually serve to strengthen anti-semitism in the present, thereby helping to generate national assertiveness via the more traditional route. Is there not a danger, they ask, of neo-Nazis 'coopting' the memorial and interpreting it as a symbolic affirmation of Hitler's achievements, indeed as a celebration of the holocaust? The proximity of the former Reich Chancellery, as well as the 'Albert-Speer'-like dimensions of some of the proposed designs for the memorial, have intensified such fears.

The noble aims of the memorial's supporters, then, may not be matched by its impact. Some critics, while sharing the conviction that the holocaust must have a prime place in German memory and identity, believe that a central monument will undermine this interest. Concentration camp memorial sites felt so threatened by the planned memorial that they set up a 'Working Community' in March 1997. On 9 April 1997 they published a warning that a 'centralization of commemoration' at a symbolic site may lead to a reduction of interest in authentic sites (Heimrod *et al.* 1999: 706); commemoration may become vague and unfocused. There is a certain danger that a centralized site of memory will detract from local and regional sites of memory. The German government's move to Berlin was accompanied by concern that the Federal system would suffer as a result of this 'pull' towards Germany's historic centre. Now, some suspected, the regional structure of memory would also suffer. There appears to be something despotic about erecting a memorial in the very heart of Berlin. Aleida Assmann has drawn attention to the need to ask whether an 'obligatory' group memory can be anchored in a liberal, secularized society (*taz*, 20 March 1996). One might also ask whether it *should* be. Berlin's memorial may act as a magnet, pulling in memory, giving it a unified shape and ruling out any other way to remember. Yet, equally, the absence of such a memorial may encourage Germans to understand anti-semitism and the holocaust only in terms of regional and local sites, not in terms of a centrally organized project and of national responsibility.

Unfortunately, some of the objections to the proposed memorial have been based on resentment towards Jews. In the course of the last ten years, the suggestion has taken root in the minds of some that the Jews are the driving force behind the memorial project – despite the fact that it was initiated by a group of Germans, and has subsequently been adopted by regional and central government. The implication behind this suggestion is that the Jews have an interest in keeping the Germans in a permanent state of shame and penance, a state from which the Jews can profit. It is true that the German government and Berlin's government did consult the Berlin and Central Jewish Councils about the project. Moreover, the Central Council of the Jews in Germany now has a right of representation in the curatorium of the Memorial Foundation set up in 1999 by Federal Parliament. Bubis, Galinski and Jerzy Kanal have all contributed their ideas to the debate, quite understandably. Clearly, the Jews would like a memorial which they can visit without feeling excluded – in contrast to the *Neue Wache*. But in no way have the Jews acted as a driving force. In fact Bubis always insisted that the memorial must remain the responsibility of the Germans. Some Jews have argued against the memorial, or both for and against (particularly Salomon Korn). There is no Jewish consensus on the issue, any more than there is a German one. Why, then, 'blame' the Jews?

The rumour that Chancellor Kohl had promised Bubis the memorial in return for the latter's attendance of the *Neue Wache* inauguration ceremony was the starting and reference point for this blame. Thus Reinhart Koselleck referred disparagingly to this promise (*Zeit*, 19 March 1998). Barbara Junge even implied that Bubis had consistently used the promise to ward off opposition to the memorial (*taz*, 20 March 1998). The notion of some shoddy 'exchange' fits the anti-semitic image of haggling, bartering Jews. In a discussion with Bubis, Walser more or less blamed him for generating unfair comparisons of the German present with the Third Reich (see Chapter Seven). The Germans, Walser seemed to imply, may be to blame for the holocaust, but the Jews are to blame for not allowing them their peace of mind in the here and now. While Kohl did come to support the memorial, his remark that it will have to be built because the American east coast 'expects it to be' also smacked of blaming the Jews (*taz*, 26 August 1998). He also said the Germans would be condemned world-wide if they reneged on the plan (*FAZ*, 17 September 1998). Rudolf Augstein wrote that no-one would 'dare to keep the heart of Berlin free' of this 'monstrosity out of respect for the New York press and the sharks in lawyers' clothing' (*Spiegel*, 30 November 1998). Augstein implied that, if the Germans build the memorial, they will do so for fear of the consequences of not doing so. On this view, the memorial is a concession to moral and legal pressure, even an emblem of Jewish tyranny. It is not a voluntary expression of shame and regret. That shame and regret should come from within, and not as knee-jerk reactions, is true. But Augstein's assumption that the memorial constitutes such a reaction is purely speculative. The tendency to accuse the Jews of pressurizing the Germans stems, one suspects, from a reluctance to own responsibility for the past.

The historiographical agenda and the 'other' victims

For the initiators of the Holocaust Memorial project, such as Lea Rosh, a 'conspicuous' central memorial to six million murdered Jews (*FR*, 30 January 1989) would reflect the centrality and singularity of the holocaust. In a sense, the memorial may represent the triumph of left-liberal historians such as Eberhard Jäckel over revisionist conservative historians such as Ernst Nolte. With a central memorial to the Jews, and nothing comparable for the victims of Stalinism, total-itarianist historiography will be dealt a symbolic blow. Jäckel, the main historian behind the memorial project, has formulated repeatedly why he thinks the holo-caust is unique: 'never before had a state decided to liquidate as comprehensively as possible a group of people, which it wilfully characterized as Jews, including old people, women, children and babies'. Unique, also, was the degree of state involve-ment, and the deportation of Jews to 'installations specially built for the purpose of killing' (Jäckel 1999: 160). Jäckel has also stressed that the Jews were 'by far the biggest group of murdered people', and that murdering them was the 'central motivation' of the Nazi era. In the same article, he even traced the idea for the genocide back to a Hitler letter of 16 September 1919, a genocide, which, accord-ing to Jäckel, ended with Hitler's final testament on 29 April 1945. The murder of European Jews 'is the prominent characteristic of that time, and the more distance we gain to the period, the clearer it becomes that this genocide determined the his-tory of the Second World War more than all military events' (*Zeit*, 7 April 1989).

It is clear that the Holocaust Memorial was understood by Jäckel as a rebuttal of structuralist historiography (see Chapter Five). Thus Jäckel, while not overlooking the role of local and regional initiatives in bringing about the holocaust, has stressed that these were responses to a central order from Hitler (Jäckel 1999: 162). Jäckel's views are in some respects not dissimilar to Goldhagen's. Where Jäckel and Goldhagen differ is in their understanding of the role played by anti-semitism within the wider historical perspective. Jäckel does not subscribe to Goldhagen's thesis of an eliminationist anti-semitism endemic to German history or the German social psyche. He places responsibility more firmly at the door of Hitler and his cronies, and of the National Socialist state itself and its organization around the anti-semitic intention. So does Lea Rosh. The Holocaust Memorial was thus originally planned as an aesthetic and commemorative enshrinement of the intentionalist paradigm. This plan has surely been enhanced by the prospective site of the memorial – near Hitler's chancellery, near bunkers for Hitler and his SS bodyguard, and on top of Goebbels's bunker. Raising a historiographical agenda to the level of a national memorial is always problematic. Against intentionalism as propagated by Jäckel and especially Rosh, it must be said that it runs the risk of exculpating the 'ordinary German' and even traditional elites. In defence of inten-tionalism, however, one can say that in some of its recent forms, notably Goldhagen's radicalization, it aims to counteract those forms of structuralism that portray the holocaust too absolutely as the result of complex interactions of vari-ous motives and sets of circumstances.

Ultimately, the relationship between the memorial and historiography will depend on the documentation centre that will accompany it (see later in the chap-ter). Moreover, whether the broad mass of Germans will conceive of the memorial as a sign of 'Hitler's guilt', or that of a nation, will depend on the interaction of memorial and public, not on Jäckel and Rosh. The second thing to say about Jäckel's argumentation is that it represents an evaluation. The view that the murder of European Jewry was unique (in its planning, its preparatory measures, its execution), central (in terms of its place in National Socialist ideology) and incomparable (in terms of the numbers of victims) is not uncontentious. Was not anti-bolshevism equally as central? When Russian Jews were killed, what role was played by racist anti-Soviet propaganda? Is it more 'unique' to die as a Jew in an Auschwitz gas-chamber than to die as a supposed Russian partisan at the hands of an SS execution squad? Does the fact that 6 million Jews were killed, but 'only' 500,000 Sinti and Roma, make the individual death of a Jew more significant than that of a Sinto? Should the percentage of those Jews and Romanies killed in relation to the total number of European Jews and Romanies be compared, or only the absolute numbers? If it is true that Nazi anti-semitic measures predated those against Romanies – and this is also a matter for debate – does this make the racism directed against Romanies less bad? On account, so to speak, of the shorter run-up? Jäckel's 'uniqueness' argument is problematic. The Holocaust Memorial project represents a laudable attempt to deconstruct the all-victims-together paradigm of West German remembrance. It disaggregates into Jewish victims and German perpetrators. Yet should it also disaggregate into Jewish and other victims, leaving the latter 'off' the memorial? Does this not make of these other victims second-class racial victims, now taking the place of the Jews who at last have reached the status of first-class victims?

The *Förderkreis* refers to the planned memorial as the 'Memorial to the Murdered Jews of Europe', though its members also use the media term Holocaust Memorial. Regardless of terminology, the Sinti and Roma are to be omitted. While the holocaust is commonly associated with the murder of Jews, it is not always exclusively identified with it. In the case of a Holocaust Memorial dedicated only to Jews, it would be. The omission of the Sinti and Roma was felt to be particularly discriminatory because they clearly belonged to the same 'category': they were persecuted purely because of their 'ethnic inferiority', rather than for any other reason. From 1989 up to the present, chairman of the Central Council of German Sinti and Roma, Romani Rose, has insisted that this omission is little short of an insult. He has taken issue with ill-considered remarks on the part of members of the *Förderkreis*. Rosh maintained that including the Sinti and Roma would lead to a generalized remembrance of the victims, and that means little, 'because then you would have to remember the soldiers or the German housewives killed in bombing raids' (*Freitag*, 20 March 1992). Jakob Schulze-Rohr asserted that there was, at first, no discrimination against the German Gypsies under Hitler. He felt bound to point out that there were Gypsies in the *Wehrmacht*, and in answer to an interviewer's objection that 500,000 Sinti and Roma were killed opined that, while this was correct, it had not been part of the National Socialist programme to kill the Roma in the same way it had been part of their programme to annihilate Jews and bolsheviks (*taz*, 13 April 1989). Jäckel argued that no-one would object to a Goethe monument which did not include Schiller. In the course of arguing the case that the holocaust was unique, Jäckel contended that Chelmno, Belzec, Sobibor and Treblinka were used exclusively for the murder of Jews (*Zeit*, 7 April 1989).

These views and comparisons are misleading. The Sinti and Roma were discriminated against in Germany long before 1933. Bavaria's Law for the Combating of Gypsies, Travellers and the Workshy of July 1926 was racist in character. After 1933, it was adopted in Bremen and Baden. While many of the racist measures introduced in the early years of the Third Reich did not explicitly address the Gypsies, they were nevertheless applied to them. This is true for instance of the Law for the Prevention of Genetically Diseased Offspring of 14 July 1933 (Reemtsma 1997: 100). The 15 September 1935 Nuremberg Laws did not mention the Sinti and Roma, but a supplementary order by the Reich and Prussian Ministry of the Interior on 'mixed-race marriages' of 16 November 1935 did (Reemtsma 1997: 103). Prior to the Berlin Olympics in 1936, many Sinti and Roma were put in a provisional camp in Marzahn on the outskirts of Berlin; the camp's inhabitants were deported to Auschwitz in 1943. Many Sinti and Roma were deported to Buchenwald and Dachau during the 'Action Workshy Reich' (*Arbeitsscheu Reich*) action of 1938. In the course of the war, there were ghetto areas for Roma, as in Lodz as of 1941, where some 5,000 Austrian and German Gypsies were held; the dead were buried in Jewish cemeteries. Around 4,000 of them were killed in gas-vans at Chelmno (Reemtsma 1997: 112; Wipperman 1999: 56) – an extermination centre which, according to Jäckel, was used only for Jews. The last transport from Lodz arrived there on 12 January 1942; 4,000 Roma were subsequently killed in gas cars. In Auschwitz, food and sanitary conditions in the 'Gypsy Camp' were particularly appalling, It had the highest mortality rate of the entire camp complex.

One would have expected more sensitivity towards the Sinti and Roma from the *Förderkreis*. After liberation in May 1945, Sinti and Roma were largely excluded both from commemoration and compensation (Krausnick 1997: 223). In the course of compensation disputes, West German authorities often claimed that the Sinti and Roma had been persecuted not for racial reasons, but because of their 'criminal and asocial' behaviour (Reemtsma 1997: 134). This implied that the National Socialists had been right to treat them as they did. Defamation and discrimination continued. Joseph Eichberger, responsible in the Reich Security Main Office under Hitler for organizing the deportation of Sinti and Roma, became head of the 'Gypsy Department' of the Regional Criminal Office in post-war Bavaria, from where he coordinated further policies against Sinti and Roma. Many *Länder*, including Bavaria, had regulations restricting Sinti and Roma freedom of movement well into the 1970s. The Memorial to the Murdered Jews, some felt, continued a tradition of discrimination. Certainly neither Rosh nor Jäckel has shown much sympathy towards the Sinti and Roma; indeed Jäckel has consistently refused to accept that as many as 500,000 Sinti and Roma were killed. The memorial sites at the concentration camps, by contrast, now include *all* camp victims in their commemorative and documentary landscape.

Günter Grass – a former supporter of the memorial – protested that the exclusion of the Sinti and Roma represented a continuation of Hitler's racial politics (*SZ*, 8 October 1997). Grass, who has set up a foundation for the Sinti and Roma in Lübeck, reinforced and amplified this view in 1998, arguing that all those persecuted and annihilated by the National Socialists should be included on the memorial, such as Sinti and Roma, homosexuals and political opponents, to prevent a continuation of 'that kind of selection undertaken by the Nazis' (*SZ*, 23 December 1998). Homosexuals have also suffered from commemorative neglect and continued discrimination in the post-war era. It was not until 1969 that West Germany toned down the anti-homosexual Article 175 of the Civil Code, and it was not abolished until 1994! The National Socialists passed 50,000 sentences on the basis of this law, and between 10,000 and 20,000 homosexuals were put in concentration camps. Homosexuals also had to wait a long time before they could apply for compensation for their sufferings. Under the terms of West German law, the injustice practised against them was not adjudged to be 'specifically National Socialist'. As for communists, the West German tradition of discriminating against KPD/DKP members and adjudged communist sympathizers is well known.

While the Germans had long resisted a central commemorative focus on the Jews, Jewish victims of Nazism had been partly compensated by West Germany, their suffering acknowledged to a degree. Was there a kind of tasteless implication that the Gypsies or the communists had no right to a place on the memorial because they had not gained this degree of acknowledgement, because they had not yet 'qualified'? Were Jews now fully accepted as 'people', Sinti and Roma and homosexuals still regarded as social outsiders, even as dangers to civil society? The plans to erect a memorial exclusively for the Jews triggered an at times vehement debate in the press, between the *Förderkreis* and Rose, or between the Jewish and Sinti Councils, about who was persecuted first, the most and in the manner deserving of the most attention. It was as if a competition had started up to find the 'best' racial victim. The result was a severe rift between the German Sinti and Roma and the German Jews, who had up to this point understood their suffering as comparable. If racist victimization is the criterion for the memorial's frame of reference, then certainly the Sinti and Roma should be on it, and so should homosexuals and euthanasia victims – the first to be gassed – because their deaths were all connected to aspects of racial ideology. Racism is not just opposition to another 'race', but opposition to what are considered genetic aberrations within one's 'own race'. There is a tendency even among leading world historians to hierarchize in a questionable manner. Saul Friedländer has argued that the campaign against Jews was qualitatively different to the euthanasia and sterilization campaign because it was 'a struggle against an active, formidable enemy' and a 'confrontation of apocalyptic dimensions' rather than merely something 'exclusively aimed at enhancing the purity of the *Volksgemeinschaft*' (Friedländer 1998: 40). While different emphases within an ideological system are relevant as a means of distinction, the identification of such differences should not imply, as Friedländer's does, that one form of persecution was somehow grander and more tragic than another.

It seemed that the only solution to the problem of the memorial's dedication would be the construction of other memorials dedicated to other groups of victims. Thus in July 1992, the Berlin Senator for Culture and the Federal Ministry of the Interior agreed on erecting one memorial to the Jews, and one to the Sinti and

Roma. But Berlin's mayor Eberhard Diepgen subsequently resisted plans for construction of a memorial to the Sinti and Roma even more vehemently than he resisted plans for one to the Jews. He was especially reluctant to countenance the construction of a 'Gypsy Memorial' near the *Reichstag*, despite original indications from the Berlin Senate that this would be a feasible site. Ignatz Bubis was not prepared to accept a memorial to the Sinti and Roma on the same site as the memorial to the Jews; nor was Rosh. In a meeting of 16 October 1993 with Chancellery State Minister Anton Pfeifer, Rosh dismissed the idea of a common memorial site as 'unacceptable', while Bubis was against a 'physical proximity' (Heimrod *et al.* 1999: 113). He insisted that the sites of the two memorials be separated by a street and be at least 200 metres apart (*BZ*, 19 November 1993). Rose subsequently accused him of apartheid during a joint visit to Israel (R. C. Schneider 1997: 125). According to the Israeli magazine *Haaretz*, Bubis refused to lay a wreath with Rose in Yad Vashem, and then called him a 'controversial gypsy' whose arguments cannot be taken seriously (*TSP*, 18 November 1993). Bubis's and Rosh's dispute with Rose created the unsavoury impression that Jews and Germans had clubbed together to protect a common understanding of the National Socialist past. They were now, in the eyes of the Sinti and Roma, partners in a separatist management of national memory.

That there should also be a separate memorial to homosexual victims is a view that has been expressed by, among others, Daniel Jonah Goldhagen (see Chapter Five). Goldhagen wrote in the *New York Times* that the monstrous fact of the persecution of the Jews is in no way belittled by erecting monuments to other victims nearby, even side by side. He called for a memorial to homosexuals, whose suffering had not yet adequately been acknowledged (see also *Zeit*, 7 February 1997). A civil rights' group – supported by Walter Jens and Bishop Wolfgang Huber – hope to bring about the construction near the Berlin Philharmonic Hall of a museum-cum-memorial commemorating the suffering of euthanasia victims (*SZ*, 22–23 January 2000). Supporters of memorials to these and other persecuted minorities can base their calls on the consensus reached by the German Federal Parliament on 25 June 1999. It decided that the memorial in the former Reich Ministries' gardens should be dedicated exclusively to Jews, but that other victim groups should also be commemorated in an appropriate manner. The foundation set up to oversee the building of the Memorial to the Murdered Jews has a twelve-member advisory committee including representatives of the Sinti and Roma, forced labourers, euthanasia victims, victims of Nazi military justice and victims of homosexual persecution. The 'Place of Information' which will accompany the Memorial to the Murdered Jews will make reference to the other groups of victims (*SZ*, 11 November 1999). It now seems likely, moreover, that a memorial to the Sinti and Roma will be constructed in Berlin's *Tiergarten*. The Berlin Senate has established first contacts to the artist Dani Karavan, and Chancellor Schröder has promised that Federal funds will be made available for a Sinti and Roma memorial. The memorial is, however, to be of modest size (*SZ*, 29–30 July 2000).

Inevitably, the call for more memorials has led to fears that Berlin will be turned into a kind of commemorative Disneyland, and Diepgen coined the term 'monumentitis' to describe what he perceived to be a worrying national sickness. On a more serious level, Salomon Korn has argued that an addition of individual monuments does not constitute a memorial ensemble against National Socialist mass murder (*FR*, 4 September 1997). Separate memorials, moreover, particularize destructive Nazi policies, obscuring common elements. Yet this may still be the best of the imperfect solutions. A total disaggregation of the victims enables each group to be distinctly visualized, its group-specific suffering recognized. Memorials to non-Jewish National Socialist victims are needed in a country which, while it started to memorialize Jewish suffering in the 1980s and 1990s, has been dilatory about other groups. It was not until 1992 that the first significant monument to the Sinti and Roma was unveiled (in Wiesbaden). The 'Frankfurt Angel', unveiled in December 1994, was the first substantial memorial to be erected to the memory of persecuted homosexuals (Initiative Mahnmal 1997). As for deserters – also represented on the advisory committee – their suffering is now remembered in belated and controversial memorials in Potsdam (as of 1990, see Soergel 1996) and Erfurt (1995). But these are not memorials in Berlin. And they can be easily overlooked (as in Erfurt).

Certainly the commitment on the part of the Federal Parliament to honouring each of the groups of victims has done much to take the heat out of the dispute between victim groups as to who should be on the memorial and who should not. As things stand at the time of writing (January 2001), it looks as if Berlin will become the site of several central memorials, each dedicated to a different set of Nazi victims – despite Diepgen's hostility to the idea, and in spite of the inevitable rows about the relative size, cost and position of the various memorials. Undoubtedly, Germans know more about the Nazi persecution of the Sinti and Roma and homosexuals as a result of the debate surrounding the Memorial to the Murdered Jews than they did before. The haggling over compensation for the forced labourers, which ended in June 2000 with an agreement between Germany and the USA (see Chapter Nine), also did much to stimulate awareness of other, excluded groups of victims.

The aesthetics of memory

In the early 1990s, and again in 1999, debate centred on the question of the Holocaust Memorial's significance within the broader debate on German identity, as well as on the issue of whom it should be dedicated to, and where in Berlin it should be situated. When the results of the first competition to find an appropriate design were published in early 1995 (Heimrod *et al.* 1999: 273–410), there was an additional point for discussion. What character should the memorial have?

All in all, there were 528 entries. They were exhibited to the general public in the former GDR State Council Building. The reaction was generally one of consternation. Henryk Broder expostulated: 'Not since the invention of the kidney-shaped table and the illuminated house-bar has so much concentrated ugliness been so shamelessly flaunted' (*Spiegel*, 17 April 1995). Given that the site for the memorial was 20,000 square metres in size, given too the enormity of the fact of

6 million murdered Jews, many artists and architects could not resist the temptation to produce correspondingly huge, even overwhelming designs. Others decided that the best thing to do was cover at least part of the area in trees or meadows. Many of the exhibits came in the shape of cubes, balls, pyramids, rectangles and other geometric forms as architects and artists went back somewhat helplessly to basics. Other designs cultivated a style of gratuitous abstraction, while some artists resorted to Jewish symbolism. Literary critic Elke Schmitter acidly observed that, after counting 37 exhibits which used the Star of David motif, she stopped counting (*SZ*, 12 April 1995). A well-meaning sense of the need to convey the horror of the holocaust had led some to construct concentration-camp-like structures, ovens and furnaces, thereby unintentionally paying homage to National Socialism. In one or two cases, Nazi swastikas were deployed, an even worse aberration. Occasionally, the proposed designs were not far short of laughable. One exhibit consisted of a 'hologram bowl' resembling a spaceship just arrived from Mars. Another, made up of 6 million Stars of David, looked, when viewed from above at least, like a massive pizza with a crack in the middle. The best example of tasteless kitsch was the much-criticized Ferris Wheel, a kind of millennium fairground feature with suspended cattle-cars in memory of the deported victims. This suggested the holocaust had been a thrills-and-spills experience.

There were, however, a number of thoughtful and thought-provoking suggestions which reflected the trend towards counter-monuments discussed earlier, even towards *non*-memorials. The most radical of these was the proposal by Renate Stih and Frieder Schnock, creators of the Bavarian Quarter memorial (see page 212). They wanted to turn the site into a bus-stop, from which visitors would be brought to 'authentic' sites of memory, notably Sachsenhausen and Auschwitz. The Memorial to the Murdered Jews, in this case, would become a self-denying homage to such sites. Some artists were aware of the contention that the holocaust is unrepresentable. Faced with the problem that they were expected to represent it nonetheless, they sought to inscribe this paradox into their designs. Other artists endeavoured to capture the dialectic between the past and the present, history and memory, remembering and forgetting. Aware that the Memorial to the Murdered Jews was to function as a warning to the German nation, some suggested adding a museum or documentation centre, sometimes underground, to ensure that any emotional response would be firmly based on historical knowledge. There were a number of interactive models. One design included a map of Europe. Each visitor would be supplied with a data-card, and would then be connected via computer to a persecuted Jew of the same age and sex. He or she would then be able to follow the course of this individual's persecution, which might end in death, or survival. Proposals which sought to link visitor and victim, individual with individual, were intriguing, but, as we shall see, could be problematic.

Ultimately, the competition's jury, composed of individuals selected by the *Förderverein*, the region of Berlin and Federal government, decided on two first prizes. One of these was awarded for an 85 by 85-metre steel structure by Simon Ungers, Christiane Moss and Christina Alt (known as the 'Ungers model'). Letters spelling the names of the concentration camps were etched into its four sides.

The other was awarded to Christine Jackob-Marks, Hella Rolfes, Hans Scheib and Reinhard Stangl for a huge slanted platform on which the names of all known Jewish holocaust victims were to be registered (known as the 'Jackob-Marks model'). A space would be left free in memory of those 1.5 million victims – principally Soviet Jews – whose names were not known. The reaction to both proposals in the press was largely negative. They were felt to be too 'monumental'. When, on 25 June 1995, the *Förderkreis*, Berlin and the Federal government expressed their preference for the Jackob-Marks model, the criticism intensified. The planned registration of the names of 4.5 million dead Jews was condemned as heartlessly bureaucratic; some felt it would even convey the unfortunate impression that the Germans wished to celebrate the outcome of Hitler's annihilation policies, or to lay the ghost of the past by inscribing the names on to what appeared to be an enormous gravestone. Particular exception was taken to the suggestion that Germans could finance the inscription process by 'buying' Jewish names. This seemed to be a modern form of a letter of indulgence. Only when this idea was dropped did Bubis relent in his opposition to the design (*FAZ*, 29 June 1995). But despite this, and despite a certain downscaling of the Jackob-Marks model, the German government declared on 30 June 1995 that, while it supported the idea of a memorial, it did not support the proposed design (Heimrod *et al*. 1999: 446). While Kohl was responsible for this act of veto, it should be remembered that the Ministry of the Interior, although it initially appeared to support the Jackobs-Marks model, was happy with neither of the winning designs. The same is true of Diepgen.

Kohl's tendency to impose cultural decrees had caused much consternation in the case of the *Neue Wache*, but in this instance it was welcomed. Kohl did not seek to stifle debate; on the contrary, the press statement issued by the government explicitly encouraged more discussion in the hope that a broader consensus could be reached. A delay was preferable to a botched job. One might, at first, be surprised at objections to a memorial on the grounds of its monumentality. Was the holocaust not an enormous crime? Was German guilt not enormous? While this is true, there is a problem with monumentality which is linked to its semantic history. For generations, nations have used vast monuments to express pride, in their great deeds, victories and worthy citizens. Monumentality is thus associated with success and self-congratulation. Clearly, such an association is undesirable in the case of a Holocaust Memorial. When a nation seeks to express regret at past aberrations, it cannot use the 'tainted' language of vastness. But the answer is not to build a 'miniment', especially when one considers that too small a memorial runs the risk of being inconspicuous, serving to reduce the significance of past atrocities rather than highlight them. Given the size of the proposed site, moreover, minimalist art would be cynical. What was required, perhaps, was a large (though not huge) memorial which problematized the monumental, taking issue with its traditional associations. Micha Brumlik objected to many of the proposed entries because they cultivated an 'aesthetics of the sublime' (*taz*, 1 April 1995). The dangers of heroizing the sufferings of the victims and glorifying their deaths were all too obvious in the Ungers and Jackob-Marks models. The latter would have acted as a multiname epitaph, a finalistic gesture. A traditional monument sets in stone. What was needed here was a monument that asked questions without providing answers, in contrast to the affirmative pomp of the traditional monument.

Faced with governmental non-cooperation, public rejection of the winning model and demands for a new competition, the competition's organizers in early 1997 arranged a three-part symposium to discuss various aspects of the memorial project. Historians, cultural theorists, as well as experts on memorials and architecture were invited to take part. Many of those invited were indignant that the organizers had set the agenda in such a way that certain issues were taboo. Thus the discussion in the first colloquium was to be about why Germany needed a memorial, not *whether* Germany needed one; the presupposition was that it did. In the second colloquium, the discussion was to focus on the historical and political context of the proposed site, and its place in Berlin's urban landscape, not on the possibility of finding an alternative site. Several of the participants felt they were being expected to accept decisions already taken, and there were walk-outs (thus Julius Schoeps, Rachel Salamander and Salomon Korn left the second colloquium in protest). The whole symposium threatened to turn into a farce. The first colloquium revealed nothing new. The second was effectively torpedoed by architect critic Bruno Flierl's dismissal of the proposed site as unsuitable. Complaints that the site was too concealed, tucked away as it was behind the Brandenburg Gate, were not new. But Flierl went further, objecting to the site's lack of spatial and historical significance, a surprising view given that the usual argument was that the site was too linked to elite Nazi buildings and bunkers (SfWFK 1997: 56). The third colloquium dealt with issues of memorial typology and iconography, and was heavily over-specialized. The day was saved by American holocaust researcher James Young, who put a positive gloss on the constant rows. Debate, he stressed, was positive and necessary. He went on to say that Germany faced the dilemma of striving to remember what it would like to forget, and that 'in the heart of a German memorial there will have to be an emptiness that must somehow be represented by the artist as his or her inspiration or concept' (SfWFK 1997: 125).

The organizers did heed some of the complaints and suggestions made during the symposium. The option of an alternative site was considered, though without any resulting change of plan. The first competition was declared ended without a winner, and in June 1997 a 'Finding Commission' was set up consisting, among others, of some of those invited to the colloquia, including Young. The job of this Commission was to define new parameters for a second competition, select a limited number of participants (including some of the previous contributors) and choose a design from the entries submitted. Also in June, the new guidelines were published. These were significantly different to the brief for the first competition in three respects. Firstly, it was made clear that 'size was not absolutely of the essence', a tame, but nevertheless palpable warning against unreflecting monumentalism. Secondly – and most importantly – there were references to the fact that the crime of the holocaust consisted not only in the horrific destruction of Jews, but also in the 'loss and emptiness this left behind', or in 'the permanent emptiness it left behind on the continent' (Heimrod *et al.* 1999: 838). This showed the influence of

Young. Thirdly, the significance of the site's location had been re-evaluated. Now, it was not so much the proximity of Hitler's Chancellery that was relevant, as the fact that the site of the proposed memorial would serve to link the traditional centre of Berlin with the west of the city, specifically with the *Tierpark*, and act as a point of rest between the Brandenburg and Potsdam Gates (Heimrod *et al.* 1999: 839). It would become a pivotal element in the new Berlin, its central and national aspect enhanced by changes in Berlin's urban topography.

Seen from the perspective of these guidelines, the weaknesses of the Jackob-Marcks model become even clearer. Dismissed in the press as the 'monstrous gravestone', it would have placed a quietist lid on the past, leaving no scope for a continuing sense of pain and loss. What was needed, arguably, was a design based on the concept of an 'open wound'. The emphasis on emptiness in the guidelines for the new competition would perhaps encourage designs that would reflect the conceptual line followed by the Jewish Museum, the New Synagogue and Berlin's other memorials to the murdered Jews. Henryk Broder, however, was quick to express alarm at the prospect of a memorial dedicated more to the German sense of loss than to this loss itself, a sense of loss he regarded rather cynically, given that Germans had profited from the Aryanization of Jewish property (*TSP*, 22 August 1997). It is worth reiterating, however, that in understanding the loss to German culture and history which resulted from the persecution of the Jews, Germans who previously regarded the Third Reich as something irrelevant to the present may find a route to appreciating the significance of the holocaust. Moreover, it is impor-tant that the central Holocaust Memorial is to be dedicated to *all* European Jews killed in the holocaust. The planned presence of European embassies near to the site will enhance this focus. The memorial is thus to be understood in terms of Europe's loss, not only Germany's. Germans will be discouraged from a purely self-reflexive sense of loss, and reminded of Germany's obligation to ideals of tolerance towards other countries. The memorial could thus help to define Germany's national identity along European lines.

In November 1997, the Finding Commission commended two winning designs, the first by Peter Eisenman and Richard Serra, the second by Gesine Weinmiller. The *Förderkreis* preferred a design by Jochen Gerz, while the Berlin Senate favoured a proposal by Daniel Libeskind. In January 1998, when the various designs were exhibited in Berlin, Kohl made straight for the Eisenman/Serra model. Again, it seemed, the Chancellor had decided to impose his authority on cultural affairs. The press response to the Eisenman/Serra proposal was also largely positive.

The Final chapter: Eisenman I, II and III

The Eisenman/Serra proposal consisted as originally planned of 4,000 upright concrete slabs or 'steles', varying in height (to a maximum of 7.5 metres) and length (between 0.92 and 2.3 metres). Both men stressed that their design was untypical of traditional monument art because it represented a departure from the idea of using just a single stone, slab or cross. After Auschwitz and Hiroshima, they claimed, no individual can be sure of dying an individual death (Heimrod *et al.*

1999: 881). Eisenman and Serra also referred to the non-symbolic nature of the design, which operates at different levels of time and space, and with a corresponding sensation of disorientation, rather than with the language of metaphor (Heimrod *et al.* 1999: 882). A further break with traditional monuments consisted in this very attempt to generate a 'living' sense of the past in the present, of its insecurities and threats, in contrast to the tendency to transfigure the past from the perspective of a nostalgic present. Thus the design is characterized by instabilities in its ground structure, and in the surfaces of the steles. Finally, the proposed memorial is non-didactic. As Eisenman and Serra pointed out in an interview, there is no single point of entry or exit, no single valid perspective, no goal or centre (*taz*, 20 January 1998). The design is open, comparable to a field of corn, or the ocean. The visitor is given no directional guidance, but left to fend for himself or herself, an experience intensified by the fact that only one person can pass between the steles at any one time.

Some still found the design too 'monumental'. Serra and Eisenman rejected such reactions as a misinterpretation. In the abovementioned interview, Eisenman stressed the isolation of the visitor within the proposed structure, which would convey what it is like to be 'out on a limb'. One might argue, then, that Eisenman and Serra had planned a memorial which actually worked against the idea of a national monument by individualizing experience, rather than creating a focal point for collective orientation. The sense of loss which Young had called for is there in the design. Eisenman and Serra have written of a 'place of loss' (Heimrod *et al.* 1999: 882). But loss is to be palpable as a physical experience, as a loss of balance, of sure-footedness. The visitor feels what it was like to lose one's moorings, as a Jew in the Third Reich lost his or hers. This ensures that loss is understood not just in terms of a post-holocaust gap in German culture and society, but also as a central experience of the victims themselves. Finally, even if the field of steles is quite large, its instability undermines any impression of enormity. At no point is it excessive in scale, or disproportionate.

Nevertheless, after meeting with Chancellor Kohl of 22 May 1998, Eisenman and Serra agreed to a reduction in the number of steles to 2,500, and in the height of the highest of these to 4 metres. An area for cars, buses and a walkway around the memorial was also planned in. Senate spokesman for Berlin Michael-Andreas Butz referred to the need to 'reduce the size' of the monument (*FAZ*, 15 June 1998). This new design was dubbed Eisenmann II in the press. Serra, for personal reasons that he insisted had nothing to do with Kohl's intervention, withdrew from the project on 3 June 1998. In the late summer of 1998, in the run-up to the national elections, prospective State Minister for Culture Michael Naumann (SPD) expressed his opposition to a central Memorial to the Murdered Jews – despite the proposed modifications. He found the very term 'bureaucratic' and reminiscent of Albert Speer's Third Reich architecture, and doubted the ability of an aesthetic project to reflect the horror of the holocaust. He feared the memorial might merely become a 'place for laying wreaths' (*TSP*, 21 July 1998). Both Bubis and Rosh began to worry that the memorial would only be built if Kohl won the elections. There were fears that the SPD had swapped roles with the CDU, traditionally the more reluctant party to confront the past. Yet Diepgen was still against both a memorial, particularly as envisaged by Eisenman and Serra, and the proposed site. On 4 September 1998, the Berlin Senate passed the decision as to whether or not the memorial should be built to Federal Parliament, while reserving the right to have a say in deciding on the site and choice of model. What had started out as a private initiative had landed on the agenda of the German Parliament – as many felt it should have done much earlier.

Once in power, Naumann and Schröder revised their stance. The most significant reason for this was the impact of Walser's October 1998 Frankfurt speech (see Chapter Seven). As a result of the far right's enthusiastic response to Walser's criticism of the memorial, Schröder was aware that opposing the project would now appear as support for right-wing extremism, at best as irresponsible. As stated at the outset of this chapter, however, the Walser–Bubis debate also helped to shift the focus from the notion of a 'pure' memorial to one of a 'combined' memorial. This idea was championed particularly by Michael Naumann. Before the 1998 elections, Naumann had argued for replacing the memorial with a branch of Steven Spielberg's Shoah Foundation, which had recorded interviews with over 48,000 holocaust survivors. James Young, in analogy to a certain kind of soft drink, opined that such a replacement would result in 'commemoration light' (*Zeit*, 29 October 1998). It is significant that Naumann wanted to substitute a memorial to the murdered with one to survivors, replacing destruction with continuity, the negative with the positive. But Michel Friedman, current Vice-President of the Central Council of the Jews in Germany, supported this idea, albeit in combination with a memorial as originally planned. Gradually, the notion of a combined solution gained in attractiveness. In December 1998, Naumann suggested building a multi-dimensional complex including a memorial, the first Leo Baeck Institute in Germany, a large library with all available books on the holocaust – but also on German-Jewish history – and a Genocide Watch centre, a kind of early warning system against future genocides (Heimrod *et al.* 1999: 1181–3). 'Nausenman' was born.

Nausenman – the forerunner of Eisenman III – came in for criticism because it apparently aimed to drive a wedge of written and recorded material between the memorial and the experience of it. There was a danger that any feeling of horror generated by the memorial would be offset by a visit to the library, whose holdings of primary and secondary literature would demonstrate to the visitor just how intensively Germans and others had set about coming to terms with the holocaust. Rational investigation and explanation would be set against emotionality and moral shock. While the memorial would seek to convey something of the original horror, the library would historicize the holocaust, parcel it up. There was a bureaucratic gigantomania in Naumann's wish to house 'all' books on the holocaust. The Germans had not quite managed to eliminate all of Europe's Jews, but they had succeeded in gathering all the books on the elimination – an unfortunate implication to say the least. The library's stress on post-holocaust intellectual and moral reflection would, moreover, have implied that the Germans had 'moved on' and were now enlightened, in all senses of the term. Nausenman would have been the story of progress, perhaps even a redemption myth, only here, in contrast to Dachau Memorial Site, redemption has been achieved by education, rather than Christianity (see Chapter One). The worst possible effect of Nausenman might have been that Germans would have glanced cursorily at the memorial, felt bad, visited the library and the Genocide Watch centre, and then felt good, in the knowledge that a nation once known for its massacres had now advanced to the self-designated status of moral watchdog.

However, it can be argued that a memorial without any additional didactic framework whatsoever is in danger of becoming meaningless. As the decades roll by, and the holocaust appears to recede more and more into the past, a memorial becomes open to misinterpretation. Depending on the nature of Germany's future problems, it might then be read as a memorial against unemployment, or as an expression of man's existential despair, of Heidegger-like *Geworfensein*. Even where its function is understood, subjective experience of the memorial may remain emotionally vapid if this experience is not also based on a reasonably detailed degree of factual knowledge. Nausenman may have attached too much significance to the value of learning, but it drew attention to the need to provide the memorial with some sort of accompanying information about the holocaust. Nausenman's library, viewed more positively, stressed the obligation for every individual to become personally involved in memory work – in analogy to the concept of active conscience discussed in the media after Walser's speech (see Chapter Seven). A memorial without documentation might, perhaps, have focused too much on guilt – a moral category, arguably, not applicable to today's or to future Germans. Nausenman reflected a shift towards a government with no experience of the war, which was itself expressive of a general generation shift within German society, a shift towards conscience. This might also explain the Genocide Watch idea. Instead of merely looking back in regret, Germans look forward in moral determination to resist future genocide. This is part of the new German 'normality'.

Nausenman was therefore overstated, but in some respects interesting. In the months before June 1999, during a series of consultative sessions of the newly established Federal Committee for Culture and Media, Nausenman came in for critical scrutiny. On 25 June 1999, the memorial issue was debated by the Federal Parliament. It decided in favour of Eisenman II – but with an added 'Place of Information', a more modest alternative to Naumann's 'House of Memory'. A compromise had been found. The indefatigable Eisenman, unperturbed by the continual renegotiation of his design, came up in July 2000 with a proposal which is as ingenious as it is simple (Eisenman III). It envisages locating the 'Place of Information' beneath the memorial, in a set of cellar-like chambers. It will therefore not be visible when visitors walk through the memorial, but some of the memorial's steles will extend downwards into the chambers, resembling stalactites. All that is at present known of the 'Place of Information' is that it will consist of four rooms entitled 'Quiet', 'Fates', 'Names' and 'Places' (*FAZ*, 8 July 2000). Certainly it will document the holocaust in some way, in the manner of an exhibition. The focus in Nausenman on the need for learning has been retained, the agenda-like stress on progress thrown overboard. The penetration of the steles into the 'Place of Information' stresses, rather, that information cannot be read without translating it back into the moral and emotional experience provided by the memorial.

There has been protest at the fact that this information, like Hitler's nearby bunker, is underground. But this is Eisenman's master-stroke. The intellectual element of Eisenman III is associated with the underworld. National Socialist racial ideology, a pseudo-rational system, is revealed to have been the product of hell, or of a sick subconscious. What 'emerged' from this system, the holocaust, is represented by Eisenman as an apparently ordered manifestation. Only when the memorial is entered does its inherent instability become palpable. In the final analysis, Eisenman III is an appeal both to empathy and to the need to be informed, but it is also a warning against over-systematization. It will seek to enhance understanding, and warn against rationalization. It will be a memorial that does not seek to engender feelings of guilt, but, in contrast, invites the visitor to take part in a dialogue. While its cost has increased from 15 to 50 million marks, its horizontal extent has been reduced. It will not glorify. It will not be divorced from its framework of reference. It may become an object of vandalism and have to be protected, but as long as this happens, it will never cease to lose its relevance as a warning to today's Germans. It may become popular with down-and-outs, as some fear, but any association of these with yesterday's social outcasts will certainly provide the media with food for thought. Nor is there a danger of the new Berlin Republic being based on national shame as a result of the memorial. It will serve to place the holocaust at the centre of national memory, but memory can have many centres.

9　The past in the present

'Anyone who persecutes or kills others is an enemy of his own country.'
(Federal President Johannes Rau in reference to racist attacks in Germany,
SZ, 10 November 2000)

The ongoing process

I have argued in this book that German unification in 1990 opened up the possibility for the projection of a more inclusive image of the National Socialist past in the public realm. This, in turn, has led to an increased awareness on the part of today's Germans of the true extent and nature of the crimes committed during the 1933–1945 period. It has also led to a broader understanding of the term 'perpetrator'. The degree of involvement of 'ordinary Germans' was greater, it is now realized, than was for a long time assumed. Equally, there was a wider range of victims than previously recognized. In the same measure, moreover, Germans have come to take leave of the self-pitying notion that they were also victims of Hitler, and there is now less inclination to place the suffering of German expellees or the victims of Allied bombings above that of Jews. The process of inclusiveness has been resisted, and I have pointed to counter-paradigms, such as Kohl's *Neue Wache*, which sought to exclude any specific focus on German crime and responsibility, preferring to label all Germans as victims. Equally, while post-1945 injustice in the east of Germany rightly found a place in the exhibition landscape of the new *Länder* after unification as Germany faced its 'double past', there have been attempts to present the German Special Camp inmates exclusively as victims. A number of new museums and memorial sites in east Germany, moreover, are designed to cast the GDR in as negative a light as the National Socialist period, thus seeking to offload responsibility for the totalitarian past onto east Germans, and to play down the crimes of Nazism. Despite these caveats, however, this book comes on balance to a positive conclusion about Germany's preparedness, as a country, to confront National Socialism and acknowledge German criminality.

The process of inclusiveness I have described is ongoing. Whatever setbacks it has to endure, it will prove hard to stop. This can be well demonstrated with reference to the continuing discussions on the issue of compensation for forced labourers. Shortly before Christmas in 1999, representatives of former forced labourers, the German government and the American government agreed that a sum of 10 billion marks, paid half by German industry and half by the state, would be shared out among those 1.5 million people still alive today who had been constrained to work in German firms during the Second World War. The bulk of the money is to go to countries such as Russia, the Ukraine, Poland and the Czech Republic. Negotiations had been under way on the issue of compensation for some time, particularly since 1998. Again, it was the end of the Cold War that raised awareness of the need to address an injustice which had largely impacted on the citizens of eastern Europe. This was an historic agreement, and a tardy one. Between 10 and 15 million people had carried out forced labour: prisoners-of-war, civilians and concentration camp prisoners. German firms had saved themselves some 16 billion *Reichsmark* in wages – around 95 billion marks by today's reckoning – thanks to this labour.

In comparison with this, the 5,000 to 15,000 marks which survivors or their families will receive seems a pittance, and getting 5 billion marks out of German industry has proved hard. By early March 2001, German firms had only paid 3.6 billion marks into the fund, which is managed by a foundation called 'Remembrance, Responsibility and the Future'. Even this money had not always been willingly provided. Some firms only agreed to contribute after the media threatened to publish, or did publish, the names of companies which had employed forced labourers. Others bowed to the domestic or international threat of trade boycotts. Many firms robustly refused to pay up despite these pressures. The main stumbling block was and is the lack of a cast-iron guarantee that German industry will be protected from legal claims in the future. In June 2000, the American government issued a so-called 'Statement of Interest' designed to discourage courts from processing such claims. But it soon became clear that this 'Statement of Interest' could only kick in effectively once German industry had paid in the full amount. Thus on 8 March 2000, US judge Shirley Kram refused to dismiss a legal claim for compensation precisely because Germany had not yet met its part of the bargain.

One commentator has pointed, rightly, to a certain 'dialectic of normality' in post-unification German political culture (Gay 2000). According to this dialectic, Germany is prepared to shoulder moral and financial debts to National Socialist victims only on the condition that 'normal' life can then resume. Hence the importance of legal closure on future compensation claims. It is not only the Schröder government that has pursued this policy. The German-Czech Agreement signed by Helmut Kohl and Vaclav Klaus on 21 January 1997 envisaged the setting up of a 'Fund for the Future' from which the 8,000 surviving Czech victims of National Socialism would be compensated. In view of the Fund, the Czechs agreed not to lodge further claims for compensation. In the case of the forced labourers, making compensation dependent on guarantees led, as shown above, to an intolerable Catch 22 situation. An important step towards resolving this situation was taken on 14 March 2001. After a meeting with Gerhard Schröder, German industry came up with the missing 1.4 million marks. Schröder's intervention aimed to prevent the system of mutual conditions degenerating into an unseemly farce played out at the expense of the forced labourers, more and more of whom are dying without having received so much as a penny in compensation. Following Schröder's intervention, Shirley Kram finally dismissed the contentious legal claim. German industry pronounced itself satisfied that there was now adequate protection from future legal action, as, at the end of May 2001, did the German Parliament, thus clearing the way for compensation payments to begin.

There is no doubting the shameful, penny-pinching prevarication of sections of German industry. But it is to the credit of the 19 firms who set up the fund that they have agreed to make up the shortfall by increasing their contributions. Nor should it be forgotten that some 6,300 firms have paid into the fund. A number of firms set up after 1945 and not linked in any way to pre-1945 industries have contributed, in line with a sense of collective industrial responsibility in the present. There can also be no doubt, moreover, that the negotiations on the issue of compensation for forced labourers have led to an intense media and public interest in the subject of such labour. It is now common knowledge in Germany that injustice was committed not just behind the front, but within the cities and towns of the *Reich* itself, within firms considered reputable, then as now, and even within the Protestant and Catholic Churches, which have had to admit that they employed forced labour. Not only 'ordinary soldiers' have a past to face, but 'ordinary German citizens' at the home front do too, and certainly ordinary German firms. When Norman Finkelstein visited Germany in February 2001 to present a book which accused some Jewish organizations of making an industry out of in part exaggerated compensation claims, his thesis was on balance rejected by the press and public (Finkelstein 2000). Even where it was felt to be partly true, there was a feeling that it would be inappropriate for German industry to use Finkelstein's arguments as an excuse for further delays. This reaction might not have been possible had not the inclusive understanding of German crime and responsibility extended to include the forced labour issue.

Moreover, while some see the 'dialectic of normality' as a questionable mechanism, whereby what should be unconditional, namely compensation, is tied to conditions, it is possible to defend it. After all, apologies on the part of one individual to another normally lead to a cessation of reproaches and accusations. Germany merely seeks to institutionalize diplomatically what is standard psychological practice. Moreover, Germany's wish to achieve a degree of freedom from the political and legal constraints and pressures resulting from the Nazi past is not unreasonable. If Germany is to act as honest broker in any European or global political process, a role which is expected of it internationally, then surely this task will be most effectively discharged on the basis of a degree of forgiveness and conciliation. Germany's contribution to this conciliation, moreover, goes beyond payment of compensation. Schröder has distanced himself from calls from the Sudeten Germans for compensation from the Czechs, and from their wish to set up a museum in the middle of Berlin focusing on the issue of expulsion. The closure on the compensation issue works two ways.

Besides, while the process of confronting the past within Germany is influenced by international conciliation politics, it is not driven by it. This book is, I hope, evidence of that. It may be that, as the National Socialist period recedes in time, confronting this past will be defined as much in terms of applying the lessons learnt from this confrontation, as in terms of that confrontation itself. Thus *Vergangenheitsbewältigung* will give way to *Gegenwarts- und Zukunftsbewältigung* – coming to terms with the present and future. Applying lessons learnt can only mean practising and actively supporting tolerance and democracy. One thing became clear from all the debates on the Third Reich after 1990: the importance of conscience. The concept was central to the discussion of German resistance in 1994, to the Goldhagen debate and to the 'Crimes of the *Wehrmacht*' exhibition. Walser's speech foregrounded conscience (in its various inflexions), and the Holocaust Memorial has been described as the 'conscience of the nation'.

Other qualities were also discussed in relation to the National Socialist past, such as empathy with the victims, and responsibility. These are linked to conscience – empathy as the trigger to conscience, responsibility as its active dimension. In the final part of this book, it seems appropriate, indeed essential, to ask whether conscience and related qualities have found a place in reactions in the present as well as in discourse on the past. In view of Germany's problems with racism, it may seem, at first glance, that they have not found a place. But I believe it can be shown that they have, and may even be helping towards a redefinition of what it means to be German.

Racism and constitutionalism

The Berlin Republic, pessimists feel, has yet to prove that the lessons of National Socialism have been adequately learnt. Quite a number of politicians and intellectuals had been against the parliamentary move to Berlin from the very first, arguing that megalomania, over-centralization, nationalism and self-aggrandizement would invade German politics. Pointing to an increase in right-wing extremism and racism, they now claim their fears were right. In early March 2001, Minister of the Interior Otto Schily released statistics which confirmed that there had been a drastic rise in the number of right-wing extremist, anti-foreigner and anti-semitic criminal acts in 2000. The number given was 15,951, an increase of 59% over 1999. Of these, 998 were acts of violence, 34% more than in 1999 (*SZ*, 3 March 2001). Other sets of statistics quoted in Germany's media suggest, in contrast to this, that there has been a steady rise in right-wing extremism over the past ten years. There is a consensus that the main problem area is the eastern Federal states, which have a higher rate of extremist right-wing crime despite the fact that only 2.2% of those living in the new *Länder* are foreigners, in comparison to 10.4% in the west (for a statistical table, see *FAZ*, 15 August 2000).

Pessimists also diagnose a swing to the right in Germany's political culture. In October 2000, the new Leader of the CDU's Parliamentary Party, Friedrich Merz, triggered ongoing discussions when he opined that foreigners in Germany should adapt their behaviour to the principles of German *Leitkultur*. While this term appears to have been coined by a non-German, Professor Bassam Tibi, to describe to immigrants what is expected of them in the country to which they emigrate,

Merz used it to imply the existence of a specifically Germanic culture of exemplary character (*FR*, 11 October 2000). This would have been a problematic notion even without the historical fact of National Socialism. Paul Spiegel, head of the Central Council of the Jews in Germany, asked pointedly if chasing foreigners through the streets, setting fire to synagogues and killing down-and-outs was a manifestation of the *Leitkultur* Merz had in mind (*SZ*, 13 November 2000). Since losing power in 1998, and since the discrediting of Chancellor Kohl, who currently stands accused of illegal financial practices in connection with party funds, the CDU has been at pains to draw attention to itself by means of questionable slogans and campaigns. In the run-up towards the 1999 regional elections in Hesse, Roland Koch – now Minister President there – spearheaded a 'signatures campaign' against immigration, while his CDU colleague Jürgen Rüttgers coined the unfortunate catchphrase *Kinder statt Inder* (Children instead of Indians) in response to the SPD's Green Card plans. Instead of employing foreigners, notably from the Third World, to solve problems of missing technical expertise, the Germans should, according to Rüttgers, produce more children.

The SPD, some fear, is drifting to the right of centre as the right drifts towards a position generally associated with the far right. Schröder's sympathy for some of Walser's comments, his remark that a Holocaust Memorial should be something people 'like' to go to, his statement to the effect that today's Germans should be allowed to run around without feelings of guilt (*Zeit*, 4 February 1999) – all of this smacked for some, like Michel Friedman, of 'a left-wing campaign to draw a line under the past' (*SZ*, 16 September 1999). Terms such as *Neue Unbefangenheit* (new lack of inhibitions) imply on one level, at least, a certain unperturbed assurance in dealing with the National Socialist past – as if the present had nothing to fear from its spectre. It was noteworthy that, following Merz's reference to *Leitkultur*, several SPD and Green politicians rejected this term in favour of 'constitutional patriotism' (*Verfassungspatriotismus*). They were even supported by Heiner Geißler of the CDU. This term, associated with political scientist Dolf Sternberger and philosopher Jürgen Habermas, had long been used in West Germany to indicate the post-war necessity for Germans to avoid nationalism in favour of loyalty to liberal and democratic values. Now, some suspected, left-wing politicians were employing the term to indicate the post-unification necessity for foreigners living in Germany to abandon their cultural and religious identity in favour of a westernized constitutionalism. In this scenario, the very value system used to re-educate the West Germans in the post-war period becomes the motor of a new repression. Such dark interpretations of recent developments in the political thinking of the CDU, SPD and Greens rest on the belief that, whereas West and East Germany were once at the geopolitical divide of Europe, united Germany is now the West's and Christianity's bulwark against the much-dreaded Islam.

How much truth is there in the fears outlined in the previous paragraphs? There can be little doubt that racism is a serious problem in Germany, as in some other European countries. But we should be wary of drawing overhasty conclusions from any diagnosed increase. Since the SPD's accession to power in 1998, it has become clear that, under the CDU government, the German police was frequently unable to recognize right-wing extremism, even when it appeared to be unmistakeable. It may also have been the case that there was a concerted effort on the part of the police and political authorities to obscure the actual number of right-wing extremist crimes, so as to maintain the impression that left-wing radicalism and right-wing radicalism were problems of equal seriousness – a desirable impression from the CDU's point of view. When Schily presented the statistics for 2000, he pointed out that, according to his Ministry, the registered increase may not mean an actual increase: the greater interest of the media and the fact that there was now greater police involvement in confronting right-wing extremism had had an effect on the figures (*SZ*, 3 March 2001). In November 2000, the Federal Agency of Criminal Investigation published a reassessment of past statistics, claiming that the official number of 25 people killed by acts of right-wing radicalism since 1990 was too low: that number should be 36. Even this number is probably too low. Unofficial statistics have suggested the number may be as high as 93. The fact of the matter is that right-wing radicalism has been a perpetual and substantial problem since unification, far more so than left-wing radicalism. Only now is the extent of this problem being recognized.

Its causes are still a matter for debate. Some point to the failure of GDR antifascism to confront the legacy of National Socialism. There have been revelations about right-wing radicalism in the National People's Army and even the *Stasi*, and the SED has come in for criticism for refusing to acknowledge the problem of such radicalism and 'passing it on' to united Germany. Others point to the impact of capitalism on the post-unification east, which led to mass unemployment and a collapse of social infrastructures. It has been argued that young east Germans have fallen prey to a new totalitarian ideology, one imported from the west by neo-Nazis. As for right-wing extremism in the west, this is also generally put down to unemployment and lack of social integration. Ethnic nationalism is too infrequently adduced as a factor, yet it surely plays a part. Nor, alas, can it be ruled out that right-wing radicals felt emboldened by their understanding of Walser's speech. Whatever the causes, the problem must be faced. Under the CDU, the tendency was to instrumentalize right-wing radicalism in the political discrediting of socialism, rather than to confront such radicalism. Any increase must be put down at least in part to this non-confrontation. Under the SPD, the policy appears to be changing.

Over the late summer and autumn months of 2000, the SPD – not least in reaction to the appalling murder in Dessau of a man from Mozambique, and the near blowing-up of a group of Ukrainian Jews in Düsseldorf – has instigated a process of political, legal and social 'coming to terms with the present'. Plans have been set in motion with the notable support of CSU-run Bavaria and some CDU-run *Länder* to ban the extreme right-wing German National-Democratic Party (NPD); this would be the first party ban since that of the German Communist Party in 1956 in West Germany. Other legal measures, including restrictions to demonstration rights and refusing to allow right-wing extremist gatherings at sites of 'national memory' such as the planned Holocaust Memorial, are under consideration. The police and Federal agencies involved in crime-fighting are being enjoined to be more vigilant, courts to be more severe. Officers in the Federal Border Protection are to be deployed at train stations and other problem areas in an attempt to detect and prevent right-wing radicalism. The CDU, forced to sit up and listen, has itself come up with suggestions. Party leader Angela Merkel expressly supported more rigorous screening of the civil service to weed out right-wing radicals. Countrywide initiatives to combat racism are under way. In August 2000, the SPD and Green Parliamentary Parties decided to set up an anti-racist foundation 'Union for Democracy and Tolerance', supporting it with an initial start-up capital of 75 million marks. In the same month, Uwe-Karsten Heye, SPD spokesman, helped to found a Civil Initiative against the Right. This inititiave unites politicians, television personalities, sports' stars including Franz Beckenbauer and Henry Maske, and writers such as Christa Wolf in a concerted action at national, regional and local level.

This is an important development. Germany's politicians, helped a little perhaps by the recent self-dissolution of the left-wing terrorist Red Army Faction, have at least understood where the true extremist threat to the social and political order lies. Moreover, not only is the problem of racism now openly acknowledged and addressed by politicians, they are also insisting on the need for the 'ordinary Germans' of today to combat the problem. This insistence may reflect the impact of the positive strand in the reception of Walser's speech. Throughout 2000, strikingly, SPD politicians have used commemorative and other occasions to direct the focus not just towards retrospective regret for the crimes of the Third Reich, but also towards proactive application of the lessons learnt. At the same time, there has been an emphasis on a need for the depoliticization of conscience, in the sense of impressing upon the population the importance of personal and civil initiative. It is as if the responsibility of a people increases as its guilt for the past decreases.

During his 8 May 2000 speech in the Centrum Judaicum, Schröder located commemoration of the end of the war firmly within the parameters of continuing German historical responsibility. '8 May cannot liberate us from our history', he maintained (*SZ*, 9 May 2000). In reference to right-wing radicalism, he went on to stress the need to fight on a daily basis for a free and tolerant society. On the occasion of the 56th anniversary of the 20 July 1944 plot, Wolfgang Thierse, after criticizing the FRG's excessive stress on Stauffenberg and the GDR's on anti-fascism, argued that resistance begins with 'small gestures of refusal'. He called for 'concrete commemoration' (*FAZ*, 21 July 2000). This was an appeal to the Germans to combat racism at grass-roots level. When Schröder spoke at the celebration of the 50th anniversary of the founding of the Central Council of the Jews in Germany, he called, no less, for the 'mobilization of civil society' (*SZ*, 22 September 2000). After the arson attack on a synagogue in Düsseldorf, Schröder asserted: 'looking away is no longer allowed. We need a rebellion of the decent' (*FAZ*, 5 October 2000). He explicitly praised a woman who had climbed over the wall of the synagogue to put out the fire. Schröder's, Thierse's and Paul Spiegel's appeals to the Germans have not gone unheeded. The police has noted an increased preparedness on the part of the public to report incidents of right-wing extremism, and there have been significant anti-racist demonstrations in the late summer and autumn of 2000, notably in Neumünster, Düsseldorf, Kassel, Berlin and Cologne.

This is active memory, as opposed to lip-service. In taking to the streets in protest at racism, as 300,000 did in November 1992 in a show of solidarity with foreigners, many Germans demonstrate determination not to allow a repetition of the past. They also draw attention to the fact that foreigners have rights under the German constitution. Similarly, the SPD's engaged resistance to right-wing radicalism in the autumn and winter of 2000 indicates that it conceives of loyalty to the constitution not just as something which one might expect of foreigners living in Germany, but also as something that must be expected of Germans. Such loyalty involves respect for minorities, their basic human rights and cultural values. The principles enshrined in the constitution do not prohibit cultural and religious difference, they are designed to protect such difference. In this context, it is worth stressing that, under the SPD/Greens government, German citizenship laws have shifted somewhat from *ius sanguinis* to *ius soli*; legislation to allow immigrants' children born in Germany access to German citizenship was introduced in early 1999. Blood-based notions of German citizenship, notions which proved so destructive under National Socialism, are at long last in the process of being revised. As it becomes easier for foreigners to attain a German passport, ethnic concepts of Germanness will become harder to sustain. Germanness will be defined more and more by shared values, such as those embodied in the constitution.

Were constitutional patriotism to become the basis for German identity in the present – and there are good grounds for believing that it might – then this identity will be an inclusive one. It will be open to all, regardless of colour or country of origin, who swear to uphold this constitution. Such an inclusive form of patriotism is perhaps a correlative to the inclusive model of remembering the National Socialist past. One might even argue that an identity based on the constitution would not be specifically German, given that this constitution is built around liberal values typical of the laws and constitutions of many countries. In one sense, however, it would retain a particularly German quality. For one of the driving forces behind loyalty to the constitution would be memory of the holocaust and German responsibility. This is the 'particular' element in any 'universal' orientation for post-2000 German democracy. It is precisely this call for an identity based on constitutional patriotism that has alarmed many in the CDU, which in the last months of 2000 frenetically insisted on the need to revive concepts of the nation and of homeland. The CSU's and CDU's wish to 'stem the tide' of immigrants can also be explained by the wish to maintain an ethnic sense of German identity. Yet if immigration legislation, as planned, is introduced, this may serve to provide a tangible acknowledgement that Germany has *de facto* long been a country of immigration. Presumably, the CDU hope that the national ticket, in the form of support for an ethnicized sense of German identity, will return them to power. But it all seems rather desperate. Friedrich Merz's idea of a *Leitkultur* has been mercilessly mocked in television cabarets, and the German press delighted in coining similar terms such as *Reitkultur* (culture of horse-riding) or *Bytekultur* (culture of computer bytes).

Resignification and reconstruction

Within the *Reichstag* building itself, the CDU and CSU are being compelled to participate in a symbolic acknowledgement that blood-based concepts of Germanness are changing. In September 2000, an art project by Hans Haacke in Germany's new seat of government was officially 'opened' by Wolfgang Thierse (SPD). Haacke has installed a huge trough containing, raised above the ground, the letters 'To the population'. This contrasts deliberately with the inscription above the portal to the *Reichstag*, which reads 'To the People', but it also sheds a critical light on the 'We are one people' of the *Wende* period. In an interview, Haacke claimed that a key experience leading to the idea for the trough was the sight, in 1984, of a group of Turks on the grass outside the *Reichstag*. It became clear to Haacke, suddenly, that the inscription above the entrance was effectively telling these Turks that the *Reichstag* had nothing to do with them (*BM*, 9 September 2000). In setting 'To the People' in relation to 'To the Population', Haacke implies that the German government has a commitment to all people living in the country, regardless of whether these are German families with centuries-old ties to Germany, second or third generation immigrant Turks, or recently arrived asylum-seekers. In the same interview, Haacke explicitly refers to Article Three of the Basic Law, which guarantees equality to all living in Germany. Population, then, is a corporate unit bound by constitutional ties which, for Haacke, must transcend or at least counteract any blood-based loyalties. In combination with Sir Norman Foster's majestic glass cupola on top of the *Reichstag*, which implies parliamentary transparency, Haacke's project will serve to enhance the sense of a need for an inclusive and open democracy in united Germany.

His project might represent not just a dialectic between 'people' and 'population', but also an attempt to redefine 'people' along the lines of 'population', thus freeing *Volk* of its historical associations with rampant ethnicity under Hitler. In another way, his project certainly seeks to redefine tainted terminology. Haacke's trough is to be filled with earth from all German parliamentary constituencies. Parliamentarians have been provided with jute sacks, and are expected to procure this earth themselves – and tip it into the trough; Wolfgang Thierse was the first to do so in September 2000. Inevitably, this has provoked comparisons with the Third Reich. Thus Heinrich Himmler, in 1940, inaugurated an SS shrine in Quedlinburg in which earth from all German districts (*Gaue*) had been deposited. But this is Haacke's point. Under Hitler, German soil was associated with purity of blood, and indirectly, then, with the rights and privileges of the 'Aryan' Germans. Jews could not claim such rights because, according to Nazi ideology, they lacked the necessary purity of lineage. Haacke resignifies soil, so that it comes to symbolize not blood-based privileges, but privileges based on democracy and parliamentarianism. Earth becomes a symbol of openness and inclusiveness, associated with generally applicable constitutional rights which obtain as soon as the individual 'touches down' on German soil. The trough has been dismissed by cynics as the 'Federal Compost Heap', and as ecological kitsch. Haacke's hope is that the seeds in the earth brought by the parliamentarians will germinate, resulting in a green biotope sprinkled with dandelions and other wild flowers. This is more than kitsch. Such wild, untrammelled growth is to be understood in relation to Haacke's notion of population, which must also be allowed to grow 'freely'. After a while, the growth will cover up the letters 'To the Population'. The message will have given way to its implementation, symbolically speaking.

It seems that the role of the National Socialist past in the present, as suggested at the start of this book, is to serve as an inbuilt negative foil. The question always is: how far have we, as Germans, moved on? The state of the health of German democracy is assessed in terms of the degree of moral and political distance to the Third Reich. We might even say that today's Germans are striving for transcendence, not in any metaphysical sense, but in a quite pragmatic one as they endeavour day in, day out to step out of the shadow of the past. Architectural developments since 1990 reflect and reinforce this striving. Dresden's famous Church of our Lady (*Frauenkirche*), destroyed by Allied bombings in 1944, is being rebuilt. Berlin's Church of Conciliation (*Versöhnungskirche*), damaged by bombs and then blown up by the GDR in 1985 because of its location at the site of the Berlin Wall, is also being reconstructed. Such reconstructions, critics say, represent a burying of the past, be this the National Socialist past, or the 'double past' of National Socialism and GDR socialism. But such a view is short-sighted. The negative past will still be present in these buildings, not least because they are being erected, partly at least, with the original bricks. In the case of the Church of Conciliation, now a chapel, some of these bricks have been crushed and reappear as fragments, flecks, in the simple clay walls of the new structure. The negative past is built into the present, but in reconstituted form, as the foil to the message of reconciliation, whether this reconciliation be between west and east Germans, or Germans and the Allies – not least the British. Outside the Chapel of Conciliation is a sculpture, 'Conciliation', donated by Richard Branson (see the cover). It is a copy of a sculpture in the School of Peace Studies in Bradford. There is also a Coventry cross of nails in the chapel, as in Berlin's Kaiser Wilhelm Memorial Church and Dresden's Church of our Lady. British donations and craftsmanship led to the construction of the Orb and Cross destined for the top of the latter.

These buildings are living manifestations of the need to maintain those values which made and make reconciliation possible. They suggest that Germany has moved on, but also that it must continue to do so. It is particularly the Berlin Chapel of Conciliation which symbolizes this ongoing process. Instead of imitating the original, the planners opted for a completely new design, a light, open, clay-walled, wooden-clad, oblong structure which hardly resembles a chapel. It has a transcultural, transreligious quality, seeming to welcome not just Christians, but also Muslims, Jews and members of other faiths [Plate 9.1]. Conciliation is written into the structure as a multi-directional message. It could be argued, by contrast, that slavishly reconstructing the Church of our Lady in Dresden represents a fetishistic love for past architectural glories, and the wish to turn the clocks back to

Plate 9.1 The new Chapel of Conciliation on Berlin's Bernauer Street.

the pre-Hitler era. Similar objections were raised in opposition to the renovation of the *Reichstag*, and are being currently raised in connection with plans to rebuild Berlin's Castle. Some fear united Germany is now set on a course of dubious glorification of the pre-1933 past, even of Prussianism – a fear first articulated in 1991 when Chancellor Kohl insisted on being present at what Berliners sarcastically called the 'repotting' (reburial) of Frederick the Great and Frederick William in Potsdam's Sanssouci. These objections must be taken seriously. But they should not be overstressed. The renovation of the *Reichstag* in preparation for its present use as the seat of the German Parliament reconnected it, and Germany, to pre-1933 parliamentary traditions; but it did not therefore glorify these. Nor did it lead to the erasure of the National Socialist past, reference to which is made in the form of an art-work by Katharina Sieverding commemorating the parliamentarians murdered, persecuted and excluded by the National Socialists. As for Berlin's Castle, it will probably only be partly rebuilt, in the form of a curious amalgamation with the GDR's House of the Republic (*Haus der Republik*) – one as ugly as the other. Something post-modern and folkloristic, tentative and experimental is likely to result, rather than a monstrous monument to Wilhelminian Germany.

Germany has the fastest-growing Jewish community in Europe, indeed the world. On its entry to the new millennium, it has a Jewish population of over 81,000; 50,000 of these came from eastern Europe over the last ten years. The regeneration of Jewish life is particularly visible in the heart of Berlin (*Berlin Mitte*), and more generally visible in the reconstruction or construction of synagogues and Jewish Centres in Berlin, Dresden, Munich and elsewhere. Arguably, this represents a move towards reconnecting to the pre-Hitler era of attempted German–Jewish symbiosis. This does not mean that Jews, or Germans (with exceptions), wish to forget that Jewish life was subsequently destroyed. Dresden's new synagogue will be built opposite the site of the original synagogue ransacked during the *Reichskristallnacht* pogrom, while Berlin's New Synagogue contains the ruins of the old one. Manifest awareness of the holocaust is inscribed into Jewish cultural identity in the present. The wish to reconnect to pre-1933 prospects of integration nevertheless reflects an acknowledgement that there were such prospects. Jews in today's Germany can derive hope not just from the fact that most of today's Germans genuinely abhor what happened between 1933 and 1945, but also from a sense of the unique role which German Jews were able to play in the life of pre-1933 Germany. The time may also have come for Germans to be trusted to reappropriate positive traditions in the pre-Hitler past *without* glorifying the Kaiser or Bismarck, or marginalizing the holocaust. A German identity based on an open-minded constitutionalism need not preclude enlightened pride in genuine historical achievements.

It is to be hoped that the evolving national identity of the Berlin Republic will be based on more liberal concepts of political, social and artistic culture than the somewhat chauvinistic *Leitkultur*. As an alternative to Merz's idea of a 'leading culture', several commentators suggested the term 'German culture'. Thus Paul Spiegel argued that he would prefer the term 'German culture' (*SZ*, 16 November 2000). Such a conceptualization would emphasize the contribution made to this culture, in the past and present, not just by Germans, but also by German Jews and recent immigrants to Germany from Turkey and elsewhere. Rudolf Augstein pointed out that, during the war, *Wehrmacht* soldiers had sung German songs written by Jewish composers and song-writers. 'My *Leitkultur*', Augstein writes, 'was Jewish' (*Spiegel*, 20 November 2000). Michael Naumann preferred the term 'world culture' to *Leitkultur* (*Spiegel*, 13 November 2000). In these various alternatives, the value of culture in Germany, in past and present, is understood to consist not in any spurious notions of ethnic purity, but in its evolution under diverse influences including the Jewish diaspora and, more recently, the influx of foreign workers and globalization. Under the roof of such a concept of culture, all will be welcome. Only such an understanding will ensure that German identity becomes an inclusive one.

Abbreviations

Given the topicality of the themes, this book makes extensive reference to newspaper reports, and occasional reference to television programmes. To prevent an 'overloading' of the bibliography, the sources for these references are given, in parentheses and italics, in the body of the text. The titles of the newspapers, magazines and TV channels have been abbreviated as follows:

AAZ = Aachener Zeitung
AN = Aachener Nachrichten
ARD = Arbeitsgemeinschaft der
öffentlich-rechtlichen
Rundfunkanstalten der BRD
BA = Bremer Anzeiger
BaZ = Badische Zeitung
BddB = Börsenblatt des deutschen
Buchhandels
BGZ = Bergedorfer Zeitung
Bild = Bild-Zeitung
BK = Bayernkurier
BM = Berliner Morgenpost
BN = Bremer Nachrichten
BraunZ = Braunschweiger Zeitung
BS = Bayerische Staatszeitung
BZ = Berliner Zeitung
DAS = Deutsches Allgemeines
Sonntagsblatt
DBP = Deutscher Bundestag,
Pressereferat
DP = Das Parlament
DWZ = Deister- und Weserzeitung
FAZ = Frankfurter Allgemeine Zeitung
FDK = Freie Demokratische
Korrespondenz
FPC = Freie Presse Chemnitz
FR = Frankfurter Rundschau
GA = Generalanzeiger Bonn
GIA = Gießener Anzeiger
HAZ = Hannoversche Allgemeine
Zeitung
JA = Jüdische Allgemeine
JF = Junge Freiheit

JW = Junge Welt
KN = Kieler Nachrichten
KR = Kölnische Rundschau
KSA = Kölner Stadt-Anzeiger
LN = Lübecker Nachrichten
LPD = Landespressedienst
MA = Märkische Allgemeine
MM = Münchner Merkur
ND = Neues Deutschland
NYT = The New York Times
OP = Oberhessische Presse
PM = SPD Pressemitteilung
Presse = Die Presse
RM = Rheinischer Merkur
RZ = Rheinische Zeitung
SächZ = Sächsische Zeitung
SBZ = Saarbrücker Zeitung
SD = Schwäbische Donauzeitung
SK = Südkurier
SPA = Senatspresseamt Berlin
Spiegel = Der Spiegel
STZ = Stuttgarter Zeitung
SZ = Süddeutsche Zeitung
taz = die tageszeitung
TSP = Der Tagesspiegel
tz = tageszeitung München
WDR = Westdeutscher Rundfunk
Welt = Die Welt
WK = Weser-Kurier
Woche = Die Woche
WP = Die Wochenpost
ZDF = Zweites Deutsches Fernsehen
Zeit = Die Zeit

Bibliography

Primary sources

Buchenwald Memorial Site Library

Buchenwald 1958: 'Rede des Ministerpräsidenten Otto Grotewohl zur Weihe der Nationalen Mahn- und Gedenkstätte Buchenwald' (1958), Bu 48(2):1, no publisher/page numbers.

Neuengamme Memorial Site Archive

Neuengamme 1951: 'Friedhofsamt: Vermerk' (30 October 1951), in *Bemühungen um eine Gedenkstätte 1951–1953*, Ng. 9.3.4.4.

Stiftung Archiv der Parteien und Massenorganisationen der DDR im Bundesarchiv (Berlin)

SAPMO 1955a: 'Politbüro des Zentralkomitees: Protokoll Nr. 16/55' (March 1955), SAPMO-BArch DY 30 J IV2/2/413.

SAPMO 1955b: 'Hauptsektor Geschichte, Brigade Widerstand: Vermerk betr.: Gründungstag für das Nationalkomitee "Freies Deutschland" in Berlin' (9 June 1955), *Institut für Marxismus-Leninismus Ideologische Kommission*, SAPMO-BArch DY 30 IV 2 9.07/152/5.

SAPMO 1958: 'Anlage Nr. 9 zum Protokoll Nr. 19/58' (April 1958), SAPMO-BArch DY 30 J IV2/2/591.

SAPMO 1961: 'Sektor Geschichte der KPD: Entwurf der Konzeption zur "Geschichte des deutschen antifaschistischen Widerstandskampfes (1933–1945)"' (December 1961), *Institut für Marxismus-Leninismus*, SAPMO-BArch DY 30 IV2 9.07/28.

SAPMO 1965: 'Politbüro des Zentralkomitees: Protokoll Nr. 15/65' (March 1965), SAPMO-BArch DY 30 J IV2/2/983.

SAPMO 1979: 'Bericht über die Begegnung mit Mitgliedern des Moltke-Kreises am 28. November 1979' (November 1979), *Büro Kurt Hager*, SAPMO-BArch DY 30 vorl. SED 38496.

SAPMO 1985: 'Politbüro des Zentralkomitees: Anlage Nr. 6 zum Protokoll Nr. 10/85' (March 1985), SAPMO-BArch DY 30 J IV 2/2/2102.

SAPMO 1988: 'Rede des Genossen Honecker am 8.11.1988' (November 1988), *Staatssekretär für Kirchenfragen*, SAPMO-BArch DY 30/IV B 2/14/177/2.

Secondary sources

AIN (Amicale Internationale KZ Neuengamme) (ed.) (1995) *'Cap Arcona': 3. Mai 1945. Spuren der Vergangenheit – Mahnung für die Zukunft*, Aukrug: AIN.

Aly, G. and Heim, S. (1991) *Vordenker der Vernichtung: Auschwitz und die deutschen Pläne für eine neue europäische Ordnung*, Frankfurt on Main: Fischer.

Apel, R. (ed.) (1995) *Es wird nicht mehr zurückgeschossen . . . Erinnerungen an das Kriegsende*, Cologne: Lingen, 1995.

Arbeitsgruppe der Neuen Gesellschaft für Bildende Kunst (eds) (1995) *Eine Streitschrift: Der Wettbewerb für das 'Denkmal für die ermordeten Juden Europas'*, Berlin: Verlag der Kunst.

Assmann, A. (1999) *Erinnerungsräume: Formen und Wandlungen des kulturellen Gedächtnisses*, Munich: Beck.

—— and Frevert, U. (1999) *Geschichtsvergessenheit, Geschichtsversessenheit: Vom Umgang mit deutschen Vergangenheiten nach 1945*, Stuttgart: Deutsche-Verlags-Anstalt.

Bamberger, E. (ed.) (1994) *Der Völkermord an den Sinti und Roma in der Gedenkstättenarbeit*, Heidelberg: Dokumentations- und Kulturzentrum Deutscher Sinti und Roma.

Barker, P. (ed.) (2000) *The GDR and its History: Die DDR im Spiegel der Enquete-Kommissionen*, Rodopi: Amsterdam and Atlanta.

Bartov, O. (1995) '"Wem gehört die Geschichte?" Wehrmacht und Geschichtswissenschaft', in Heer, H. and Naumann, K. (eds), *Vernichtungskrieg: Verbrechen der Wehrmacht 1941 bis 1944*, Hamburg: Hamburger Edition, 601–19.

—— (ed.) (2000a) *The Holocaust: Origins, Implementation, Aftermath*, Routledge: London and New York.

—— (2000b) 'Introduction', in Bartov, O. (ed.), *The Holocaust: Origins, Implementation, Aftermath*, Routledge: London and New York, 1–18.

—— (2000c) 'German Soldiers and the Holocaust; Historiography, Research and Implications', in Bartov, O. (ed.), *The Holocaust: Origins, Implementation, Aftermath*, Routledge: London and New York, 162–84.

—— et al. (2000) *Bericht der Kommission zur Überprüfung der Ausstellung 'Vernichtungskrieg. Verbrechen der Wehrmacht 1941 bis 1944'*, unpublished report (available on the internet under http://www.his.de).

Bauche, U., Brüdigam, H., Eiber, L. and Wiedey, W. (eds) (1991) *Arbeit und Vernichtung: Das Konzentrationslager Neuengamme 1938–1945: Katalog zur ständigen Ausstellung im Dokumentenhaus*, Hamburg: VSA-Verlag.

Baumann, L. and Messerschmidt, M. (1999) 'Stellungnahme der Bundesvereinigung Opfer der NS-Militärjustiz zum Wettbewerb für eine gemeinsame Gedenkstätte in Torgau Fort Zinna', *Gedenkstättenrundbrief*, 91/10: 32–4.

Bautzen-Komitee (ed.) (1992) *Das Gelbe Elend: Bautzen-Häftlinge berichten 1945–1956*, Halle: Buchverlag Union.

Bechtel, M. (ed.) (1997) *Das Ende, das ein Anfang war: Das Jahr 1945*, Bonn: Bundeszentrale für politische Bildung.

Beckermann, R. (1998) *Jenseits des Krieges: Ehemalige Wehrmachtssoldaten erinnern sich*, Vienna: Döcker.

Benz, W. (ed.) (1995) *Die Vertreibung der Deutschen aus dem Osten. Ursachen, Ereignisse, Folgen*, Frankfurt on Main: Fischer.

—— (ed.) (1996) *Jahrbuch für Antisemitismusforschung 5*, Frankfurt on Main and New York: Campus.

Bergander, G. (1998) *Dresden im Luftkrieg. Vorgeschichte – Zerstörung – Folgen*, Würzburg: Flechsig.

Berger, S. (1997) *The Search for Normality: National Identity and Historical Consciousness in Germany since 1800*, Providence and Oxford: Berghahn.

Biddiscombe, P. (1998) *Werwolf: The History of the National Socialist Guerilla Movement 1944–1946*, Toronto and Buffalo: University of Toronto Press.

Birn, R. B. (1997) 'Revising the Holocaust', *The Cambridge Historical Journal*, 40/1: 195–215.

Blaschke, O. (1998) 'Die Elimination wissenschaftlicher Unterscheidungsfähigkeit: Goldhagens Begriff des "eliminatorischen Antisemitismus" – eine Überprüfung', in Heil, J. and Erb, R. (eds), *Geschichtswissenschaft und Öffentlichkeit: Der Streit um Daniel J. Goldhagen*, Frankfurt on Main: Fischer, 63–90.

Bredthauer, K. and Heinrich, A. (eds) (1997) *Aus der Geschichte Lernen: How to Learn from History*, Bonn: Blätter-Verlags-Gesellschaft.

Brink, C. (1998) *Ikonen der Vernichtung: Öffentlicher Gebrauch von Fotografien aus nationalsozialistischen Konzentrationslagern nach 1945*, Berlin: Akademie Verlag.

Brochhagen, U. (1994) *Nach Nürnberg: Vergangenheitsbewältigung und Westintegration in der Ära Adenauer*, Hamburg: Junius.

Broszat, M. (1979) 'Hitler and the Genesis of the "Final Solution": An Assessment of David Irving's Thesis', *Yad Vashem Studies*, 13: 73–125.

—— (1981) *The Hitler State: The Foundation and Development of the Internal Structure of the Third Reich*, London and New York: Longman.

Browning, C. (1992a) *Ordinary Men: Reserve Police Batallion 101 and the Final Solution in Poland*, London: Harper-Collins.

—— (1992b) *The Path to Genocide: Essays on Launching the Final Solution*, Cambridge: Cambridge University Press.

—— (1996) 'Review Essay: Daniel Goldhagen's Willing Executioners', *History and Memory*, 8/1: 88–108.

—— (2000) *Nazi Policy, Jewish Workers, German Killers*, Cambridge: Cambridge University Press.

Burleigh, M. (2000) *The Third Reich: A New History*, London: Macmillan.

Courtois, S. *et al.* (eds) (1998) *Das Schwarzbuch des Kommunismus: Unterdrückung, Verbrechen und Terror*, Munich and Zurich: Piper.

Cullen, M. (1999) *Das Holocaust-Mahnmal: Dokumentation einer Debatte*, Zurich and Munich: Pendo.

Dawidowicz, L. (1975) *The War against the Jews, 1933–1945*, New York: Holt, Rinehart and Winston.

Diepgen, E. (1998) 'Grußwort', in Jüdisches Museum Berlin and MD Berlin (eds), *Jüdisches Museum Berlin*, Berlin: Jüdisches Museum Berlin, 4.

Dietzsch, M., Jäger, S. and Schobert, A. (eds) (1999) *Endlich ein normales Volk: Vom rechten Verständnis der Friedenspreis-Rede Martin Walsers. Eine Dokumentation*, Duisburg: DISS.

Dreissinger, S. (ed.) (1992) *Von einer Katastrophe in die andere. 13 Gespräche mit Thomas Bernhard*, Weitra: Bibliothek der Provinz.

Drobisch, K. and Wieland, G. (1993) *System der NS-Konzentrationslager 1933–1939*, Berlin: Akademie Verlag.

Dubiel, H. (1999) *Niemand ist frei von der Geschichte: Die nationalsozialistische Herrschaft in den Debatten des Deutschen Bundestages*, Munich and Vienna: Hanser.

Eberlein, M., Haase, N. and Oleschinski, W. (1999) *Torgau im Hinterland des Zweiten Weltkriegs: Militärjustiz, Wehrmachtsgefängnisse, Reichskriegsgericht*, Leipzig: Kiepenheuer.

Enzensberger, H. M. (ed.) (1995) *Europa in Ruinen. Augenzeugenberichte aus den Jahren 1944–1948*, Munich: dtv.

Evans, R. (1989) *In Hitler's Shadow: West German Historians and the Attempt to Escape from the Nazi Past*, London: I. B. Tauris.

—— (1997) *Rereading German History 1800–1996: From Unification to Reunification*, London and New York: Routledge.

Fachbeirat Dachau (1996) 'Vorbemerkung', in *KZ-Gedenkstätte Dachau: Empfehlungen für eine Neukonzeption, vorgelegt vom wissenschaftlichen Fachbeirat*, Munich: no publisher specified.

Fest, J. (1996) *Plotting Hitler's Death: The German Resistance to Hitler 1933 to 1945*, London: Weidenfeld and Nicolson.

Filmer, W. and Schwan, H. (eds) (1995) *Besiegt, befreit . . . Zeitzeugen erinnern sich an das Kriegsende 1945*, Munich: Bertelsmann.

Finkelstein, N. (1997) 'Daniel Jonah Goldhagen's "Crazy" Thesis: a Critique of Hitler's Willing Executioners', *New Left Review*, 224: 39–87.

—— (2000) *The Holocaust Industry: Reflections on the Exploitation of Jewish Suffering*, London and New York: Verso.

—— and Birn, R. B. (1998a) *A Nation on Trial: The Goldhagen Thesis and Historical Truth*, New York: Henry Holt and Company.

—— and Birn, R. B. (1998b) *Eine Nation auf dem Prüfstand: Die Goldhagen-These und die historische Wahrheit. Mit einer Einleitung von Hans Mommsen*, Hildesheim: Claassen.

Finker, K. (1984) 'Politischer Realismus und Verantwortungsbewußtsein', *Die Wahrheit*, 14–15 July: 4–5.

Finker, K. (1994) *Der 20. Juli 1944: Militärputsch oder Revolution?*, Berlin: Dietz.

Fleming, G. (1984) *Hitler and the Final Solution*, Berkeley: University of California Press.

Frei, N. (1996) *Vergangenheitspolitik: Die Anfänge der Bundesrepublik und die NS-Vergangenheit*, Munich: Beck.

Friedländer, S. (1998) *Nazi Germany and the Jews: The Years of Persecution 1933–39*, London: Phoenix.

Fulbrook, M. (1999) *German National Identity after the Holocaust*, Cambridge: Polity.

Gärtner, K.-H. *et al.* (1995) *Berliner Straßennamen: Ein Nachschlagewerk für die östlichen Bezirke*, Berlin: Christoph Links.

Gay, C. (2000) 'Remembering for the Future, Engaging with the Present: National Memory Management and the Dialectic of Normality in the Berlin Republic', speech given at The Nottingham Trent University in September 2000. To be published in Niven, B. and Jordan, J. (eds), *Politics and Culture in 20th Century Germany*, Rochester: Camden House, no pagination as yet.

GB (Gedenkstätte Buchenwald) (ed.) (1992a) *Jahresinformation der Gedenkstätte Buchenwald 1991*, Weimar-Buchenwald: Repro und Verlag GmbH.

—— (ed.) (1992b) *Zur Neuorientierung der Gedenkstätte Buchenwald*, Weimar-Buchenwald: Weimardruck.

—— (ed.) (1997) *Speziallager 2, 1945–1950, Rundbrief Nr. 15/16/17*, Weimar-Buchenwald: Keßler.

—— (ed.) (1999) *Konzentrationslager Buchenwald 1937–1945: Begleitband zur ständigen historischen Ausstellung*, Göttingen: Wallstein.

GDW (Gedenkstätte Deutscher Widerstand) (ed.) (1984) *Der 20. Juli 1944: Reden zu einem Tag der deutschen Geschichte. Band 1*, Berlin: Möller.

Gerlach, C. (2000a) *Kalkulierte Morde: Die deutsche Wirtschafts- und Vernichtungspolitik in Weißrußland 1941 bis 1944*, Hamburg: Hamburger Edition.

—— (2000b) *Krieg, Ernährung, Völkermord. Forschungen zur deutschen Vernichtungspolitik im Zweiten Weltkrieg*, Hamburg: Hamburger Edition.

Giordano, R. (1987) *Die zweite Schuld oder Von der Last Deutscher zu sein*, Hamburg: Rasch und Röhring.

Goldhagen, D. J. (1996a) *Hitler's Willing Executioners: Ordinary Germans and the Holocaust*, London: Little, Brown and Company.

—— (1996b) *Hitlers willige Vollstrecker. Ganz gewöhnliche Deutsche und der Holocaust*, Berlin: Siedler (German translation with new foreword by Goldhagen).

—— (1996c) 'Das Versagen der Kritiker', *Die Zeit*, 32: 9–14.

——— (1997a) 'Modell Bundesrepublik: National History, Democracy, and Internationalization in Germany', in Bredthauer, K. and Heinrich, A. (eds), *Aus der Geschichte Lernen: How to Learn from History*, Bonn: Blätter-Verlags-Gesellschaft, 56–83.

——— (ed.) (1997b) *Briefe an Goldhagen*, Berlin: Siedler.

Graml, H. (1998) *Reichskristallnacht: Antisemitismus und Judenverfolgung im Dritten Reich*, Munich: dtv.

Gropp, D. (2000) '20 Jahre KZ-Gedenkstätte Laura: von der Dokumentensammlung zur internationalen Begegnungstätte', *Gedenkstättenrundbrief*, 93/1: 3–6.

Haase, N. (1999) 'Bemerkungen zu dem Artikel von Ludwig Baumann und Manfred Messerschmidt', *Gedenkstättenrundbrief*, 91/10: 35–7.

——— and Oleschinski, B. (eds) (1993a) *Das Torgau-Tabu: Wehrmachtstrafsystem, NKWD-Lager, DDR-Strafvollzug*, Leipzig: Forum Verlag.

——— and Oleschinski, B. (1993b) 'Das Torgau-Tabu: Zur Einführung', in Haase, N. and Oleschinski, B. (eds), *Das Torgau-Tabu: Wehrmachtstrafsystem, NKWD-Lager, DDR-Strafvollzug*, Leipzig: Forum Verlag, 11–28.

——— and Paul, G. (eds) (1995) *Die anderen Soldaten: Wehrkraftzersetzung, Gehorsamsverweigerung und Fahnenflucht im Zweiten Weltkrieg*, Frankfurt on Main: Fischer.

Habermas, J. (1995) *Die Normalität einer Berliner Republik*, Frankfurt on Main: Suhrkamp.

Hackett, D. (ed.) (1995) *The Buchenwald Report*, Boulder, San Francisco and Oxford: Westview Press.

Hartmann, G. (ed.) (1986) *Bitburg in Moral and Political Perspective*, Bloomington: Indiana University Press.

——— (1996) *The Longest Shadow: In the Aftermath of the Holocaust*, Bloomington and Indianapolis: Indiana University Press.

Heer, H. (1995) 'Killing Fields: Die Wehrmacht und der Holocaust', in Heer, H. and Naumann, K. (eds), *Vernichtungskrieg: Verbrechen der Wehrmacht 1941 bis 1944*, Hamburg: Hamburger Edition, 57–77.

——— (ed.) (1997) *Im Herzen der Finsternis. Victor Klemperer als Chronist der NS-Zeit*, Berlin: Aufbau.

——— (1999a) *Tote Zonen. Die Deutsche Wehrmacht an der Ostfront*, Hamburg: Hamburger Edition.

——— (1999b) 'Das letzte Band: Kriegsverbrechen und Nachkriegserinnerung', in HIS (ed.), *Eine Ausstellung und ihre Folgen: Zur Rezeption der Ausstellung 'Vernichtungskrieg. Verbrechen der Wehrmacht 1941 bis 1944'*, Hamburg: Hamburger Edition, 123–62.

——— and Naumann, K. (eds) (1995) *Vernichtungskrieg: Verbrechen der Wehrmacht 1941 bis 1944*, Hamburg: Hamburger Edition.

Heil, J. (1996) 'Die Einzigartigkeit der Täter: Anmerkungen zu Daniel Goldhagens "Hitlers Willing Executioners"', in Benz, W. (ed.), *Jahrbuch für Antisemitismusforschung 5*, Frankfurt on Main and New York: Campus, 242–51.

——— and Erb, R. (eds) (1998) *Geschichtswissenschaft und Öffentlichkeit: Der Streit um Daniel J. Goldhagen*, Frankfurt on Main: Fischer.

Heimrod, U., Schlusche, G. and Seferens, H. (1999) *Der Denkmalstreit - das Denkmal? Die Debatte um das Denkmal für die ermordeten Juden Europas: Eine Dokumentation*, Berlin: Philo.

Herf, J. (1997) *Divided Memory: The Nazi Past in the Two Germanys*, Cambridge (Massachusetts) and London: Harvard.

Hillgruber, A. (1986) *Zweierlei Untergang: Die Zerschlagung des deutschen Reiches und das Ende des europäischen Judentums*, Berlin: Corso bei Siedler.

HIS (Hamburger Institut für Sozialforschung) (ed.) (1995) *200 Tage und 1 Jahrhundert: Gewalt und Destruktivität im Spiegel des Jahres 1945*, Hamburg: Hamburger Edition.

—— (ed.) (1996) *Katalog zur Ausstellung 'Vernichtungskrieg. Verbrechen der Wehrmacht 1941 bis 1944'*, Hamburg: Hamburger Edition.

—— (ed.) (1998a) *Besucher einer Ausstellung: Die Ausstellung 'Vernichtungskrieg. Verbrechen der Wehrmacht 1941 bis 1944' in Interview und Gespräch*, Hamburg: Hamburger Edition.

—— (ed.) (1998b) *Krieg ist ein Gesellschaftszustand: Reden zur Eröffnung der Ausstellung 'Vernichtungskrieg. Verbrechen der Wehrmacht 1941 bis 1944'*, Hamburg: Hamburger Edition.

—— (ed.) (1999) *Eine Ausstellung und ihre Folgen: Zur Rezeption der Ausstellung 'Vernichtungskrieg. Verbrechen der Wehrmacht 1941 bis 1944'*, Hamburg: Hamburger Edition.

Hoffmann, C. (1992) *Vergangenheitsbewältigung in Deutschland 1945 und 1989*, Bonn and Berlin: Bouvier.

Hofhaensel, K. (1999) 'The Diplomacy of Compensation for Eastern European Victims of Nazi Crimes', *German Politics*, 8/3: 103–24.

Initiative Mahnmal Homosexuellenverfolgung (ed.) (1997) *Der Frankfurter Engel: Mahnmal Homosexuellenverfolgung*, Frankfurt on Main: Eichborn.

Jäckel, E. (1999) 'Die Einzigartigkeit des Mordes an den europäischen Juden', in Rosh, L. (ed.), *'Die Juden, das sind doch die anderen': Der Streit um ein deutsches Denkmal*, Berlin and Vienna: Philo, 153–70.

Jacobeit, S. and Philipp, G. (eds) (1997) *Ravensbrück: Beiträge zur Geschichte des Frauen-Konzentrationslagers*, Berlin: Edition Hentrich.

Jäger, H. (1997) 'Die Widerlegung des funktionalistischen Täterbildes', *Mittelweg 36*, 6/1: 73–85.

Jüdisches Museum Berlin and MD Berlin (eds) (1998) *Jüdisches Museum Berlin*, Berlin: Jüdisches Museum Berlin.

Kautz, F. (1998) *Goldhagen und die 'Hürnen Sewfriedte'*, Berlin and Hamburg: Argument.

Kershaw, I. (1987) *The 'Hitler Myth': Image and Reality in the Third Reich*, Oxford: Clarendon Press.

Kirsch, J.-H. (1999a)*'Wir haben aus der Geschichte gelernt': Der 8. Mai als politischer Gedenktag in Deutschland*, Cologne, Weimar and Vienna: Böhlau.

—— (1999b) 'Identität durch Normalität. Der Konflikt um Martin Walsers Friedenspreisrede', *Leviathan*, 27/399: 309–54.

Klee, E. (1991) *Persilscheine und falsche Pässe*, Frankfurt on Main: Fischer.

Klemperer, V. (1995a) *Ich will Zeugnis ablegen bis zum letzten: Tagebücher 1933–1941*, Berlin: Aufbau.

—— (1995b) *Ich will Zeugnis ablegen bis zum letzten: Tagebücher 1942–1945*, Berlin: Aufbau.

Klotz, J. (ed.) (1998) *Vorbild Wehrmacht? Wehrmachtsverbrechen, Rechtsextremismus und Bundeswehr*, Cologne: PapyRossa.

—— and Schneider, U. (eds) (1997) *Die selbstbewußte Nation und ihr Geschichtsbild: Geschichtslegenden der Neuen Rechten*, Cologne: PapyRossa.

—— and Wiegel, G. (eds) (1999) *Geistige Brandstiftung? Die Walser-Bubis-Debatte*, Cologne: PapyRossa.

Knechtel, R. and Fiedler, J. (eds) (1991) *Stalins DDR: Berichte politisch Verfolgter*, Leipzig: Forum Verlag.

Kohl, H. (1996) *Ich wollte Deutschlands Einheit*, Berlin: Ullstein.

Köhler, K. (1999) 'Die poetische Nation: Zu Martin Walsers Friedenspreisrede und seinen neueren Romanen', in Klotz, J. and Wiegel, G. (eds), *Geistige Brandstiftung? Die Walser-Bubis-Debatte*, Cologne: PapyRossa, 65–117.

Kramer, S. (1999) *Auschwitz im Widerstreit: Zur Darstellung der Shoah in Film, Philosophie und Literatur*, Wiesbaden: Deutscher Universitäts-Verlag.

Krausnick, H. and Wilhelm, H.-H. (1981) *Die Truppe des Weltanschauungskrieges: Die Einsatzgruppen der Sicherheitspolizei und des SD, 1938–1942*, Stuttgart: Deutsche Verlagsanstalt.

Krausnick, M. (1997) 'Der nationalsozialistische Völkermord an den Sinti und Roma', in Lichtenstein, H. and Romberg, O. (eds), *Täter–Opfer–Folgen: Der Holocaust in Geschichte und Gegenwart*, 223–54.

Kulturamt der Stadt Marburg (ed.) (1998) *Formen von Erinnerung. Eine Diskussion mit Claude Lanzmann. Ein anderer Blick auf Gedenken, Erinnern und Erleben. Eine Tagung*, Marburg: Jonas.

Kulturreferat der Landeshauptstadt München (ed.) (1998) *Bilanz einer Ausstellung: Dokumentation der Kontroverse 'Vernichtungskrieg. Verbrechen der Wehrmacht 1941 bis 1944'*, Munich: Knaur.

Kunstamt Schöneberg, Schöneberg Museum and Gedenkstätte Haus der Wannsee-Konferenz (eds) (1994) *Orte des Erinnerns: Das Denkmal im Bayerischen Viertel*, Berlin: Edition Hentrich.

Küntzel, M., Thörner, K. *et al.* (eds) (1997) *Goldhagen und die deutsche Linke*, Berlin: Elefanten Press.

KZ-Gedenkstätte Neuengamme (ed.) (1998) *Abgeleitete Macht - Funktionshäftlinge zwischen Widerstand und Kollaboration*, Bremen: Edition Temmen.

Lagergemeinschaft Ravensbrück (ed.) (1991) *Dokumentation zur Auseinandersetzung um die privatwirtschaftliche Zweckentfremdung des Geländes der Mahn- und Gedenkstätte Ravensbrück*, Stuttgart (unpublished).

Leo, A. (1996) 'Das kurze Leben der VVN', in Morsch, G. (ed.), *Von der Erinnerung zum Monument: Die Entstehungsgeschichte der Nationalen Mahn- und Gedenkstätte Sachsenhausen*, Berlin: Edition Hentrich, 93–100.

—— and Reif-Spirek, P. (eds) (1999) *Helden, Täter und Verräter: Studien zum DDR-Antifaschismus*, Berlin: Metropol.

Libeskind, D. (1998) 'Between the Lines. Das Jüdische Museum', in Jüdisches Museum Berlin and MD Berlin (eds), *Jüdisches Museum Berlin*, Berlin: Jüdisches Museum Berlin, 6–11.

—— (1999) 'Daniel Libeskind talks with Doris Erbacher and Peter Paul Kubitz', in Studio Libeskind, Binet, H. and G + B Arts International (eds), *Jewish Museum Berlin*, Berlin: G + B Arts International, 17–45.

Lichtenstein, H. and Romberg, O. (eds) (1997) *Täter–Opfer–Folgen: Der Holocaust in Geschichte und Gegenwart*, Bonn: Bundeszentrale für politische Bildung.

Maier, C. (1988) *The Unmasterable Past: History, Holocaust, and German National Identity*, Cambridge (Massachusetts) and London: Harvard University Press.

Manoschek, W. (1993) *'Serbien ist judenfrei': Militärische Besatzungspolitik und Judenvernichtung in Serbien 1941/2*, Munich: Oldenbourg.

—— (ed.) (1996) *Die Wehrmacht im Rassenkrieg*, Vienna: Picus.

Markovits, A. and Reich, R. (1997) *The German Predicament: Memory and Power in the New Europe*, New York: Cornell University Press.

Marrus, M. (1993) *The Holocaust in History*, Harmondsworth: Penguin.

Mazower, M. (1996) 'Fighting Demonization with Demonization: Daniel Jonah Goldhagen's "Hitler's Willing Executioners"', *Patterns of Prejudice*, 30/2: 73–5.

Messerschmidt, M. (1969) *Die Wehrmacht im NS-Staat: Zeit der Indoktrination*, Hamburg: Verlag von Decker.

MfWFK (Ministerium für Wissenschaft, Forschung und Kultur des Landes Brandenburg) (ed.) (1992a) *Brandenburgische Gedenkstätten für die Verfolgten des NS-Regimes*, Berlin: Edition Hentrich.

—— (ed.) (1992b) *Die brandenburgischen Gedenkstätten: Empfehlungen der Expertenkommission zur Neukonzeption*, Berlin: Edition Hentrich.

Mohler, A. (1996) *Der Nasenring: Die Vergangenheitsbewältigung nach dem Fall der Mauer*, Munich: Langen Müller.

Möller, H. (ed.) (1999) *Der rote Holocaust und die Deutschen. Die Debatte um das 'Schwarzbuch des Kommunismus'*, Munich: Piper.

Moller, S. (1998) *Die Entkonkretisierung der NS-Herrschaft in der Ära Kohl*, Hannover: Offizin.

Morsch, G. (ed.) (1994) *Konzentrationslager Oranienburg*, Berlin: Edition Hentrich.

—— (ed.) (1995) *Die Baracken 38 und 39: Geschichte und Zukunft eines geschändeten Denkmals*, Berlin: Edition Hentrich.

—— (ed.) (1996) *Von der Erinnerung zum Monument: Die Entstehungsgeschichte der Nationalen Mahn- und Gedenkstätte Sachsenhausen*, Berlin: Edition Hentrich.

Müller, J. (1999) 'From National Identity to National Interest: The Rise (and Fall) of Germany's New Right', *German Politics*, 8/3: 1–20.

Münch, I. von (ed.) (1991) *Dokumente der Wiedervereinigung Deutschlands*, Stuttgart: Kröner.

Musial, B. (1999) 'Bilder einer Ausstellung', *Vierteljahreshefte für Zeitgeschichte*, 47/4: 563–91.

—— (2000) *'Konterrevolutionäre sind zu erschießen'*, Berlin: Propyläen.

Naumann, K. (1999) '"Wieso erst jetzt?" oder Die Macht der Nemesis. Der geschichtspolitische Ort der Ausstellung', in HIS (ed.), *Eine Ausstellung und ihre Folgen: Zur Rezeption der Ausstellung 'Vernichtungskrieg. Verbrechen der Wehrmacht 1941 bis 1944'*, Hamburg: Hamburger Edition, 262–88.

Nedelmann, B. (1999) 'Die Ausstellung "Vernichtungskrieg. Verbrechen der Wehrmacht 1941 bis 1944" und die Konstruktion öffentlicher Diskurse', in HIS (ed.), *Eine Ausstellung und ihre Folgen: Zur Rezeption der Ausstellung 'Vernichtungskrieg. Verbrechen der Wehrmacht 1941 bis 1944'*, Hamburg: Hamburger Edition, 230–61.

Neuss, R. (1996) 'Wem gehört der deutsche Widerstand? – Der Streit zum 50. Jahrestag des 20. Juli 1944', *German Life and Letters*, 49/1: 111–19.

Niemetz, D. (1999) 'Besiegt, gebraucht, gelobt, gemieden: Zum Umgang mit ehemaligen Wehrmachtoffizieren im DDR-Militär', *Deutschland Archiv*, 32/3: 378–92.

Niethammer, L. (ed.) (1994) *Der 'gesäuberte' Antifaschismus: Die SED und die roten Kapos von Buchenwald*, Berlin: Akademie Verlag.

—— (1999) 'Alliierte Internierungslager in Deutschland nach 1945: Ein Vergleich und offene Fragen', in Reif-Spirek, P. and Ritscher, B. (eds), *Speziallager in der SBZ: Gedenkstätten mit 'doppelter Vergangenheit'*, Berlin: Christoph Links, 100–23.

Niven, B. (1995) 'The Reception of Steven Spielberg's "Schindler's List" in the German Media', *Journal of European Studies*, XXV: 165–89.

—— (2000) 'Redesigning the Landscape of Memory at Buchenwald: Trends and Problems', in Barker, P. (ed.), *The GDR and its History: Die DDR im Spiegel der Enquete-Kommissionen*, Rodopi: Amsterdam and Atlanta, 159–83.

—— and Jordan, J. (eds) (forthcoming) *Politics and Culture in 20th Century Germany*, Rochester: Camden House.

Nolte, E. (1995) *Die Deutschen und ihre Vergangenheiten: Erinnerung und Vergessen von der Reichsgründung Bismarcks bis heute*, Berlin and Frankfurt on Main: Propyläen.

Oleschinski, B. and Pampel, P. (1997) *'Feindliche Elemente sind in Gewahrsam zu halten': Die sowjetischen Speziallager Nr. 8 und Nr. 10 in Torgau 1945–1948*, Leipzig: Kiepenheuer und Witsch.

Pohl, D. (1997) 'Die Holocaust-Forschung und Goldhagens Thesen', *Vierteljahreshefte für Zeitgeschichte*, 1: 1–48.

Puvogel, U. and Stankowski, P. (1995) *Gedenkstätten für die Opfer des Nationalsozialismus. Eine Dokumentation*, Bonn: Bundeszentrale für politische Bildung.

Raettig, H. (1997) *Eine Stellungnahme zu dem Buch von Daniel Jonah Goldhagen 'Hitlers Willige Vollstrecker: Ganz gewöhnliche Deutsche und der Holocaust': Wie erlebte ein deutscher Bürger das 20. Jahrhundert*, Frankfurt on Main: Fischer.

Rahe, T. (1997) 'Vergessen und unterschlagen? Die Darstellung des Schicksals lesbischer und homosexueller Häftlinge in den KZ-Gedenkstätten in Deutschland', *Gedenkstättenrundbrief,* 76/4: 10–21.

Reemtsma, J. P. (1997) 'Turning away from Denial', in Bredthauer, K. and Heinrich, A. (eds), *Aus der Geschichte Lernen: How to Learn from History*, Bonn: Blätter-Verlags-Gesellschaft, 38–55.

Reemtsma, K. (1996) *Sinti und Roma: Geschichte, Kultur, Gegenwart*, Munich: Beck.

Reichel, P. (1999) *Politik mit der Erinnerung: Gedächtnisorte im Streit um die nationalsozialistische Vergangenheit*, Frankfurt on Main: Fischer.

Reif-Spirek, P. and Ritscher, B. (eds) (1999) *Speziallager in der SBZ: Gedenkstätten mit 'doppelter Vergangenheit'*, Berlin: Christoph Links.

Ritscher, B. (1986) *Buchenwald: Rundgang durch die Nationale Mahn- und Gedenkstätte*, Erfurt: no publisher specified.

——, Lüttgenau, R.-G. and Hammermann, G. (1999) *Das sowjetische Speziallager Nr. 2 1945–1950: Katalog zur ständigen historischen Ausstellung*, Göttingen: Wallstein.

Roon, G. van (1994) *Widerstand im Dritten Reich*, Munich: Beck.

Rosh, L. (ed.) (1999) *'Die Juden, das sind doch die anderen': Der Streit um ein deutsches Denkmal*, Berlin and Vienna: Philo.

Roth, A. and Frajman, M. (1998) *The Goldapple Guide to Jewish Berlin*, Berlin: Goldapple.

Rürup, R. (ed.) (1996) *Topography of Terror: Gestapo, SS and Reichssicherheitshauptamt on the 'Prinz-Albrecht-Terrain': A Documentation*, Berlin: Willmuth Arenhövel.

—— (ed.) (1997) *10 Jahre Topographie des Terrors*, Berlin: Stiftung Topographie des Terrors.

Schafft, G. E. and Zeidler, G. (1996) *Die KZ-Mahn- und Gedenkstätten in Deutschland*, Berlin: Dietz.

Schirrmacher, F. (ed.) (1999) *Die Walser-Bubis-Debatte: Eine Dokumentation*, Frankfurt on Main: Suhrkamp.

Schlant, E. (1999) *The Language of Silence: West German Literature and the Holocaust*, London and New York: Routledge.

Schley, J. (1999) *Nachbar Buchenwald: Die Stadt Weimar und ihr Konzentrationslager 1937–1945*, Böhlau: Cologne, Weimar and Vienna.

Schmidbauer, W. (1998) *'Ich wußte nie, was mit Vater ist': Das Trauma des Krieges*, Reinbek bei Hamburg: Rowohlt.

Schneider, M. (1997) *Die 'Goldhagen-Debatte': Ein Historikerstreit in der Mediengesellschaft*, Bonn: Friedrich-Ebert-Stiftung.

Schneider, R. C. (1997) *Fetisch Holocaust. Die Judenvernichtung–verdrängt und vermarktet*, Munich: Kindler.

Schoeps, J. (ed.) (1996) *Ein Volk von Mördern: Die Dokumentation zur Goldhagen-Kontroverse um die Rolle der Deutschen im Holocaust*, Hamburg: Hoffmann und Campe.

Schwilk, H. and Schacht, U. (eds) (1994) *Die selbstbewußte Nation: 'Anschwellender Bocksgesang' und weitere Beiträge zu einer deutschen Debatte*, Frankfurt on Main: Ullstein.

Seferens, H. (1995) *Ein deutscher Denkmalstreit: Die Kontroverse um die Spiegelwand in Berlin-Steglitz*, Berlin: Edition Hentrich.

Seibt, F. (1997) *Deutschland und die Tschechen: Geschichte einer Nachbarschaft in der Mitte Europas*, Munich and Zurich: Piper.

SfVuB (Senatsverwaltung für Verkehr und Betriebe) (ed.) (1994) *Unabhängige Kommission zur Umbenennung von Straßen: Abschlußbericht vom 17. März 1994*, Berlin: Krüger + Partner.

SfWFK (Senatsverwaltung für Wissenschaft, Forschung und Kultur) (ed.) (1997) *Colloquium: Denkmal für die ermordeten Juden Europas. Dokumentation*, Berlin: Senatsverwaltung.

Soergel, F. (1996) 'Tabuthema Deserteure: Denkanstöße durch Deserteure-Initiativen', *AKP-Fachzeitschrift für Alternative Kommunalpolitik*, 1: 1–8.

Sojka, K. (ed.) (1998) *Die Wahrheit über die Wehrmacht: Reemtsmas Fälschungen widerlegt*, Munich: FZ-Verlag.

Stadt Fürstenberg/Havel, Land Brandenburg und BRD (eds) (1998) *Dokumentation: Internationaler Landschaftsplanerischer Ideenwettbewerb 'Ehemaliges Frauen-Konzentrationslager Ravensbrück'*, Fürstenberg/Havel: Amt Fürstenberg/Havel.

Steinbach, P. (1994) *Widerstand im Widerstreit: Der Widerstand gegen den Nationalsozialismus in der Erinnerung der Deutschen*, Paderborn: Schöningh.

—— and Tuchel, J. (eds) (1994) *Lexikon des Widerstands 1933–1945*, Munich: Beck.

—— and Tuchel, J. (1998) 'Georg Elser – Tat und Erinnerung', *Gedenkstättenrundbrief*, 83/6: 3–10.

Stern, F. (1996) 'The Goldhagen Controversy: One Nation, One People, One Theory?', *Foreign Affairs*, 11/12: 128–38.

Stern, H. (1998) *KZ-Lügen: Antwort auf Goldhagen*, Munich: FZ-Verlag.

Stiftung Haus der Geschichte der Bundesrepublik Deutschland (ed.) (1999) *Einsichten*, Leipzig: Schleiner + Partner.

Stiftung Sächsische Gedenkstätten (ed.) (1996) *Spuren Suchen und Erinnern*, Leipzig: Kiepenheuer.

Streim, A. (1995) 'Saubere Wehrmacht? Die Verfolgung von Kriegs- und NS-Verbrechen in der Bundesrepublik und der DDR', in Heer, H. and Naumann, K. (eds), *Vernichtungskrieg: Verbrechen der Wehrmacht 1941 bis 1944*, Hamburg: Hamburger Edition, 569–97.

Streit, C. (1978) *Keine Kameraden: Die Wehrmacht und die sowjetischen Kriegsgefangenen, 1941–1945*, Stuttgart: Deutsche Verlagsanstalt.

Studio Libeskind, Binet, H. and G + B Arts International (eds) (1999) *Jewish Museum Berlin*, Berlin: G + B Arts International.

Studt, C. (ed.) (1995) *Das Dritte Reich: Ein Lesebuch zur deutschen Geschichte 1933–1945*, Munich: C. H. Beck.

Taberner, S. (1999) '"Wie schön wäre Deutschland, wenn man sich noch als Deutscher fühlen und mit Stolz als Deutscher fühlen könnte". Martin Walser's Reception of Victor Klemperer's *Tagebücher 1933–1945* in "Das Prinzip Genauigkeit" and "Die Verteidigung der Kindheit"', *Deutsche Vierteljahrsschrift für Literaturwissenschaft und Geistesgeschichte*, 73/4: 710–32.

Thiele, H.-G. (ed.) (1997) *Die Wehrmachtsausstellung: Dokumentation einer Kontroverse*, Bremen: Edition Temmen.

Thomaneck, J. K. A. and Niven, B. (2001) *Dividing and Uniting Germany*, London and New York: Routledge.

Titz, W. (1995) 'Zur Geschichte der Baracken 38 und 39: Aufbau, Belegung und museale Nutzung', in Morsch (ed.), *Die Baracken 38 und 39: Geschichte und Zukunft eines geschändeten Denkmals*, Berlin: Edition Hentrich, 15–24.

Trampe, G. (1995) *Die Stunde Null: Erinnerungen an Kriegsende und Neuanfang*, Stuttgart: Deutsche Verlags-Anstalt.

Ueberschär, G. (ed.) (1998) *Der 20. Juli: Das andere Deutschland in der Vergangenheitspolitik nach 1945*, Berlin: Elefanten Press.

Ungváry, K. (1999) 'Echte Bilder–problematische Aussagen. Eine quantitative und qualitative Analyse des Bildmaterials der Ausstellung "Vernichtungskrieg–Verbrechen der Wehrmacht 1941–1944"', *Geschichte in Wissenschaft und Unterricht*, 10: 584–95.

Walser, M. (1996) *Das Prinzip Genauigkeit: Laudatio auf Victor Klemperer*, Frankfurt on Main: Suhrkamp.

—— (1998) *Ein springender Brunnen*, Frankfurt on Main: Suhrkamp.

—— (1999) *Friedenspreis des Deutschen Buchhandels 1998: Erfahrungen beim Verfassen einer Sonntagsrede*, in Schirrmacher, F. (ed.), *Die Walser–Bubis–Debatte: Eine Dokumentation*, Frankfurt on Main: Suhrkamp, 7–17.

Wehler, H.-U. (1996) 'Wie ein Stachel im Fleisch', in Schoeps, J. (ed.), *Ein Volk von Mördern: Die Dokumentation zur Goldhagen–Kontroverse um die Rolle der Deutschen im Holocaust*, Hamburg: Hoffmann und Campe, 193–209.

Weigelt, A. (1999) 'Die Asche der jüdischen Häftlinge auf dem "Galgenberg" in Lieberose: Zum Umgang mit dem KZ-Nebenlager Jamlitz in der DDR', in Leo, A. and Reif-Spirek, P. (eds), *Helden, Täter und Verräter: Studien zum DDR-Antifaschismus*, Berlin: Metropol, 37–64.

Weiss, C. (ed.) (1995) *'Der gute Deutsche': Dokumente zur Diskussion um Steven Spielbergs 'Schindlers Liste' in Deutschland*, St Ingbert: Röhrig.

Werkentin, F. (1998) *Recht und Justiz im SED-Staat*, Bonn: Bundeszentrale für politische Bildung.

Wette, W. (1998) 'Wehrmachtstraditionen und Bundeswehr: Deutsche Machtphantasien im Zeichen der neuen Militärpolitik und des Rechtsradikalismus', in Klotz, J. (ed.), *Vorbild Wehrmacht? Wehrmachtsverbrechen, Rechtsextremismus und Bundeswehr*, Cologne: PapyRossa, 126–54.

Wiedmer, C. (1999) *The Claims of Memory: Representations of the Holocaust in Contemporary Germany and France*, Ithaca and London: Cornell University Press.

Wielenga, F. (1995) *Schatten deutscher Geschichte: Der Umgang mit dem Nationalsozialismus und der DDR-Vergangenheit in der Bundesrepublik*, Greifswald: SH-Verlag.

Wippermann, W. (1997) *Wessen Schuld? Vom Historikerstreit zur Goldhagen-Kontroverse*, Berlin: Elefanten Press.

—— (1999) *Konzentrationslager: Geschichte, Nachgeschichte, Gedenken*, Berlin: Elefanten Press.

Wise, M. Z. (1998) *Capital Dilemma: Germany's Search for a New Architecture of Democracy*, New York: Princeton Architectural Press.

Wolffsohn, M. (1995) *Die Deutschland-Akte: Juden und Deutsche in Ost und West. Tatsachen und Legenden*, Munich: Bruckmann.

Young, J. E. (1993) *The Texture of Memory: Holocaust Memorials and Meaning*, New Haven and London: Yale University Press.

ZAM (Zentrum für audio-visuelle Medien) (ed.) (1993) *Die Grunewald-Rampe: Die Deportation der Berliner Juden*, Berlin: Edition Colloquium.

Zimmer, H. (1999) *Der Buchenwald-Konflikt*, Münster: agenda.

Zitelmann, R. and Prinz, M. (eds) (1991) *Nationalsozialismus und Modernisierung*, Darmstadt: Wissenschaftliche Buchgesellschaft.

Zorn, M. (ed.) (1994) *Hitlers zweimal getötete Opfer: Westdeutsche Endlösung des Antifaschismus auf dem Gebiet der DDR*, Freiburg: Ahrimann.

Zur Nieden, S. (1996) 'Das Museum des Widerstandskampfes und der Leiden des jüdischen Volkes', in Morsch, G. (ed.), *Von der Erinnerung zum Monument: Die Entstehungsgeschichte*, Berlin: Edition Hentrich, 272–8.

Index